Bowyer

J. A. TURNER S. S.

SOCIAL SCIENCE

SPOTLIGHT CANADA

Third Edition

J. Bradley Cruxton

W. Douglas Wilson

Toronto
Oxford University Press

For Dianne and Mary for your encouragement and constant support.

Oxford University Press
70 Wynford Drive, Don Mills, Ontario M3C 1J9

Oxford   New York   Toronto
Athens   Auckland   Bangkok   Bombay
Calcutta   Cape Town   Dar es Salaam   Delhi   Florence
Hong Kong   Istanbul   Karachi   Kuala Lumpur
Madras   Madrid   Melbourne   Mexico City
Nairobi   Paris   Singapore   Taipei   Tokyo

and associated companies in
Berlin   Ibadan

Oxford is a trademark of Oxford University Press

This book is printed on permanent (acid-free) paper. ∞

CANADIAN CATALOGUING IN PUBLICATION DATA
Cruxton, J. Bradley
    Spotlight Canada

3rd ed.
ISBN 0-19-541041-6

1. Canada - History - 20th century.[*] I. Wilson, W. Douglas.
II. Title.

FC600.C78 1996   971.06   C95-930662-5
F1034.2.C78 1996

Cover illustration: David Craig
Project editor: Monica Schwalbe
Photo research: Patricia Buckley Editorial Services
Design: Heather Delfino/Paul Sneath
Page composition, cartographic and graphic art: free&Creative
Illustrations: Brian Hughes/Christine Alexiou

Printed and bound in Canada

        3   4   5   97 98 99 00

CONTENTS

SPOTLIGHT CANADA

Third Edition

Acknowledgements

The authors would like to acknowledge a long-standing and stimulating relationship with the editorial and production staff of Oxford University Press (Canada). In particular, we would like to thank our editor, Monica Schwalbe; Susan Froud, Managing Director; Gerard Shkuda, Acquisitions Editor; Joanna Gertler, Production Director; and Heather Delfino, Designer for their creative advice, encouragement, and constant support.

We would also like to thank the following reviewers for their helpful comments on the manuscript.

Dr. Philip Cull, Program Co-ordinator, Bonavista-Trinity-Placentia School District, Clarenville, Newfoundland

Jackie Moore Daigle, First Nation Education Consultant, University of Toronto (Ph.D. student)

Bruce W. Gillespie, Social Studies Department Head, Saint Mary's High School, Calgary Separate School Board, Alberta

William D. Grant, Nepean High School, Ottawa, Ontario

Bruce E. Hill, Ontario Ministry of Education and Training (retired)

Peter Hill, Curriculum/Native Advisor, Haldimand Board of Education, Ontario

Dennis J. Monteith, Department Head of History, Hamilton Board of Education, Ontario

Richard W. Woods, Head of History and Contemporary Studies, Sir Frederick Banting Secondary School, London Board of Education, Ontario

Unit 1

Confederation and the Early Growth of the Nation 1860–1900

TIMELINE

1864 — Confederation conferences at Charlottetown and Quebec

1866 — Colonial delegates attend London Conference

1867 — Confederation
John A. Macdonald is sworn in as Canada's first prime minister

1869 — Canada purchases Hudson's Bay Company lands
Rebellion at Red River begins

1870 — Manitoba enters Confederation

1871 — British Columbia enters Confederation
First of the numbered treaties between Canada and Native peoples

1873 — Prince Edward Island enters Confederation
Treaty of Washington comes into effect

1876 — Indian Act is passed

1879 — Macdonald introduces the National Policy

1885 — Canadian Pacific Railway is completed
Rebellion breaks out in the North-West
Louis Riel is executed at Regina

1890 — Manitoba Schools Act

1896 — Wilfrid Laurier becomes prime minister
Immigration boom begins

In the mid 1800s, British North America was a scattered collection of colonies and territories. On the Atlantic coast were Newfoundland, Prince Edward Island, Nova Scotia, and New Brunswick. Farther west were the united provinces of Canada East and Canada West. In the vast interior were Rupert's Land, the North-Western Territory, and the Red River Colony, all controlled by the Hudson Bay Company. On the Pacific coast was British Columbia.

Each colony was part of the British Empire but had its own local government. Each was struggling to forge its own path. But some people had a dream that all the colonies could be united into one country. This dream was for Confederation. **Confederation** is the joining of provinces or states into a unified country under a central government.

The decision of whether or not to support Confederation was not an easy one for the colonies. All had to weigh the advantages and disadvantages. Many French-speaking people in Canada East, for example, felt that they would be swamped by an English-speaking majority if the colonies united. People in Prince Edward Island were concerned that their small population would have little voice in a central government. Other colonies strongly supported a union. The years leading to Confederation in 1867 were stormy ones.

In 1867, four colonies joined to form the new Dominion of Canada. In following years, new provinces were added and the young country grew at an astonishing pace. A railway was built to the Pacific Ocean and hundreds of thousands of settlers moved into the West. The make-up of Canada's population changed because of this wave of immigration. By 1912, almost one-fifth of the people of Canada were not of British or French origin.

But the growth was not without struggle and conflict. The expansion westward disrupted the lives of Métis and Native peoples. Rebellions broke out. Conflicts arose between French and English Canadians in the new country. Canada also struggled to forge its own identity and define its relationship with Britain and the United States.

LEARNING OUTCOMES

By the end of this unit, you will be able to:

- explain the main reasons for Confederation
- demonstrate an understanding of why some colonies supported Confederation and others strongly opposed it
- describe the model of government chosen for Canada
- show how Confederation was extended after 1867
- analyze the causes of the rebellions in the West and their results
- explain the changes brought about by the railway, settlement, and immigration
- understand and apply timelines and brainstorming techniques
- demonstrate an appreciation for differing points of view
- recognize key themes that are important in understanding Canadian history

KEY THEMES

Social Issues

- immigration boom
- Métis life and culture
- effects of immigration on Native nations
- Red River and North-West Rebellions
- role of Chinese workers on the Canadian Pacific Railway
- early African Canadian communities

The Economy

- effects of Confederation on economies of the colonies
- construction of the Canadian Pacific Railway
- Macdonald's National Policy

French-English Relations

- French Canadian culture and nationalism
- guarantees to Quebec at Confederation
- debate over the trial and execution of Louis Riel
- Manitoba Schools Act

Canadian-American Relations

- American expansionism and Manifest Destiny
- Fenian raids
- Reciprocity (trade)
- Treaty of Washington 1873

Canada and the World

- trade with Britain
- British attitudes to the colonies

National Growth and Identity

- Confederation debate
- British North America Act establishes the Dominion of Canada 1867
- building of the Canadian Pacific Railway
- new provinces join Confederation

Regional Development

- settlement of the West
- construction of railways
- Manitoba is created 1870; British Columbia (1871) and Prince Edward Island (1873) join Confederation

Citizenship, Government, and Law

- passage of the British North America Act 1867
- structure of Canada's government at Confederation

Technological Change

- railway building
- new strains of wheat developed for the Canadian prairies
- important Canadian inventors

The Arts

- early Canadian artists and literature about Canada's early years

CHAPTER 1

The Road to Confederation

CONFEDERATION DAY—1 JULY 1867

The bells started to ring at midnight. Early in the morning guns roared a salute from Halifax in the east to Sarnia in the west. Bonfires and fireworks lit up the sky in cities and towns across the new country. It was the birthday of the Dominion of Canada and the people of New Brunswick, Nova Scotia, Ontario, and Quebec were celebrating.

It was a day of blue skies and sunshine. People of all religious faiths gathered to offer prayers for the future of the nation and its people. Through the crowded streets of Ottawa, the new prime minister, John A. Macdonald, and his government made their way to the Parliament Buildings. There, the new governor-general, Lord Monck, was sworn into office.

A royal proclamation was read declaring that the British North America Act was now in effect. Cheers went up for Canada and Queen Victoria. Banners everywhere proclaimed "Good Luck to Confederation!" and "Bienvenue à la Nouvelle Puissance!"

Factors Leading to Confederation

What events led to this celebration of a new nation on 1 July 1867? The idea of a union or confederation of all the British colonies in North America had been talked about for many years. Lord Durham, a former governor of British North America, had dreamed about some day uniting all the colonies under a central government. In the 1860s, five major factors provided the final push for Confederation.

1 War and Expansionism in the US

From 1861 to 1865, people in the United States were fighting a civil war. A civil war is a war between people who live in the same country. In the **American Civil War**, the Northern states were fighting the Southern states. The issue was whether North and South should remain united or separate into two countries. By 1865, the North had won the war and the United States remained one country.

The American Civil War had nothing to do with Canada or Britain directly. But wars have a habit of affecting many countries.

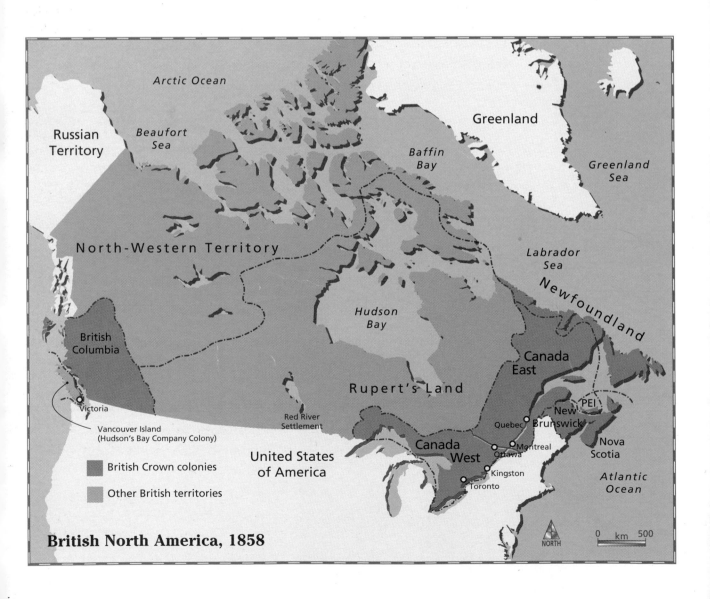

British North America, 1858

Russian Territory

Arctic Ocean

Beaufort Sea

Greenland

Baffin Bay

Greenland Sea

North-Western Territory

Labrador Sea

Newfoundland

Hudson Bay

British Columbia

Rupert's Land

Canada East

Victoria

Red River Settlement

PEI

Vancouver Island (Hudson's Bay Company Colony)

United States of America

Canada West

Quebec

New Brunswick

Montreal
Ottawa

Nova Scotia

Kingston

Atlantic Ocean

Toronto

■ British Crown colonies
□ Other British territories

NORTH

0   km   500

During the American Civil War, Britain appeared to support the Southern states. British shipyards built armed cruisers for sale to the South. One of these, the *Alabama*, captured and destroyed 65 Northern ships. The North demanded that Britain pay damages. After the war, Britain did pay over $15 million to the United States to settle the claims.

When the North won the war in 1865, British North Americans were worried. With the tense relations between Britain and the Northern states, the colonies wondered whether the North would turn its vast armies against them. Would Americans attack the British North American colonies as a way of getting revenge on Britain?

A number of American newspapers and politicians had been talking about the takeover of Britain's territories to the north. Some Americans believed in **Manifest Destiny**. That is, they believed it was natural that the United States would one day expand to control all of North America.

In 1867, the United States purchased Alaska from the Russians. Next, some British North Americans feared the United States would take over the plains northwest of Canada. American settlers, railways, and trade were steadily pressing in on the Red River Settlement near what is now Winnipeg. On the west coast of North America, the discovery of gold in British Columbia brought thousands of Americans into that colony. Now that the Americans owned Alaska, British Columbia was hemmed in to the north and south by the United States.

If the colony of British Columbia and the northwestern plains were to be kept British, something would have to be done quickly. The fear of an American takeover was one factor drawing the colonies together.

2 Fenian Raids

British North American colonies were actually raided by Irish American troops after the Civil War. These troops were members of an organization called the **Fenians**. The Fenians were some of a large number of Irish who had settled in the United States to get away from British rule. At this time, Britain controlled all of Ireland.

The Fenians were a small group determined to fight for a free Ireland. They believed that if they captured the British North American colonies, they might force Britain to free Ireland. Many Fenians were experienced soldiers. They had just been released from the victorious Northern army.

The Fenians planned to invade the colonies at a number of points: at Niagara, along the St. Lawrence River, along the New Brunswick-Maine border, and in the Eastern Townships of Canada East. In May 1866, 1500 Fenians crossed the border at Buffalo. They captured Fort Erie and won a victory over a Canadian force at Ridgeway. Six Canadians were killed and 30 were wounded.

When reinforcements failed to arrive, the Fenians turned back across the border. The same year, British warships prevented a Fenian attack in New Brunswick. For the next several years, people along the border were always on the alert for Fenian raids.

The Fenian attacks had two major effects on the British North American colonies. First, John A. Macdonald turned the raids into an argument for union of the colonies. He asserted that a united country would be better able to resist such invasions.

Second, there was a growing feeling of resentment against the United States government. Many people in the colonies felt that American newspapers encouraged the Fenians. They believed that the United States government should have stopped the Fenians at the border. Thus, the Fenians provided another push toward Confederation.

3 The Trouble With Trade

Another concern to the British North American colonies was the problem of trade. Before 1846, the colonies had enjoyed a

Fenian soldiers clash with British soldiers at Ridgeway in the Niagara Peninsula. Why were the Fenians a factor in pushing the colonies toward Confederation?

special trading position with Britain. Britain allowed wheat and flour from the British North American colonies to enter Britain with a very low tax. This special favour was called a preference.

Suddenly, in 1846, Britain cancelled the preference and established free trade. Britain would allow goods from any country into its markets without a tax.

Britain's new free trade policy caused serious problems for the economy of the British North American colonies. The colonies would no longer have a guaranteed market in Britain. They would have to find new trading partners. The most obvious choice was their rapidly expanding neighbour to the south, the United States.

In 1854, the British North American colonies signed a **Reciprocity Treaty** with the United States. Reciprocity is an agreement between countries allowing trade in certain goods without tariffs or taxes.

By the Reciprocity Treaty, it was agreed that the United States could fish along the shores of Atlantic Canada and that British North Americans could fish in some US waters. Both countries would allow the products of farms, mines, and sea to cross the border tax-free. Fish, timber, grain, and cattle were sent to the United States. American coal and pork were sent north. The treaty was for a 10-year trial period. After that, either side could break the bargain.

During the 1860s, the colonies began to worry that the United States might end the Reciprocity Treaty. Americans were saying they were losing money by allowing British North American goods into their country tax-free. Americans were also upset because of the British support of the South during the Civil War. In 1865, the United States announced that it intended to end the Reciprocity Treaty.

The British North American colonies were thrown into a panic. The only solution seemed to be free trade among themselves.

Strange as it may seem, there was very little trading among the colonies. When they did exchange goods, they always charged high tariffs. When wheat was sent from Canada into the United States, it crossed tax-free into that foreign country. But when wheat was shipped to New Brunswick or Nova Scotia, it was taxed! If the colonies were united, it would be easier for them to trade with one another.

4 The Need for Rail Links

If there was to be trade among the colonies, there had to be a railway link. In 1850, British North America had only 106 km of track. Much of the railway business was going to the American railways. It was time, the colonists thought, to build their own railways.

Between 1850 and 1867, 3570 km of track were added in the colonies. The most ambitious railway project was the **Grand Trunk Railway**. It was to be an all-British route linking Canada West with the Atlantic Ocean at Halifax. By 1860, the Grand Trunk had stretched from Sarnia only as far east as Rivière du Loup. It cost a tremendous amount of money to build and was on the verge of bankruptcy.

Many people thought that the only way the Grand Trunk could be completed to Halifax was if the colonies were united. Then expenses could be shared. The railways would also provide a communication and trade link among the colonies. Some even dreamed of one day extending the railway right across the continent to British Columbia and the Pacific Ocean.

A railway connection with the Maritime colonies was essential for the defence of British North America. If the colonies were attacked by the United States during the winter, the St. Lawrence River would be blocked by ice. There would be no way British troops could get to the colonies from Halifax by rail without crossing through the United States. A railway link between the colonies was essential for trade and defence. It was another reason for Confederation.

5 Changing British Attitudes

In England, a small but vocal group called the **Little Englanders** believed the colonies were a great burden to Britain. One of the biggest expenses of colonies was their defence. The Little Englanders felt it was time that the British North American colonies became independent and paid their own way.

Many people in Britain agreed with the Little Englanders. This was bad news for the colonies. It came at the very time that the Fenians were raiding their borders and Americans were threatening to expand into the West. The views of the Little Englanders also helped to push the colonies toward Confederation.

The Charlottetown Conference 1864

In the summer of 1864, politicians from Nova Scotia, New Brunswick, and Prince Edward Island were planning to meet in Charlottetown to discuss a union of the Maritime colonies. These colonies had been talking about a union for several years. Unexpectedly, they received a request from politicians in Canada asking if they could join the discussions. The Canadians wanted to talk about an even wider union. The Maritime delegates agreed to hear the Canadians.

On 29 August 1864, the *Queen Victoria* left Quebec City for Charlottetown carrying several important Canadian politicians. Among them were George Brown, John A. Macdonald, George-Étienne Cartier, Alexander Galt, and D'Arcy McGee. They had worked out a plan for a union of all the British North American colonies and hoped to convince the politicians of the Maritime colonies to consider the idea.

For a week, the Canadians put forward

SOCIETY AND SOCIAL CHANGE

Early African Canadian Communities

Most of Canada's population at Confederation was of either French or British heritage. But the new country was already home to people from other diverse cultures.

The first major wave of immigration into British North America by people of African descent occurred at the end of the American Revolution in 1763. During the Revolution, the British promised freedom to any African American slaves who joined the British forces. After the revolutionary war, several groups of African American Loyalists settled in Nova Scotia around Birchtown and Digby. Others also came after the War of 1812 and settled around Amherst and Truro.

In 1796, hundreds of Black Jamaicans came to Halifax. They were known as Maroons. Many were hired to help with the building of the Citadel in Halifax. Today, a part of the Citadel is still known as the Maroon Bastion. The Maroons found it difficult adjusting to the climate and the life in Nova Scotia. After a few years, at their own request, they went to Sierra Leone, a small country on the west coast of Africa.

Between 1840 and 1860, another 30 000 Black settlers came to British North America by way of the **Underground Railroad**. This "railroad" was not a real railroad. It was the name given to the network of safe houses and people who helped escaped slaves from the United States come to Canada. Slavery had been abolished in the British Empire in 1834, but had not been abolished in the United States.

American slaves escaping to Canada by way of the Underground Railroad.

Two of the most important African Canadian communities were the Elgin settlement near Chatham, Ontario, and Africville in the north end of Halifax, Nova Scotia. Descendants of the settlers still live in these areas today.

Like other immigrants in this period, many of the people who arrived by way of the Underground Railroad became farmers. Often shut out from society, however, they established their own schools and churches and formed strong communities. By 1921, there were approximately 21 000 African Canadians. The next major wave of Black immigration did not come until after World War II.

1. Harriet Tubman was a famous "conductor" on the Underground Railroad. Find out more about her and how people came to Canada on the Underground Railroad.
2. What difficulties did early African Canadian settlers face? How were some of these difficulties overcome?

Delegates to the Charlottetown Conference, 1864.

the reasons why the Maritime colonies should join in a union with Canada. The Saint John daily newspaper reported that the arguments of Macdonald, Brown, Cartier, and the other Canadians were "almost irresistible." As they talked, the delegates became convinced that Confederation could work.

The parties and social festivities of the conference also added to the friendly atmosphere. The luncheon on the *Queen Victoria* was arguably the most important piece of shipboard hospitality in Canadian history. Most of the delegates decided that afternoon that Confederation was a real possibility.

As a result of the **Charlottetown Conference**, the Maritime delegates set aside the idea of a Maritime union. They agreed to meet with the Canadians for further discussions at Quebec City in October.

The Quebec Conference 1864

At Quebec City that October, seven delegates from New Brunswick, seven from Prince Edward Island, and five from Nova

Scotia met the twelve delegates from Canada East and Canada West once again. Newfoundland, which had not been represented at Charlottetown, also sent two officials.

At the **Quebec Conference**, the Fathers of Confederation agreed on one point. The union must be a strong one that could not be broken by any one province. The central government must be more powerful in every way than the governments of the provinces.

There were other factors to be worked out. How many representatives would each province have in the central government? Where would the money come from to run the central government? What powers would the prime minister have? Would they have two houses of Parliament as the British system had? Would there be an elected House of Commons to make the laws? Would there be an appointed House of Lords to double-check all laws passed by the House of Commons? Would other colonies, such as British Columbia, be able to enter Confederation in the future?

When these and many other questions

had been discussed, the delegates drew up the **Seventy-two Resolutions**. These resolutions provided a plan for the new partnership of the colonies.

During the summer and fall of 1864, the idea of Confederation caught on. Before that time, most of the politicians had been strangers to one another. Now they found themselves working together for something bigger than they had ever known before. For Confederation, there were still many hurdles ahead.

The Quebec Conference was a beginning, but the Seventy-two Resolutions had to be accepted by the government of each colony. The Fathers of Confederation went home to convince their people of the idea. Would the people of the colonies be as excited about Confederation as were the delegates to the Charlottetown and Quebec conferences?

Seesaw in New Brunswick

In New Brunswick, Premier Leonard Tilley was a staunch supporter of Confederation. After the Quebec Conference, Tilley called an election in New Brunswick. Confederation was the main issue. Those who were opposed to Confederation **(anti-Confederationists)** made fun of the whole idea. At the Quebec Conference, it had been decided that each province would receive a sum of money each year from the central government. This money was called a subsidy. The amount of the subsidy was based on the population of the colony. In the case of New Brunswick, the subsidy amounted to 80¢ per person. Opponents of Confederation complained that Tilley was selling New Brunswickers out to the Canadians for 80¢ each.

On election day in 1865, the anti-Confederationists won easily. It was a black day for those who dreamed of a great united country. Without New Brunswick, there could be no Confederation. New Brunswick was the land link between Canada and the other Atlantic colonies.

But Leonard Tilley did not give up. In the months that followed, he travelled throughout the colony talking to people and explaining Confederation. He was a sincere and honest speaker. Tilley's personal efforts helped to win many people over to the idea of a union.

Three other events helped to convince New Brunswickers that they should reconsider Confederation. First, the United States ended reciprocity with the British North American colonies. Second, the British government sent a message encouraging New Brunswickers to join Confederation. Third, the Fenians attacked New Brunswick in 1866. While the Fenian threat was still present, an election was called in 1866. The people had another chance to say if they wanted Confederation. This time, people in New Brunswick voted in favour of Confederation.

Success in Canada West

In Canada, the politicians spent more than a month debating the Quebec Conference resolutions. One of the most impressive speeches in the Assembly was given by George Brown.

Brown gave six main reasons why he was in favour of Confederation:
1. Confederation would change five unimportant colonies into a great and powerful nation.
2. It would remove the barriers to trade among the colonies and provide a market of four million people.
3. Canada would become the third largest sea-going nation in the world after Britain and the United States.
4. A strong new country would encourage people to come from other countries to settle in Canada.
5. Since the United States had cancelled

THE ARTS

Cornelius Krieghoff, Merrymaking, *1860. The inn in this painting still stands near Montmorency Falls in Quebec.*

Early Canadian Artists

Cornelius Krieghoff, 1815-1872
Cornelius Krieghoff was one of Canada's most famous painters of the mid-nineteenth century. Born in Amsterdam in 1815, he arrived in Canada about 1846 and settled in Quebec. He was very taken with French Canadian rural society in Quebec and painted many scenes of everyday life. His paintings depict farm life, festive celebrations, tavern scenes, and country customs. The scenes are packed with details and crowded with lively figures. His paintings were popular as souvenirs for tourists and soldiers.

Homer Watson, 1855–1936
Homer Watson was also inspired by rural life and landscapes. He became intensely interested in art at age 15 and spent hours pouring over the illustrated magazines of the day. Born in Doon, Ontario, many of his paintings focussed on what he saw around him. His scenes became known for their detail, intensity, and the sense of mystery in land and sky that they captured.

Homer Watson,
Log-cutting in the Woods, *1894.*

1. a) Describe the scenes in the paintings.
   b) What similarities and differences can you identify?
   c) What do the paintings tell you about life in nineteenth century Canada?
2. Examine paintings of other artists from this period. What are the most common subjects of the paintings?

reciprocity with the colonies, Confederation would provide other markets for their goods.

6. In case of war, all the colonies would stand strong together.

The people of Canada West listened to respected leaders such as George Brown and John A. Macdonald. When the vote was taken in 1865, the Quebec Resolutions were approved by a vote of 91 to 33.

Debate in Canada East

In Canada East, there were bitter critics of the plan for Confederation. A. A. Dorion complained that Canada East was being sold out. He argued that French-speaking Canadians would be completely outnumbered in Confederation because the new government would be based on representation by population. The provinces with the largest population would receive the most seats in the legislature.

A majority of French Canadians were eventually won over to the idea of Confederation by George-Étienne Cartier. Cartier travelled around Canada East trying to persuade the French-speaking people that they had nothing to worry about. He explained that in Confederation French and English Canadians would be equal partners. He promised they would not lose their language, their religion, or their schools. He warned them that if they did not join Confederation, Canada East could be swallowed up by the United States. The Roman Catholic Church also added its voice in support of Confederation.

When it came time to vote in 1865, 26 of the 48 French-speaking members of the combined Assembly of Canada East and Canada West voted for

Confederation. Cartier and the supporters of Confederation had carried the day.

Division in Nova Scotia

Charles Tupper was the Premier of Nova Scotia. He was excited and enthusiastic about the possibility of a union. But, when he returned to Halifax from Quebec, he found trouble. Opposition leaders, especially Joseph Howe, were fiercely opposed to union. A powerful separatist movement had come to life in Nova Scotia. Opponents objected to the subsidy. In Nova Scotia, this subsidy amounted to 40¢ per person. "Tupper has sold out to central Canada for a grant of 40¢ per person—the price of a sheepskin," roared Joseph Howe. Tupper knew that if he tried to introduce the Seventy-two Resolutions in the Assembly, he would be defeated.

Instead, he stalled for time. He travelled

In Nova Scotia, Joseph Howe led the campaign against Confederation.

throughout the colony trying to destroy the arguments of Howe and the anti-Confederationists. This was the fight of Tupper's life. Bitter statements were written and spoken on both sides. The people of Nova Scotia were deeply divided. Friendships were broken up when people disagreed over the need for union.

About that time, word reached Nova Scotia of the Fenian threat to New Brunswick. Many thought that there was a real possibility Nova Scotia would be invaded too. Some people in Nova Scotia began to hint that they would reconsider if they received a better deal from Ottawa.

Tupper suggested that delegates from the colonies should meet in London, England, to work out a plan that would satisfy them all. In London, Tupper worked with the delegates from Canada, New Brunswick, and Nova Scotia to make final plans for union.

While the delegates were in London, Howe continued his fight. Nevertheless, in 1866 Nova Scotia agreed to enter the partnership.

Rejection in Newfoundland and Labrador

Newfoundland and Labrador flatly rejected the Quebec Resolutions and waited 82 years before it joined Canada. The colony had not sent representatives to Charlottetown. However, two delegates had attended the Quebec Conference. One of them, F.B.T. Carter, became the colony's premier in 1865. Although Carter personally was in favour of Confederation, he could not convince his independent people. They were very proud of their historic ties with Britain and the fact that they were Britain's first overseas colony.

A wealthy St. John's merchant, C.F. Bennett, led the fight against Confederation. He warned that the new government would probably tax their boats, fish, and fishing tackle. Goods from Canada, he said, would be so cheap that products from Newfoundland and Labrador would not sell. He hinted that young people from the colony would be expected to give up their lives "in defence of the desert sands" of Canada, though Canada promised that they would not have to serve in the army on the mainland.

On the night Confederation was defeated in Newfoundland in 1866, a huge parade wound through the streets of St. John's. Anti-Confederationists pushed a large coffin labelled "Confederation." The coffin was buried during a fake funeral. Confederation was a dead issue in Newfoundland and Labrador. It stayed buried until 1949 when Newfoundland and Labrador joined Canada as the tenth province.

Rejection in Prince Edward Island

Prince Edward Island also rejected the Quebec Resolutions in 1866. It was not until six years after Confederation, in 1873, that Prince Edward Island entered the union.

Prince Edward Islanders felt Charlottetown should be considered as the new capital of Canada. It was not. The idea of a union had been born at the Charlottetown Conference and many Islanders thought their city deserved the honour.

A more important reason for turning down Confederation was the sheer size of the new country. Prince Edward Islanders feared they would be swamped in the union. The Fathers had agreed on representation by population in the new Parliament. Prince Edward Island had a very small population, smaller than the city of Montreal. With representation by population, Prince Edward Island would have only 5 members in the House of Commons out of a total of 194 members. How could the voice of the island be heard with only 5 members in Parliament?

The people of the island listened to all the talk of a railway from Canada to the Maritimes. Since their province was an island, the railway was of no great interest to them. What they needed was a railway to join the places on the island. There was no mention of that in the Quebec Resolutions.

SOCIETY AND SOCIAL CHANGE

An Anti-Confederation Song from Newfoundland

Hurrah for our own native isle, Newfoundland!
Not a stranger shall hold one inch of its strand!
Her face turns to Britain, her back to the Gulf,
Come near at your peril, Canadian Wolf!

Ye brave Newfoundlanders who plough the salt sea
With hearts like the eagle so bold and so free,
The time is at hand when you'll all have to say
If Confederation will carry the day.

Cheap tea and molasses they say they will give,
All taxes take off that the poor man may live;
Cheap nails and cheap lumber our coffins to make,
And homespun to mend our old clothes when they break.

If they take off the taxes how then will they meet
The heavy expense of the country's upkeep?
Just give them the chance to get us in the scrape
And they'll chain us like slaves with pen, ink, and red tape.

Would you barter the rights that your fathers have won,
Your freedom transmitted from father to son?
For a few thousand dollars of Canadian gold,
Don't let it be said that your birthright was sold.

Then hurrah for our own native isle, Newfoundland!
Not a stranger shall hold one inch of its strand!
Her face turns to Britain, her back to the Gulf,
Come near at your peril, Canadian Wolf!

1. What main objections does this song suggest Newfoundlanders had to Confederation?
2. Why is a folk song an effective way to express feelings and concerns about key issues? Suggest other examples of folk songs that have expressed a strong stand on an issue.
3. Write one other stanza to go before the final refrain in the song or write a stanza for a pro-Confederation song from one of the other colonies.

Nor was there any mention of buying out the absentee landlords of the island. Though the Islanders worked the farms, the land was owned by wealthy landlords in Britain. Not until the last minute was it suggested that the new union should buy the land. But it was too late. The Islanders had made up their minds. They wanted no part of Confederation.

Three Fathers of Confederation from Prince Edward Island tried their best to convince the Islanders to join. But nothing that John H. Gray, William H. Pope, or Edward Whelan could do or say seemed to make any difference. Prince Edward Island preferred "to stand off and watch the game for a little while."

Confederation Won— The London Conference 1866

The British North American colonies still belonged to Britain. The union could not become official until the British Parliament approved it. Sixteen delegates went to talk over the matter with members of the British Parliament.

Britain was in favour of Confederation. If the colonies were united, the British hoped they could look after themselves. Many of Britain's responsibilities would be over. In the spring of 1867, the **British North America Act**, often called the **BNA**

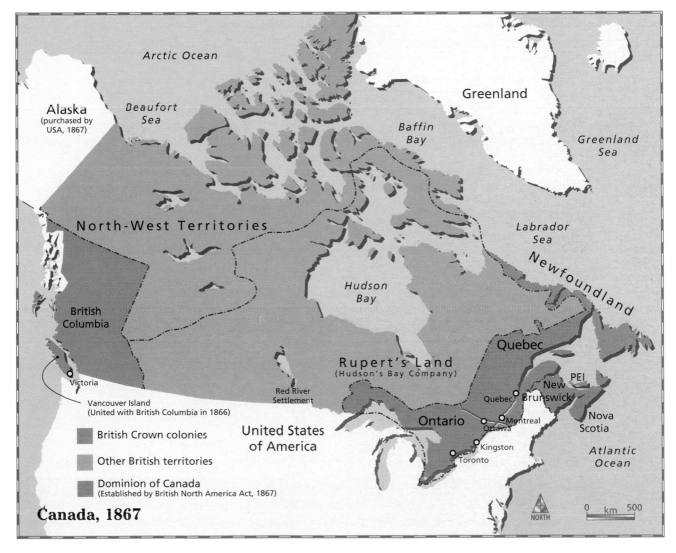

Canada, 1867

British Crown colonies

Other British territories

Dominion of Canada
(Established by British North America Act, 1867)

Act, was introduced in the British Parliament. The Dominion of Canada was created by the BNA Act. It united four provinces: New Brunswick, Nova Scotia, and the two Canadas, renamed Ontario and Quebec.

The Act was built on the Seventy-two Resolutions worked out at the Quebec Conference. It passed quickly without any major changes. Queen Victoria put her signature on it and 1 July 1867 was proclaimed as the day the Act would come into effect.

Celebration!

On 1 July 1867, most of the people in the new country of Canada took a holiday. In Toronto, a great celebration took place at the Horticultural Gardens. The gardens were lighted with Chinese lanterns. Fresh strawberries and ice cream were served.

A concert was followed by dancing. In Quebec, boat races on the St. Lawrence River, horse races, and cricket matches were held. In the Maritimes, many families travelled to the sea for a day of swimming and a picnic supper of salads, cold meat, pies, and cakes. Almost everywhere, there was the feeling that this day was just the beginning of great things for Canada.

But in some parts of the new Dominion, the mood was not one of rejoicing. Anti-Confederationists displayed flags at half-mast. They wore black clothes as a sign of mourning. A likeness of Dr. Tupper was burned side-by-side with a rat in Nova Scotia.

In New Brunswick, a newspaper carried a death notice on its front page: "Died—at her residence in the city of Fredericton, The Province of New Brunswick, in the eighty-third year of her age."

DEVELOPING SKILLS: USING TIMELINES

Can you recall all the jumbled events of the movement for Confederation? So much was happening quickly that it is not easy to sort out the events. A timeline is an excellent way to record the most important events in chronological order, that is, the order in which they occurred. A timeline can give you a clear overall picture of what happened at a glance.

Suppose you wanted to develop a timeline to record the important events that led to Confederation. How would you do it?

■ Step 1
First, you need to decide what period your timeline will cover. For a timeline of important events leading to Confederation, you could start your timeline with the planned talks about Maritime Union and end it with the celebrations on 1 July 1867, for example.

■ Step 2
Use a long strip of paper or tape two sheets end to end. Draw a line down the page and divide it into the years 1864 to 1867. Timelines can also be divided into days, months, or decades depending on your topic and the amount of detail you want to show.

■ Step 3
Give your timeline a title that clearly describes its content.

■ Step 4
Select the most important events leading to Confederation. Record these events on the timeline in point form and in chronological order. A sample timeline has been started for you on the next page.

■ Step 5
Add sketches, symbols, or pictures to your timeline to illustrate some of the events. Be creative.

■ Step 6
Compare your timeline with that of a classmate.

Have you identified the same events? Why or why not? Do you have the events in the same order? If in doubt, double check by rereading the text.

■ Step 7

Discuss why a timeline is a useful tool for history students. Examine other examples of timelines. Examine the timelines at the beginning of each unit in this book to get an overview of what you will be studying and for review when you have completed your study.

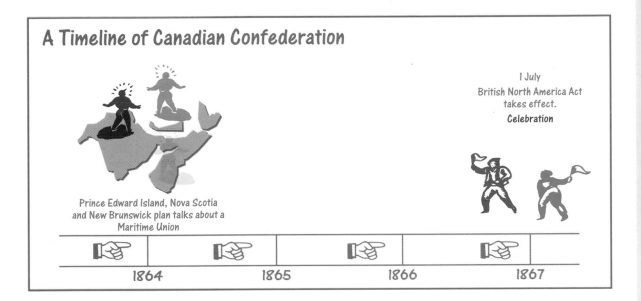

A Timeline of Canadian Confederation

1 July
British North America Act
takes effect.
Celebration

Prince Edward Island, Nova Scotia and New Brunswick plan talks about a Maritime Union

| 1864 | 1865 | 1866 | 1867 |

Models for Government

Before Confederation, the British North American colonies had responsible government. Members were elected by the people to a Legislative Assembly. Executive and Legislative councils were chosen from the party with the most members in the Assembly. The governor was the representative of the Queen or King of Britain and the head of the colonial government. He was required, however, to follow the advice of the councillors and the Assembly. The Fathers of Confederation kept responsible government, but the organization of the government changed.

In forming the new government for Canada, the Fathers of Confederation had two models: the British and the American.

They selected what they believed were the best features from both.

The British Model

Canada was still loyal to Britain so the Queen would continue to be the head of state for the Canadian government. There was no talk of separation from Britain. A Governor General would be the Queen's representative in Canada.

It was also decided that Canada would have a **parliamentary government** fashioned on the example of the British system. The British government had a prime minister and a cabinet of senior ministers who controlled government policy. They were all members of the political party that had the most representatives in the House of Commons.

The House of Commons was made up of

representatives elected by the people. The government would be responsible to the people of Canada. If the prime minister and his party lost the support of a majority of the members in the House of Commons, they could be voted out of power.

In Canada, the House of Commons would consist of elected representatives from each of the provinces. Quebec was guaranteed 65 members to ensure a strong voice for the French-speaking population. The other provinces would elect members on the basis of their populations.

The British government also had a second house of Parliament called the House of Lords. Canada would also have a second house, but it would be called the Senate. The name was taken from the American system. There were to be 72 lifetime members in the Senate—24 from Quebec, 24 from Ontario, and 24 from the Maritimes. The main function of the Senate was to double-check all laws passed by the elected House of Commons.

The American Model

From the American system of government, Canadians chose the idea of a **federal union**. In a federal union, a federal or central government deals with matters of concern to the whole nation. But each province or state deals with its own affairs independently of the central government. In other words, the Canadian provinces could make their own decisions on roads, for example, without having to ask permission of the federal government.

The questions then arose: What powers should the federal government have? What powers should the provincial governments have? Here again, the Fathers of Confederation learned from the American example.

In their federation, the Americans gave wide powers to the states. Macdonald

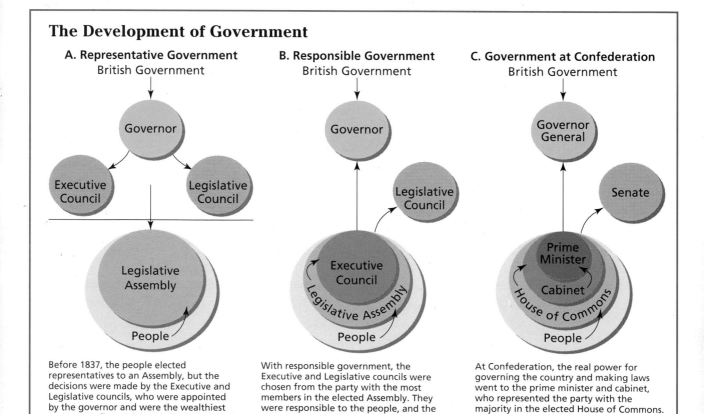

The Development of Government

A. Representative Government
British Government

Governor

Executive Council

Legislative Council

Legislative Assembly

People

Before 1837, the people elected representatives to an Assembly, but the decisions were made by the Executive and Legislative councils, who were appointed by the governor and were the wealthiest and most influential people in the colony.

B. Responsible Government
British Government

Governor

Legislative Council

Executive Council

Legislative Assembly

People

With responsible government, the Executive and Legislative councils were chosen from the party with the most members in the elected Assembly. They were responsible to the people, and the governor was obliged to follow their advice.

C. Government at Confederation
British Government

Governor General

Senate

Prime Minister

Cabinet

House of Commons

People

At Confederation, the real power for governing the country and making laws went to the prime minister and cabinet, who represented the party with the majority in the elected House of Commons. The government was based on features from the British and American systems.

Can you identify each Canadian prime minister pictured here? Which are not pictured?

Prime Ministers of Canada

1. Sir John A. Macdonald   Conservative   1867–1873, 1878–1891
2. Alexander Mackenzie   Liberal   1873–1878
3. John Abbott   Conservative   1891–1892
4. Sir John Thompson   Conservative   1892–1894
5. Sir Mackenzie Bowell   Conservative   1894–1896
6. Sir Charles Tupper   Conservative   1896
7. Sir Wilfrid Laurier   Liberal   1896–1911
8. Robert Borden   Conservative   1911–1920
9. Arthur Meighen   Conservative   1920–1921, 1926
10. W. L. Mackenzie King   Liberal   1921–1926, 1926–1930, 1935–1948
11. R. B. Bennett   Conservative   1930–1935
12. Louis St. Laurent   Liberal   1948–1957
13. John G. Diefenbaker   Conservative   1957–1963
14. Lester B. Pearson   Liberal   1963–1968
15. Pierre Elliott Trudeau   Liberal   1968–1979, 1980–1984
16. Joseph Clark   Conservative   1979–1980
17. John Napier Turner   Liberal   1984
18. Brian Mulroney   Conservative   1984–1993
19. Kim Campbell   Conservative   1993
20. Jean Chrétien   Liberal   1993–

thought this was the great weakness of the American system. The Civil War that had just ended arose out of a dispute over the rights of individual states. This mistake must be avoided in Canada at all costs. Canada must have a strong central government and the provinces should be weaker.

The Division of Powers

The Fathers of Confederation made a list of the powers the provinces could have. Provinces were responsible for education, property rights, mines and forests, the licensing of businesses, raising money by taxes (such as a provincial sales taxes) for provincial purposes, and other matters of provincial concern. All other powers belonged to the federal government.

The federal government would control trade, defence, foreign affairs, banks, shipping, fisheries, and criminal law. It was also given the power to tax people. The federal government could disallow any law passed by the provinces.

Finances

By the BNA Act, the federal government took over all the debts of the provinces. It also took over most of the provinces' sources of income, such as customs duties. Therefore, every province was given a sum of money or subsidy by the federal government every year. The amount of money was based on the population of the province.

Other Matters

The British North America Act promised that an Intercolonial Railway connecting the St. Lawrence River with Halifax would be started within six months. It also allowed for other provinces to join the Dominion in the future.

The Fathers of Confederation were careful to protect the rights of the French-speaking people of Quebec. French Canadians would keep their own province, language, religion, and schools. Both Roman Catholic and Protestant schools were guaranteed. English and French languages were to be used in the central Parliament, in the Parliament of Quebec, and in federal courts. The new country of Canada was firmly established.

ACTIVITIES

Check Your Understanding

1. Start a *Factfile* on Canadian history. This *Factfile* will be your personal file of key terms, their meanings, and their historical importance. Set aside a section of your notebook for your *Factfile* or create it on computer. You will be adding to your file as you encounter new terms throughout your study. Refer to your *Factfile* for quick reference any time you need a reminder about some key information.
   a) Divide the pages in your notebook or on your computer into three columns. Make the middle column the widest.
   b) In the left column, write the key term. In the middle column, write a definition or description of the term. Include a picture, sketch, or computer graphic to help you describe the term if you can.
   c) In the third column, write a brief point-form note about the historical importance of the term.

Start your *Factfile* with the following terms.

Confederation	Charlottetown Conference 1864
American Civil War	Quebec Conference 1864
Manifest Destiny	Seventy-two Resolutions
Fenians	anti-Confederationists
Reciprocity Treaty 1854	British North America Act (BNA Act)
Grand Trunk Railroad	parliamentary government
Little Englanders	federal union
Underground Railroad	

2. Why were the British North American colonies concerned about an American invasion in 1865?

3. a) Who were the Fenians and what were their goals?
   b) How did they try to achieve these goals?
   c) In which British North American colonies did the Fenians have the greatest effect on public opinion? Why?
   d) How did the Fenians help the cause of Confederation?

4. a) Who were the Little Englanders? What were their main beliefs?
   b) Why did they cause Canadians to worry?

5. a) What problems with trade were the colonies facing in the 1860s? How did these problems provide a push for Confederation?
   b) Why were more railway links important?

6. What major decisions were made at
   a) the Charlottetown Conference
   b) the Quebec Conference
   c) the London Conference?

Confirm Your Learning

7. George-Étienne Cartier said:"When all colonies are united the enemy will know that if he attacks any province he will have to deal with the combined forces of the Empire."
   a) Who was "the enemy?"
   b) Who were "the combined forces of the Empire?"
   c) Why were British troops stationed in the colonies?
   d) Why would it be difficult for an individual colony to defend itself?

8. What arguments might each of the following give for preferring a Maritime union rather than a union of all the colonies? Explain your answers.
   a) a Nova Scotia merchant
   b) a Prince Edward Island farmer
   c) a New Brunswick railway worker
   d) a Newfoundlander who earns a living from fishing

9. a) Why did the people of Newfoundland and Prince Edward Island reject Confederation?
   b) Outline reasons why the Canadas, New Brunswick, and Nova Scotia supported the union of the colonies.

10. a) The BNA Act set out the powers of the federal and provincial governments. Create a two-column chart with the headings "Federal Powers" and "Provincial Powers." Place the items in the following list in the correct columns.

   Defence   Banks
   Education   Taxation
   Mines and Forests   Licensing of Businesses
   Fisheries   Immigration
   Customs Duties   Trade
   Criminal Law   Foreign Affairs
   Property Rights   Native Affairs

   b) Which government received the greatest powers? Why?

   c) Do you agree this division of powers was a good one? Explain.

11. a) On what kind of union did the Fathers of Confederation decide? Why?

   b) How was it different from the American one? Why?

12. *Extra, Extra! Read all about it!* Write newspaper headlines reflecting the mood and events in each of the colonies after the Confederation votes.

Challenge Your Mind

13. a) What are the advantages and disadvantages for Canada of reciprocity with the United States?

   b) Does Canada have reciprocity with the United States today? Do the provinces have reciprocity with each other today?

14. Create posters that could have appeared in the colonies in the 1860s both supporting and denouncing Confederation. Be creative. Remember that posters often use strong images or symbols to get their message across.

15. a) The Native peoples of British North America were not consulted about Confederation. They were not given a chance to decide whether or not it would be good for them or how they might be part of it. How do you think they felt?

   b) How might Canada be different today if Native peoples had been able to give their point of view?

   c) How might the position of Native peoples be different today if they had been given a chance to participate directly in the affairs of Canada?

16. If your town or city is older than Confederation, try to find out how the birth of Confederation was celebrated (or mourned). Local libraries and old newspapers will help you. Create a mural depicting the event.

CHAPTER 2

The Nation Expands

Go West!

What does this poster suggest about the growth of Canada after Confederation?

The Greatest Land Deal in History

Confederation in 1867 established the new nation of Canada. In the years following, thoughts turned to expanding the nation westward into the vast lands controlled by the Hudson's Bay Company. People dreamed of turning that land into farms where their children could settle.

The Hudson's Bay Company had owned the vast territory known as **Rupert's Land** since 1670. The territory included all the land drained by the rivers that flowed into Hudson Bay. For almost 200 years no one, except Native peoples and fur traders, cared very much about Rupert's Land. Then, at the time of Confederation, Canadians began to think seriously about settling the West.

The Hudson's Bay Company lands also included the **Red River Settlement** around Fort Garry (near the present city of Winnipeg). About 12 000 settlers lived in the colony. The settlers had sent petitions to London protesting the way the Hudson's Bay Company was ruling their settlement. They felt they did not have the rights and privileges British subjects should enjoy. They preferred to be part of Canada.

Canada's new prime minister, John A. Macdonald, feared that Canada and Britain would lose the West if they did not act. In a letter in 1865 he wrote:

> *I am perfectly willing to leave Rupert's Land a wilderness for the next half century, but I fear that if the Canadians do not go in, the Yankees will.*

Canada decided to send delegates to England to find out if the Hudson's Bay Company would sell its empire to Canada. The Company was in no hurry to give up its claim to the land. But finally, a price was agreed upon. The Hudson's Bay Company would be paid 300 000 pounds and keep one-twentieth of the fertile land or about 2.5 million ha. Eventually, it would sell parts of that land to settlers. The Company also kept its trading posts and the land immediately around them. The whole region was to be transferred to Canada on 1 December 1869 and renamed the **North-West Territories**. Canada decided the North-West Territories would be ruled by a lieutenant-governor and council appointed by the federal government.

Thus one of the greatest land deals in history was completed. Before its third birthday, Canada would stretch almost from sea to sea.

Trouble at Red River

But the expansion westward was not so simple as this deal signed on paper suggested. Long before the Hudson's Bay lands were sold to Canada in 1869, Native peoples had lived in and travelled over this vast territory. Most of the Native groups in the West were nomadic. They moved from place to place hunting buffalo and trapping fur-bearing animals.

The few European settlers in the region were Hudson's Bay Company employees working at lonely, scattered trading posts. Their job was to buy furs from the Native peoples in exchange for goods. Only at Red River was there a large populated settlement in the 1860s. Many of these settlers were farmers or merchants.

A large number of people living in the Red River Settlement were **Métis**. The Métis were people of mixed heritage—Native and European. They had a distinct culture that was a blend of European and Native ways. They called themselves the "Métis Nation."

In the early days, the Métis formed the backbone of the fur trade in the West. They acted as agents between the Native groups and the Europeans. They bought furs from the Native peoples and sold them to the Hudson's Bay Company agents. Some transported goods in their Red River carts.

A Red River cart on the prairie. The Red River carts were made entirely of wood with the parts held together by wooden pegs and strips of rawhide.

These were the days before the railroad reached the West.

Background to Rebellion

The Hudson's Bay Company had withdrawn its rule from Rupert's Land in January 1869. The Canadian government was not entitled to establish rule until December. For almost 12 months, the people of the territory had no legal government. Who would protect their rights?

On sunny June days in 1869, crews of Canadian surveyors appeared on the farms of the Métis in the Red River Settlement. The Canadian government was eager to survey the land recently bought from the Hudson's Bay Company. This was ground the Métis people thought was theirs to use.

The Métis were told by the surveyors that the land would be marked out in large squares as it was in Ontario. This would mean an end to their narrow river farms. Métis farms were laid out in narrow strips facing the rivers, in the same way the people of New France had laid out farms along the St. Lawrence River.

Métis people were worried because they had no papers to prove they owned their homes and their lands. The thought of settlers coming in and taking over their lands alarmed them. Many were also disturbed by the rumours that the Canadian government was planning to build a railroad right through the buffalo country. Some were ready to fight to keep what they thought was rightfully theirs.

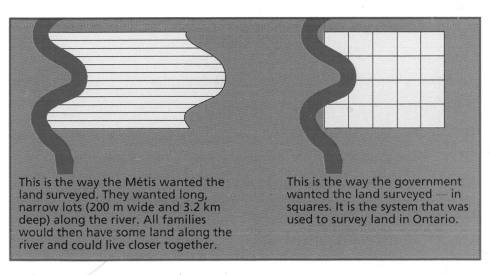

This is the way the Métis wanted the land surveyed. They wanted long, narrow lots (200 m wide and 3.2 km deep) along the river. All families would then have some land along the river and could live closer together.

This is the way the government wanted the land surveyed — in squares. It is the system that was used to survey land in Ontario.

The Métis of the Red River Settlement gathered in a council meeting. They turned for leadership to a 25-year-old Métis man, Louis Riel. On 11 October 1869, the crew of Canadian surveyors stepped onto André Nault's land. He saddled his horse and rode for help. Nault returned with Riel and 16 Métis. Riel placed his moccasined foot on the surveyor's chain and said, "You go no farther."

Afterwards, Riel was asked why he had done this. He said that the Canadian government had no right to make surveys before the land had been transferred to Canada. With that act, Louis Riel stepped onto the stage of Canadian history. He became the champion of the Métis people. The **Red River Rebellion** was about to begin.

The Red River Rebellion, 1869-70

One week after Louis Riel stepped on the surveyor's chain, he formed the **National Committee of the Métis**. The committee was to decide how to protect Métis lands. Shortly afterwards, the Métis heard that William McDougall was coming from Ottawa to Fort Garry to govern the territory.

When McDougall arrived at the border of the settlement, he found the road to Fort Garry blocked by representatives of the National Committee of the Métis. The Métis told him to return to Ottawa. They would not have any governor without being consulted first. McDougall had no choice. He turned back to the closest American frontier town and waited for orders from Ottawa.

In the meantime, Louis Riel and the Métis took up their position in the fortress of Fort Garry. They set up a government of their own to replace the Hudson's Bay Company's rule of the colony. It was known as the **Provisional Government**. Riel said it spoke for their area in any dealings with the Canadian government.

Some people in the settlement thought that this was an act of rebellion. Riel never considered himself a rebel. His people were loyal citizens of the Queen. They were fighting against two things. First, the Hudson's Bay Company had sold their land to Canada without telling them. Second, the Canadian government was taking over without consulting them.

People thought that Macdonald would rush troops to the Red River to remove Riel from Fort Garry. But Macdonald chose another course. The Red River Settlement did not belong to Canada until 1 December 1869. Canada would not accept the region before there was peace.

The Thomas Scott Affair

Most of the people of the Red River Settlement supported Riel's government. Only a small group who had come from Ontario refused to accept it. They were known as "the Canadians." One of these Canadians was Thomas Scott. When riots broke out, a number of Canadians, including Thomas Scott, were jailed by Riel.

Louis Riel was the leader of the Métis in the West. Why did he become one of the most controversial figures in Canadian history?

The people of Red River drew up a **Métis Bill of Rights** and sent it to Ottawa. The major demands were as follows:

1. the territory must have the right to enter Canada's Confederation as a province;
2. the people should be able to send four members of Parliament to Ottawa;
3. they should have control over their local affairs;
4. French and English languages should be equal in schools and law courts; and
5. above all, the Métis should be able to keep their customs and their way of life.

These requests were considered fair in Ottawa. But a serious incident then occurred. Thomas Scott, who was in jail on a charge of taking up arms against Riel's government, struck his guards, called the Métis a pack of cowards, insulted their Roman Catholic religion, and threatened to murder Riel. Riel ordered Scott brought to trial. The court found him guilty and demanded the death penalty. Within 24 hours, Thomas Scott was brought before a firing squad.

Why would Riel allow such a sentence to be carried out so quickly? Riel may have felt he had to prove that his Provisional Government must be obeyed. He had to show the Canadian government that he was in charge. Then Ottawa would have to work out the terms of the colony's entrance into Confederation with the Provisional Government.

When the news of Thomas Scott's execution reached Ontario, the uproar started. Scott was English-speaking and a member of the Protestant religion. People in his home province were outraged by his death. Newspapers throughout the province called for revenge. People in Ontario demanded that Riel be hanged for Scott's murder. They even offered a reward for Riel's arrest.

On the other hand, in the Roman Catholic province of Quebec, many people said Riel's actions were justified. They felt sympathetic toward Riel and his government. They placed the blame for the problem in the Red River Settlement on the "troublemakers" from Ontario.

The execution of Thomas Scott aroused bitter feelings between English and French Canadians. It would be a long time before the case of Thomas Scott was forgotten.

Aftermath of the Rebellion

Riel's Provisional Government worked out an agreement with Ottawa called the **Manitoba Act**. On 15 July 1870, the Red River Settlement entered Confederation. The small settled region around Fort Garry became known as Manitoba—Canada's fifth province.

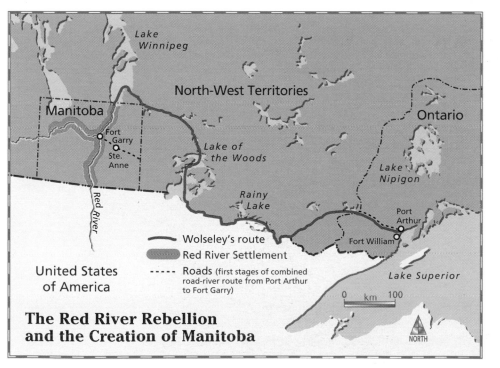

Lake Winnipeg

North-West Territories

Manitoba

Fort Garry

Ste. Anne

Red River

Lake of the Woods

Rainy Lake

Ontario

Lake Nipigon

Port Arthur

Fort William

Lake Superior

— Wolseley's route
▬ Red River Settlement

United States of America

- - - - Roads (first stages of combined road-river route from Port Arthur to Fort Garry)

0   km   100

NORTH

The Red River Rebellion and the Creation of Manitoba

In time, however, many Métis became dissatisfied as more settlers moved into Manitoba. They moved farther west to join other Métis in the area of Canada we now know as Saskatchewan. They hoped to be able to hunt buffalo and follow their traditional way of life.

Riel was pleased with the Manitoba Act. He believed that he had founded a new province. He had won for his people the right to be represented in Ottawa. They had received land, French schools, and protection of the French language. Now he was prepared to turn over control of the settlement to the new lieutenant-governor sent from Ottawa.

Meanwhile, Macdonald decided to send troops to the Red River in case of further trouble. The troops would be made up of British and Canadian men headed by Colonel Garnet Wolseley. With the troops there, it would also be clear to the United States that Canada was claiming the West.

It took 13 weeks for Colonel Wolseley to reach Manitoba. Since there was no railroad, the soldiers had to build a road as they went along. As the troops neared Winnipeg, Riel began to fear that he might be seized and punished for the death of Thomas Scott. Riel's followers begged him to flee. He leaped on his horse and rode away to the United States.

British Columbia Enters Confederation

On 10 May 1870, three delegates left the town of Victoria on Vancouver Island for Ottawa. They told Macdonald that British Columbia was interested in joining Confederation. They asked for responsible government, just as the other provinces had. Responsible government meant that the representatives elected to the assembly would be responsible to the people of the province, not to the upper house or to Britain. If the people became unhappy with the politicians, they could be voted out of office. The British Columbians also wanted Canada to build a wagon road across the prairies and through the mountains to link British Columbia to the East.

It had been Macdonald's dream to link Canada to the Pacific Ocean. The new province would also provide Canada with natural resources such as gold and lumber. Canada accepted British Columbia's terms and went further. Macdonald promised a railway. A railway would be started in two years and be completed within ten. The new province would be linked to the rest of Canada by a ribbon of steel. On 20 July 1871, British Columbia entered the Dominion of Canada.

Prince Edward Island Joins Confederation

In 1867, Prince Edward Island had turned Confederation down flat. During the next six years, Islanders began to have second thoughts.

By 1873, Prince Edward Island was hopelessly in debt trying to build a railway. When the people of Prince Edward Island heard that they would have to pay heavier taxes or join Canada, the prospects of joining Canada started to appear very good. Canada was still interested in having Prince Edward Island as part of Confederation. As long as it was outside of Confederation, Prince Edward Island could be used as a base for an attack on Canada.

On 1 July 1873, Prince Edward Island joined Confederation. By the terms of the agreement, Canada provided $800 000 to buy the land on the island from the absentee landlords. Canada took over the province's debts, most of which had been caused by the new railway. It promised, too, that there would be a year-round ferry boat service from the mainland to the island, as well as a telegraph service.

In 1880, more territory was added to the

nation. Britain presented the Arctic islands to Canada. There were dozens of islands named and unnamed in the frozen north. It had taken only 13 years for Canada to fulfill the dream of "stretching from sea to sea," and from "the river to the ends of the earth."

The Treaty of Washington 1873

Canada was also taking its first steps on the international stage. In 1871, British and American commissioners met to discuss problems between Britain and the United States. For the first time a Canadian, John A. Macdonald, was a member of the British Commission. Canada was participating in the handling of its external affairs.

The United States wanted payment for the losses caused by the *Alabama* during the American Civil War. It also wanted fishing rights in Canadian and Newfoundland waters lost in 1866 with the end of the Reciprocity Treaty. Macdonald hoped to use the United States' interest in the Atlantic fishery to obtain a new free trade agreement from the United States. But he was not supported by the other British commissioners. Britain was more interested in ironing out its own problems with the United States than in Canadian affairs.

The **Treaty of Washington** did restore good relations between Britain, Canada, and the United States. After the Treaty, Canada was free from the danger of attack by its neighbour and could turn its attention to the development of the West. The Treaty gave the United States access to the inshore fishery of Canada and Newfoundland for 12 years. In return, Canadian fish could enter into American markets without tariffs.

The new Canadian provinces and Newfoundland complained that this was a much more valuable deal for the Americans. In 1877, the Americans agreed to pay Canada $5.5 million and Newfoundland $2.5 million for the use of the fisheries on the Atlantic coast. These payments so irritated Americans that by 1885, they cancelled the fishing clauses of the Treaty of Washington.

The Dream of a Railway

At home, plans were underway for westward expansion and settlement. The largest project was the railway to the Pacific. A railway would move settlers west and bring their farm products to eastern markets.

But what a task the railway was! Surveyors were required to find the best route through swamps, forests, mountains, and plains. It would take expert engineers to build bridges and blast tunnels. Thousands of workers would be needed to put down the track. Above all else, it would cost a lot of money.

A group of business people under Sir Hugh Allan formed the **Canadian Pacific Railway Company** to do the job. But the plan soon came crashing down. Some people found out that Allan and his friends had given large amounts of money to Macdonald's government. It looked as if Allan was bribing the government for the right to build the railway. The event became known as the **Pacific Scandal**. The scandal forced Macdonald and the Conservatives to resign in 1873.

It appeared that the railway to the west coast would never be built. It also looked as if Sir John A. Macdonald, a Father of Confederation, would end his career in disgrace.

For the next five years, Alexander Mackenzie was the prime minister and the Liberal party formed the government of Canada. The Liberals were less enthusiastic about pouring large amounts of money into the railway.

The National Policy and the CPR

In the election of 1878, Macdonald was returned to power. The Conservatives had put forward a **National Policy** to solve the country's problems. The plan was this. Keep cheaper American goods out of Canada. Encourage Canadians to buy goods made by other Canadians. Fill the rich prairie lands with settlers. Encourage these settlers to buy manufactured goods made in eastern Canada and to sell their agricultural products to eastern Canadians. Help to make all this possible by building an east-west railway.

Not all Canadians supported the National Policy. The policy encouraged an east-west economy. Natural resources flowed into central Canada and manufactured goods flowed out. A problem was that many of the provinces produced the same goods. The Maritime provinces, in particular, opposed the National Policy. For someone in Nova Scotia, it made more sense to trade north-south with the United States. The Maritimes had a long history of trade with their southern neighbour. It was cheaper to transport goods south than across the vast distances to central Canada.

With the National Policy in place, the railway project was on again. In 1880,

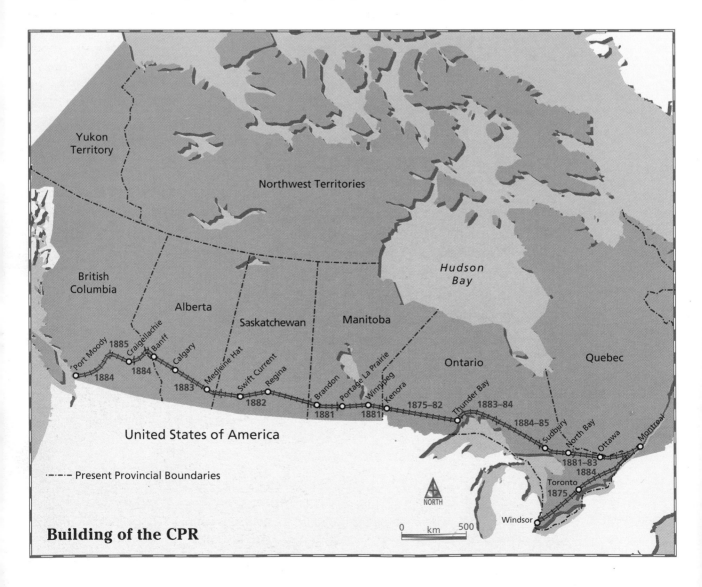

Building of the CPR

George Stephen and Donald A. Smith formed a company to build the railroad. This new company was also called the Canadian Pacific Railway Company.

Stephen and Smith worked out a deal with Macdonald's Conservative government. In return for building the railway, the company would own and operate it. In addition, the government would give the company 10 million ha of land. This land would be sold later to settlers to raise money for the company. Also, the 1100 km of railway lines that had already been finished were transferred to the Canadian Pacific Railway Company.

The Conservative government granted the company a 20-year monopoly. This meant that the Canadian Pacific would have complete control of all east-west rail traffic in the southern part of the prairies for 20 years. All materials for the railway, such as steel tracks and spikes, could be brought into Canada free of taxes. All Canadian Pacific stations, sidings, and lands were to be tax-free forever.

In return, the railway company promised to complete the line to British Columbia within 10 years. About 3040 km of track were yet to be built.

Building Problems

The CPR hired a remarkable railroader to supervise the construction process. His name was William Cornelius Van Horne. Canadian geography presented gigantic problems for Van Horne and the railroad builders. On the flat, open prairies it was fairly easy to lay the track. But in northern Ontario and in the western mountains, it was quite a different matter!

When Van Horne first saw the region north of Lake Superior, he called it "two hundred miles of engineering impossibility." The workers had to cut down hills, fill in swamps, blast through very hard granite, and lower lake levels. To make matters worse, day and night they were driven mad by mosquitoes.

Massive trestle bridges were built to carry the trains through the Rockies.

Chinese workers played an important role in the construction of the CPR.

Northern Ontario rock was a major challenge. It took $7.5 million worth of dynamite to move the Ontario granite. In one stretch of 80 km, more than 30 labourers lost their lives! They were killed by explosions or falling rocks. This was the human cost of building a transcontinental railway.

The British Columbia section of the line was the most difficult and dangerous. The mountains had to be crossed. Wooden trestles had to be built over deep river canyons. A trestle is a framework used as a bridge to support the railway tracks.

In places, the railway was forced to creep along the edges of cliffs. Below, torrents and rapids roared. Workers had to blast a way for the tracks through the rocks. They had to be lowered on ropes down the slippery canyon walls to set the dynamite charges. Then they were hauled back up to the surface and everyone ran for cover. Many railroaders died or were injured by pieces of flying rock. The work was so dangerous that some claimed "every kilometre of tunnel and track was stained with blood along the British Columbia section of the line."

The Role of Chinese Workers

Several thousand Chinese workers were brought in to work on the British Columbia stretch of railway. They were willing to work hard for half the wages that other workers expected. The Chinese were often assigned the most backbreaking and high risk jobs. Almost 200 Chinese were killed in railroad construction accidents. Without them, British Columbia would not have had a railway.

Some people objected to the Chinese because they appeared different. Their clothing, language, queue hairstyle (which Canadians called "pigtails"), customs, and skin colour set them apart. Railroad officials and citizens of British Columbia often treated the Chinese harshly.

When work on the railway was complete, most Chinese had no choice but to stay in Canada. They faced a grim future in a country where they seemed unwanted. Many had to take low-paying jobs that most people found disagreeable. Some worked as servants, in canning factories, and in laundries.

Over the years, these Chinese Canadians and many others who immigrated to

Canada have contributed to the country's growth. They established and worked in thousands of businesses and highly skilled industries across the country. They worked in the professions and many became prominent citizens.

The Last Spike!

The last railway spike was driven at 9:22 a.m. on 7 November 1885. The brief ceremony took place high in the Eagle Pass at Craigellachie, British Columbia. At last, Montreal and the Pacific were linked by a ribbon of steel.

What did the completion of the CPR mean for Canada?

- It meant that one of British Columbia's conditions for joining Confederation had been honoured. Now the province was linked to Canada.
- The new railway made it easier for people to settle in western Canada.
- Movement was now faster and easier between the west and east coasts. This would encourage trade within the country.

The North-West Rebellion 1885

After Manitoba joined Confederation, many Métis moved farther west into present-day Saskatchewan and Alberta. They were looking for wide open spaces and freedom to live in the traditional Métis way. Canadian surveyors started to appear in the North-West, dividing the land for settlement. The railway was coming through. It would be only a matter of time before settlers would flood into the area. It was the same old problem for the Métis.

The Métis, other Native nations, and the settlers of the North-West, wanted Ottawa to listen to their concerns. The Métis wanted legal proof that they owned the land on which they lived. Native peoples were struggling because of the loss of the buffalo and they wanted food and money from the government in exchange for use of their lands. Settlers wanted higher prices for their wheat and a stronger voice for the North-West in Ottawa.

But Ottawa did not act until it was too late. The Métis had persuaded Louis Riel to return as their leader. In 1885, Riel decided to use the same methods that had been successful earlier in 1870. He would set up his own government and arm his followers to pressure the Canadian government.

It was a risky move. Conditions had changed since 1870. A new police force, the North-West Mounted Police, had been set up to support the Canadian government. There was also a railroad to bring troops from eastern Canada.

Riel's call to take up arms lost him the support of the settlers. They wanted to see changes come in a lawful way. Riel also lost the support of the Roman Catholic Church when he encouraged the use of arms. Only the French-speaking Métis and some Native people continued to support him.

The **North-West Rebellion** began in March 1885. A small group of North-West Mounted Police officers were defeated in a skirmish with Métis and Natives. When news of the Mountie defeat reached Ottawa, the government decided to send troops immediately to put down the rebellion. Within 10 days, 5000 armed troops had arrived in the West.

In battles at Fish Creek, Batoche, and Cut Knife Hill, government troops confronted Riel and his supporters. The Métis and Natives held out for quite some time, but they were eventually overcome by the superior weapons of the troops. In a hundred days, the rebellion had been put down. Riel was a prisoner of the Canadian government and he was charged with treason—the crime of taking up arms against the government.

SOCIETY AND SOCIAL CHANGE

Treaties with Native Peoples

After Confederation, the Canadian government wanted to open western lands for settlement. To make this possible, government agents had to persuade Native nations to give up their rights to the land. They wanted Native peoples to move onto reserves. Reserves were lands set aside for Native peoples and on which they would have special rights. Others would not be able to hunt, fish, or settle on these lands.

In 1876, the Canadian government introduced the **Indian Act**. The act set out the rules that controlled Native communities. Native peoples were already the most regulated people in Canada. Now the Indian Act introduced more regulations. Traditional ceremonies, such as the potlatch, were banned. It was decided that Native children must go to special residential schools. The government was acting like a parent managing the affairs of children. The government said that the Native peoples should move onto reserves.

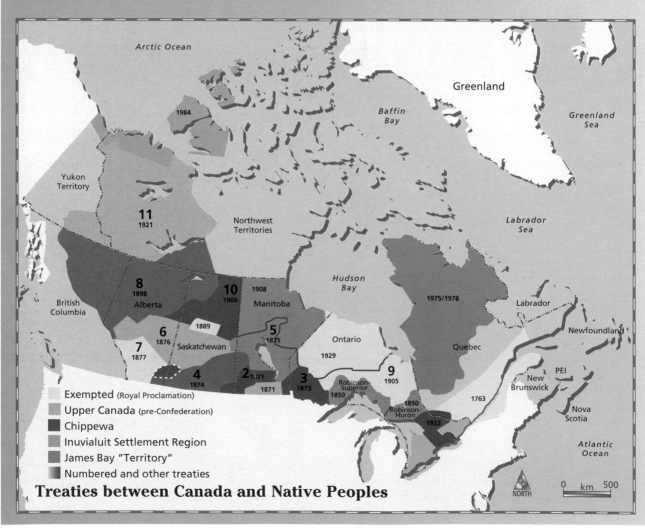

Legend:
- Exempted (Royal Proclamation)
- Upper Canada (pre-Confederation)
- Chippewa
- Inuvialuit Settlement Region
- James Bay "Territory"
- Numbered and other treaties

Treaties between Canada and Native Peoples

Chief Crowfoot of the Blackfoot with his family. The Blackfoot were one Native nation directly affected by western settlement. They signed Treaty No. 7 in 1877. At the signing, Crowfoot said, "We cannot sell the lives of men and animals, and therefore we cannot sell the land. It was put here by the Great Spirit …"

Native groups on the prairies faced a crisis. For centuries, their way of life had been based on the buffalo. But in the 1870s, with increasing settlement and overhunting by settlers, the buffalo began to disappear. In less than 10 years, the buffalo were almost wiped out. The way of life of the Native peoples was changed forever. With the buffalo gone, they were facing starvation. The government said farming on reserve lands would provide them with a source of food. The land on many reserves, however, was often poor and unproductive.

In addition, settlers were pouring into the West. In the United States, Native groups were fighting a losing battle against the settlers. Native lands were taken and many Native people were killed.

In Canada, the struggle was less violent. Eleven treaties were made between Canada and Native groups of the plains between 1871 and 1921. These were the so-called numbered treaties. A treaty is an agreement between parties or nations for the purchase or transfer of land or property. Over 2 million km² were turned over to Canada by the terms of these treaties.

Did the Native peoples believe they were giving up the land forever? Most Native people say no. To them, land is like the air, the sky, and the water. It cannot be owned by any one person or group. It is part of Nature and to be shared with all living things. The Native peoples believed they were making a friendship agreement—an agreement to share the land with other people as they shared it with the animals. In return for sharing the land, the government was to provide food, clothing, medicines, and money to help them establish a new way of life.

Adjustment to life on the reserves was difficult. For many Native peoples, the treaties were "broken promises." Government food supplies often did not arrive or were inadequate. Native people believe their treaty rights have been violated many times. In some areas of Canada, no treaties were ever signed with Native nations. Today, Native nations are actively working for a better and fairer deal for their lands.

1. Examine the map showing the lands covered by treaties between Canada and Native nations. When were the majority of the treaties signed? What areas are not covered by treaties?
2. Why would the Native nations see the treaties as "broken promises?"

The Trial of Louis Riel

Riel's trial aroused great interest and excitement across Canada. Held in Regina, it has been called the most important trial in Canadian history. Six settlers were chosen to act as Riel's jury. All were English-speaking and of the Protestant religion. Riel was French-speaking and of the Roman Catholic religion. His friends feared he would not get a fair trial.

Riel's lawyers wanted him to plead insanity. If he were insane, he could not be held responsible for his actions. They believed it was the only way to save him. But for Riel, to plead insanity would be a disgrace.

Debate raged across the country. In Ontario, many people saw Riel as a rebel and said "Hang him!" They remembered the execution of Thomas Scott. To many people in Quebec, Riel was a hero. He had fought to protect the rights of the French-speaking Métis.

Riel's jury took only one hour and twenty minutes to reach a decision. They declared him guilty and sentenced him to death. On 16 November 1885, the execution of Louis Riel was carried out. The outcome of the trial is still debated.

The Manitoba Schools Question 1890

When Manitoba became a province in 1870, most of the people living there were French-speaking and Roman Catholic. They had been promised Roman Catholic schools paid for with money raised by taxes. Over the next 20 years, large numbers of English-speaking Protestants moved to Manitoba. The French Canadians in Manitoba gradually became a minority.

In 1890, the Manitoba provincial government passed the **Manitoba Schools Act**. This act set up a single school system not connected with any church and with instruction only in English. The government would no longer pay for separate Roman Catholic schools. Roman Catholics would have to pay for separate schools themselves if they wanted them.

Supporters of Roman Catholic schools in Manitoba took their case before the Canadian courts. However, the courts ruled that the BNA Act gave each province the right to manage its own education system. The issue of Manitoba schools was hotly debated by French and English Canadians across the nation.

In 1896, Wilfrid Laurier was elected prime minister. Laurier worked out a compromise solution. Manitoba would no longer have a complete system of Roman Catholic schools supported by taxpayers. However, Roman Catholic teachers would be allowed to provide religious instruction to Roman Catholic children for part of the school day. French-speaking teachers would be provided where 10 or more students spoke French. These rights, however, were later taken away and English was made the official language in schools. The Manitoba Schools Question, like the Riel affair, was an issue dividing French and English Canadians.

Settling the West

After Laurier and the Liberal party swept to power in 1896, they continued to govern the country for 15 years. These years were a time of prosperity for Canada and are sometimes referred to as the "Golden Age of Laurier."

Clifford Sifton was the Minister of the Interior in Laurier's new government. His main task was to find ways to fill the West with settlers. The Canadian prairies were ready to produce large amounts of wheat. All that was needed were people to grow it.

DEVELOPING SKILLS: BRAINSTORMING

Suppose your class wants to raise money for a trip. What is the first step? You need suggestions for ways to raise the money. Try brainstorming. Brainstorming is a technique to help you find creative solutions to problems. It involves pooling as many ideas as possible, however outrageous they may seem, and then selecting the best solution to the problem. It is best to brainstorm in groups so you have more people to come up with good ideas. Often, one person's idea sparks another and another. Brainstorming can be fun and creative.

■ Step 1
Have a clear idea of the problem you want to solve. State it as a question. For example: How can we raise money for our class trip?

■ Step 2
Choose someone in the group to record all the ideas.

■ Step 3
List as many possible ideas or solutions as you can. Ideas can range from serious to "far-out." All ideas are acceptable. Quantity helps to produce quality.

■ Step 4
Don't discuss or criticize any ideas until after you have finished brainstorming. Get everyone in the group involved.

■ Step 5
Combine or improve upon ideas. This is called piggy-backing. An idea to put on a concert to raise money, for example, might lead to the idea of making it a variety show so that more people can get involved and it will have wider appeal.

■ Step 6
Don't give up when you first run out of ideas. There is usually a break between coming up with the obvious solutions and finding the less obvious ones.

■ Step 7
Once you have as many ideas as possible, evaluate them. Discuss the pros and cons of each one and eliminate those that may not be workable. Continue the process until you come down to the best solutions.

■ Step 8
Discuss the brainstorming process when you are finished. Do you think it helped you to come up with the best solutions?

Try It!
In groups, brainstorm answers to these questions.
1. a) Why would people leave their homelands and set out for Canada in the 1890s?
   b) What kind of preparations would you have to make before you set out to settle in the Canadian West in the 1890s?
   c) Why do people move to Canada from other countries today?

Sifton and his agents set out to persuade people from other parts of the world to come and settle the prairies. The government was looking for strong, healthy settlers experienced in farming. They would have to break up the soil, put up farm buildings, and survive through the Canadian winters.

The government ran advertising campaigns in Britain, Europe, and the United States describing the opportunities available in western Canada. Eventually, the advertising paid off. Sifton's policies started a flood of immigration to the Canadian West. Other factors also helped to make Canada's immigration plan work.

1. There was not much good farmland left in the United States, while a great deal of good free land was available in Canada.

2. In Europe, the demand for Canadian wheat increased. The price of wheat almost doubled. Growing wheat became more profitable for the Canadian farmer.

3. Canada had a transcontinental railroad to ship grain to markets. Steam-powered ocean vessels transported wheat to Europe cheaply and quickly.

4. More modern farm machinery, such as ploughs and reapers, was invented. These machines helped to make the farmers' work easier and more efficient.

5. Millions of Europeans were looking for new homes and better opportunities. Some were fleeing cruel treatment, compulsory service in the army, economic hardships, and overcrowding. Many chose Canada.

Sifton's policy, however, was selective. It favoured Europeans and Americans with farming experience and tended to restrict the entry of Asians, Blacks, Jews, East Indians, and southern Europeans. People from these groups came to Canada later when Canada's immigration policy changed and became more open.

In 1881, Calgary was just a stockaded police fort.

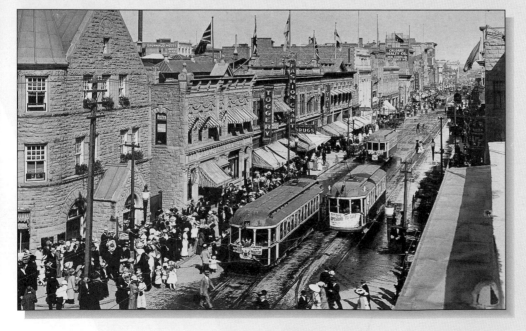

By 1912, it was a thriving centre.

The West developed rapidly with the in-rush of settlers. Roads and railway branch lines were built. Towns and villages sprang up. Regina, Edmonton, Calgary, and Saskatoon were once small and isolated outposts. Now they became large and thriving trading centres. The West was booming and the population of Canada was growing as the country prepared to move into the next century.

SCIENCE AND TECHNOLOGY

Canadian Inventors

Jane and David Fife

If the Fife's cow had taken one more bite, Canada might never have become a great wheat-producing country. It happened like this. Jane and David Fife came from Scotland in 1820 and settled near Peterborough, Ontario. David Fife spent a lot of time experimenting with wheat. He was trying to develop a strong and healthy kind of wheat that would grow well in Canada. Although his neighbours laughed at him, he continued to mix different strains.

In 1843, Fife sowed a few wheat seeds that he had received in the mail from a friend in Glasgow. The seed had come originally from somewhere in Europe. Fife planted them behind his house. Only one plant had healthy stalks with good fat heads. Fife decided to save the seeds from that plant.

Shortly before the wheat was ripe, the Fife's cow broke into the garden. Jane Fife looked out the window just as the cow was about to munch the heads of the experimental wheat. She ran from the house waving her apron and shooing the cow out of the yard. The precious wheat had been saved.

From the seeds of that one plant came a new type of wheat known as Red Fife. It was a very hardy strain that did not come down with common wheat diseases. Most important, it matured 10 days earlier than other kinds of wheat. This was a key factor on the prairies where the frost-free growing season is short. Soon many prairie farmers were growing and harvesting Red Fife.

Charles Saunders

Charles Saunders was a quiet, studious man in charge of the government's experimental farm in Ottawa. At the turn of the twentieth century, Saunders took Red Fife wheat and crossed it with a variety from India. It grew into a healthy strain that Saunders called Marquis. Marquis wheat was the discovery of the century. It was even better for the Canadian season because it took just 100 days to ripen. The most northern areas of the prairies could now be opened for farming. With the development of Marquis wheat, Canada was to become one of the greatest wheat-producing nations of the world.

Abraham Gesner

Abraham Gesner was a Nova Scotia doctor, geologist, author, and inventor. In 1842 in New Brunswick, he opened one of the first museums in British North America. It featured a collection of minerals and wildlife specimens that he had collected on his travels through the countryside.

However, Gesner's greatest accomplishment came in 1854. He patented the process for manufacturing kerosene oil from petroleum. Kerosene was inexpensive to manufacture. It burned with a light that was both brilliant and white. In fact, when the first kerosene lamp was lit in a home at the Red River Settlement, it gave off such a glow that the neighbours ran to help put out the flames. They thought the house was on fire. Soon kerosene lamps replaced candles and whale oil lamps. The light from a kerosene lamp was much easier to read and work by. Gesner's invention made him an important forerunner of today's giant petrochemical industry.

1. Find out about other important Canadian inventors from the turn of the twentieth century. Examples include the following.

Elijah McCoy	Alexander Graham Bell
Reginald Fessenden	Mabel Bell
Sandford Fleming	Guglielmo Marconi

ACTIVITIES

Check Your Understanding

1. Add these new terms to your *Factfile*.

Rupert's Land	Manitoba Act
Red River Settlement	Treaty of Washington 1873
North-West Territories	Canadian Pacific Railway Company
Métis	Pacific Scandal
Red River Rebellion 1869-70	National Policy
National Committee of the Métis	Indian Act
Provisional Government	North-West Rebellion 1885
Métis Bill of Rights	Manitoba Schools Act

2. a) Why did Canada want to buy the Hudson's Bay Company lands?
   b) Why did the Hudson's Bay Company want to keep some of its land instead of turning it over to Canada?

3. Imagine you are a Métis sent to Ottawa from the Red River Settlement. Make a list for the government of the problems faced by your people in 1869.

4. Describe the Thomas Scott affair. How did it arouse bitter feelings between French and English Canadians?

5. a) Why did Macdonald introduce the National Policy? What did it claim it would do?
   b) How did Canadians react to the National Policy?

6. a) Why did the North-West Rebellion break out in 1885?
   b) How were the results different from those of the Red River Rebellion in 1869-70?

7. Explain why Clifford Sifton's immigration advertising campaign was largely successful.

Confirm Your Learning

8. Did these new provinces—Manitoba, British Columbia, and Prince Edward Island—get a fair deal when they entered Confederation? Why or why not? Explain your view.

9. Explain how each of the following factors affected the building of the railroad in Canada:
   a) climate
   b) physical features of the land
   c) money
   d) personalities (Van Horne, Stephen, Macdonald)
   e) labourers.

10. List some of the difficulties that the Chinese railroad workers faced in Canada. Why do you think Chinese workers were not treated as well as workers from other countries?

11. Arrange the following events in chronological order. Then add them to the timeline you started in the last chapter (page 19). Add illustrations or sketches.
    a) The Manitoba Act 1870
    b) The North-West Rebellion 1885
    c) the Rebellion in the Red River Settlement 1869-70
    d) the last spike ceremony at Craigellachie 1885
    e) the hanging of Louis Riel 1885
    f) the Pacific Scandal 1873
    g) British Columbia enters Confederation 1870
    h) Prince Edward Island enters Confederation 1867
    i) Treaty of Washington 1873
    j) Manitoba Schools Act 1890
    k) John A. Macdonald's National Policy 1878
    l) formation of the North-West Territories 1869

Challenge Your Mind

12. Imagine you are government agents attempting to encourage settlement in the Canadian West. Divide into three groups—the first to work in Britain, the second in Europe, and the third in the United States. Develop an advertising campaign including posters, newspaper advertisements, etc., to attract settlers from your area of the world. If you have knowledge of other languages, use them on your posters.

13. A monument to Louis Riel on the grounds of the Manitoba Legislature is inscribed with the following words of Riel:

    Yes, I have done my duty. During my life I have aimed at practical results. I hope that after my death my spirit will bring practical results. All that I have done and risked, and to which I have exposed myself, rested certainly on the conviction that I was called upon to do something for my country... I know that through the grace of God I am the founder of Manitoba.

    Discuss the statement: Louis Riel deserves the title "Founder of Manitoba." Support your point of view.

14. a) Do you think that the Métis should have fought against the government? Can you think of anything they could have done instead? Explain.

    b) Collect information about Métis culture and modern Métis in Canada. Make a bulletin board display.

15. Divide your class into groups and put Riel on trial. You will need a judge, a prosecuting lawyer, a defending lawyer, Riel, a six-person jury, witnesses, reporters, and spectators. If you decide not to hang Riel, what else would you do with him? Did Riel get a fair trial in your class? In Regina in 1885? Explain your answers.

Unit 2

The Twentieth Century Dawns

1900–1913

TIMELINE

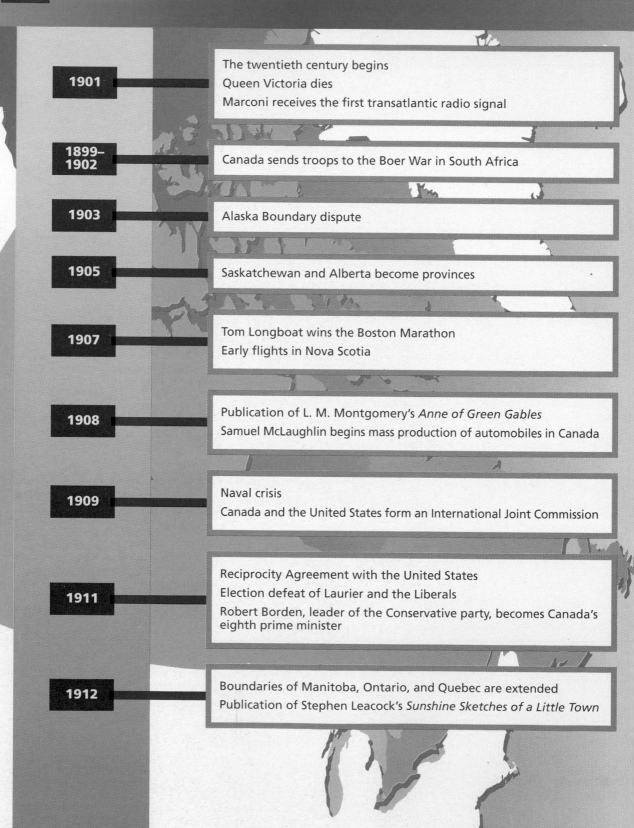

1901
The twentieth century begins
Queen Victoria dies
Marconi receives the first transatlantic radio signal

1899–1902
Canada sends troops to the Boer War in South Africa

1903
Alaska Boundary dispute

1905
Saskatchewan and Alberta become provinces

1907
Tom Longboat wins the Boston Marathon
Early flights in Nova Scotia

1908
Publication of L. M. Montgomery's *Anne of Green Gables*
Samuel McLaughlin begins mass production of automobiles in Canada

1909
Naval crisis
Canada and the United States form an International Joint Commission

1911
Reciprocity Agreement with the United States
Election defeat of Laurier and the Liberals
Robert Borden, leader of the Conservative party, becomes Canada's eighth prime minister

1912
Boundaries of Manitoba, Ontario, and Quebec are extended
Publication of Stephen Leacock's *Sunshine Sketches of a Little Town*

During the twentieth century, the lives of Canadians and of people around the world have changed dramatically. At the beginning of the century, the total population of the world was approximately 1.4 billion. By the end of the century, it is expected to be 7 billion! The twentieth century has seen a population explosion, and along with it astounding social, economic, and technological changes.

In 1900, the young Dominion of Canada was only 33 years old. But Canadians were feeling very confident about their future. Prime Minister Wilfrid Laurier said that the twentieth century would belong to Canada. In some ways he was right.

The first decade, 1900 to 1910, was a time of incredible prosperity and growth. The population of Canada increased by 1.8 million, from just over 5 million in 1901 to over 7 million by 1911. Industrial production in eastern Canada was growing at a phenomenal rate. Canada's west was harvesting bumper crops of wheat for the tables of the world. Women were organizing to improve their social positions and to fight for the right to vote. New inventions were bringing dramatic changes. The automobile, airplane, and telephone were just three of the developments that would change the lives of people throughout the century.

In this first decade, the young country of Canada was also struggling to find its own identity. Could Canada begin to cut its ties with Britain and become an independent country? Could French and English Canadians stay together as one nation? Could Canada survive as an independent country beside a very powerful neighbour, the United States? Could the forces that brought the provinces together in Confederation continue to hold them together?

By the end of this unit, you will be able to:

- describe what it was like to live in Canada in 1901
- recognize social changes brought about by immigration and urbanization
- describe major developments in the arts and technology
- evaluate the contribution of Prime Minister Wilfrid Laurier
- analyze the crises in Canada's relations with Britain and the United States
- understand the differences between French and English Canadians over issues such as imperialism
- apply good note-making skills
- effectively analyze and interpret political cartoons
- appreciate the early struggles in Canada's growth as a nation

47

KEY THEMES

Social Issues
- life at the turn of the century
- immigration boom
- urbanization
- differences between rich and poor
- role of women and actions for change

The Economy
- prosperity in the first decade of the century
- industrialization

French-English Relations
- Henri Bourassa and French-Canadian nationalism
- imperialists vs anti-imperialists
- differences over participation in the Boer War and the Naval Service Bill

Canadian-American Relations
- Alaska Boundary Dispute 1903
- International Joint Commission 1909 to settle disputes
- Reciprocity

Canada and the World
- Canada's foreign policy largely determined by Britain
- participation in the Boer War 1899-1902
- Naval crisis

National Growth and Identity
- nationalism vs imperialism—Canadians still British?
- anti-American feelings over the Alaska Boundary Dispute 1903
- Naval Service Bill establishes a Canadian navy
- economic prosperity
- new inventions and developments in the arts

Regional Development
- Alberta and Saskatchewan become provinces 1905
- boundaries of Ontario, Manitoba, and Quebec extended 1912
- transatlantic wireless station established in Nova Scotia

Citizenship, Government, and Law
- Wilfrid Laurier's leadership as prime minister

Technological Change
- new inventions—telephones, wireless, automobiles, aircraft

The Arts
- Canadian writers such as L.M. Montgomery and Stephen Leacock publish important books
- first movie theatres open with silent films

CHAPTER 3

Life at the Turn of the Century

THE END OF AN ERA

In the evening hours of 22 January 1901, a powerful queen died. She was Victoria, queen of England and empress of India— ruler of the British Empire. Victoria had been queen for 63 years. Over a quarter of the human race in Britain and British colonies around the world were her subjects, including 5.3 million Canadians.

Queen Victoria had always tried to keep things as they were. Though her husband, Albert, had been dead for 39 years, she left his room exactly as it had been. Albert's clothes were laid out as if he were alive. Victoria even ordered that hot water for shaving be brought to his room every morning. Now Victoria herself was dead, and with her death came the end of an age.

Among the people who watched her funeral procession, very few could remember a time when she was not their queen. But now that Victoria was dead, people sensed that nothing could ever be the same again. Victoria's eldest son "Bertie" became King Edward VII. Edward was a new king in a new century.

Queen Victoria. Her death in 1901 marked the end of an age.

Life in Canada

What was it like to live in Canada at the turn of the century? Changes were occurring in almost every aspect of life.

Horses

Horses played an important role in everyone's life. When a baby was born, a horse-drawn carriage brought the doctor to the house. At the end of a person's life, the undertaker's sleek black horses pulled the hearse to the cemetery. Farmers used horses to pull their ploughs and town dwellers kept them for transport. Every bakery, dairy, and coal company had to have horses to pull its delivery wagons.

Horse-drawn streetcars were still in use in many Canadian towns and cities. Montreal and Toronto, however, were beginning to make the switch to the electric railway. Horse-drawn fire engines racing through the streets were exciting to behold. A more common cause of excitement was a runaway horse that had to be stopped by a police officer or a brave passerby.

Wheels

By the turn of the century, the bicycle craze was sweeping Canada. One in every 12 persons owned "a wheel." Police found the bicycle useful for patrolling city streets. Bicycles were cheaper to buy and operate than horses, which had to be fed and housed. For many city residents, a bicycle solved the problem of transit. People could now live farther from their place of work and get to their jobs more easily.

Yet bicycles were more than transportation, they were romance. Couples honeymooned on them. On summer Sundays the roads were dusty from cyclists heading into the countryside for picnics. Those willing to take up the sport found a new sense of freedom and mobility.

Automobiles

The automobile was just being introduced. Henry Ford had founded the Detroit Automobile Company in 1899, nine years after Daimler started his company in Germany. King Edward VII was an enthusiastic supporter of "**horseless carriages**" and helped to make them popular. In Ontario the first motorist was John Moodie of Hamilton, who imported a $1000 Winton from the United States in 1898.

By 1908, an Oshawa carriage-maker, Sam McLaughlin, was producing automobiles in Canada. McLaughlin had signed a contract with the Buick Motor Company in the United States. McLaughlin built the body of the

A horse-drawn fire engine roars down a street in 1912.

Bicycles were used for transportation and romantic picnics in the country.

cars and Buick provided the engines. The Oshawa firm in 1908 produced only 200 automobiles, but it was the beginning of the mass production of cars in Canada.

Until the 1920s, the automobile was considered a rich person's toy. But with the development of the assembly line, the prices of cars dropped and moved to within the grasp of nearly everyone. Certainly no one at the turn of the century could predict the problems of accidents, parking, and congestion that the new invention would bring.

Flight

In 1903 the American brothers, Orville and Wilbur Wright, successfully flew the first airplane. That flight, on the beach of Kitty Hawk, North Carolina, lasted just 12 seconds. But the Wright brothers proved that a machine heavier than air could fly. The air age had begun.

Meanwhile in Canada, Alexander Graham Bell, the inventor of the telephone, also worked on the problem of flight. At Baddeck, Nova Scotia, he formed a group known as the **Aerial Experiment Association (AEA)**. In 1908 Casey Baldwin, a member of the AEA, flew a plane called the ***Red Wing***. It travelled a distance of 97 m! By the summer of 1909, Douglas McCurdy was making flights of 32 km over the water at Baddeck in the ***Silver Dart***. The *Silver Dart* was the finest and most easily flown aircraft of its day. McCurdy and Baldwin tried hard to convince the Canadian government of the military value of an air force. However, when the *Silver Dart* crash-landed during the flight trials, military officials rejected the idea of using airplanes in warfare. Thirty years later, the Canadian government asked McCurdy to become the director of government aircraft production during World War II.

A collision in Vancouver. Automobile traffic was getting heavier on city streets.

First flight of the Silver Dart at Baddeck, Nova Scotia, 1909.

Communications

Around the turn of the century, more people were getting telephones. Household needs could now be ordered by telephone and delivered to the home. Storekeepers hired youngsters with bicycles to deliver packages. Party lines, where more than one household shared a line, were common. All calls had to be channelled through the telephone exchange. Operators sitting at boards connected the callers. The telephone had an important social impact. It greatly improved communication and provided employment for women as operators.

In 1901, at Signal Hill in St. John's, Newfoundland, Guglielmo Marconi received the first radio signal sent across the Atlantic Ocean. The following year, with the backing of the Canadian government, Marconi built a wireless station at Glace Bay, Nova Scotia. From there, he set up official transatlantic wireless communication.

Entertainment

Twenty years elapsed before radio broadcasting became a means of mass entertainment. In the first years of the twentieth century, people were more dependent on home-made entertainment such as the piano,

banjo, and amateur theatrical productions. The phonograph or gramophone was coming in, but the thick, flat discs sounded scratchy and tinny. Not until the invention of electrical recording in the 1920s did the sound made from records improve.

The first movie theatres were opened in the early years of the century. The films were silent and the dialogue had to be shown on the screen as captions. A pianist often accompanied the film and provided important sound effects. It was 20 years before talking films arrived. Canada's own Mary Pickford made her first film in 1909, and Charlie Chaplin made his in 1911.

Lifestyles

In the early 1900s, changes were taking place in life around the home as well. Modern bathrooms and other household conveniences became more common.

Marconi waits for the first transatlantic radio message from England at Signal Hill in St. John's, Newfoundland.

THE ARTS

Anne of Green Gables *Published*
June 1908

A delightful new novel by a Prince Edward Island writer, Lucy Maud Montgomery, has just been published. The novel is *Anne of Green Gables*. It is the enchanting story of Anne Shirley, a lively and talkative red-haired orphan. By mistake, Anne is sent to live with the Cuthbert family who have requested a boy to help on their farm. The adventures that follow are hilarious and heartwarming. The novelist captures the spirit of growing up in Prince Edward Island in Victorian times. Lucy Maud Montgomery's novel is so successful that she is already working on the sequel, *Anne of Avonlea*.

Sunshine Sketches of a Little Town *Hailed*
1912

Stephen Leacock is the funniest man in Canada. His new book, *Sunshine Sketches of a Little Town,* is a wonderful satire of life in a small Ontario town. The town is called Mariposa. Many people believe it is inspired by Leacock's home town of Orillia, Ontario. Leacock's satire makes fun of characters and small town life in a good-natured way. The people described in Leacock's story are just like people all of us know. Leacock allows us to laugh at ourselves and our everyday follies.

1. Lucy Maud Montgomery and Stephen Leacock are only two of many writers who published important novels and poems at the turn of the century in Canada. Find out more about one of the following. Write a short review like those above about one of his or her works or create a history card with a picture and short biography of the writer. You could also research writers not in this list.

Pauline Johnson	Robert Service
Frederick Philip Grove	Bliss Carman
Louis Hémon	Isabella Valancy Crawford
Charles G. D. Roberts	Archibald Lampman
Duncan Campbell Scott	Phillipe-Joseph Aubert de Gaspé

2. Every summer, the Stephen Leacock Medal for Humour is given to a Canadian writer for the most humorous book of the year. Find out who the most recent winner is and present a short report about the writer.

Electric washing machines took some of the drudgery out of washday. Other gadgets included sewing machines, electric hearing aids, and vacuum cleaners.

Canadians who could afford them purchased these gadgets from the Eaton's catalogue. The catalogue was considered by several generations to be the most popular book in Canada. Rural families in particular depended on the catalogue for everything from fence posts to fashionable hats. For Canadian children and adults, the Eaton's catalogue became a "wish book" that they could gaze at for hours.

Growth of the Nation— Immigration and Urbanization

Between 1901 and 1911, Canada experienced the greatest wave of immigration in its history to that point. **Immigration** is the movement of people into a country from other lands. Almost 2 million people moved to Canada from Europe, Britain, and the United States between 1901 and 1911. They were looking for new homes, land to farm, and better opportunities. Not only did the number of people in Canada grow rapidly, but the make-up of the population also changed. By 1912, almost one fifth of the population was neither British nor French in origin.

PROFILES

Tom Longboat—Long-Distance Runner

Watching professional sport was a very popular form of entertainment at the turn of the century. In Canada, tremendous attention was focussed on Tom Longboat. He was the greatest long-distance runner of his day. Tom Longboat was an Onondaga born in 1877 on the Six Nations Reserve near Brantford, Ontario. As a boy he raced at local town field days. By age 19, Tom could outrun a horse around a 19 km course.

In 1906, Longboat burst onto the Canadian sporting scene by winning the Hamilton Around-the-Bay race. Longboat had a deceptive running style with long, slow strides. In 1907 he raced the tough, hilly course of the Boston Marathon. Against 125 opponents, Longboat set a record of 2 hours, 21 minutes, 24 seconds, battling snow, rain, and slush. He ended the race 400 m ahead of the second place runner. His record was not broken until the course of the Boston Marathon was changed to make it easier.

In 1908 he ran in the Olympics in London, England, but collapsed after 32 km. However, later that year in New York, he won the professional marathon championship. In 1909 at Madison Square Gardens in New York, he took part in the "race of the century." He raced against a professional runner, Alfie Shrubb. At the 39 km mark, Longboat passed Shrubb and went on to win the race. Longboat was proclaimed the world's best long-distance runner. Each time Tom Longboat ran, crowds flocked to see him.

Tom Longboat later enlisted in the Canadian army and fought overseas in World War I. He served on the Western Front as a dispatch runner. He got a job with the Toronto streets department in 1926, and retired from there in 1945. He died in 1949 at the Six Nations Reserve.

1. Research other famous Canadian sports figures of the early twentieth century. Prepare a mural with photos and captions telling about the individuals or teams and their accomplishments.

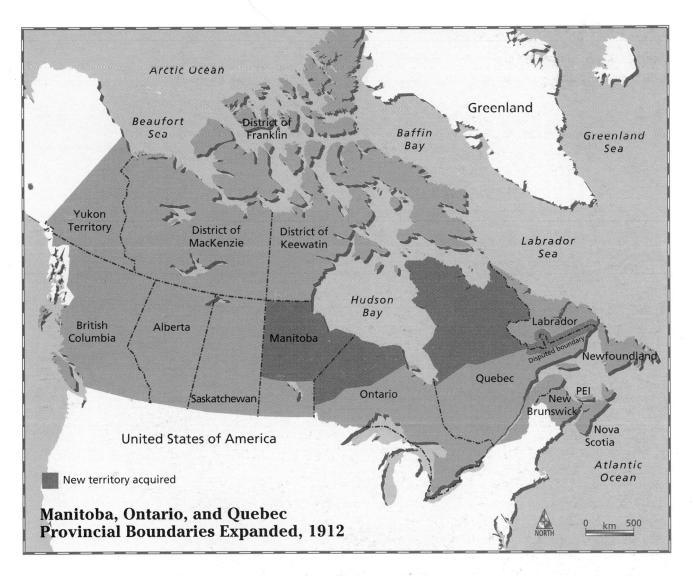

New territory acquired

Manitoba, Ontario, and Quebec Provincial Boundaries Expanded, 1912

0   km   500

Many of the new settlers moved to the West and the population of western Canada increased rapidly. Towns sprang up, roads were built, and railway lines branched out. Regina, Saskatoon, Calgary, and Edmonton mushroomed in size. The West was booming. Two new provinces were created. In 1905, Alberta and Saskatchewan became the newest members of Confederation. In 38 years, Confederation had grown from the joining of four provinces in eastern Canada to the union of nine provinces coast to coast. In 1912, the boundaries of Manitoba, Quebec, and Ontario were extended. With their larger territories, these provinces also gained new resources and new opportunities for development.

Canada was also becoming more urbanized. **Urbanization** is the movement of people into cities and towns. The rapid increase in the number of immigrants coming to Canada meant that more people had to find homes. In 1913, over 400 000 immigrants arrived. Many settled in the cities, including Montreal, Toronto, and Winnipeg. Housing was often pitifully inadequate for them. Some immigrants were forced to live in slums and work in basement or attic factories. Urban poverty and related problems of high unemployment and poor housing became very serious.

New immigrants on a Winnipeg street. Why did many new immigrants have difficulties finding homes?

Equality and Inequality

Perhaps what would strike you most if you were to step back into the Canada of 1901 would be the inequalities in society. People were divided by their work and by their wealth. The rich were very rich. Taxes were so low that the wealthy were left with almost all of their money to spend. Most of it went on clothes, houses, horses, and carriages.

Sir Henry Pellatt was a prime example of the wealthy in Toronto. Pellatt is reported to have made millions in the Toronto Electric Light Company and mining stocks. In 1910 he sank $2 000 000 into the building of Casa Loma, a palatial home in Toronto. Casa Loma contained 30 bath-rooms, 3 bowling alleys, 52 telephones, and the world's finest indoor rifle range. The stables had mahogany stalls and Persian rugs, and Pellatt once had a custom set of false teeth made for his favourite horse.

However, the average Canadian at the turn of the century still lit a kerosene or gas lamp and cooked on a wood stove.

Immigrants to Canada, 1900-1913	
Year	**Number of immigrants**
1900	41 681
1901	49 149
1902	89 102
1903	138 660
1904	131 252
1905	136 266
1906	211 653
1907	272 409
1908	143 326
1909	173 694
1910	286 839
1911	331 288
1912	375 756
1913	400 870

Source: Dominion Bureau of Statistics

Population of Canada by Census Dates, 1871-1911			
Year	**Rural**	**Urban**	**Total**
1871	2 967 000	722 000	3 689 000
1881	3 215 000	1 110 000	4 325 000
1891	3 296 000	1 537 000	4 833 000
1901	3 357 000	2 014 000	5 371 000
1911	3 934 000	3 273 000	7 207 000

Note: Figures rounded to nearest thousand.
Source: Dominion Bureau of Statistics

Women shopped every day, scrubbed clothes on a washboard, put up pickles and fruit preserves, and beat their rugs with a wire whip.

At the bottom of the economic ladder were the recent immigrants. Most immigrants came to Canada with very little. Many who decided to live in towns or cities were forced to live in terrible conditions, crowded into basement rooms where sanitation and ventilation were poor.

Native people also faced difficulties. Their traditional way of life was disappearing. Many had been forced to move onto reserves. In the West, the buffalo were almost extinct and settlers were moving into traditional Native lands. Diseases new to North America reduced Native populations drastically. Facing poverty and ill-health, life for many Native people in Canada at the turn of the century was full of difficulties.

Women Organize for Change

Inequality between men and women was also evident. For a woman to enter a tavern, pool room, or even a bowling alley was considered unrespectable. To go alone to a concert or the theatre was frowned upon. Women in Canada had just begun to fight for an education equal to that available to men. Women in professions, such as medicine, were still a rarity. Women tended to work in stores and factories, and girls from poorer families became domestic servants. Girls from wealthy or middle-class families had to choose between nursing and teaching as a possible career.

The early twentieth century was still very much a man's world, run by men for men. Women in Canada could not vote or stand for political office. In New Zealand and Australia, women had recently won the right to vote (1893 and 1902 respectively).

But some Canadian women were working to improve their situation in society. In 1876, Dr. Emily Stowe had formed the **Toronto Women's Literary Club**. The purpose of this club was to teach women their rights and to help them secure these rights. The organization persuaded the University of Toronto to admit women in 1886. The Club also struggled for laws to improve wages and working conditions for women.

In 1897, Adelaide Hoodless had formed the world's first **Women's Institute**. This was a group of farm women who organized themselves to study nutrition, child care,

Canada Post stamp recognizing the achievements of Emily Stowe.

Emily Stowe

CANADA postage postes 17

household management, and sanitation. Adelaide Hoodless's eighteen-month-old son had died from drinking contaminated milk. She was determined to help prevent such deaths. She worked to persuade public schools to introduce courses in domestic science.

Another important organization was the **Women's Christian Temperance Union** **(WCTU).** Its aims were to combat the problems created by alcohol in society. Nellie McClung, Canada's great social reformer, got her start in the WCTU. McClung argued that women should have exactly the same freedom as men, and she led in the fight for women's rights. The twentieth century was to bring great changes in the role and status of women.

DEVELOPING SKILLS: NOTE-MAKING

Everyone needs to take notes at some point. We often need notes on what we read, hear, or see. You might take notes, for example:

- when someone calls on the phone and leaves a message
- when you are going shopping and need a list
- when you are invited to a friend's house and are given directions
- when your teacher or other students are making a presentation
- when you are reading from a text or other resource and need to record some information.

Note-making skills will be very valuable to you in the future. In almost every job or career, people use note-making skills. They need to be able to record instructions, summarize written reports, make written reports of a meeting or discussion, or record observations from field work.

Making notes involves four main skills. The first is comprehension. You need to understand what you read, hear, or see and recognize the main idea. Then you need to record the statements that support the main idea. A simple example for the section on "Horses" from page 50 of the text would look like this:

Horses

Horses were important to everyone in 1901
- at birth and death
- for farming
- for delivering goods
- streetcars
- fire engines

Sometimes what you read, hear, or see includes a lot of detail that you don't really need to remember. Then you use the skill of categorizing. When you categorize, you pick out only the most important statements that support the main idea and leave out the less important statements. An

---

These are the main steps in note-making.

■ **Step 1**
Write the topic at the top of your note.

■ **Step 2**
Decide on the main idea and write it down.

} Comprehension

■ **Step 3**
Decide on the most important supporting statements or ideas.

} Categorizing

■ **Step 4**
Organize the ideas and summarize them in your own words in point form.

} Organizing and Summarizing

example for the section on "Wheels" from page 50 of the text would look like this:

Wheels
Why the bicycle craze swept Canada
- bicycles were cheaper to buy and operate than horses
- people could live farther from their jobs
- bicycles provided freedom and mobility

(Note that less important ideas were left out: police on bicycles; honeymooners on bicycles; picnics on bicycles)

Finally, note-making also involves the skills of organizing and summarizing. Organizing means that you select your material and put it together in your own words in a logical way. Summarizing means that many words are reduced to a few. The main idea has to be expressed in such a way that in six months you can still understand what you have written. An example for the section on "Automobiles" from pages 50–51 of the text would look like this:

Automobiles
Horseless carriage coming in
- Ford founded in 1899
- Samuel McLaughlin mass produced in Canada by 1908
- rich person's toy
- automobiles not affordable for most people until the 1920s

(Note that the section in the text, containing 179 words, has been summarized in 29 words.)

Practise It!

1. Use your skills to make notes on other sections of this chapter. You could work in groups of six, with each person working on one of the sections outlined below. When you are finished, provide everyone in your group with a copy of your note. You don't need to put your name on it.

Flight	Immigration and
Communications	Urbanization
Entertainment	Equality and Inequality
Lifestyles	

2. Take time to go over everyone's notes and then discuss them in your group. Was there anything you didn't understand in any of the notes? Which do you think were the best? Why?

3. Select one occupation or career from the list below or choose a different one. Describe how you would use note-making skills on a typical day in this job.

police officer	electrician	computer
nurse	actor	programmer
journalist	salesperson	carpenter

ACTIVITIES

Check Your Understanding

1. Add the following terms to your *Factfile*.

horseless carriage	urbanization
Aerial Experiment Association (AEA)	Toronto Women's Literary Club
Red Wing	Women's Institute
Silver Dart	Women's Christian Temperance
immigration boom	Union (WCTU)

2. a) The first decade of the twentieth century was not a time of prosperity for everyone. Which groups in society did not share in the prosperity? Why?

   b) Contrast the lifestyles of the rich and poor in the first decade of the twentieth century.

3. a) What roles did women have in Canadian society at the turn of the twentieth century?

   b) In what ways did women work to change their social conditions?

Confirm Your Learning

4. a) Changes were occurring in all aspects of life at the turn of the twentieth century. Copy the organizer below and add examples of changes that were occurring in each area.

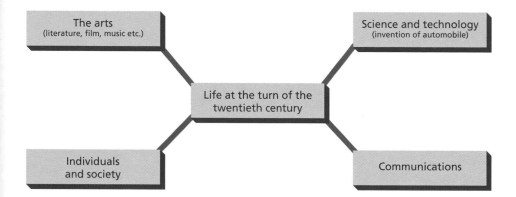

   b) The changes in one aspect of life often have an effect on other aspects. For example, the invention of the automobile changed people's lives dramatically. Choose two items from your completed chart and explain what effects they had.

   c) How did these changes contribute to Canada's growth and development?

5. Compare Canadian lifestyles at the beginning of the century with Canadian lifestyles today. Use the following criteria in a comparison organizer: transportation, entertainment, sports, and inventions. See if you can find illustrations in catalogues or books that would allow you to compare female and male fashions then and now.

6. a) If you had been an adult woman in 1910, would you have had the right to vote? How would you have felt about this? Why?

   b) Would you have tried to do anything about it? Why or why not?

   c) If you were an adult male who could vote, how would you have felt about those who could not vote?

Challenge Your Mind

7. Do some additional research to create history cards for one or more of the following people. Your history cards can be like sports cards or cards of major movie or television stars. They should include a picture or sketch of the person on one side, and a brief paragraph describing some key facts about the individual's life and his or her major contributions on the other side. Be creative in designing your cards. You can add to your class's collection of history cards throughout your study.

Alexander Graham Bell   Adelaide Hoodless
Douglas McCurdy   Nellie McClung
Guglielmo Marconi   Tom Longboat
Samuel McLaughlin   Mary Pickford
Dr. Emily Stowe

8. New inventions had a great effect on life at the turn of the century. Can you think of a modern invention that is affecting your life as much as the telephone or automobile changed the lives of people at the turn of the century? Explain.

9. Build a model or draw a diagram of some important inventions from the early twentieth century, such as the *Silver Dart*, telephone, gramophone, wireless, or electric streetcar. Explain to a group of your classmates how the invention worked and why it was important.

10. In groups, create a page from a city newspaper published in 1901. Include headlines, news items, and photos to cover the major events and issues that you have read about in this chapter. For example, you might have been a reporter present at the first flight of the *Red Wing* in Nova Scotia, or you might be writing a letter to the editor about the conditions in the city for new immigrants.

CHAPTER 4

Canada—Between Britain and the United States

PROFILE OF A PRIME MINISTER

In 1896 Wilfrid Laurier had entered the House of Commons in Ottawa to the sound of cheering and applause. He had made his way to the seat Sir John A. Macdonald had occupied for 19 years. Laurier, the leader of the Liberal party, was Canada's seventh prime minister. He was in power for the next 15 years. No prime minister except Macdonald had been in power longer. Those 15 years became known as the "Golden Age of Laurier."

Wilfrid Laurier was Canada's first French Canadian prime minister. He was born near the village of St. Lin in the province of Quebec. When he was 11, his father had sent him to school in the English-speaking settlement at New Glasgow. There he studied English and became fluently bilingual. He lived with the Murray family, who were Scottish Protestants, and worked as a clerk in a village store. Laurier learned a great deal about the culture and religion of English-speaking Protestants. He also learned to be tolerant of people different from himself.

Later, Laurier chose to study law at McGill University in Montreal. He graduated in 1864 and gave the valedictory address. In his speech, he touched on a concern that was to dominate his life. "Two races share today the soil of Canada," he said. These people had not always been friends. "But I hasten to say it… There is no longer any family here but the human family. It matters not the language people speak, or the altars at which they kneel."

Following graduation, Laurier opened a law practice at Arthabaskaville, Quebec. The townspeople were impressed with his honesty, courage, and sense of fair play. They chose him to represent them in the federal government in Ottawa. In 1887, he became the leader of the Liberal party and was known as an excellent speaker. Sir John A. Macdonald admired his political opponent and recognized him as one of Canada's most promising politicians.

Laurier tried to see both English and French Canadian points of view. His main aim was to keep both language groups together and to make sure each treated the other fairly. Laurier continually tried to work out compromises that he hoped would be acceptable to both English and French Canadians.

In 1897, Laurier travelled to England and was knighted by the queen. Before he returned to Canada, he wanted to visit France. It was the country of his forebears, and he had never been there. In a speech in Paris, Laurier said, "French Canadians have not forgotten France… Here in France people are surprised at the attachment French Canadians feel for the Queen of England. We are faithful to the nation which gave us life (France), and we are faithful to the great nation that gave us liberty (Britain)."

Wilfrid Laurier was a new prime minister in a new age for Canada. The worldwide economic depression of the early 1890s was over. Prosperity was returning to Canada. Once again factories began to hum, people had jobs, and there were markets for Canadian products. But though the years around the turn of the century were a "Golden Age," Canada was still a young nation struggling to find its own identity. Problems arose in Canada's relations with both Britain and the United States. These problems also divided French and English Canadians at home.

Imperialism and French Canadian Nationalism

One major issue was imperialism. **Imperialism** is a policy of establishing colonies away from the homeland and building an empire. In the nineteenth and early twentieth centuries, many European countries established colonies around the world. Colonies provided a source of raw materials, a market for manufactured goods, and a great deal of prestige, glory, and military strength for the home country. At the turn of the twentieth century, Canada was part of the British Empire.

Most English Canadians supported the imperialist movement. They were proud to be part of the British Empire. But for many French Canadians, there was less pride and responsibility in belonging to the British Empire. They felt a stronger sense of pride and loyalty in their French Canadian culture and language. As a minority, they felt isolated within Canada and the British Empire. Quebec had been conquered by British soldiers, but for many French Canadians Quebec was still the homeland of French Canadian culture. Incidents such as the execution of Louis Riel and the Manitoba Schools Act made many French Canadians feel that their culture and rights were threatened in Canada. A French Canadian nationalist movement gained strength, particularly in Quebec. French Canadian nationalists were determined to preserve their language and culture.

Henri Bourassa, who founded the newspaper Le Devoir, *was an outspoken supporter of French Canadian rights and an opponent of Canada's involvement in Britain's imperialist wars.*

The Boer War, 1899-1902

When the **Boer War** broke out in 1899, it created a crisis in Canada that centred on the issue of imperialism. The Boer War was fought in South Africa. Many British settlers had immigrated to South Africa and were moving into the areas where gold and diamonds had been discovered. Trouble developed between the British settlers and the Boers, who were the descendants of the early Dutch colonists. As tensions increased, the Boers declared war on Britain. While the war did not directly concern Canada, the British government asked Canada to send soldiers. This military support would prove that the British Empire stood together in times of trouble.

English Canadian imperialists were anxious for Canada to take part. But while many English Canadians said "Yes" to the British government's request, many French Canadians said "No!" Quebec politicians such as Henri Bourassa argued that Canada should not get involved in Britain's imperialist wars.

Laurier tried to provide a compromise solution that would satisfy both English and French Canadians. Canada would not send an official army to South Africa. However, Canada would equip and transport 1000 volunteers. These volunteers would be part of the British forces once they arrived in South Africa. In the end, Canada sent about 7300 volunteers to South Africa and spent $2.8 million in their support.

Laurier's compromise did not fully satisfy anyone. Imperialists felt that Canada had let Britain down. Many French Canadian nationalists felt Laurier had done too much. In spite of the differences in attitude to Laurier's compromise solution, his government was returned to power in the election of 1900.

A painting shows Boer troops surrendering to Canadian forces during the Boer War.

The Naval Crisis

By 1909, Britain was facing a serious crisis. The possibility of a war between Britain and Germany was very real. Britain and Germany were in a race to have the largest navy in the world. The British wanted Canada and other colonies to contribute funds to help build more ships for the British navy. Without help from its colonies, Britain would soon fall behind in the naval race with Germany.

Should Canada add to the British navy, or should Canada develop its own navy? Every aspect of the problem threatened to divide English and French Canadians. It was just as serious an issue as the Boer War had been.

Again Laurier offered a compromise— the **Naval Service Bill**. Canada would have a navy of its own under the control of the Canadian government. In an emergency, the Canadian navy could be placed under British control with the consent of Canada's parliament. Service in the navy would be voluntary. Five cruisers and six destroyers would be built immediately. Canadian naval bases would be established at Esquimalt, British Columbia, and Halifax, Nova Scotia.

First Canadian navy recruiting poster, 1911. Why was Canada's navy a source of conflict in the country?

A storm of protest greeted Laurier's Naval Service Bill. Bourassa and some French Canadian nationalists complained that this policy meant Canadians could be sent anywhere at any time to fight Britain's imperialist wars. The Conservatives, led by Robert Borden, also attacked the bill. They thought Canada should make an outright contribution to the British navy. The Conservatives accused Laurier of setting up a "tin-pot Canadian navy" when an immediate contribution to the British navy was urgently needed. Laurier agreed that when Britain is at war, Canada is also at war. However, he made it clear that Canada would decide how much it would participate in future wars.

Canadian-American Relations— The Alaska Boundary Dispute, 1903

In the early years of the new century, Canada also came into conflict with its southern neighbour, the United States. A dispute developed over the border between Alaska and Canada. The United States had purchased Alaska from Russia in 1867. The deal included the "panhandle," the strip of coastline extending south from Alaska as far as Prince of Wales Island off the coast of British Columbia. The wording of the treaty was fuzzy, but no one cared very much until the discovery of gold in the Yukon Territory.

During the Gold Rush in 1898, thousands of prospectors flooded into the Klondike area of the Yukon Territory. Suddenly, the ownership of the land through which they passed became very important. Gold seekers needed outfits and supplies. Both Canadian and American merchants wanted to take advantage of this new business.

The Americans said that the ports of Skagway, Dyea, and Juneau belonged to them. The Canadians argued that these ports belonged to Canada. Whoever owned these ports could charge customs taxes on all goods going into the area and all the gold going out.

The Canadians argued that the boundary should be measured from the mountains nearest the ocean. This boundary would give Canada direct access to the Pacific Ocean by way of several deep inlets. Gold could be brought out of the Yukon Territory and supplies brought in without passing through American ports. The Americans were determined to keep as much land as they could. President Theodore Roosevelt threatened to send troops to Alaska to protect the American claim.

Eventually the dispute was submitted to a court of six judges. Three judges were appointed by the United States and three were chosen by Britain. Two of the judges appointed by the British government were Canadians; the third was Lord Alverstone, an Englishman.

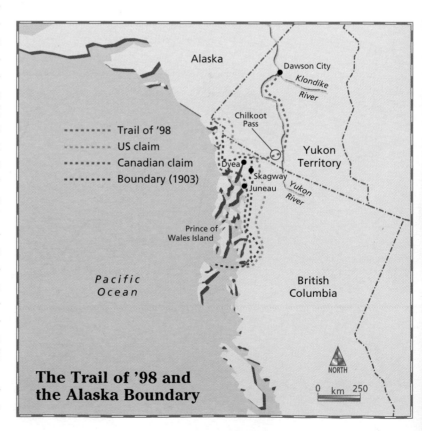

The Trail of '98 and the Alaska Boundary

Legend:
- Trail of '98
- US claim
- Canadian claim
- Boundary (1903)

Alaska · Dawson City · Klondike River · Chilkoot Pass · Yukon Territory · Dyea · Skagway · Juneau · Yukon River · Prince of Wales Island · Pacific Ocean · British Columbia · NORTH · 0 km 250

After a full month of discussion, the tribunal decided 4 to 2 against Canada. Lord Alverstone had sided with the Americans. Britain was facing growing problems with Germany in Europe. Britain knew it would need American support if a war developed with Germany. Therefore, Britain was not willing to risk losing its friendship with the United States at this time.

When the decision was announced, Canadians were outraged. Many thought they had been bullied by their more powerful southern neighbour. At the same time, Canadians felt bitter resentment toward Britain and Lord Alverstone. It appeared that Britain had let Canada down in this dispute with the United States. The reaction in Vancouver was so hostile that the *Victoria Colonist* reported on 23 October 1903 that some citizens had pledged "they will not sing 'God save the King' again until England has justified itself in the eyes of Canada."

In 1909, an **International Joint Commission** was set up to settle peacefully any future disputes between Canada and the United States. This permanent commission would deal with any disagreements over boundary waters or rivers along the Canadian-American border. Though this commission would help to solve future controversies in a friendly manner, Canadian resentment toward both the United States and Britain remained. Canadians were becoming more determined that Canada must make its own decisions in the future.

Reciprocity

Another issue that faced the Laurier government was reciprocity. Reciprocity is an agreement between two countries to trade certain products without tariffs (taxes). In 1854, the British North American colonies had signed a Reciprocity Treaty with the United States, but the United States had ended the Treaty in 1866. A great deal of trade business had been lost. Canadian farmers and business people wanted a new agreement.

In 1910, a large group of western farmers demonstrated on Parliament Hill in Ottawa. They demanded lower tariffs on goods traded between Canada and the United States. High tariffs, they complained, were causing high prices for farm products and materials. Tariffs can help to protect home industries by limiting foreign competition, but they can also mean that prices on the protected home goods rise.

The farmers in western Canada had a legitimate complaint. They were paying eastern railway companies a lot of money to ship their grain and supplies. They were charged high interest rates on money they borrowed from banks. When they visited friends or relatives across the border, they were annoyed to discover that farm machinery cost half as much in the United States as it did in Canada. High costs were blamed on Ontario and Quebec manufacturers who grew rich because tariffs kept out foreign competition.

Laurier's response to the farmers' complaints was to work

What does this cartoon suggest about some Canadians' attitudes to reciprocity with the United States?

A NEW FIELD FOR CONQUEST.

PROFILES

James Naismith—The Canadian Inventor of Basketball

Few people realize that the game of basketball was created by a Canadian, Dr. James Naismith. In 1891, Naismith was teaching physical education at the YMCA college at Springfield, Massachusetts. He was looking for a competitive indoor team sport for his students to play between the baseball and hockey seasons. He set out deliberately to invent a new sport. The ball used was a soccer ball. The nets were peachbaskets nailed to the gymnasium balcony. That was the beginning of basketball.

In 1892, the first rule book was published. There were 13 basic rules. The dribble was not part of the original game. When players tired of climbing up to the balcony to retrieve the ball each time someone scored, Naismith cut the bottoms out of the peachbaskets. In 1900, the iron ring and the bottomless net replaced the peachbaskets. The game caught on quickly. In 1894, the Montreal YMCA started its first basketball house league and by 1900 hosted junior, intermediate, and senior leagues. By 1907, the Canadian Amateur Athletic Union appointed a Dominion Basketball Committee as part of its structure. Today, some people believe that basketball has become the most popular sport in the world.

James Naismith, the creator of the new game, was a modest man. He was born in 1861 on a farm west of Ottawa near Almonte. He earned university degrees in medicine, theology, and physical education but never sought fame and fortune from his new invention. There is a school named after James Naismith in Almonte, Ontario, but there is not even a roadside plaque at the farm where he was born and raised. His memory is best preserved at Springfield, Massachusetts, site of the Basketball Hall of Fame.

1. Many people think of basketball as an American sport. Why do you think this is so?
2. Are there sports that people think of as particularly Canadian? Which ones? Why?

out a **reciprocity agreement** with the United States in 1911. Products of Canadian farms, fisheries, forests, and mines would be allowed into the United States free of tariffs. Taxes on American items coming into Canada, such as farm implements, automobiles, building materials, and canned goods would be lowered. It was the kind of tariff deal that every Canadian government since Confederation had been trying to make with the United States.

When news of the proposed agreement became known, the leader of the Conservative party, Robert Borden, became so discouraged that he wanted to resign. It seemed impossible that the Laurier Liberals could be defeated in the next election. But Borden was persuaded to stay and fight.

Then things began to go wrong. Clifford Sifton, a Liberal cabinet minister, was opposed to reciprocity. He joined other wealthy Liberals in fighting the idea. Business people, manufacturers, and bankers of both political parties were afraid that cheaper American goods in Canada would put them out of business. Canadian railway builders, such as Canadian Pacific Railways' president William van Horne, were worried. For years Canadians had been building east-west railway lines. Now they feared the railway business would be ruined if trade suddenly became north south. Canadian nationalists thought that Canadian natural resources should be kept at home and not shipped across the border. Anti-American feelings were still strong in Canada from the decision made over the Alaska boundary dispute.

President Taft of the United States forecast that Canada was at the parting of the ways with Britain. A prominent American politician named Champ Clark declared full support for reciprocity, saying "I hope to see the day when the American flag will float over every square mile of the British North American possessions, clear to the North Pole."

That was enough ammunition for the Conservatives. They waved the British flag in every campaign speech during the **election of 1911**. They preached an anti-American policy. They warned that if reciprocity passed, it would mean a political as well as economic takeover of Canada by the United States. Borden campaigned with the slogan "No truck or trade with the Yankees." In other words, he wanted no shipments or trade of goods with the Americans.

The headlines of 22 September 1911 told the election results: "Laurier's government goes down to defeat" (*The Globe*), "Conservatives sweep country, reciprocity killed" (*The Mail and Empire*).

Two issues were central in the Liberals' defeat: the Naval Service Bill and the reciprocity deal with the United States. French Canadians did not want to become involved in British imperialist disputes. English Canadians did not want to be taken over by American economic interests. Anti-imperialists such as Bourassa joined forces with the Conservatives to defeat the Liberals. Neither Laurier's personal leadership nor his program could save the Liberals from defeat in 1911. Sir Wilfrid Laurier was never again to be prime minister of Canada. He died on 17 February 1919.

DEVELOPING SKILLS: INTERPRETING POLITICAL CARTOONS

The art of political cartoons began early in Canada. By the 1890s, political cartoons were regular features in Canadian newspapers and magazines. One of Canada's most noted cartoonists was J.W. Bengough. He made his mark with his caricatures of Sir John A. Macdonald in his weekly magazine *Grip*. Caricature involves exaggerating certain characteristics of people to create humour. Through humour, the cartoons made statements about significant issues or events of the day.

At the turn of the century, political cartoons were very popular. They not only poked fun at politics and politicians, they helped people put issues into perspective. Cartoons often accompanied the editorials that expressed opinions on key issues.

Political cartoons are still popular today. They appear in newspapers across the country. Leading cartoonists today choose their own subject matter and make their own comment on it, rather than illustrating the editorials.

Cartoons can be fun to interpret. When you look at political cartoons, ask yourself the following questions.

1. Does the cartoon have a title? If so, what does it mean?

2. What issue or event is referred to in the cartoon?

3. What is the setting? Describe what you see.

4. Where and when does the action in the cartoon take place?

5. Who are the people or figures in the cartoon? What is their mood? What are they saying?

6. What other objects, symbols, or words are in the cartoon? What do they mean?

7. What comparisons, if any, are being made?

8. Who or what is the cartoonist poking fun at?

9. What is the message of the cartoon? Summarize it in one or two sentences.

10. Does the cartoonist get the message across effectively? Why or why not?

11. How does the cartoonist create humour? What techniques are used to get the message across?

12. Does the cartoonist's viewpoint differ from yours? Explain.

Try It!

1. Now you can try to interpret a political cartoon yourself. The following cartoon appeared at the time that reciprocity was being discussed. Using the 12 questions, interpret what the cartoon is saying.

2. Interpret the cartoon on page 67 of this chapter.

3. Clip modern political cartoons from your local newspaper. Use the same questions to interpret these cartoons. Discuss similarities and differences between these modern cartoons and those from the early twentieth century.

UNCLE SAM—"I CAN ALMOST HEAR THEM SINGING 'THE STAR SPANGLED BANNER' IN OTTAWA, BE GOSH."

ACTIVITIES

Check Your Understanding

1. Add these new terms to your *Factfile*.

   imperialism
   Boer War
   Naval Service Bill
   Alaska Boundary Dispute

   International Joint Commission
   Reciprocity Agreement 1911
   election of 1911

2. What qualities and characteristics did Laurier possess that prepared him for the position of prime minister?

3. What were some advantages for Canada of belonging to the British Empire? What were the disadvantages?

4. Explain the major reasons why a French Canadian nationalist movement gained strength in Quebec around the turn of the century.

5. Identify the major problems that caused conflicts in the first decade of the twentieth century:
   a) between French and English Canadians
   b) between Canada and the United States
   c) between Canada and Britain.

Confirm Your Learning

6. a) What were the causes of the Boer War?
   b) How did English and French Canadians react to the British request for Canadian assistance in South Africa? Why?
   c) Make a list of the possible solutions open to the Laurier government. What might have been the outcome of each solution?
   d) Explain and evaluate the eventual compromise worked out by Prime Minister Laurier.

7. a) Why did neither French Canadian nationalists nor pro-British Canadians approve of the Naval Service Bill?
   b) Was the bill a step forward for Canada's independence? Explain.

8. In 1903, F. H. Turnock, a Canadian journalist, discussed the anti-British feeling caused by the Alaska boundary dispute.

   The callousness, the selfishness, and the bad faith with which Canadians consider Britain has treated Canada in this matter will long rankle in the breasts of Canadians. It is bound to affect Canada's destiny. What the ultimate outcome may be, it is perhaps too early yet to predict. But it will sensibly loosen the tie which binds Canada to Great Britain. It will quench the spirit of Imperialism which has for some time been growing in Canada. Canadians now realize how little their services in the cause of the British Empire have been appreciated.

   a) Account for the anti-British feeling triggered by the Alaska boundary dispute.
   b) What effect do you think the dispute had on Canada's struggle for national identity?

9. Have various members of the class role play the following characters in a debate over reciprocity. Prepare arguments for or against reciprocity depending on your role. Then stage a public meeting in the class. Debate the statement:"Reciprocity is a good policy for Canada in 1911." Following the debate, take a class vote to reach a consensus.
   i) president of the CPR
   ii) a Saskatchewan wheat farmer
   iii) an individual who earns a living fishing in Prince Edward Island
   iv) an Ontario manufacturer of farm machinery

v) a woman working in the home

vi) an owner of a meat canning factory in Quebec

vii) a worker on the docks of British Columbia

viii) a worker in a Canadian steel company

ix) a pro-British imperialist

x) a wealthy Conservative business person

xi) a French Canadian nationalist

xii) a Native leader

10. How would you have voted in the election of 21 September 1911? Explain your reasons.

Challenge Your Mind

11. Slogans are short catchy phrases used to express a strong idea or feeling. In groups, create slogans that might have been written by each of the following in the first decade of the twentieth century.

a) a French Canadian nationalist

b) an English Canadian nationalist

c) a Canadian imperialist

d) a British imperialist

e) an American nationalist

12. Try creating your own political cartoon. Decide on an issue or a character from this chapter or from current events to be the focus of your cartoon. Think about what you want the cartoon to say and how you can say it simply and clearly. Don't make it too complicated. You want your audience to get your message almost immediately. Present your cartoons to the class.

Unit **3**

Canada and World War I
1914–1919

TIMELINE

1914
- Assassination of Archduke Ferdinand; World War I begins
- Britain declares war on Germany
- Canada is also automatically at war

1915
- German U-boat sinks the British luxury liner *Lusitania*
- Gas attack at Ypres

1916
- Battle of the Somme
- Major British and German naval battle off Jutland, Denmark
- Canadian women win the right to vote in Manitoba
- Saskatchewan, Alberta, British Columbia, and Ontario also grant women the right to vote

1917
- Canadians take Vimy Ridge
- Battle at Passchendaele
- Conscription crisis
- Halifax explosion
- United States enters the war
- Wartime Elections Act passed

1918
- Women gain right to vote in federal elections
- Canadian Wop May shoots down Germany's Red Baron
- Last major offensive by German forces fails; Germany surrenders on 11 November

1919
- Treaty of Versailles
- League of Nations formed

The twentieth century has seen two major wars fought at points all over the globe: World War I, 1914-1918, and World War II, 1939-1945. You will be reading about the horrors of World War I in this unit. Memories of such scenes as the one on page 93 haunted people for many years afterwards. World War I was different from every other war ever fought before it. It was total war, which meant that it involved civilians almost as much as soldiers. This war had an effect on everyone. When at last it was over, life was never the same again.

The war that began in August 1914 at first involved seven European countries. By its end, 30 countries were involved, including Canada and the United States. It was a world war in the sense that fighting was not limited to Europe. Battles were also fought in Africa, Asia, and on the Atlantic and Pacific oceans.

The war changed the history of most countries involved in it. Out of World War I came revolutions, changes of government, the loss of empires, and the rise of great new powers. At the end of the war, Canada had grown economically. It had also gained a greater degree of independence, but the loss of lives was a high cost and would never be forgotten.

The peace treaty that ended the war in 1919 reshaped the map of Europe. While it solved some problems, it also created new ones. Germany, the defeated power, especially resented the peace settlement. This resentment was a major reason for the later rise of Adolf Hitler. It was an important cause of World War II in 1939. When you come to study the causes of World War II, you will need to review the results of World War I.

At the end of this unit, you will be able to:

- analyze the causes of World War I
- recognize Canadian contributions to the war
- appreciate how ordinary Canadians supported the war effort at home
- understand why the issue of conscription divided the country
- determine the major effects of the war on Canada
- apply mind mapping techniques to understand key issues
- recognize and analyze bias
- appreciate how reading historical fiction can enrich the study of history
- prepare and evaluate a research report

Social Issues

- horrors of the war and the loss of lives
- effects of the Halifax explosion
- changes in the role of women
- treatment of "enemy aliens"
- Native and African Canadian participation in World War I

The Economy

- war production
- economic boom and industrial development
- women in the workforce

French-English Relations

- different feelings of commitment to the war
- controversy over Sir Sam Hughes's policies
- conscription crisis

Canadian-American Relations

- United States enters the war 1917
- trade with Canada

Canada and the World

- effects of European nationalism, imperialism, and militarism on Canada
- Canada enters World War I on behalf of Britain
- Canada's contribution to the war gains international respect

National Growth and Identity

- feelings of patriotism
- Canadian war heroes
- economic development
- Canada participates as a separate nation at the peace talks

Regional Development

- shipping boom in the Maritimes
- industrial development in central Canada
- wheat and food production in the West

Citizenship, Government, and Law

- financing the war—Victory Bonds, introduction of the income tax
- women's suffrage movement
- Wartime Elections Act 1917 and Dominion Elections Act 1920
- conscription

Technological Change

- technological developments (aircraft, tanks, submarines, etc.)
- industrialization

The Arts

- Canadian war art
- war poetry
- posters
- historical fiction about World War I

CHAPTER 5

War Breaks Out!

MURDER AT SARAJEVO

Assassination of Archduke Ferdinand and Archduchess Sophia at Sarajevo, 1914—an artist's impression.

It was Sunday morning, 28 June 1914. The citizens of Sarajevo, a sleepy little town in Austria-Hungary, were getting ready to welcome Archduke Franz Ferdinand and the Archduchess Sophia. The archduke was an important visitor. He would someday be their ruler, the emperor of all Austria-Hungary. That day in 1914 the archduke was in uniform—a light-blue tunic, black trousers, and a hat topped with large green ostrich feathers.

At 10:00 a.m., the royal couple drove toward the town hall in a four-car motorcade. Suddenly, someone threw a bomb. The bomb exploded against the hood of the limousine, but the archduke was not hurt. The tour continued. At the town hall the archduke complained angrily to the mayor, "I come here on a visit and get bombs thrown at me. It is outrageous!" Both the mayor and the chief of police assured the archduke there would be no more danger.

The motorcade moved on to the governor's palace. Several minutes later, a 19-year-old, Gavrilo Princip, stepped up to the car and fired two shots from a pistol at pointblank range. The first shot hit the archduke in the throat; the second hit Sophia in the stomach. Franz Ferdinand, blood pouring from his mouth, saw that his wife was wounded. "Sophia," he cried, "don't die! Keep alive for our children." Both Franz Ferdinand and Sophia died on the way to the hospital.

The assassin, Gavrilo Princip, swallowed poison, but the poison failed to work. Within minutes Princip and five others were rounded up by the police. They were members of a Serbian terrorist group known as the Black Hand. Their plan had been to murder the archduke and then to commit suicide.

That day, a friend of the assassin sent a message in code to the Serbian capital. It read, "Excellent sale of both horses." Members of the Black Hand in Serbia knew exactly what this code meant. What they could not know was the terrible effect those two shots would have on world history.

Causes of World War I

The shots fired that day in 1914 were the immediate cause of World War I. But in explaining a historical event as complex as a world war, many different causes need to be investigated. No one cause ever adequately explains why a historical event happens. To understand World War I, some of the causes have to be traced back to the late nineteenth century.

Alliances

The countries that went to war in 1914 were in two camps. Britain, France, and Russia were on one side; Germany and Austria-Hungary were on the other. France and Germany had been involved in conflicts for centuries. Each had tried to find other countries to be its allies in case of future wars. **Alliances** are formed when countries band together against a common threat, just as two or three children sometimes band together for protection against a bully or when neighbours join together to form a neighbourhood watch against crime.

France formed alliances with Russia and Britain in what was known as the **Triple Entente**. These three countries were also often called **"the Allies."** Germany joined with Austria-Hungary and Italy to form the **Triple Alliance** or the **Central Powers**. When the war started, Italy left the Central Powers to join the Triple Entente.

Thus at the time of Archduke Franz Ferdinand's assassination, Europe was already clearly divided into two hostile camps. The alliances were dangerous because they increased fear and suspicion among rival nations. With these alliances, a war between two countries would likely involve many more!

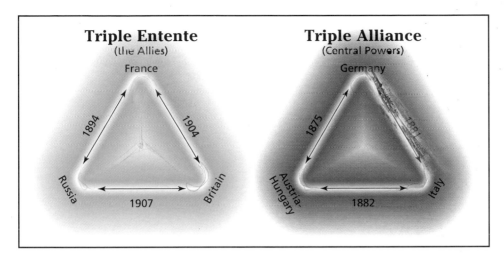

Triple Entente
(the Allies)

France

1894

1904

Russia

1907

Britain

Triple Alliance
(Central Powers)

Germany

1875

1882

Austria-Hungary

Italy

consisted of more than 200 small states in the eighteenth century. Gradually, feelings of nationalism drew these states together to form one strong nation.

But by the early twentieth century, extreme nationalism was causing problems. Some people seemed willing to take any action to support their nation, regardless of the effects on others. They were even ready to go to war to promote the interests of their homelands.

Nationalism was strong in the small country of Serbia in the early 1900s. Serbia was a small country bordering on the Austrian province of Bosnia. Many people of

Nationalism

Nationalism is a feeling of deep loyalty to one's people and homeland. In nineteenth century Europe, nationalism was a powerful force. Germany, for example, had

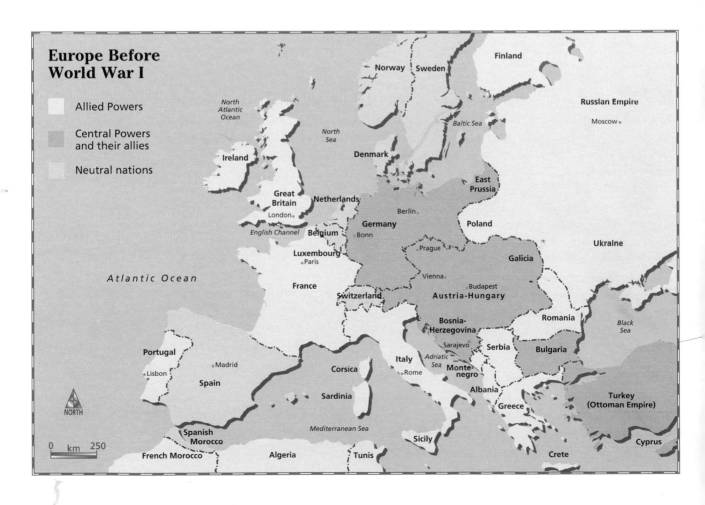

Europe Before World War I

- Allied Powers
- Central Powers and their allies
- Neutral nations

North Atlantic Ocean

Norway
Sweden
Finland

North Sea

Baltic Sea

Russian Empire

Moscow

Ireland

Denmark

East Prussia

Great Britain

London

Netherlands

Berlin

Germany

Poland

Ukraine

English Channel

Belgium

Bonn

Prague

Galicia

Luxembourg

Paris

Vienna

Budapest

Atlantic Ocean

France

Switzerland

Austria-Hungary

Romania

Black Sea

Bosnia-Herzegovina

Sarajevo

Serbia

Bulgaria

Portugal

Madrid

Lisbon

Spain

Corsica

Italy

Rome

Adriatic Sea

Monte-negro

Albania

Greece

Turkey (Ottoman Empire)

Cyprus

NORTH

0   km   250

Sardinia

Mediterranean Sea

Sicily

Crete

Spanish Morocco

French Morocco

Algeria

Tunis

Serbian descent lived in Bosnia and bitterly resented being under Austrian control. Some Serbs and Bosnians thought Bosnia should break away from Austria. They formed the terrorist organization known as the **Black Hand**. A terrorist organization is a group that supports violent action to gain its goals. Sometimes these groups feel that violence is the only way open to them. Terrorist groups, however, do not always represent the wishes of all people in their country.

The motto of the Black Hand was "Union with Serbia or Death." Gavrilo Princip belonged to the Black Hand, which claimed responsibility for the assassination of Archduke Ferdinand. The Austrians were also expressing feelings of nationalism when they strongly opposed the attempts of Bosnia to break away from their empire.

Imperialism

During the late nineteenth and early twentieth centuries, the nations of Europe became more industrialized. As a result, the spirit of imperialism gained momentum. European countries became increasingly interested in gaining control of lands away from the home country and building huge empires. These lands or colonies were a source of raw materials and a market for manufactured goods. They also gave the home country glory and military strength.

France had colonies in northwest Africa and east Asia. Russia controlled a vast empire stretching across northern Europe and Asia. The largest empire was controlled by Britain. The British Empire included Canada, Australia, New Zealand, India, Burma, Malaya, South Africa (as well as other parts of Africa), the East and West Indies, and islands in the Pacific.

The United States had gained power in the Pacific by taking control of the Hawaiian and Philippine islands. Germany also wanted colonies and world markets. But by the time Germany began to build an empire, all that remained were some territories in Africa and the Pacific that were not particularly valuable.

Imperialism led to frequent quarrels among the great powers of Europe in all parts of the world. Arguments over colonies and trade constantly threatened peace.

Militarism

Closely related to nationalism and imperialism was the rise of militarism. **Militarism** is the belief in the power of strong armies and navies to decide issues. It was thought that the only way to guarantee peace was by preparing for war. Militarism is based on the idea that if a nation is strong, no enemy would dare attack it. If war does break out, the militarized nation is able to defend itself.

This kind of thinking led to an **arms race** in Europe. Each country produced steel battleships, high-powered cannons, and explosives. Each tried to build a larger and more deadly war machine than its rivals. The size of armies and navies determined who would be the most powerful nation in Europe.

Britain therefore became nervous when Germany started building a huge navy. Since Britain was an island nation, it depended on its giant navy to "rule the waves" and guarantee its safety. By building a powerful navy, Germany challenged Britain's supremacy at sea. The nations of Europe were becoming increasingly suspicious and alarmed by the others' military power.

A stamp shows the extent of the British Empire in the early 1900s.

Ultimatum

When Gavrilo Princip fired those two fateful shots on the morning of 28 June 1914, the assassination set off a chain reaction of events. It gradually entangled the Central Powers and the Triple Entente in a major war.

The Austro-Hungarian government blamed Serbia for the deaths of the archduke and the archduchess. Austria-Hungary saw a chance to crush Serbian nationalism. With the support of its ally, Germany, Austria-Hungary sent Serbia an **ultimatum**. An ultimatum is a demand by one government that another government accept its terms or face war. In the ultimatum, Austria-Hungary insisted that Serbia:

1. put down all nationalist hatred against Austria-Hungary
2. punish all those involved in the assassination plot
3. allow Austro-Hungarian officials into Serbia to help crush the Black Hand.

The Serbs were given 48 hours to reply to the ultimatum. They agreed to all the conditions except the third. They refused to allow Austro-Hungarian officials into their country. Austria-Hungary took this as a complete refusal of its ultimatum and declared war on Serbia on 26 July 1914. Russia, considering itself an ally of the Serbs, started to mobilize its armies. France, as Russia's ally, also mobilized its forces. Germany now felt threatened by the actions of its two neighbours, France and Russia. Germany ordered them to stop mobilizing. When they refused, Germany declared war on Russia on 1 August 1914, and on France the next day.

Since the French border was heavily fortified, Germany planned to attack France through the small, neutral nation of Belgium. To this point, Britain was not yet involved in the war. However, Britain had signed a treaty guaranteeing that it would protect the neutrality of Belgium. Neutrality means a country does not help or support any side in a war or dispute. When Belgium was invaded, Britain declared war on Germany.

In London, England, that evening, Sir Edward Grey, British foreign secretary, told a friend, "The lamps are going out all over Europe. We shall not see them lit again in our lifetime." By midnight on 4 August 1914, all the countries of the two alliances, except Italy, were at war. World War I had begun!

A British battleship, HMS Dreadnought *—"Queen of the seas." It carried a crew of 862 and 36 guns. Canada's navy had very few ships in 1913.*

DEVELOPING SKILLS: MIND MAPPING

A group of sports fans is talking about the school's championship basketball game last weekend. Rita took a videotape of the game and is replaying it on the VCR. The group is amazed that the team actually did it! What was the secret of its success?

The group analyzes the tape. Leon says he is convinced it was the great offence. Rita thinks it was the team's defensive play. She sketches out some of the key plays on the board, showing how the players blocked the other team's offence. Leon sketches out some of the key offensive plays. Sharma argues that excellent coaching was a factor and Karl says it was luck—the last three point shot in the final seconds of the game. After a lot of discussion, the group decides the team success was due to a combination of all factors, but especially great defence.

What the group has done is analyze the causes of an event. Any event can have several causes. Causes are reasons or factors which produce an effect, action, or condition. Understanding why events happen, especially very complex events, requires a careful investigation and analysis of all possible causes.

People have argued for a long time over the major causes of monumental events such as World War I. How did the shooting of Archduke Ferdinand lead to world war? Why were so many nations dragged into full-scale war over what should have been just a squabble between two countries, Austria-Hungary and Serbia? What other factors contributed to the war?

A mind map is one technique you can use to help you analyze the causes of World War I. A mind map is a way of sketching ideas to provide a visual picture. Organizing information visually helps because it:

- highlights important points
- shows how ideas are connected
- triggers or cues your mind to remember key information.

The beginnings of a mind map to analyze the causes of World War I are set out on the next page.

Work It Through!

1. Examine the mind map. Notice that the main idea, "CAUSES OF WORLD WAR I," is written in capital letters at the centre of the diagram. All other ideas are connected to it. Drawing shapes around the ideas or using symbols can help to create a visual reminder of what they mean and show their importance. For example, two hands shaking can be used to represent "Alliances."

2. The first cause listed is "Alliances." Copy the mind map and fill in the other main causes. Use the information in this chapter as a resource. Include a question mark after each cause to remind you that you need to investigate further. Develop your own shapes to symbolize each cause.

3. The information provided under Alliances presents a visual picture of the two camps that were formed in Europe. The battle symbol between them indicates that they were hostile camps. The arrow from Italy shows that that country changed allegiances just before the war.

   The point form notes summarize important information and answer the question: "How did alliances help to cause World War I?" In your mind map, you use the note-making skills you learned in the last chapter.

   Fill in the key information for the other causes in your mind map. Use a different colour for each cause. Also include sketches, arrows to connect ideas, and any other symbols you find helpful.

4. Notice the arrows pointing out from the diagram. What do these represent? Fill in the important information to replace the question marks.

5. When your mind map is complete, review it and compare it with those of your classmates. Discuss similarities and differences. What is the value of having a visual layout of your notes?

6. Discuss the question: "Was any one cause more important than others? Why or why not?" Justify your answers.

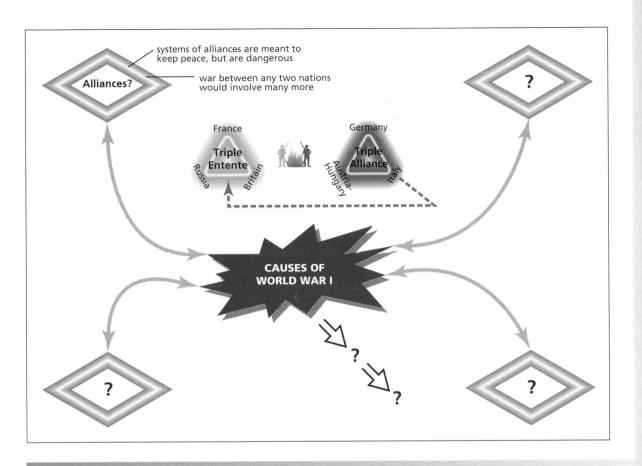

War!

In Canada, the giant headline on the front page of newspapers across the country announced the news: WAR! When Britain declared war on Germany, Canada and the other countries of the British Empire were automatically at war too. The British colonies were not independent nations, so they could neither declare war nor make peace on their own. They were subject to the rule of the home country.

In Canada, support for Canada's involvement in the war was widespread. Laurier was on record as saying, "There is in Canada but one mind and one heart.... When Britain is at war, Canada is at war also." Even Henri Bourassa, the French Canadian nationalist, agreed that it was Canada's duty "to contribute within the bounds of her strength... to the combined efforts of France and England." In Montreal, both French and English Canadians linked arms in the street and sang "La Marseillaise," the French national anthem, and the patriotic song "Rule Britannia."

When the call went out, recruiting offices were flooded with volunteers willing to fight for a private's pay of $1 a day. Wealthy and patriotic citizens donated money for machine guns and trucks. Everyone believed the war would be short, glorious, and full of adventure. Within the first two months, over 30 000 soldiers were on their way across the Atlantic. Most thought that the war would be over by Christmas. Who could have known it would take more than four years and the involvement of another 400 000 Canadians before peace would return to the world.

SOCIETY AND SOCIAL CHANGE

Native and African Canadians in World War I

Almost all Canadians who went to war in 1914 were volunteers. The majority of those who enlisted first were of British descent. But by the end of the war, Canadians from many different backgrounds had participated and distinguished themselves.

Native people went to France with the first contingent of the Canadian Expeditionary Force. Over 4000 Natives and many Métis saw active service in World War I. Among them was Patrick Riel, a grandson of Louis Riel. Patrick Riel was killed at Vimy Ridge. Francis Pegahamagabow, an Ojibway from Parry Island in Ontario, won a military medal and several bars for his skill and courage as a scout and expert shot. He was the most decorated Native soldier in World War I. "Ducky" Norwest, a Cree, also won recognition as an excellent sniper.

In 1916, the Department of Militia and Defence authorized the formation of the No. 2 Construction Batallion in Pictou, Nova Scotia. It was the first African Canadian unit. This unit contributed to the war effort by specializing in logging, milling, and shipping.

African Canadians who wanted to fight overseas met with resistance and racism. Some, however, managed to break through the barriers. Sixteen joined the 106th Battalion of Nova Scotia Rifles. One, Jerry Jones, served in France. He wiped out a machine gun post at Vimy Ridge and was wounded at Passchendaele.

1. Find out more about the individuals and battalions mentioned above.
2. What other groups made significant contributions to the war effort, but are not always remembered?

Native members of the Canadian Expeditionary Force with their elders.

Some African Canadian soldiers served with the fighting units. This illustration, from a 1919 issue of The Veteran, *is a reminder of their contribution and participation.*

Canadian soldiers set off to fight. Most went in an upbeat mood, thinking the war would be over quickly.

ACTIVITIES

Check Your Understanding

1. Add these new terms to your *Factfile*. Explain their historical importance to events surrounding World War I.

alliances	Black Hand
Triple Entente	militarism
Triple Alliance	arms race
nationalism	ultimatum

2. The diagram on page 79 shows how the Triple Entente and the Triple Alliance were formed.
   a) Which alliance was made first?
   b) Which two nations formed the first agreement? In which year?
   c) When was the Triple Alliance completed?
   d) Which European nation was the last to join an alliance?

3. Why did the system of alliances make countries feel safer? At the same time, how did alliances make a major war more likely?

4. Explain the reasons why an arms race developed in Europe early in the twentieth century.

5. How did French and English Canadians react when war was declared? Why?

Confirm Your Learning

6. When the Triple Entente was formed, Germany complained that it was being surrounded. Examine the map of Europe on page 79. How justified was Germany's complaint?

7. In 1914, Europe was divided into two armed and hostile camps. Were the alliances the cause or the effect of the arms build-up? Explain your answer.

8. When officials of Austria-Hungary proposed to enter Serbia to track down the archduke's assassins, Serbia insisted this would violate its national sovereignty. National sovereignty is a nation's right to run its own affairs. Does this seem like a reasonable position to you? Explain your answer.

Challenge Your Mind

9. a) Research and listen to a recording of the patriotic song "Rule Britannia." Why is this song described as patriotic? What does it suggest about the mood of people who sang it when war was declared in 1914?
   b) What are your impressions of this song?

10. a) Nationalism was very strong at the beginning of the twentieth century. Examine your own feelings of nationalism. Would you say they are strong? How do you express them?
    b) Would you be willing to go to war for Canada? Under what circumstances, if any?
    c) Are there any instances in the world today where nationalism has played a part in war or violence? Find out more about them. Do you feel these wars are justified?

11. Imagine you were a foreign correspondent sent to report on the visit of Archduke Ferdinand to Sarajevo in 1914. Write the news bulletin you would have telegraphed to your home newspaper following the fateful events on 28 June. Include the effects you believe the event will have. Write your bulletin from the point of view of one of the following.
    a) a Canadian reporter
    b) a reporter for the Serbian national newspaper
    c) a correspondent for a major British newspaper
    d) a member of the Black Hand writing for an underground paper
    e) a German reporter writing for a German paper

CHAPTER 6

Horror on the Western Front

GAS ATTACK AT YPRES

The First German Gas Attack at Ypres, *by artist William Roberts. What impressions does this painting create of the battle?*

One of the most famous battles involving Canadian soldiers in World War I was fought on the front lines near the Belgian town of Ypres. Deadly poison gas was used for the first time in the war during this battle. Here is one soldier's vivid memoir.

I saw the whole picture of the gas attack as probably no one else did. I have never been in a battle—and I have been in many—where the men were suffering in such numbers that their crying and groaning could be heard all over the battlefield. None of us had ever seen gas before. It was the first gas attack in history.

But not a single unit skipped out—some individuals, yes, but formations, no... Suddenly we saw the gas rolling up in a brownish yellowish bank. It was between 1 and 3 m high and it wouldn't rise higher unless it was puffed up by the wind.

I went over to where the line had been broken and where there was confusion. No Canadian troops were running.

> *The gas was dreadful and suffering was immediate. The only thing we could do was soak our handkerchiefs in urine and hold them over our noses.*
>
> *Thousands were lying around gasping and crying. They were being drowned by the gas. They didn't know how to protect themselves.*
>
> *But we held our position.*

The War on Land

The battle at Ypres on 22 April 1915 was only one of many battles fought during the long years of the war. Troop movements began during August 1914 when German forces swept through Belgium and into northeastern France. Germany wanted to capture Paris before the British and Russians could fully mobilize their armies. Within a few short weeks, German forces had advanced almost to the outskirts of Paris. But the Allies moved faster than Germany expected. Using every available vehicle including Paris taxicabs, the French rushed troops to the front. The British and French eventually managed to stop the German advance.

In the Trenches

In October 1914, both sides began to secure their positions and "dig in" before winter. They dug rows of deep trenches protected by machine guns and barbed wire. Parallel lines of trenches soon stretched several hundred kilometres from

Soldiers had to struggle through barbed wire and mines to cross no-man's land.

Canadian troops wash in a shell hole. There was little opportunity to wash in fresh water.

The trenches were laid out in a zigzag pattern to prevent enemy fire from sweeping along the whole length of the trench. As the diagram below shows, the front-line trenches were usually about 2 m deep and protected by sandbags. Firing lines were linked by traverses or joining sections. From the front-line trenches, communication trenches were dug back to a line of support trenches. Here at the rear were command posts and reserve companies of soldiers. Sometimes small trenches, known as saps, probed out into no-man's land to serve as lookout posts.

the English Channel to the border of Switzerland. The trenches twisted and turned across the countryside, separating the opposing forces in some places by only 25 m. Soldiers in World War I fought mainly by **trench warfare**.

The corridor between the enemy trenches was called **"no-man's land."** This strip of land was armed with buried land mines and covered with barbed wire entanglements. Any soldier who ventured into this area was an easy target for enemy fire. Sometimes the wounded caught in no-man's land could not be brought back to safety. The soldiers in the trenches could do nothing but listen to the cries of agony from their dying comrades.

In wet weather, the trenches became slippery and waterlogged. Wooden floorboards (duckboards) were placed in the bottom of the trenches, but troops often stood in water up to their knees. The soldiers slept where and when they could, often standing up or slumped against the sandbags. At other times, they crawled into crude underground dugouts carved in the walls of the trenches.

The early days there, for the first winter, oh boy, I want to tell you, primitive living alright. [The soldiers] were packed into a lot of dugouts, six or

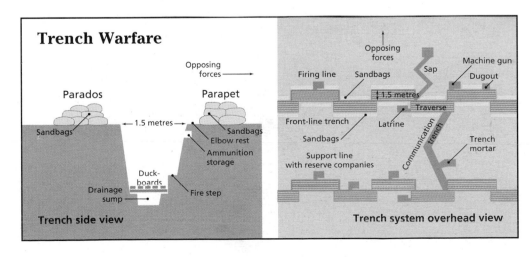

Trench Warfare

Parados

Parapet

Sandbags

←1.5 metres→

Sandbags
Elbow rest
Ammunition storage

Duck-boards

Drainage sump

Fire step

Trench side view

Opposing forces →

Opposing forces

Firing line   Sandbags   Sap   Machine gun
Dugout

1.5 metres

Traverse

Front-line trench   Latrine

Sandbags

Support line with reserve companies

Communication trench

Trench mortar

Trench system overhead view

seven or eight men all pushed in together as tight as they could go, and wet right straight through. We never took off our shoes or our clothes, we just slept in them. But we'd take any sandbags that were halfway dry and pull them over our feet and tie them one on top of the other, four or five on each leg. Your body heat and that of the other men would more or less heat the place, provided it wasn't too drafty. And in the morning when you woke up, why the outside sandbag would be soaking wet...

Soldiers huddled in the trenches, sometimes sleeping sitting up.

Since the soldiers were constantly cold, wet, and dirty, sickness and disease spread rapidly. Two of the most common illnesses were trench foot and trench mouth. Trench foot was rotting of the flesh between and around the toes. Trench mouth was a painful infection of the gums. Everyone had body lice living in their mud-caked uniforms. Rats ran through the trenches feeding on the garbage and human waste. Some soldiers suffered from shell-shock, a nervous breakdown caused by the immense stress of battle.

Meals had very little variety. Most times the meals consisted of "bully" beef (tinned corned beef), bread or hard biscuits, and hot tea. Occasionally there was stew, which was mostly vegetables and not much meat. The soldiers looked forward to packages from friends and families at home in Canada. Then they received treats of chocolate, fruit cakes, and tins of jam.

Night was the worst time in the front-line trenches. Everyone was tense and watchful for any signs of attack. Raiding parties would creep across no-man's land at night. They would cut through the barbed wire with wire cutters and make a surprise attack with their bayonets.

After a month or so in the trenches, units would be allowed to go to the rear for the chance to sleep in a dry place, rest, eat a decent meal, and above all, bathe and clean up. The soldiers in the trenches must often have wondered what they were doing there. On Christmas Eve 1915, Canadian and German soldiers joined in singing "Silent Night" across the shell-torn no-man's land. A soldier put his feelings this way:

It seemed that the Germans didn't want to be there any more than we did. But it seemed to be that somebody else was manipulating the strings behind the line, and we were just put there to work out a game. It wasn't really hatred. Only sometimes you did hate, when you see your chums and your friends get shot. It would be pretty hard on you that way, and you could say you'd hate for a while, but not necessarily hate that you wanted to kill. But you had to kill or be killed, if you wanted to survive….

Sometimes at that time I felt, well, it's so unnecessary. A bunch of men… a hundred yards away… you could talk to them and you could hear them talking, hear them working, and here you was [sic], you've got to make an attack. And you had to kill them or get killed. And you would sometimes wonder what it was all about.

Battles on the Western Front

The first division of 20 000 Canadian troops took up places alongside their allies on the front lines in mid-April 1915. In the horror of the months and years that followed, they were joined by another 400 000 fellow Canadians. Some of Canada's most prominent moments in the war are associated with battles along the **Western Front**. Canada's contribution will never be forgotten at Ypres, Festubert, the St. Eloi craters, Mount Sorrel, the Somme, Courcelette, Vimy Ridge, the Scarpe, Passchendaele, Amiens, Arras, the Canal du Nord, and Cambrai. The following are a few of the major battles in which Canadians were involved.

Ypres

The Canadian First Division was assigned to the front lines near the ancient city of **Ypres** in Belgium. Their task was to hold about 3.5 km of the line in the face of heavy German attack. They had only been in action for a few weeks when they faced the first deadly poison gas. You read a soldier's account of the attack at the beginning of this chapter. Made of chlorine, the poison gas was released from canisters when the breeze was blowing toward the Allied trenches. The chlorine gas burned the eyes and throats and destroyed the lungs. Those who breathed the gas choked, gagged, gasped, coughed, and died. The Canadians, with makeshift gas masks, managed to hold their position.

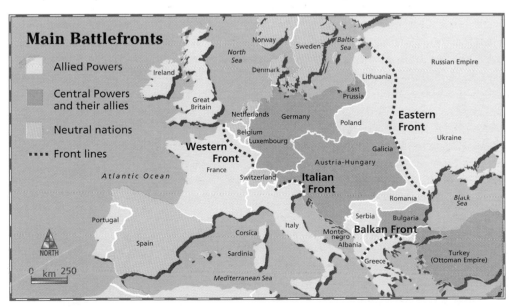

The Canadian troops suffered dreadful casualties at Ypres on 22 April 1915. More than 5200 died, and one in five was listed as killed in action, gassed, missing, or wounded.

Later in the war, even more deadly poison gases were used by both sides. Worst of all was mustard gas. This burned the skin and the respiratory tract, and caused blindness. Eventually, more effective gas masks were invented. These masks had filters through which the air could be purified.

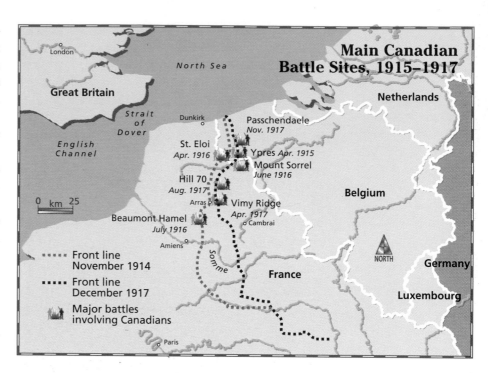

Main Canadian Battle Sites, 1915–1917

- ····· Front line November 1914
- ▪▪▪▪▪ Front line December 1917
- 🔥 Major battles involving Canadians

Battle of the Somme

The first day of the **Battle of the Somme** in France—1 July 1916—was the most disastrous the British army had ever suffered. The Canadian corps fought as part of the British forces under the command of General Douglas Haig. The pictures on the next page, taken at the Somme attack, record what happened in the first few minutes. At exactly 7:30 a.m., the British officer leapt to the top of the trench, and with a wave of his cane ordered his troops to go forward. The soldiers went over the top.

One man was hit as soon as his head appeared over the trench, and he fell back into the mud. The soldiers stumbled through the barbed wire of no-man's land heading for the German trenches. They faced a hail of German machine gun fire. A British sergeant recorded, "Our dead were heaped on top of each other... In places three and four deep." Only a few Allied soldiers ever reached the German trenches. By nightfall British and Canadian casualties totalled 57 470, the heaviest ever in warfare for one day's fighting.

Troops from Newfoundland and Labrador also played a major part in the Battle of the Somme. These troops faced a particularly strong part of the German line at Beaumont Hamel. They were mowed down by German machine gun fire as they advanced across no-man's land toward the German trenches. Ninety percent of the Royal Newfoundland Regiment were killed or wounded. It was the greatest single disaster in the 500 plus year history of Newfoundland and Labrador. July 1 is still marked as a solemn memorial day in that province.

Soldiers display some of the first gas masks. A range of different gas masks was developed after the experience of Canadian and other troops at Ypres.

Soldiers go over the top at the Battle of the Somme. Some never made it out of the trenches.

When the Battle of the Somme ended five months after it began, both armies were exhausted. Casualties for both sides had reached 1.25 million, of whom 24 000 were Canadians. The British had advanced no more than 11 km. People at home were horrified by this massacre. Many blamed General Haig; others blamed the politicians who had started the war. To many soldiers, the real enemy was not the Germans or the Austrians, but the war itself.

At the Somme, tanks were used for the first time in warfare. A British invention, tanks were huge armed "land ships" weighing over 25 t. They lumbered along at less than 5 km/h. Though they often got stuck in the mud, tanks were able to break through the barbed wire of no-man's land. Although the British High Command did not at first appreciate the potential value of the tank, this new weapon eventually helped to win the war.

In spite of the heavy losses, hardly any ground had been captured. General Haig, however, insisted that the attack go on. For 141 days, the Battle of the Somme continued. Canadians fought so heroically at the Somme that they were marked out as storm troops. During the rest of the war, they were often brought in to lead an attack. British Prime Minister Lloyd George later wrote in his war memoirs, "Whenever the Germans found the Canadian corps coming into their line, they prepared for the worst." He also singled out the troops from Newfoundland and Labrador for their contribution and valour.

Vimy Ridge

Today a white stone Canadian war memorial stands high on **Vimy Ridge**. Here on 9 April 1917, Canada won its most celebrated battle. German forces had dug in on the height of land at Vimy. From this vantage point, they could control all the surrounding areas. Several unsuccessful attempts had been made by both British and French troops to push out the German forces.

Finally, after months of preparations, 100 000 Canadians launched an attack. For the first time, all four Canadian divisions fought together. In a blinding sleet storm, the Canadians forced their way up the hill. In a few hours, they had captured the ridge. That day more ground, more guns, and more German prisoners were taken than in the first two-and-a half years of the war.

Four Canadians won the Victoria Cross (the most prestigious award given by Britain to its heroes) at Vimy. The victory was a great morale booster and focussed international attention on Canada. Some people said that at that moment, Canada became a nation.

A painting shows the great power of the tank. Tanks were used for the first time in World War I and proved to be a formidable weapon.

Passchendaele

One of the most bitter disasters for Canadians occurred at **Passchendaele** in the fall of 1917. This Belgian area of land had once been beneath the North Sea. When the shelling destroyed drainage ditches, the land became waterlogged. Soldiers sometimes wept with the sheer frustration of trying to advance through the mud. Narrow duckboards were placed as pathways over the mire. Nevertheless, thousands of soldiers and horses who slipped into the mud were sucked in and drowned. Locomotives sank to their boilers and tanks quickly bogged down.

A British official, seeing the battlefield for the first time, cried out, "Good God! Did we really send soldiers to fight in that?" Almost 16 000 Canadians lost their lives at Passchendaele. The offensive gained 7 km of mud which the Germans soon won back again.

Canadian soldiers fire a heavy howitzer gun in battle.

THE ARTS

Canadian War Art

During World War I, it was common for newspapers and magazines to send artists and photographers to record images of the fighting. The government offered artists the pay and rank of officers if they would go to the front. Several artists, including some who later became part of the famous Group of Seven, went to the front lines.

War correspondents and war artists shared the same hardships and risks as front-line soldiers. Often they sent back rough sketches along with their notes and news stories. Other artists sometimes completed the work for publication. The scenes were frequently copied in quantity and sold to patriotic Canadians.

The war artists did not glorify war. They portrayed the grim horror of the battlefield. The painting entitled *The Stretcher Bearer Party* by Cyril Henry Barraud, for example, captures the desolation of the battlefield, the smoke from the exploding shells, the huge craters left behind, and the wounded and exhausted troops. Yet there is also in the picture a sense of pride in the Canadian troops and a hint of victory and accomplishment. Some artists also painted scenes showing the effects of the war at home.

1. Why would artists have been called upon to act as reporters during World War I?
2. Describe the scenes shown in the paintings by A.T.J. Bastien and Henrietta Mabel May. What impressions do they create of the war?
3. Research other Canadian war paintings. Display copies of the paintings and add captions to describe the events and the artists.

The paintings are, top to bottom:
Women Making Shells *by Henrietta Mabel May*
The Stretcher Bearer Party *by Cyril Henry Barraud*
Canadian Gunners in the Mud
(at Passchendaele) *by A.T.J. Bastien.*

DEVELOPING SKILLS: READING HISTORICAL FICTION

When you do a research assignment, you usually look for sources of *factual* information. You need to know what happened, when, how, and why. Resources you search out for the facts are non-fiction resources. They can include books, newspapers, videos, maps, and photographs, for example.

When these resources are actual documents or accounts from people experiencing the events, they are primary sources. The words of Canadian soldiers involved in the battles of World War I that you have read in this chapter are examples of primary sources. When accounts are written *about* events and are based on primary sources, they are secondary sources. Biographies and books written about World War I by people who did not experience it, for example, are secondary sources.

But what about novels, short stories, poems, movies, and dramas? Novels don't give you the facts, you say, they are fiction. Works of fiction are imagined. They do not try to be true and actual accounts of real people or events. But writers of fictional novels, movies, or plays can *base* their stories on actual events. Novels written about historical people or events, for example, are historical fiction. Writers of historical fiction often do a lot of research about the period, people, and events they are writing about. Then, when they create their scenes and characters, they have a real sense of what people would have been feeling and doing. Fiction can often fill in the details and feelings that we can only imagine because we do not have complete records of the past.

Historical fiction can help to make some of the people and events you learn about come alive. By recreating the events, the writers can make you feel like you are there. You can identify with the characters.

An Example

Erich Maria Remarque told the story of World War I from the German point of view. His novel is called *All Quiet on the Western Front*. It is narrated by Paul Baumer, a 19-year-old German soldier. Paul and his friends left high school and volunteered to go to the front lines to fight for their country. It wasn't long before they saw the horror of the war and came to despise everything it stood for.

In the passage below, Paul is alone in the front-line trenches. A French soldier falls into the shell hole where Paul is sheltering. Paul stabs him to death to prevent any noise from giving away his position. But the man does not die right away and looks at Paul with terror in his eyes. Paul feels terrible. This is the first time he has killed with his own hands someone whom he can see face to face. He talks to the dying man.

> *Comrade, I did not want to kill you. If you jumped in here again, I would not do it, if you would be sensible too. But you were only an idea to me before, an abstraction that lived in my mind and called forth its appropriate response. It was that abstraction I stabbed. But now, for the first time, I see that you are a man like me. I thought of your hand grenades, your bayonet, of your rifle; now I see your wife and your face and our fellowship. Forgive me, comrade. We always see it too late. Why do they never tell us that you are just poor devils like us, that your mothers are just as anxious as ours, and that we have the same fear of death, and the same dying and the same agony? Forgive me, comrade; how could you be my enemy? If we threw away these rifles and this uniform you could be my brother just like Kat and Albert....*
>
> *... Comrade,... today you, tomorrow me. But if I come out of it comrade, I will fight against this, that has struck us both down; from you, taken life and from me? Life also.*

Source: Erich Maria Remarque, *All Quiet on the Western Front*.

1. How do you know that Paul is in despair at having taken another human being's life?

2. How does Paul justify doing what he has done?

3. What lessons about war does Paul learn from this incident?

4. a) What are your thoughts and feelings about the war after reading this passage?

   b) Is the incident realistic? Do you think it could actually have happened? How does the writer make you feel it is real?

   c) Is this an effective passage? Why or why not?

5. How would you feel if you were in Paul's position?

6. Read, listen to, or view some other works of fiction dealing with World War I and report on them for the class.

The War in the Air

When war broke out in 1914, the airplane was a new and unproven invention. Few military leaders had any confidence in the airplane as a weapon of war. The Canadian Colonel Sam Hughes is reported to have said, "The airplane… will never play any part in such a serious business as the defence of a nation."

Canada had no air force of its own, but Canadians who wanted to fly joined the British Royal Flying Corps. The earliest planes were usually singleseaters. Their maximum speed was between 95 and 125 km/h, and they could stay airborne for only an hour without refuelling. At first unarmed airplanes were used just to scout enemy positions behind the lines. Some pilots carried pistols, rifles, and shotguns. Others caught in battle threw bricks or links of rusty chain at the propellers of opposing planes to bring them down.

At the beginning of the war, Germany seemed to have several advantages in the air battles. It had the most aircraft (400 compared with 156 French and 113 British). The Germans had also developed a superior plane called the Fokker, a monoplane with one set of wings. It was armed with a machine gun with a firing mechanism timed so that bullets did not hit its own propeller blades. The Germans also had gasfilled balloons called **Zeppelin dirigibles** or **airships**. These were used on observation missions and bombing raids. Eventually, both sides used airships.

By 1917, the Allies had developed the Sopwith Camel, an excellent fighter plane. The pilots' fighting technique was to engage in aerial dogfights or duels, manoeuvring their light planes to dive on the enemy from the rear.

The percentage of pilots killed was higher than in any other branch of the military. In late 1916, it was said that the average life of a pilot was three weeks. There were no parachutes to save those unlucky enough to be shot down. The great air aces included Germany's Manfred von Richthofen, Britain's Alfred Ball, and Canada's Billy Bishop. An ace was a fighter who had shot down at least five enemy planes. Von Richthofen, known as the Red Baron, downed 80 planes in his career.

Few people know that it was a Canadian air ace who finally shot down the Red Baron. On 21 April 1918, von Richthofen, flying about the Somme Valley, spotted an Allied plane far below. He put his Fokker into a steep dive and moved in. His target was an inexperienced Canadian flier, Wilfred ("Wop") May. May's gun jammed, but behind von Richthofen was another Canadian pilot, Captain Roy Brown. Brown, in his Sopwith Camel, opened fire on von Richthofen. The Red Baron fell into a

Zeppelins were huge balloons with a metal frame and were filled with hydrogen. Some had platforms on the top from which guns could shoot at airplanes overhead.

deadly spin. The German ace was dead at the age of 26.

Today the seat of the Red Baron's plane is displayed at the Royal Military Institute in Toronto. You can put your finger through the bullet hole in the seat.

Billy Bishop

During World War I, a young pilot named Billy Bishop became a Canadian hero. As a boy in Owen Sound, Ontario, Billy Bishop practised shooting at moving targets with his rifle in the woods. His firing expertise made him one of the greatest fighter pilots of the British Commonwealth. On his first day behind the front lines, he shot down a German plane. In one five-day period, Bishop destroyed 13 planes.

Billy often flew the skies alone. On one occasion, he attacked a German air base near Cambrai, France. Two enemy planes rose to chase him, and Bishop shot down both of them. Two more enemy planes came up to attack the single raider. One fell from the deadly fire from Bishop's gun, and the other was driven off, out of ammunition. Billy Bishop returned safely to his home field.

By the end of the war, Billy Bishop was awarded the Victoria Cross by Britain and the highest honours of France. He was among the top three Allied air aces. He went on to become Director of Recruiting for the Royal Canadian Air Force in 1940.

As a group, Canadian fighter pilots brought down 438 enemy aircraft during World War I. Four of the top seven leading aces of the Royal Air Force were Canadians. It was a remarkable record!

The War at Sea

In early May 1915, the British luxury liner **Lusitania** was crossing the Atlantic Ocean. The unarmed ship carried almost 2000 passengers. Suddenly a torpedo streaked through the waves toward the hull of the *Lusitania*. Moments later there was an explosion, panic, chaos, and death. Eleven hundred and ninety-eight people drowned. At sea, there was a new terror. A deadly weapon had been added to naval warfare—the submarine.

German submarines had been prowling the seas since the beginning of the war. They had downed 200 British ships by the end of 1914 and they warned that passenger ships would not be spared. But the

Billy Bishop, World War I flying ace, stands in front of his Nieuport 17 Scout plane.

sinking of the *Lusitania* was different. More than half the passengers on board the *Lusitania* that day were Americans. The United States, still neutral at this stage of the war, did not want to get involved with European wars. But the attack on American citizens shocked the American people. It turned public opinion in the United States against Germany. Eventually, it helped to bring the United States into the war.

Germany knew that command of the seas was of supreme importance to Britain. As an island nation, Britain depended on its navy to keep the sea lanes open for supplies of food and raw materials. German submarines attacked British ships in an attempt to cut off supplies. At the same time, the British navy tried to blockade the German coast so that food and war supplies could not get into Germany by sea.

Both Britain and Germany had strong fleets of battleships. But only once during the war, off the coast of Denmark at **Jutland**, did these two great fleets face each other. Neither side could risk massive losses to their fleets. In May 1916, 149 British warships met 99 German warships head on at Jutland. It was one of the most dramatic

nights of the war. Britain suffered greater losses both in ships and sailors. However, after Jutland, the Germans risked no more major sea battles with their fleet. German shipyards stopped producing surface ships and started producing more submarines.

The submarine or **U-boat** *(Unterseeboot)* was Germany's most deadly weapon. The early submarines could stay submerged for two and a half hours. Submarines carried a crew of 35 and 12 torpedoes. Torpedoes were very expensive, but could be fired underwater at a moving target. However, U-boats preferred to come to the surface and sink their enemies by gunfire. By late 1916, German submarines were sinking an average of 160 ships per month. Germany was predicting an early defeat for Britain.

The U-boat Menace

By 1917, the war on the Western Front still had not been won. Germany decided that some more drastic action had to be taken to defeat the Allies. The German navy introduced a policy of "unrestricted submarine warfare." This meant that German U-boats would sink any Allied or neutral ship approaching Britain. The results of

SCIENCE AND TECHNOLOGY

Submarines

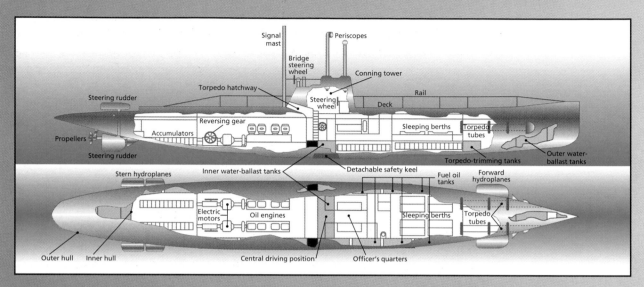

World War I submarines were relatively small, but their torpedoes could sink the largest ships. All navies developed hydrophones (listening equipment) to pick up the sound of the submarines' engines underwater. By the end of the war, they also used sound echoes to find the position of the submarines and then dropped depth charges (explosive devices) to destroy them.

this policy were almost disastrous for Britain. In the first four months the policy was in operation, Germany sank over 1000 British ships. Britain had to find a way to counter the U-boats, or it would be starved into surrender.

One answer was the **convoy system**. Instead of cargo ships sailing alone from Canada and the United States to Britain,

Ships Sunk by German U-boats	
Month	**Number of ships**
February 1917	212
March 1917	297
April 1917	335
May 1917	230
Total	**1074**

they began to sail in fleets. Supply ships were escorted by armed destroyers which kept constant watch like sheepdogs guarding a flock of sheep. The convoy system helped get necessary supplies through to Britain again.

The U-boats did tremendous damage to British and Allied shipping. However, the sinking of American ships by U-boats brought the United States into the war against Germany. The entrance of the Americans in 1917 helped to turn the tide in favour of the Allies.

Canada's main contribution to the war at sea was providing sailors and ships for the Royal Navy. Canadian shipyards built more than 60 anti-submarine ships and more than 500 smaller anti-submarine motor launches. Several thousand Canadians served in the British Royal Navy, in the Royal Naval Canadian Volunteer Reserve, and in the Royal Naval Air Service.

DEVELOPING SKILLS: PREPARING A RESEARCH REPORT

You are about to start on a bicycle trip and you discover something is wrong with your bike. What do you do? Cancel your trip? Pull out your hair? No. Head to the local library. You can borrow a bicycle repair manual that gives step-by-step instructions on how to fix your bike.

Resource centres are valuable sources of information on just about any topic. The trick is to find the information you need quickly and efficiently. You are asked to write a research report about World War I. What do you do? Here are some key steps to follow.

■ Step I *Purpose*

1. Be sure you understand your assignment. For example, you need to know that a report summarizes and presents important information on a particular topic. It is different from an essay, which develops a particular point of view or argument. Also ask yourself these questions.

   • What exactly am I being asked to do?
   • When is the assignment due?
   • How long should it be?
   • How is it to be presented—written, oral, etc.?
   • How will it be evaluated?

   Highlight key words in your assignment so you are absolutely clear on what you need to do.

■ Step II *Preparation*

2. Often you will have options. You may be given a choice of topics, for example. Choose your topic carefully. Ask yourself:

   • Will I find this topic interesting?

   • Is this topic manageable?
   • Will I be able to find resources?
   • Will I have enough time to complete the assignment?
   • Is the topic specific or too broad? Do I need to define it more carefully?

Suppose your topic is new technology used in World War I. By asking the above questions, you will come to the conclusion that this topic is not manageable. It is too broad. So much new technology was introduced that it would be impossible to cover it all. You need to define your topic more carefully. You might decide to focus on types of airplanes used in World War I, for example.

■ Step III *Process*

3. Once you have a clear idea of your topic, you can start your research. Use the card or computer catalogue in your resource centre to identify possible resources. The catalogue is the nucleus of any library. It lists all resources by author, title, and subject.

   For information on types of airplanes used during World War I, there are several possible subjects to look under. You could look under "airplanes," "World War I," or "weapons." [Hint: Always have a pencil and paper with you when using the catalogue. Jot down the call numbers of the books so you can locate them on the shelves.]

   Check periodical indexes and computer databases for magazines, audio-visual resources, newspaper reports, and journal articles. Check the vertical information files. You will probably be surprised by the amount of information that you discover.

4. Next, get an overview of your topic by browsing and skimming through a number of the resources you locate. The idea is to familiarize yourself with the information available on your topic. Then you can decide where you will focus your attention in your research.

   For example, you may discover that encyclopedia articles, special reference books on World War I and airplanes, and films are the best sources of information.

5. Make point-form notes from your resources. Try to use your own words. Gather references for illustrations as well. Always note the source of the information (author, title, date, and page number).

■ Step IV *Product*

6. Once you have gathered your information, develop a working outline for your report. This becomes the framework of your report. Organize your information into a few main ideas.

   For example, you may decide to focus on three types of planes. Enter your main ideas on an organizer like the one below. Your subpoints would include descriptions of the planes, illustrations, and information on how they were used. As a conclusion, you could present your ideas on how effective the planes were and how technology can be used for both positive and negative purposes.

7. Prepare a draft copy of your report. Decide on an introduction that will grab the reader or listener's attention. It should give a clear and concise statement of the focus topic.

   Develop each of your main ideas or subtopics. Be sure the main idea is clearly expressed in a topic sentence and the subpoints refer to and develop the main idea. Put the main ideas in the most effective order, leaving the best idea to the last.

   Write a conclusion that summarizes your main points, reinforces what you have said, and leaves your audience with something interesting to think about.

8. Edit your draft. Be sure that:

   - you have met the requirements of the assignment
   - the report is organized logically and makes sense to the reader

Names in group: _____	Teacher's Name: _____
_____	Class: _____
_____	Due Date: _____

Focus Topic/Question: Types of airplanes used in World War I

Main Idea/Sub-Topic: *Fokker*	Main Idea/Sub-Topic: *Sopwith Camel*	Main Idea/Sub-Topic: *Airships*
Subpoints:	Subpoints:	Subpoints:

Conclusion:

- the sentences vary in length and structure
- the spelling, grammar, capitalization, and punctuation are correct.

9. Consider a variety of possible formats or a combination of ways to present your research report. See the suggestions in the box below.

■ **Step V** *Personal Learning*

10. Once you have completed or presented your report, reflect on it. Evaluate what you have done and think about what you might do differently next time to improve your work. Classmates or your teacher can also help you with this evaluation process.

Try It!

1. Choose one of the following topics on World War I and prepare a research report.
   - i) trench warfare
   - ii) poison gas
   - iii) tanks
   - iv) airplanes
   - v) submarines
   - vi) role of women

2. a) As a class, discuss how the skill of a research report will be important to you in various careers and occupations.
   b) The following are some careers in which you could be expected to write reports. Choose one that interests you and describe a situation in which you would need to prepare a report. Outline what the report might contain.
   Salesperson • Computer programmer • Lawyer • Accountant • Architect • Construction Foreperson • Police Officer • Detective • Engineer • Politician • Teacher • Chef • Recreational director • Newspaper or television reporter • Doctor • Nurse • Flight Attendant • Curator • Manager

Oral	Visual	Written
panel discussion	slide show or overhead trans- parencies	report
dramatization		booklet
role play	picture story	newspaper
radio broadcast	models/ diagrams	letter or diary
interview	charts, graphs, maps	poem
talk with visuals	film or video	play
	bulletin board display	memoir

The Last Hundred Days

By the spring of 1918, Germany's leaders realized a crisis had come. German submarine attacks on supply ships had failed to force Britain to surrender. Now the United States had entered the war. Austria-Hungary and Turkey, Germany's allies, were on the point of collapse. The only hope for Germany was to launch a mighty offensive on the Western Front before the United States army could arrive in Europe in large numbers. The German generals launched a devastating attack all along the Western Front.

Thousands of German soldiers poured into France. They were stopped only 80 km from Paris. On 8 August 1918, Canadian and Allied troops launched a counterattack. Fresh American troops with tanks had arrived and were a great encouragement for the Allies. Supported by 500 tanks, the Allies swept north and east toward Germany. The Germans fought hard, but they fell back steadily. Eventually, the Allies won back France and then Belgium.

By November, the Allies had reached the frontiers of Germany. On **11 November 1918**, at a predawn ceremony, Germany formally surrendered. Hostilities ceased at 11:00 a.m. on that morning. Five minutes before 11:00 a sniper killed George Price, the last Canadian to die in World War I. For some Canadian troops, the war ended on the streets of the Belgian town of Mons. The Belgians flew flags that had been hidden for four years while their country was occupied by German forces. Grateful Belgians shouted, "Vive les braves Canadiens!"

THE ARTS

War Poetry

John McCrae was a 43-year-old member of the Canadian Medical Corps from Guelph, Ontario. He was a war veteran, having fought in the Boer War. On 3 May 1915, he was sitting on the step of an ambulance. The Battle of Ypres was in its ninth day. The previous night McCrae had buried his best friend who had been blown to bits by an artillery shell.

Looking over the desolate scene of the crosses in the fields, he wrote the lines of a poem that started, "In Flanders Fields the poppies blow…" The poem was completed in about 20 minutes. The poem's lines are enshrined in the hearts of all soldiers who heard them. McCrae made copies of the poem and gave them to all his friends. The poem was published in 1915, and is one of the most memorable war poems ever written.

"In Flanders Fields" was read at the first observance of Armistice Day in 1918. This poem and the poppies described in it have been part of the 11 November ceremonies ever since. A soldier who was there said, "It seemed to me that this poem was an exact description of the scene."

In Flanders Fields

In Flanders fields the poppies blow
Between the crosses, row on row,
That mark our place; and in the sky
The larks, still bravely singing, fly
Scarce heard amid the guns below.

We are the Dead. Short days ago
We lived, felt dawn, saw sunset glow,
Loved and were loved, and now we lie
In Flanders fields.

Take up our quarrel with the foe;
To you, from failing hands we throw
The torch; be yours to hold it high.
If ye break faith with us who die
We shall not sleep, though poppies grow
In Flanders fields.

Lieutenant Colonel John McCrae

1. What images does this poem create? Describe the scene in your own words or create a sketch.
2. Who is speaking in the poem? Why do you think the poem is written from this point of view?
3. What makes this poem memorable?
4. John McCrae wrote the poem while battles were still raging in World War I. He never witnessed the peace. In 1918, he was killed while on active service in France. Write a one stanza response to John McCrae's poem, telling of the peace.

ACTIVITIES

Check Your Understanding

1. Add these new terms to your *Factfile*.

trench warfare	dirigibles
no-man's land	*Lusitania*
Western Front	Jutland
Ypres	U-boat
Battle of the Somme	convoy system
Vimy Ridge	11 November 1918
Passchendaele	

2. All of the following words are related to trench warfare. Write a descriptive paragraph using all of the words. Refer to the diagram on page 89 for help.

duckboards	sap
trench foot	trench mouth
communication trench	traverses
parapet	parados

3. a) Describe the various roles played by the air force in World War I.
   b) Outline the problems that might be encountered by pilots in wartime flying.

4. a) In what ways was the submarine a revolutionary new weapon?
   b) Explain the defensive measure that had to be taken against the threat of submarines.

5. Describe the contribution of Canadians to the war in the air and at sea.

Confirm Your Learning

6. a) Explain why Germany thought it was necessary to sink the *Lusitania*.
   b) Describe the reaction of Britain and the United States to the sinking of the *Lusitania*.
   c) Was the sinking of a civilian ship a justifiable act in a time of war? Explain your answer.

7. Working in groups, choose a single battle such as the Somme, Passchendaele, or Vimy Ridge. Gather information on the battle and prepare an account of the part Canadians played. Record your account on audiotape and include a short dramatization of a few minutes during the battle with dialogue and sound effects.

8. You are a Canadian soldier, nurse, reporter, or war artist on the front lines. Write a letter home in which you describe events, living conditions, and your reactions.

9. a) Billy Bishop is considered a Canadian hero. Why?
   b) Define what you think makes a hero. List other individuals involved in World War I who you would consider to be heroes and explain why.
   c) Who are your heroes today?

10. Soldiers are frequently expected to fight in intolerable conditions. At Passchendaele, it was almost impossible to carry on trench warfare in the mud of the battlefield. Many believe the battle should have been stopped because of the conditions and the high number of casualties. Yet, the commander ordered the fighting to continue.

   a) Would soldiers ever be justified in refusing the order to fight? Why?

   b) Do you think military leaders were to blame for the high number of casualties? Why? Stage a panel discussion in your class.

Challenge Your Mind

11. Memorials are objects (often statues or plaques) or customs (special holidays) established in memory of important people or events. People have created many memorials associated with World War I. Each year on 11 November, for example, we celebrate Remembrance Day. With a few moments of silence and special ceremonies around the world, we remember the many people who died in the war.

   a) Discuss why memorials are important. Which people or events do you feel should be remembered about World War I?

   b) Find more information about some famous World War I memorials or visit some memorials in your community. How do they make you feel?

   c) Create your own memorials for World War I. You can use a variety of media—sculptures, stories, collages, videos, audiotapes, or ceremonies.

12. Research the lives of prominent Canadian individuals associated with World War I. Consider soldiers, artists, leaders, and social reformers. Examples include Sir Arthur Currie, Billy Bishop, Francis Pegahamagabow, Wop May, Sam Hughes, and Nellie McClung. Prepare a short biography or role play interviews with these people for the class.

CHAPTER 7

War on the Home Front

THE WAR EFFORT AT HOME

FISH & VEGETABLE MEALS
WILL SAVE WHEAT, MEAT & FATS
FOR OUR SOLDIERS AND ALLIES

Back Him Up!
Buy VICTORY BONDS

Advice for the Home

1. Use nut-butter or margarine.
2. Remake leftover bread into new bread, cake, or pudding.
3. Instead of one beefless day, why not try for six to make up for people less patriotic?
4. Eat as little cake and pastry as you can.
5. Use oats, corn, barley, and rye instead of wheat.
6. Use ham and pork bones in other dishes.
7. Chew your food thoroughly—you will be satisfied with less.
8. All kinds of cold cereal can be saved, and when not enough to roll into balls to fry, they can be used in batter cakes and corn breads.
9. Cut each slice of bread as required.
10. Mix your own cleanser (use white sand, washing soda, soap, and chalk).
11. Fifty million dollars is thrown away in garbage cans annually.
12. Do not display the roast of meat on the table. It is an inducement to eat more than you need.
13. Do not eat both butter and jam with bread.

Effects on Everyday Life

Canadians at home supported the troops overseas in many different ways. Posters, community groups, and government campaigns suggested that no sacrifice should be spared to ensure a victory in Europe. Many people planted "victory gardens" to produce as much food as possible. Canadians were sending large amounts of food to the fighting forces and civilian populations of other Allied countries. At home, people were trying to waste nothing and to reduce their own food consumption.

Students in Saskatchewan and other wheat-producing areas were often dismissed from school early to replace the farm workers who were overseas. Groups of women of all ages met regularly to organize community fund raisers and roll bandages for the troops. Every community held card games, dances, and variety shows. The profits from these evenings were used to send soap, writing paper, pencils, and candy to the troops.

The Economics of War

By 1918, the war was costing Canada over $1 million a day! Workers helped to pay the enormous costs by buying **Victory Bonds**. Victory Bonds were issued by the government. By buying them, citizens were loaning money to the government for the war effort. After the war, the bonds could be cashed in at a profit.

Private and commercial investors together also loaned over $1 billion to the government. The loans would be paid back with interest when the war was over. Children played a part by buying Thrift Stamps. Each stamp cost 25¢ and was stuck on a card. When $4 worth of stamps were bought, the child received a War Savings Stamp. A War Savings Stamp could be cashed in for $5 in 1924.

The Canadian government also introduced the practice of an income tax during World War I. The tax was supposed to be a "temporary measure" to help finance the war. But as we know, the income tax has never been abolished.

Who Did You Do In the Great War?

Canada's tremendous wartime production was not without its scandalous side. This 1917 cartoon shows Joseph Flavelle, chair of the Imperial Munitions Board. Flavelle's meat-packing company was said to have done very well as a result of the war and gained Flavelle the title of "Sir Lardship."

SOCIETY AND SOCIAL CHANGE

The Halifax Explosion

Early on the morning of 6 December 1917, a terrible explosion rocked the city of Halifax. Halifax was a major shipping port in the war. Most of the North American convoys with supplies for Europe set out from Halifax.

On that morning in 1917, the *Mont Blanc*, a French munitions ship carrying a cargo of explosives, collided with the Belgian vessel *Imo* in the harbour. Almost 3000 t of explosives were set off. The blast levelled large sections of Halifax and was heard all over the province. It was even felt in Sydney, over 320 km away.

Fires roared through the wooden buildings of the city. A huge tidal wave swamped other ships in the harbour and tossed them in pieces onto the shore. Two thousand people were killed and thousands more were injured or left homeless.

The explosion was one of the worst disasters in Canadian history. It is said that, until the atomic bomb was dropped on Hiroshima in 1945, the explosion in Halifax was the biggest artificial explosion ever recorded. All that was ever found of the *Mont Blanc* was a cannon and part of an anchor that landed over 3 km away.

1. "The Halifax Explosion brought the horrors of the war to the doorsteps of Canadians at home." Discuss this statement.
2. How would you have reacted if you had been in Halifax at the time of the explosion? Write a brief journal entry or create an illustration to describe the event.

Halifax, after the devastating explosion in 1917.

Industrial production reached dramatic new heights during World War I. Especially important for the war effort was the production of munitions (military weapons and equipment). Plants manufacturing airplanes, shells, and ships sprang up across the country. By 1918, 300 000 Canadians were employed in these factories and one-third of the shells fired by the armies of the British Empire were made in Canada.

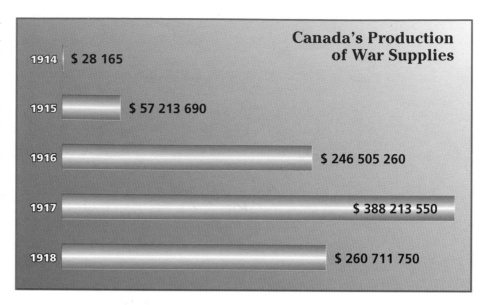

Canada's Production of War Supplies

1914	$ 28 165
1915	$ 57 213 690
1916	$ 246 505 260
1917	$ 388 213 550
1918	$ 260 711 750

Women During the War Years

World War I brought great changes to the lives of Canadian women. As soon as the war began, hundreds of Canadian women volunteered to work overseas as nurses or ambulance drivers. Many worked in field hospitals just behind the front-line trenches. One operating room nurse wrote in a letter home, "We… had 291 operations in ten nights, so that will give you a fair idea of a week's work."

Women also played an important part in the war effort at home. With the general shortage of labour in Canada, the number of women employed in industry rose dramatically. Thirty thousand Canadian women worked in munitions factories and other war industries. These jobs in heavy industry would have been considered unsuitable for women before 1914. Working conditions were difficult and sometimes dangerous. Women also drove buses and streetcars. They worked in banks, on police forces, and in civil service jobs.

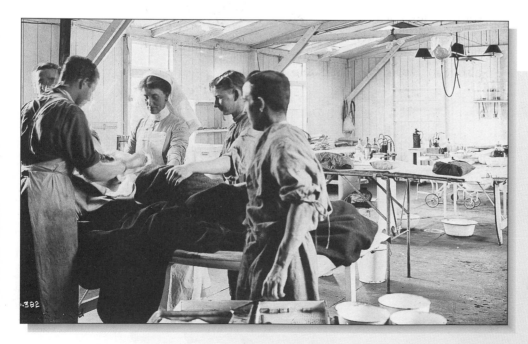

Many women worked in wartime hospitals near the front lines.

During the war, women worked in munitions factories, sometimes under very dangerous conditions.

I had a very hard job. It had to be that you run a machine of weights into the shell, and the weight had to be just exact. Quite a few of them didn't have the patience.

It was interesting work but very hard on your nerves. There was a machine went on fire. This friend from Beaverton was on the machine that blew up, and I run to her and we had to go down on our hands and knees and crawl out of the place. So we had a little experience of what it was to be right in a war.

In wartime, there were few men left to work on the farms. Women on the farms brought in the harvests and city women were also recruited to go out and help.

We decided to become farmerettes when we read in the paper that there was a big crop and they needed people to come, and there were no men. So this friend and I said that we would go. We volunteered. Masses of young people went out and brought that all in.

Groups of women of all ages met regularly to knit socks for the soldiers and to roll bandages. They arranged many of the card games, dances, and variety shows that helped fund the parcels sent to the troops.

I wanted to help do my share, and I joined the Red Cross and helped roll bandages and knit socks. My first ones were big enough to fit an elephant, and after that, I became very proficient—so proficient that I knit a pair of socks a day without any trouble.

You see, everybody felt they had to do something. You just couldn't sit there.

There was a phrase, 'Doing your bit.' Well, that was pretty well the keynote feeling all through that First World War. Everybody was extremely patriotic, and everybody wanted to 'do a bit.' If there's anything we could do to help, we must do it.

The Struggle for Women's Rights

Since women were doing so much for the war effort, they wanted a share in making decisions about the country. It was during World War I that an important step forward was taken in Canada for women's rights. At the beginning of the twentieth century, women in many countries had begun to organize themselves to gain the right to vote. Members of this movement in Canada were called **suffragists**.

Nellie McClung was a suffragist and one of Canada's great social reformers. She wrote, "Certainly women belong in the home, but not 24 hours a day. They should have exactly the same freedom as men." When World War I broke out, it helped to prove that Nellie McClung was right. Women did jobs once performed only by men. The war brought women together in volunteer organizations and employment. They began to share ideas and work for political equality with men. They also took active roles in journalism and campaigned for better public health, working conditions, and wages. They pushed for equal opportunities in careers such as medicine and law, and for the right to own property.

Nellie McClung, Alice Jamieson, and Emily Murphy. This famous photo was taken on the day women won the right to vote in Manitoba, 1916.

Suffragists campaigned enthusiastically for women's suffrage (the right to vote). Their leaders included Dorothy Davis in British Columbia, Margaret Gordon in Ontario, Emily Murphy and Alice Jamieson in Alberta, and the dynamic Nellie McClung in Manitoba. The first breakthrough for women's suffrage came in Manitoba. In 1916, women were given the right to vote in that province. Within a few months, Saskatchewan, Alberta, British Columbia, and Ontario also granted women suffrage.

But the main goal was to win the right to vote in federal elections. In the federal election of December 1917, the **Wartime Elections Act** had granted the vote to the mothers, sisters, and wives of soldiers in the Armed Forces. Canadian nurses serving in the Forces could also vote. By the time the war had ended, the right to vote in federal elections had been extended to almost all women in Canada over the age of 21. The **Dominion Elections Act** (1920) also gave women the right to run for election to Parliament. However, Native women and most Native men were not allowed to vote.

Conscription

At the beginning of the war, Canadians were very enthusiastic about the war effort. Thousands rushed out to volunteer for service. The country was flooded with patriotic appeals. Volunteers marched behind brass bands to the enlistment offices. But as the war dragged on into 1916, it became obvious that it was not going to be as short as Canadians first thought. The death toll was mounting. The number of volunteers was dwindling.

Canadian Women Win the Right to Vote in Provincial Elections	
Manitoba	28 January 1916
Saskatchewan	14 March 1916
Alberta	19 April 1916
British Columbia	5 April 1917
Ontario	12 April 1917
Nova Scotia	26 April 1918
New Brunswick	17 April 1919
Prince Edward Island	3 May 1922
Newfoundland	13 April 1925
Quebec	25 April 1940
Federal Dominion of Canada	24 May 1918

Early in 1917, Prime Minister Robert Borden left to visit the Canadian soldiers at the front. Borden was shocked by the information he received. Casualties were mounting daily on the Western Front. Military officials urged Borden to send even more Canadian troops to Europe. In Canada, volunteer enlistments were not keeping up with the number of men killed or wounded.

Borden returned home and asked Parliament to pass a conscription bill. **Conscription** means that all able-bodied men would be required to join the army. They would have no choice. Enlistment would no longer be on a voluntary basis only.

SOCIETY AND SOCIAL CHANGE

Canada's "Enemy Aliens"

When war broke out, there were about 500 000 German and Austrian citizens living in Canada. At first, the government urged that these citizens be treated fairly. But feelings ran high. Some Canadians were afraid that these immigrants might still be loyal to their homelands and might secretly work for the enemy side. Feelings of intolerance grew for those who became known as "enemy aliens."

Mr Spade, who was German, lived at 2 or 4 Jersey Avenue in Toronto. At that time we lived at number 14. This happened after supper because I didn't see it, but I heard them talk about it. A whole gang of men came around and got him and took him over to Clinton Street. They tarred and feathered him. Why I don't know. Except he was a German.

The Wartime Elections Act denied or took away the vote from those born in countries considered to be the enemy and those of European birth who spoke the language of an enemy country. Many people of Austrian, German, and later Italian, Russian, and Ukrainian descent lost their jobs or had their homes or businesses vandalized. Some were put in internment (holding) camps.

People of German ancestry tried to show they were loyal to the British side in the war. In Ontario, the town of Berlin changed its name to Kitchener, after the British War Minister. Carlstadt in Alberta also changed its name to Alderson after the British commander of the Canadians at Ypres.

1. a) Define civil rights. In 1917, the Wartime Elections Act took away the civil rights of Canadians who had come from countries with whom Canada was at war. Was this action justified? Explain your point of view.
   b) List some examples in which people's civil liberties are taken away today. Is it ever right to take away an individual's civil rights? How can we prevent our civil liberties from being lost?
2. Women, Native people, and Asian Canadians also did not have the right to vote during World War I, even though many fought in the war or made significant contributions to the war effort. Why was this so?

Enlistment/Casualty Rate for 1917		
Month	Enlistments	Casualties
January	9 194	4 396
March	6 640	6 161
May	6 407	13 457
July	3 882	7 906
September	3 588	10 990
November	4 019	30 741

A Country Divided

The mention of conscription brought a storm of protest in some parts of Canada, especially among French Canadians. Many English Canadians believed that Quebec was not doing its part in the war. English Canadian newspapers pointed out that Ontario had provided 63 percent of the volunteers in proportion to its population. Manitoba and Saskatchewan provided 81 percent, Alberta 92 percent, British Columbia 104 percent, and the Maritime provinces 38 percent. Quebec had provided only 20 percent of the volunteers in proportion to its population.

Why were there fewer volunteers from Quebec? The majority of Quebeckers were farmers, many with large families. Fewer farmers than city people joined the Armed Forces since farmers were considered essential to produce food for the war effort. But most French Canadians also did not share the enthusiasm that English Canadians felt for Britain's war. They did not believe that their sons should be forced to join the war. Many also did not feel any real tie to their country of origin, France. They felt they had been deserted by France when they were conquered by British forces in 1760. French language rights had been taken away in Manitoba, other western provinces, and in Ontario schools. French Canadians felt they were being treated like second-class citizens in Canada.

Sir Sam Hughes, minister of militia, stirred further protest in Quebec when he appointed a Protestant clergyman to supervise recruiting in that province. Quebeckers were mostly Roman Catholics. Training programs for French Canadian volunteers were also in English, even though the men often did not speak the language.

Very few French Canadian officers received important army posts. Only one French Canadian regiment—the 22nd, the famous "Vandoos"—had been sent to the Western Front to fight. It seemed to many French Canadians that Hughes's policies were doing little to encourage their greater participation in the war. Eventually, Hughes was dismissed by Borden, but not before he caused long-term resentment in Quebec.

Borden knew that conscription was a dangerous policy. It could divide French and English Canadians. Farmers would

Conscription brought a storm of protest in Quebec.

also protest the loss of their remaining sons and farm hands. Still, Borden felt the shortage of troops was so severe that he had no other choice. The **Military Service Bill** was passed in the summer of 1917. The Bill made conscription a law. Military service became compulsory for all males between the ages of 20 and 45. Only men in vital wartime production jobs, those who were sick, or conscientious objectors did not have to join the Forces. Conscientious objectors were those people who refused to fight on the grounds that war went against their moral and religious beliefs.

The opposition to conscription in Quebec was led by Henri Bourassa. Bourassa summarized his position in a pamphlet published on 4 July 1917.

We are opposed to further enlistments for the war in Europe, whether by conscription or otherwise, for the following reasons:

~ Canada has already made a military display, in men and money, proportionately superior to that of any nation engaged in the war

~ any further weakening of the labour force of the country would seriously handicap agricultural production and other essential industries

~ an increase in the war budget of Canada spells national bankruptcy

~ it threatens the economic life of the nation and, eventually, its political independence

~ conscription means national disunion and strife, and would thereby hurt the cause of the Allies to a much greater extent than the addition of a few thousand soldiers to their fighting forces could bring them help and comfort.

More moderate French Canadian opinion was represented by Sir Wilfrid Laurier, the leader of the federal Liberal party and former prime minister. Laurier had struggled all his life to keep Canada united. He did not support conscription. He realized it was an issue that could tear the country apart. Laurier was disillusioned when 22 Liberals from Ontario, the West, and the Maritimes voted with the government for the Military Service Bill. Only the Liberals in Quebec and a handful of English-speaking Liberals stood with Laurier against conscription.

The Election of 1917

With a general election coming in December 1917, the government passed two further bills. They were both meant to strengthen Borden's position on conscription. The **Military Voters' Act** allowed soldiers overseas to vote. More important was the Wartime Elections Act. It gave the vote to female relatives of soldiers. These women could be expected to vote for conscription and a government that promised to support their loved ones overseas.

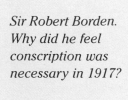

Sir Robert Borden. Why did he feel conscription was necessary in 1917?

THE ARTS

Posters in World War I

During World War I, the Canadian government found that colourful posters were an effective way of reaching a widely scattered population. Many people did not own radios and television had not been invented. Printed posters were the most effective way of advertising. They were put up in post offices and other public places where everyone could see them. They were also printed in magazines and newspapers. Examine the posters on this page.

1. List four different purposes for which posters were used by the government.

2. Describe what you see in each poster. What major images are used?

3. What emotions does each poster evoke?

4. a) Summarize the message of each poster in a sentence.
   b) What reasons do the posters suggest for supporting the war effort?
   c) Do the posters show a bias? Explain.

5. How successful do you think these posters would be? Why?

6. What methods might the government use today to achieve the same purpose? Gather some examples.

7. Design your own posters! In groups, create posters which could be used to:
   • recruit soldiers
   • encourage the purchase of war bonds
   • help reduce food consumption
   • recruit children to work in the war effort.

1917 Election Results
Number of Seats in House of Commons

	Liberal	Union (Conservatives plus some Liberals)
PEI	2	2
Nova Scotia	4	12
New Brunswick	4	7
Quebec	62	3
Ontario	8	74
Manitoba	1	14
Saskatchewan	0	16
Alberta	1	11
British Columbia	0	13
Yukon	0	1
Totals	82	153

The Conservatives were now joined by the Liberals who had deserted Laurier. Conservatives and Liberals who believed in conscription formed a **Union government**. The election of 1917 was particularly bitter. Voters were asked by the Union government: "Who would the Germans vote for?" Laurier and his followers were accused of letting down the soldiers at the front. The election results saw Borden and the Union government returned with an overwhelming majority, but with only three seats in Quebec.

The split in Canada that Laurier had feared for so long had occurred. There were riots in Montreal and Quebec City against conscription. Four people were killed and many were injured. Troops had to be sent in with machine guns to restore order. In years to come, the passage of conscription continued to anger French Canadians. When the war ended in November 1918, Canada was a divided nation.

Did conscription work? The call for conscripts did not begin until 1918. Thousands of men, both French and English Canadians, claimed exemption from service. A man could be excused from military service if he had a physical disability, an essential occupation (e.g., farmer), or was a member of the clergy. By the time the war ended in November 1918, only about 45 000 conscripts had reached the battlefield.

Was conscription a success in Canada? Most historians would say no. English Canadians were arguing against French Canadians, Protestants against Roman Catholics, majority against minority. There was widespread disagreement about conscription between farmers and city dwellers, and between civilians and soldiers. National unity seemed a high price to pay for 45 000 soldiers.

DEVELOPING SKILLS: RECOGNIZING AND UNDERSTANDING BIAS

What is bias? Suppose a friend tells you that video games are excessively violent. You should not be buying them. You disagree. Not all video games are violent and besides, they are just games. Are either of you biased? Both of you are.

A bias is a person's viewpoint or way of seeing an event, person, or thing. A person's bias is shaped by his or her frame of reference. Personal experiences, background, family, friends, knowledge, concerns, and interests all go into making up a person's frame of reference.

Bias is not necessarily negative. Different viewpoints should invite discussion and critical thinking. But bias can be dangerous if the viewpoint is based on distorted facts, incomplete information, or if it suggests that it is the only right view and excludes all other viewpoints. Any point of view should carefully consider all available facts and all other viewpoints. Viewpoints should always be open to change.

Many things that you read, hear, or see express a bias, including books, articles, films, TV shows, advertisements, posters, paintings, speeches, and even games. Use the following questions as a guide to help you recognize and understand bias.

1. a) What is the source and who is the author? What was the author's intention?
   b) Who is the intended audience?
   c) Does this information tell you anything about the point of view being expressed?

2. When was the material written or created? How might the time period and circumstances colour the view of events?

3. Are emotionally charged words or phrases used? Find examples. Which present a positive point of view? Which present a negative view?

4. What is fact and what is opinion? Are opinions supported by facts? Remember that facts are information or statements that can be proven. Opinions are thoughts or feelings that may or may not be supported by facts.

5. Does the author oversimplify? Are important facts left out?

6. Are both sides of the issue considered or is only one side presented and not the other?

7. a) Check other sources. Do they agree? If sources disagree, consider why.
   b) Which sources do you trust? Why?

8. a) What is the bias? Try to state it in one sentence.
   b) How might frame of reference account for the bias?

9. How could a more balanced view be presented?

Frequently, French and English Canadians have looked at issues from different sides or points of view. Many people in Quebec have always felt like outsiders in Canada. They became part of the British Empire because of military defeat. Their frame of reference has been formed by their background, French Canadian culture, and their experiences in Confederation. English Canadians also have a frame of reference shaped by their background, culture, and experiences. This frame of reference can lead to bias.

Two reporters writing about Sir Sam Hughes, the minister of militia, may have very different frames of reference. A person of British descent, who is Protestant and lives in Ontario, might see Hughes as a hero. A French Canadian Roman Catholic living in Quebec may see Hughes as a crook and a threat to French Canadian survival.

Read the two fictional newspaper accounts of the dismissal of Hughes as minister of militia in 1916. Use the questions outlined above to help you determine the bias and frame of reference in the articles.

Montreal Matin
Hughes fired from the Cabinet
Montreal, November 1916

Prime Minister Borden has finally fired Sir Sam Hughes from the Cabinet. Hughes will be unable to do any more damage to Canadian unity. As minister of militia, Hughes had antagonized French Canadians. He ordered that training and instruction manuals for volunteers should be supplied in English only. More importantly, promotions were given only to the English-speaking officers. Those French Canadians who volunteered for the war have been insulted. How could Hughes and other Canadians expect French Canadians to join in the war effort when they are treated so poorly?

Hughes also disgraced the nation by rewarding his friends with munitions contracts. These shady deals have allowed his friends to make millions at the taxpayers' expense.

Why should French Canadians spill more blood in Europe? Canada only wants French Canadians in Confederation when we are willing to sacrifice for the British Empire. Britain started this war. Let Britain finish it!

Toronto Times
Sir Sam steps down!

Toronto, November 1916

Sad news was announced in Ottawa today. Sir Sam Hughes is no longer the minister of militia. The prime minister, bending to howls of protest from Quebec, has dismissed Hughes—despite the fact that Hughes has done more for the war effort than any other Canadian. He recruited thousands of volunteers and raised thousands of dollars.

Canada entered the war with only 3000 men in the armed forces. By the end of 1915, Hughes had managed to put more than 100 000 on the battlefield. He had also persuaded reluctant industrialists to invest heavily in the production of much needed war materials. We should be thankful that, through the contracts negotiated by the minister, tons of vital munitions are making their way to our soldiers at the front.

Peace: The Treaty of Versailles

Almost five years after the assassination of Archduke Ferdinand at Sarajevo, government leaders met at Versailles, near Paris, to sign the peace treaty. Thirty-two victorious countries were represented, including Canada. Canada was not content just to be part of the British delegation. Borden demanded that Canada be represented as a separate nation at the meetings and at the official signing of the treaty. He argued that Canada deserved a voice in the peace talks because of its strong support for the war effort. The main decisions, however, were made by the leaders of three countries—Britain, France, and the United States. These countries were referred to as **"The Big Three."** Germany, a defeated country, was not invited to the peace talks.

Woodrow Wilson, the American president, was determined to make a settlement that would ensure lasting peace. He argued that the defeated countries should be treated justly so that they would not try to get revenge in the future. Wilson suggested "Fourteen Points" that included complete disarmament and free trade among nations. He suggested that a **League of Nations** be set up to settle future disputes. The League of Nations would be an organization promoting international co-operation.

The prime minister of France, Georges Clemenceau, also wanted to avoid another war. He was determined, however, that Germany should pay for starting the war and for the damage that had been done. Twice in his lifetime, Clemenceau had seen Germany invade his homeland. He wanted to ensure that Germany would be too weak ever to attack France again.

Lloyd George, the British prime minister, believed that many British people felt much the same way. His country had lost many citizens in the war. However, George was concerned that a harsh treaty might cause bitterness and lead Germany to seek revenge in the future. He helped to work out many of the compromises that made the peace treaty possible.

Crowds across the country, like this one in Winnipeg, celebrated the peace.

The following are the major terms of the Treaty of Versailles.

Article 42

Germany is forbidden to build any military fortifications on the left bank of the Rhine River. It may not build any fortifications on the right bank for a distance of 50 km.

Article 45

To pay for the destruction of the coal mines in the north of France, Germany turns over to France its coal mines in the Saar Basin for 15 years.

Article 51

The territories of Alsace and Lorraine taken from France in 1871 are restored to it.

Article 80

Germany must accept the complete independence of Austria.

Article 81

Germany must accept the complete independence of Czechoslovakia.

Article 87

Germany must accept the complete independence of Poland.

Article 89

Poland will allow persons, goods, vessels, carriages, wagons, and mail to pass freely between East Prussia and the rest of Germany over Polish territory. (This was necessary because Poland was given a strip of German territory to provide it with access to the sea at the city of Danzig. This was called the **Polish Corridor**. It separated East Prussia from the rest of Germany.)

Article 118

Germany must give up all its rights and titles to its overseas possessions (colonies in Africa and East Asia).

Article 180

After 31 March 1920, the German army must not exceed 100 000 soldiers. The army shall be used only to maintain order within Germany and to control the frontiers.

Article 181

German naval forces must not exceed 6 battleships, 6 light cruisers, 12 destroyers, and 12 torpedo boats. Germans are forbidden to have any submarines.

Article 198

The armed forces of Germany must not include any military air force.

Article 231

Germany must accept the responsibility for causing all the loss and damage that the Allies and their citizens have suffered. (This is known as the **War Guilt Clause**.)

Article 232

The Allied governments require Germany to pay for all wartime damages to the civilian population and the property of Allied powers. (These payments are known as **reparations**.)

Article 233

The amount of the above damage will be determined by an Allied Commission.

Article 428

A guarantee is needed to make sure the treaty be carried out by Germany. Therefore, the German territory west of the Rhine River will be occupied by Allied troops for 15 years.

Other Peace Treaties

The Treaty of Versailles was just the first of a series of agreements. Peace treaties with the other Central Powers also brought major territorial changes in Europe. Four new independent nations were created out of the old Austro-Hungarian Empire. These were Czechoslovakia, Poland, Hungary, and Yugoslavia. Austria itself was reduced to a small nation.

The peacemakers justified changing the boundaries of nations by the principle of self-determination. This principle means that people of similar language and culture should have the right to rule themselves. By the Treaty of Versailles, Germany was required to accept the complete independence of Austria, Czechoslovakia, and Poland. The principle of self-determination, however, did not always work out as planned. Over 3 million Germans found they now lived in Czechoslovakia.

The Russian empire was also broken up after World War I. Finland, Estonia, Latvia, and Lithuania were given independence as new nations. Russia also lost large regions to Poland, Czechoslovakia, and Romania. It may seem strange that Russia, one of the Allies, lost so much territory after the war. This happened because Russia had come under Communist rule in 1917. The new Communist government had withdrawn from the war and made peace with Germany. The delegates to the peace conference hoped that the new nations in the centre of Europe would keep communism from spreading westwards from Russia.

Europe After World War I, 1919

Developing Skills: Interpreting and Comparing Maps

When we look at a world map, we tend to think that the world has always been as it is pictured and always will be. It is difficult to imagine that the boundaries between countries could change overnight—but they have. New countries have been created and some destroyed many times in history.

In 1990, the Soviet Union was dissolved and several new countries emerged. If Quebec separates, the map of Canada could change dramatically. At the end of World War I, the map of Europe also changed dramatically. These changes had a tremendous effect on the way people lived and related to one another.

By comparing maps before and after the changes, you can begin to hypothesize (think) about the effects the changes had on people living in these countries or regions.

Try It!

Select maps of the same area from two different time periods. We can compare maps of Europe in 1914 before World War I (see page 79) and Europe in 1919 after the war (see page 121), for example.

■ Step I *Comprehension*

The first step is understanding the maps. Ask yourself these questions.

1. What does each map show? At what period of time?

2. What countries or regions are shown? What symbols are used and what do they represent?

■ Step II *Interpretation*

The next step is to gather important information from the maps. In this case, you compare two maps to determine the major changes that occurred over a period of time.

3. Compare the size of Germany before and after the war. Locate and name two countries that received territory in 1919 which formerly belonged to Germany.

4. What happened to Austria-Hungary in 1919? Name the newly independent nations that were created in Europe.

5. Name and locate four new countries that were created from former Russian territory. To what other countries did Russia lose territory?

■ Step III *Hypothesizing*

At this stage, you use the information you have gathered from the maps to draw some conclusions and speculate about possible effects in the future. Consider these questions.

6. Locate the Polish Corridor on the map. How might the creation of the Polish Corridor lead to problems among nations in the future?

7. How might the creation of a number of new small nations in Europe lead to future territorial disputes?

Effects of the War on Canada

What was the cost of the war to Canada? The heaviest cost was in the numbers who died. A total of 60 661 Canadians lost their lives. Another 173 000 were wounded or gassed. Many thousands of the injured lived on for years in veterans' hospitals. For these people, the suffering of war never ended.

They were victims who had lost limbs, whose lungs had been destroyed by gas attacks, or who had experienced severe emotional trauma.

Another disastrous effect of the war was the deepening resentment between French and English Canadians over conscription. The gulf between Quebec and the rest of the country steadily widened. The hurt, pain, and distrust lingered after the war.

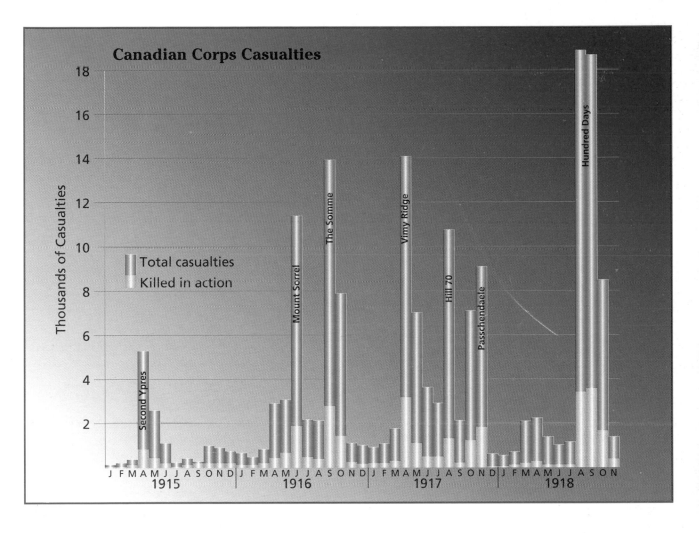

Canadian Corps Casualties

Thousands of Casualties

Total casualties
Killed in action

Second Ypres
Mount Sorrel
The Somme
Vimy Ridge
Hill 70
Passchendaele
Hundred Days

J F M A M J J A S O N D | J F M A M J J A S O N D | J F M A M J J A S O N D | J F M A M J J A S O N
1915 | 1916 | 1917 | 1918

On the positive side, World War I had produced a great boom in Canadian industry. Steel and munitions production and manufacturing had grown fantastically. During the war, almost everyone who could work had a job.

Canada also emerged from the war a more independent country. Canada's war effort had earned the country international respect. The outstanding contribution of Canada's soldiers won a separate seat for Canada at the peace conference following the war. Previously, Britain would have signed the peace treaty on behalf of all the British Empire. Now Canada signed the treaty as a separate nation. Canada had achieved a degree of national sovereignty—the right to control its own affairs with-

out interference. Canada was still part of the British Empire, but Britain had agreed to grant the colonies "autonomy (the right to self-government) within the Empire."

As the decade drew to a close, three of the most important Canadian leaders were also leaving the spotlight of politics. On 17 February 1919, Sir Wilfrid Laurier died of a stroke. With his main opponent gone, Henry Bourassa became less involved in the political scene. Sir Robert Borden, exhausted from leadership during wartime, resigned as leader of the Conservative party in 1920. Three new leaders in Canada were about to emerge—William Lyon Mackenzie King, Arthur Meighen, and J.S. Woodsworth.

Canada's Economic Growth, 1913–1919

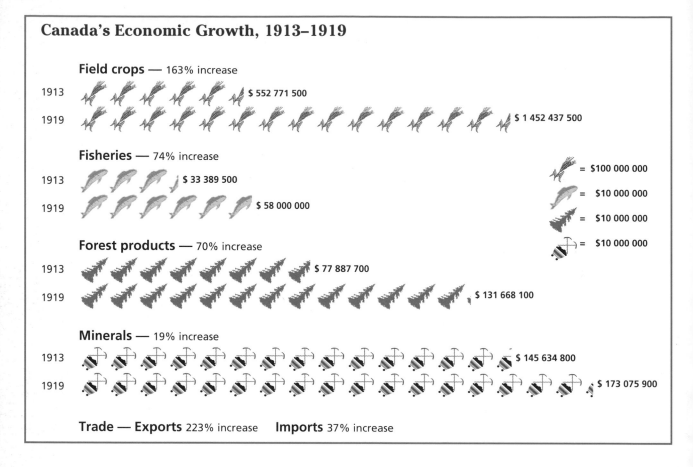

Field crops — 163% increase

1913 — $ 552 771 500

1919 — $ 1 452 437 500

Fisheries — 74% increase

1913 — $ 33 389 500

1919 — $ 58 000 000

= $100 000 000

= $10 000 000

= $10 000 000

= $10 000 000

Forest products — 70% increase

1913 — $ 77 887 700

1919 — $ 131 668 100

Minerals — 19% increase

1913 — $ 145 634 800

1919 — $ 173 075 900

Trade — Exports 223% increase   **Imports** 37% increase

ACTIVITIES

Check Your Understanding

1. Add these new terms to your *Factfile*.

Victory Bonds	Union Government 1917
Halifax Explosion	Treaty of Versailles 1919
suffragists	"The Big Three"
Wartime Elections Act 1917	League of Nations
Dominion Elections Act 1920	Polish Corridor
conscription	War Guilt Clause
Military Service Bill 1917	reparations
Military Voters' Act 1917	

2. Describe how each of the following contributed to the war effort at home.

   a) women
   b) workers
   c) children
   d) families in their homes

3. Why did a spirit of excitement and confidence exist in Canada at the outbreak of the war in 1914? How and why did this mood change?

4. Explain why these statements are true or false.
   a) British-born Canadians volunteered more promptly than Canadian-born citizens.
   b) Only French Canadians opposed conscription.
   c) The conscription issue caused a split in Canada.
   d) The war helped women gain the right to vote in Canada.

5. a) Explain why Canadians were considered to be part of the British army.
   b) How did this relationship between Britain and Canada change by the end of the war?

Confirm Your Learning

6. How did ordinary people feel about conscription? Describe in your own words how you would have felt about conscription if you were the following people in 1917 Canada.
   a) a young man, age 21, living on a farm and who is part of a family of four
   b) the young man's parents
   c) the young man's fiancée
   d) the young man's younger brother, age 19

7. a) In a chart, summarize the terms of the Treaty of Versailles. Use these headings.
   - military terms
   - territorial terms inside Europe
   - territorial terms outside Europe
   - economic terms
   - other terms
   b) Compare the attitudes of "The Big Three" towards defeated Germany. After you have examined the terms, decide whose views had most influence on the treaty. Why?

8. Which of the following terms of the Treaty of Versailles do you consider fair treatment of Germany? Explain why.
   a) the Allies took away all Germany's colonies
   b) Germany's army was limited to 100 000 soldiers
   c) Germany was held responsible for causing World War I
   d) Germany was required to pay reparations
   e) Germany would not be allowed to have troops in the Rhineland for 15 years

9. a) Refer to the bar graph on page 123 showing Canadian casualties during World War I. In which year did Canada suffer the most casualties? Why were the number of casualties in this year significant?
   b) Refer to the pictograph on page 124 showing the growth in Canada's economy during the war years. Which two areas of the economy showed most growth? Suggest why.

10. a) Present evidence that Canada emerged from World War I as a more independent and respected nation.

b) Present three facts to support the following statement:"The growth in Canada's economy from 1914 to 1919 was mainly due to World War I."

Challenge Your Mind

11. Stage a mock parliament to debate the conscription issue, 1917.
    Participants: Sir Robert Borden
    Sir Wilfrid Laurier
    English-speaking Conservatives
    Liberals who refuse to support Laurier
    French-speaking Conservatives and Liberals

12. It has been said that the Treaty of Versailles contained within it the seeds of another war. What do you think this statement means? Do you think it is correct? Why?

13. Canada's economy boomed during World War I largely because of the great demand for food and war products. What problems might arise when the war ended? Why?

14. Why might Canadians feel that the experiences of World War I made the country better prepared to take control of its own affairs?

15. List ways in which the government became involved in the everyday lives of Canadians during World War I. Do you think these actions were justified? Explain your point of view.

16. Refer to the outline of key themes for each unit you have studied so far on pages 4, 48, and 76. Choose three themes and in chart form or as a timeline, outline the major developments in these themes from Confederation to the end of World War I. For example, you could create a timeline showing the major events in Canada's growth as a nation from Confederation to 1919.

The Roaring Twenties and the Dirty Thirties

TIMELINE

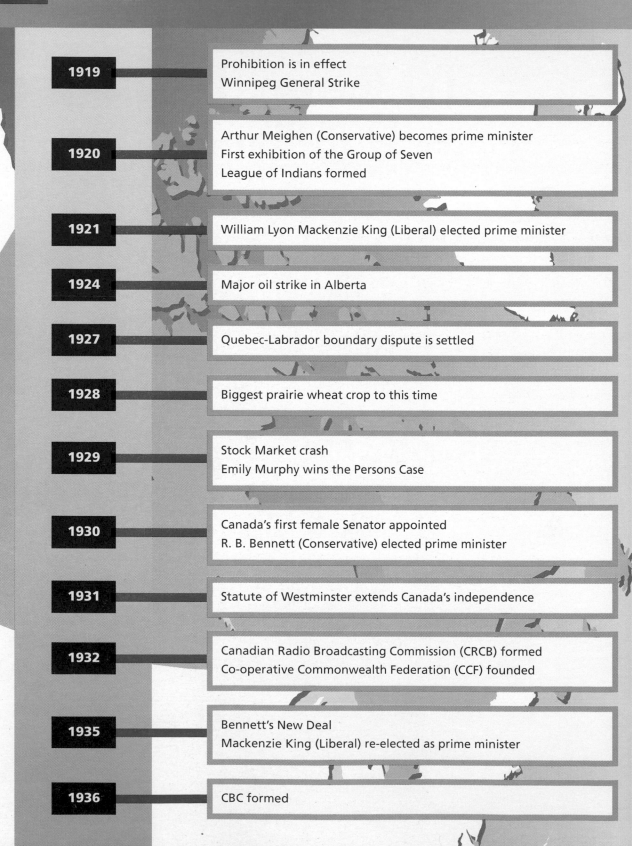

1919	Prohibition is in effect Winnipeg General Strike
1920	Arthur Meighen (Conservative) becomes prime minister First exhibition of the Group of Seven League of Indians formed
1921	William Lyon Mackenzie King (Liberal) elected prime minister
1924	Major oil strike in Alberta
1927	Quebec-Labrador boundary dispute is settled
1928	Biggest prairie wheat crop to this time
1929	Stock Market crash Emily Murphy wins the Persons Case
1930	Canada's first female Senator appointed R. B. Bennett (Conservative) elected prime minister
1931	Statute of Westminster extends Canada's independence
1932	Canadian Radio Broadcasting Commission (CRCB) formed Co-operative Commonwealth Federation (CCF) founded
1935	Bennett's New Deal Mackenzie King (Liberal) re-elected as prime minister
1936	CBC formed

This unit examines life in the "Roaring Twenties" and the "Dirty Thirties." The story begins at the end of World War I in 1919 and closes with the outbreak of World War II in 1939. In these two decades, Canadians experienced both the high excitement and confidence of prosperity, and the disaster of economic collapse and depression.

After World War I, returning soldiers expected to find good jobs and economic security. Instead, they were faced with the problems of unemployment, rising prices, and strikes. Lifestyles were changing too. The new role of women, prohibition (the ban on liquor), and urbanization had brought significant changes to Canada.

It wasn't until the mid-1920s that the economy began to turn around. Gradually, more people could afford new luxuries such as automobiles and radios. They could enjoy the excitement of investing in the stock market. Business was booming. Canada was becoming more independent. It seemed that the prosperity would last forever.

When the stock market crashed in 1929, people's hopes were dashed. Businesses went bankrupt. Many people lost everything. Workers were laid off. People roamed the country looking for work. To make matters worse, the West was hit with devastating drought and plagues of grasshoppers. Life was bleak for many Canadians during the Great Depression of the 1930s.

At the end of the unit, you will be able to:

- appreciate the problems facing post-war Canadians
- understand the economic swing from prosperity to the Great Depression
- explain how the role of women changed in the 1920s and 1930s
- describe developments in technology and the arts
- analyze concerns over the "Americanization" of the Canadian economy and culture
- understand how Canadians survived during the "Dirty Thirties"
- apply sound decision-making skills
- use simulation games and role play techniques to understand events in the past
- develop effective presentations using a variety of media
- analyze and construct useful charts and graphs

KEY THEMES

Social Issues

- problems for returning war veterans
- Prohibition and the rumrunners
- women's rights and the Persons Case
- struggles of Native peoples
- fads, fashions, sports, and entertainment
- hardship in the Great Depression

The Economy

- unemployment and rising prices after the war
- Winnipeg General Strike, 1919
- prosperity and resource development in the 1920s
- stock market crash, 1929
- Great Depression

Canadian-American Relations

- American investment in Canada
- branch plant system
- controversy over "Americanization" of the Canadian economy and culture

Canada and the World

- American investment surpasses British investment in Canada
- Statute of Westminster 1931; Canada gains independence in its foreign affairs

National Growth and Identity

- growing independence
- industrial development in the 1920s
- growing cultural identity (Group of Seven, formation of CBC, etc.)

Regional Development

- oil and gas development in Alberta
- prairie wheat boom in 1920s, drought in the 1930s
- hydroelectric power development in Ontario and Quebec
- economic difficulties in the Maritimes
- Quebec-Labrador boundary dispute is settled

Citizenship, Government, and Law

- Prohibition
- Emily Murphy and the Persons Case
- R.B. Bennett's New Deal
- new political parties formed
- leadership of Mackenzie King and R.B. Bennett

Technological Change

- new inventions (radio, mass production of automobiles, talking films)

The Arts

- formation of the Group of Seven
- establishment of CBC
- debate over influence of American culture
- golden age of Hollywood

CHAPTER 8

Moving into the Twenties

GANGSTERS OF THE TWENTIES

The legendary gangster, Al Capone.

Al Capone rode around Chicago in an armour-plated limousine. He was accompanied by a body-guard who sat with a machine gun on his lap. A flashy dresser, Capone wore a priceless diamond ring and carried $50 000 cash in his wallet. Al Capone was a gangster, head of a Chicago crime organization that made and sold illegal liquor. He crushed all rival gangs with ruthless threats and torture, and is said to have been responsible for more than 400 murders.

In Canada, the most notorious gangsters were Rocco Perri and Bessie Starkman. Perri was the "Canadian Al Capone." Perri and Starkman ran a vast bootleg (illegal) liquor operation that stretched from Ontario to New York, west to Chicago, and east to the Maritimes and beyond. They were involved in a trail of brutal killings and crimes. In 1930, Bessie Starkman was shot to death in the garage of their Hamilton, Ontario, mansion—the victim of a brutal gangland murder. Capone, Perri, and Starkman were symbols of the wild and lawless 1920s.

Prohibition and the Rumrunners

People called the 1920s the "Roaring Twenties." It was a time of glamour and prosperity for many. This was the age of "hot" jazz and dance halls. New forms of entertainment became available for almost everyone—movies, radio, dance clubs, and cars. It looked as if people were making up for the misery of war by enjoying themselves as much as possible. But at the same time, the 1920s were years of crime, corruption, and extreme poverty for some.

Much of the crime and corruption centred around **Prohibition**. The Prohibition era in Canada started in 1916 and 1917 during World War I. Prohibition made the production and sale of alcohol illegal. During the war, many women's groups had campaigned against drinking. The Women's Christian Temperance Union worked to ban the use of intoxicating liquor. It was argued that grain should be used to feed soldiers and civilians rather than to make alcohol. Also, money needed to feed families was often spent on drink and there

were many arrests for drunkenness. The women's groups were supported by farm, church, lodge, and merchant associations. They persuaded provincial governments to introduce Prohibition.

But people could always find a drink if they had the money. They bought "bootleg booze"—illegal liquor made and sold by organized bootleggers like Rocco Perri and other small-time operators. Elegant private clubs called "speakeasies" sprang up. Customers were approved through a peephole in the front door. Inside, the surroundings were fashionable and drinks were readily available. Some druggists did a roaring business by filling prescriptions of alcohol as a tonic.

The United States was also officially "dry" from 1919 to 1933. Some Canadians made fortunes smuggling Canadian liquor south of the border. Under the cover of dense woods, **rumrunners** used horse-drawn sleighs and snowshoes to smuggle booze across the Quebec border into Maine, New Hampshire, and Vermont. From ports along the shores of Lake Ontario and Lake Erie, fast boats ran cargoes of rum to the American shores. Estimates suggest that

A secret distillery is raided at Elk Lake, Ontario. Over 150 kegs of illegal liquor were seized.

almost $1 million of liquor crossed from Windsor to Detroit each month.

On the Atlantic coast, schooners from Halifax, Charlottetown, and St. John's in Newfoundland ran cases of liquor to Americans at meeting points off the coast. A small fleet of World War I planes was used to fly the illegal cargo to out-of-the-way landing fields in the United States. Individual Canadians were also ready to take a chance at smuggling liquor across the border. At Buffalo, some tried to saunter through customs wearing coats with hidden pockets packed with liquor bottles. If they got through customs, they could sell Canadian rye for $20 to $30 a bottle.

Prohibition had some positive social effects. The crime rate dropped, and arrests for drunkenness decreased dramatically. More workers took their pay cheques home instead of to the tavern. Industrial efficiency improved because fewer work days were missed. However, it became obvious during the 1920s that Prohibition was impossible to enforce. Underworld characters on both sides of the border were making fortunes in illegal liquor.

Provincial governments realized that they were losing millions of dollars in potential taxes on liquor sales. Prohibition was also unpopular with many citizens. Pressures increased for a more moderate liquor policy. People argued that legalizing liquor under strict government controls would be easier to enforce than total Prohibition. Gradually, individual provinces dropped Prohibition throughout the 1920s. Prince Edward Island was the last province to eliminate the law in 1948.

Smugglers sometimes carried liquor bottles across the border in hidden pockets under coats.

Other Post-War Problems

When World War I ended, wartime industries such as munitions factories closed down. Many workers were laid off their jobs. Women, who had played an important role in the wartime factories, were under pressure to return to household duties so that men could have jobs. Thousands of returning soldiers were looking for work, but jobs were hard to find.

Many war veterans were unemployed and bitter. Some looked at their medals and wondered why there were no jobs for them in the country they had fought to defend. They also resented the fact that some business people at home had made huge profits in war industries while the soldiers risked their lives in Europe. Veterans felt that the country at least owed them a job and a chance to make an honest living.

People who did have jobs in Canada in 1919 were not much better off. The problem was rapid inflation. This meant that prices of basic items such as food and clothing had increased greatly, while wages had not. The cost of living had more than doubled from 1914 to 1919. Housing was scarce and costly, and rents were high. Workers and returning soldiers wanted their share of prosperity. They joined unions to fight for better living and working conditions.

In 1919, workers across the country staged strikes. Miners and steelworkers in Cape Breton Island, machinists in Toronto, loggers in West coast lumber camps, and streetcar drivers in Windsor, Ontario, all went on strike.

The Winnipeg General Strike

The **Winnipeg General Strike** in 1919 was one of the most important and dramatic strikes in Canadian history. Building and metal trades workers voted to strike in May 1919. To show their support, 30 000 other workers in Winnipeg walked off the job. The workers organized a general strike in which almost all industries and key services were shut down. Streetcar operators, garbage collectors, postal workers, telephone operators, firefighters, and hydro workers refused to work. Ottawa sent Mounties and soldiers to put down the strike.

On June 21, a day known as **Bloody Saturday**, violence erupted in Winnipeg. The Mounted Police charged a parade. Shots were fired. One striker was killed. Strike leaders were arrested and sentenced to jail terms. The combined force of government, factory owners, and Mounted Police had defeated the strikers. The workers were ordered to return to their jobs.

When strikers went back to work, some were forced to promise not to become a union member or to become involved in union activities. Others found they no longer had a job. Employers branded them as troublemakers and fired them on the spot.

The strike, however, did draw attention to the social and economic conditions faced by many working people. A royal commission was appointed to investigate the causes of the strike. H. A. Robson,

A streetcar is overturned during the rioting on Bloody Saturday in Winnipeg.

who headed the commission, concluded that the strike was caused by the high cost of living, poor working conditions, and low wages. Labour leaders turned to politics to make their voices heard. Many were elected to all levels of government in the 1920s.

Economy on the Upswing

Gradually however, by the mid-1920s, life started to get better for most Canadians. The after effects of the war were beginning to wear off. Business picked up as foreign investors gained new confidence in Canada. By the middle of the decade, the economy was on the upswing. In regions across the country, industries were growing.

Wheat on the Prairies

The prairie provinces enjoyed huge wheat crops from 1925 to 1928. War-torn Europe was hungry for Canadian wheat, and the world price of wheat moved steadily upward. Farmers began to buy trucks and mechanical harvesters. They replaced their horses with tractors. The development of early maturing strains of wheat meant that wheat could be grown in more northerly regions. Railway branch lines were extended and settlers moved into the region around the Peace River in northern Alberta.

Some farmers organized wheat pools and co-operatives. These co-operatives were businesses owned by farmers. Their goal was to loan money to other farmers at lower interest rates than eastern Canadian bankers charged. Farmers also hoped that the co-operatives would be able to find customers for their grain, cattle, and dairy products. In this way, they could skip the dealers by marketing their own products and receiving a greater share of the profits. By 1928, Canada had a record wheat crop and a major share of the world market. Grain elevators were bursting at the seams

and prices of wheat remained at an all-time high through the first half of 1929.

Pulp and Paper

In the 1920s, the production of newsprint became Canada's largest industry after agriculture. From Nova Scotia to British Columbia, vast forests of softwoods such as spruce, pine, and poplar were used to make newsprint. Most of the American sources of pulpwood had been used up. Giant American newspapers provided a ready market for Canadian pulpwood. By 1929, exports of Canadian pulpwood equalled total pulp exports from the rest of the world. So much newsprint was shipped across the border that the Canadian government finally had to urge Canadian producers to save some of the supply for our own newspapers.

The boom did have a down side. Canada's forests were being destroyed. Canada's economy was also becoming more and more dependent on the export of raw materials. Thousands of Canadian workers were following the materials to the United States and finding jobs in American industries.

Hydroelectric Power

Quebec and Ontario saw a dramatic increase in the production of hydroelectric power in the 1920s. Niagara Falls had been used for power since 1895. Rivers such as the Saguenay and the St. Maurice were developed as resources for water power in the 1920s. Industries were beginning to use hydroelectric power instead of coal. People were demanding electricity for their homes, especially as new electrical appliances became available. Canada's output of hydroelectric power became the second largest in the world.

Oil and Gas

People called the 1920s the "Oil Age." As more Canadians took to the road in automobiles, the demand for gasoline and oils soared. Oil and gas were also being used for heating and cooking. An all-out search for new sources of thin "black gold" was on.

In October 1924, oil speculators in Alberta struck it rich. The well they were drilling in the Turner Valley south of Calgary exploded into flames and burned out of control for several weeks. Eventually, the fire was brought under control and the well became a great moneymaker. It produced a million barrels of oil and large quantities of natural gas. The confidence and optimism of the Alberta oil speculators grew. They continued to pour investment dollars into exploration and development of oil resources.

The oil boom and growing hydroelectric power industry, however, had a devastating effect on the economy of the Maritime provinces. The demand for coal, a major product of the Maritimes, was drastically reduced. Maritimers also struggled with rising freight rates and tariffs on their fish and farm products going to central Canada and the United States. Government policies tended to favour the development of manufacturing industries in central Canada while Maritime industries were hard hit. Many workers had to move to other parts of Canada to find work.

Mining

Exciting new mining discoveries were made in the 1920s. Large deposits of copper were found in the Canadian Shield near Noranda along the Ontario-Quebec border and at Flin Flon in northern Manitoba. At Sudbury, Ontario, by 1929, Canada was producing almost 80 percent of the world's supply of nickel. Kimberley, in British Columbia, produced lead and zinc in one of the world's largest mines. Many of these rich mining deposits were developed with American financing.

A natural gas flare lights up an oil derrick in the Turner Valley of Alberta. The oil strike marked the beginning of a major oil and gas boom in the province.

Foreign Investment in Canada

At the beginning of the twentieth century, the biggest foreign investors in Canada were the British. Bankers from Britain had invested in Canadian government bonds and railroads. They invested less in industrial enterprises because of the greater uncertainty of making a profit.

With the outbreak of World War I, British investment in Canada slowed down. But as British investment fell off, American investment increased. Americans preferred to put money into the rapidly expanding areas of the Canadian economy. These included mining, pulp and paper, and hydroelectric power.

There was another difference between American and British investors. American investors took greater control over the industries. British investors usually left Canadian business people to run the businesses in their own way. Americans introduced

SOCIETY AND SOCIAL CHANGE

The Dispute over Labrador

In March 1927, the Privy Council in Britain settled a long dispute between Canada and the Dominion of Newfoundland. For years, Canada and Quebec had argued with Newfoundland over who owned Labrador. Newfoundland boats had fished off the Labrador coast from the earliest days of settlement. In 1763, the Treaty of Paris gave Newfoundland Anticosti Island, the Magdalen Islands, and the Labrador "coast." The coast ran from the St. Jean River to the Hudson Strait. Newfoundland claimed its territory was defined by the watersheds of rivers running to the ocean.

Over the next 160 years, disputes over the boundary continued. In 1925, Quebec turned down a chance to buy Labrador from Newfoundland for $30 million. Finally, the Judicial Committee of the Privy Council handed down a decision in 1927. It ruled in Newfoundland's favour. The boundary was to run from Blanc Sablon on the coast to the Hudson Strait and include a large inland area. Quebec was outraged at the decision. Labrador had abundant natural resources. Surveys had shown that there were rich iron ore deposits and waterpower potential in the territory.

The Quebec-Labrador Boundary

1. Why was the settlement of the dispute over Labrador important?
2. How might the dispute affect relations between Quebec and the new province of Newfoundland and Labrador when it later became part of Canada?

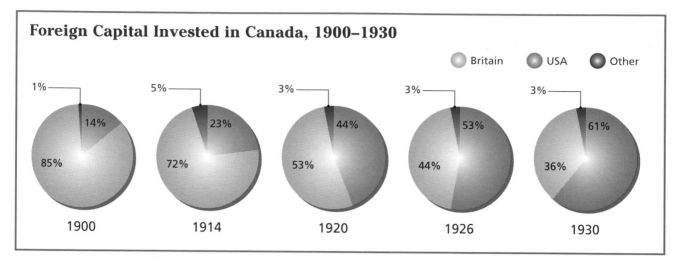

Foreign Capital Invested in Canada, 1900–1930

Britain   USA   Other

1900   1914   1920   1926   1930

the **branch plant** system. These branch industries were copies of the American parent company. They produced the same product as the parent company in the United States, but the products could be marked "Made in Canada." In this way, the parent company avoided paying high tariffs on imports at the border.

Canadian opinions about American investment differed widely. Some people believed the foreign capital was essential to develop industries and provide jobs in Canada. They felt American capital could develop Canada into a powerful nation.

Other Canadians were deeply concerned about the increasing "Americanization" of the Canadian economy. They argued that many important decisions concerning Canadian branches were made in the United States. Top management jobs frequently were held by Americans. Profits earned by the Canadian branch plants were often sent back to the United States. Some people feared a complete economic takeover of Canada by the United States. Some Canadians felt the government should be seriously looking for ways to curb American control of the economy.

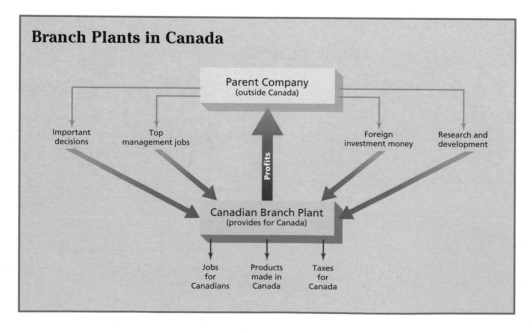

Branch Plants in Canada

DEVELOPING SKILLS: DECISION-MAKING

You have probably come up against some tough decisions in your life and have more ahead of you. Can you join a club or sports team and still keep up your grades? What do you do if you can't find a summer job? What occupation or career do you want to pursue? Often, these decisions can be easier to work through if you follow a careful reasoning process.

Let's take an example. Suppose you have a friend who you know has been shoplifting. You want to help her.

■ Step 1

First, state the problem as a question. Remember it should begin with something like, "In what ways might…?", or "How might…", or "How should…?" Try out a few problem questions and choose the one that is most relevant and meaningful.

Sample question:
"How should we help our friend with her shoplifting problem?"

■ Step 2

Brainstorm alternative solutions to the problem. Try to generate as many ideas as you can, even if they seem outrageous at first.

Alternatives:
- Tell a teacher whom you trust and ask for advice
- Persuade your friend to see a counsellor
- Tell your friend's parents
- Talk with your friend about her problem
- Go with your friend to her parents or a counsellor
- Don't do anything

■ Step 3

You have no doubt produced more alternative solutions than you can deal with. You need some basis for making your decision, some way of working out what is important to you in this situation. In other words, you need criteria to judge by. List criteria that you think are important in evaluating your alternative solutions.

Criteria:
- The friendship is maintained
- Your friend gets help
- As few people as possible know about the problem
- Your friend stays out of trouble
- Your friend is not suspended from school
- Your friend feels supported
- The solution does not cost too much
- The solution is practical
- Your friend maintains her dignity

Alternatives					
Criteria	1 Get advice from a teacher	2 Talk with your friend	3 Tell her parents	4 Persuade her to see a counsellor	5 Go with her to a counsellor
Friendship is maintained	4	1	5	3	2
Friend gets help					
Friend feels supported					
Friend stays out of trouble					
As few people as possible know					
Total					

■ Step 4

Choose five of your most promising solutions and your five most important criteria. Now you need to evaluate your alternative solutions according to your criteria. Write your criteria and your alternatives in a matrix like the one on page 139.

■ Step 5

Rank each of your alternatives from 1 through 5 on the first criterion. Score 5 for the best and 1 for the poorest solution. Next, rank each alternative on the second criterion in the same way. Continue until you have ranked all your alternative ideas according to your criteria. Make sure all the numbers from 1 to 5 are used in each column. Now total the numbers for each alternative. Which alternative scores highest?

■ Step 6

State your decision and make a plan for how you would carry it out.

■ Step 7

Evaluate your decision. If your plan was carried out, what would be the desired results?

Apply It!

Now you can use this model to help you decide what you would do about the Americanization of the Canadian economy. In groups, follow the steps in the decision-making process. Come to a group decision on this issue and present it to the class. Discuss the usefulness of the decision-making model.

PROFILES

Entrepreneurs and Reformers of the Twenties

Joseph-Armand Bombardier

Joseph-Armand Bombardier was the son of a prosperous farmer in Valcourt, Quebec. In 1922, when he was only 15, Bombardier built his first snow machine. His father had given him an automobile and young Armand removed the engine and mounted it on the family sleigh. He attached a hand-made propeller to the engine drive shaft. To the astonishment of his neighbours, Armand and his brother Leopold raced this primitive snowmobile through the town.

In 1934, Bombardier's son Yvon died of appendicitis during a raging winter storm. All the roads were blocked with snow. Bombardier's snow machines were lying in pieces in the garage. There was no way to transport his son to the hospital. Spurred on by the death of his son, Bombardier set out to work on developing a machine that would end the isolation of winter.

Bombardier converted this 1928 Model T Ford into a snow machine with the help of his brother-in-law, who is shown in this picture.

The next year he travelled through Quebec taking his invention with him. Everywhere he went he became front page news. He was granted a patent for his snowmobile which was called the B7. "B" stood for Bombardier and "7" stood for the number of passengers it could hold.

A later version of the B7 was used during World War II. In 1959, he introduced a two-passenger sport model, the now famous Bombardier Ski-Doo. Bombardier's inventions have been used around the world.

Business tycoon Herbert Holt and his family.

Sir Herbert Holt

One of the most powerful business tycoons of the 1920s was Sir Herbert Holt. Holt arrived in Canada from Ireland as a 19-year-old in 1875. One of his first jobs was working on railroad construction. Eventually, Holt built up a multimillion-dollar empire which included railroads, banks, mines, hotels, utilities, and the Famous Players theatres. He was the president of 27 major business enterprises.

A Montrealer in the late 1920s stated: "We get up in the morning and switch on one of Holt's lights, cook breakfast on Holt's gas, smoke one of Holt's cigarettes, read the morning news printed on Holt's paper, ride to work on one of Holt's streetcars, sit in an office heated by Holt's coal, then at night go to a film in one of Holt's theatres." Holt had few hobbies or close friends. Although he was the richest man in Canada, few people really knew him well.

Emily Murphy

Emily Murphy was the first woman magistrate in the British Empire.

Emily Murphy was a writer, journalist, magistrate, reformer, and famous crusader for women's rights. In her early career, Murphy published a series of popular and delightful books of personal impressions under the pen name "Janey Canuck." Born in Cookstown, Ontario, she later moved west with her family and spent a large part of her life in Edmonton, Alberta. It was there that she developed her interest in law and women's rights.

One afternoon, when Murphy was visiting a prairie farm, she met a bitterly distraught woman. The woman's husband had, without warning, sold their land and gone off to the United States. The woman was left penniless and homeless. Women at that time had no property rights. Men could sell land and home without their wives' consent and without giving her any part. It was law. Murphy determined that day to change that law. Seven years later, she had won the fight. In 1911, Alberta passed the Dower Act giving women rights to one-third share of their husband's property.

Emily Murphy went on to become the first woman magistrate in the British Empire. She led the battle to have a woman judge preside over cases involving women and children so that their cases could be fairly heard and their interests protected. She also campaigned against drug addiction and fought to prove that women were "persons" under the law and could therefore be appointed to the Senate. You will read more about the famous "Persons Case" later in this chapter.

Effects of the Boom Years

One result of the industrial boom in the 1920s was that Canadians gradually regained confidence in their country. The mood was generally optimistic. People were willing to take risks. Some Canadian entrepreneurs (business owners) built large and successful business enterprises. Financial success stories inspired ordinary citizens to believe that they too could get rich. Two dollar bets on horses, investing in stocks and bonds, and hockey pools were all seen as ways for the ordinary working man and woman to strike it rich quickly. The bubble of prosperity, however, was not to last.

Politics of the 1920s

In July 1920 Arthur Meighen, a Conservative, was sworn in as prime minister of Canada. He took over from Sir Robert Borden, who had resigned. The Canada that Meighen inherited was restless and torn apart by strikes and regional interests.

French Canadians were still seething over the conscription crisis of 1917. Maritimers were demanding more jobs and better working conditions. Prairie farmers were suffering from a postwar slump. They claimed that high tariffs increased their costs of operation. Farmers also demanded that railways be taken over by the government and freight rates reduced. Organized labour saw Meighen as a friend of big business and an enemy of the worker. With so many groups opposed to him, Meighen and the Conservatives lost the federal election in 1921.

The man who became prime minister for most of the 1920s was destined to be the most successful political leader of his age. He was the grandson of William Lyon Mackenzie, the leader of the 1837 Rebellion in Upper Canada. For almost 30 years until his death in 1950, William Lyon Mackenzie King dominated the Liberal

William Lyon Mackenzie King and his parents. King was a powerful personality on the Canadian political scene through the 1920s and 1930s.

party and political life in Canada. King was Canada's longest-serving prime minister.

On the surface, King seemed to possess few qualities that would attract large numbers of voters. He was a pudgy man, some said "dumpy" in appearance. He was cautious and careful, and extremely shrewd. He had a strong interest in spiritualism and sometimes, through mediums and seances, tried to contact the dead. There were times when King believed he had been in contact with his dead mother and had received political advice from important figures of the past, including Laurier.

King's political genius lay in making Liberal policies acceptable to various groups and regions across the nation. He listened to what various regions of Canada wanted. Often, he put off reaching a decision until he worked out compromises among the diverse interests.

Canada's Growing Independence

In 1926, all the countries of the British Empire met at an Imperial Conference. King insisted that the delegates talk about the powers of the dominions and the nature of their relationships to each other and to Britain. King was determined that Canadians should make their own decisions about foreign policies as well as policies at home.

At the conference, Canada and the other dominions were declared self-governing and independent nations. They all agreed, however, to remain a part of a **Commonwealth** of nations. Commonwealth nations were equal in status and united by their common allegiance to the king or queen of Britain. The Commonwealth was a voluntary family of nations from around the world.

By the **Statute of Westminster**, passed by Britain in 1931, Canada became fully independent in all but two legal details. There was still one court higher than the Supreme Court of Canada. That was the Judicial Committee of the Privy Council in Britain. Canadian citizens could appeal cases to the Privy Council. Also, Canada still had to ask the British Parliament to amend the Canadian Constitution (BNA Act). However, it

THE ARTS

The Group of Seven

At the turn of the century, art and especially painting was changing considerably. Some of the old rules were breaking down. Artists around the world were experimenting with new techniques and ways of expressing themselves. Impressionists, for example, wanted to express their feelings for their subjects through their art. They were less concerned about representing their subjects to look exactly as they were. Canadian artists, particularly members of the **Group of Seven**, were influenced by the Impressionists.

Members of the Group of Seven were also determined to create art that dealt with the Canadian experience. They took their inspiration from the Canadian landscape. The first exhibition of paintings by the Group was held in May 1920 at the Art Gallery of Ontario. All of the pictures portrayed Canada as a land of spectacular open spaces, rivers, lakes, and forests.

Lawren Harris was one member of the Group. In 1912, Harris saw an exhibition of paintings by J. E. H. MacDonald that changed his life. Not only was he impressed with the work, but through MacDonald he was introduced to other Toronto-based artists. Franklin Carmichael, Frank Johnston, Arthur Lismer, and Fred Varley became members of the Group. In 1913, MacDonald wrote to a Montreal friend, A. Y. Jackson, whose work they admired. Jackson soon moved to Toronto to join the other six. A. J. Casson joined the Group of Seven in 1926. By that time, Frank Johnston had left the Group.

Stormy Weather, Georgian Bay by Frederick Varley.

Some of the most inspiring pictures were produced on sketching trips in northern Ontario, but members of the Group also illustrated other parts of Canada including areas of Quebec, Nova Scotia, and the Rocky Mountains. The painters used bright, strong colours to portray the forces of nature. Often the paint was applied thickly with vivid brush strokes. They captured the vitality and ruggedness of the landscape by using simple, bold shapes.

Later, West coast artist Emily Carr also exhibited with the Group. Many of her paintings took their inspiration from Native life and culture on the West coast.

The Group of Seven were the first to create a Canadian national style in painting. Their influence and popularity spread steadily during their lifetimes. Today, Canadian art collectors eagerly seek out and pay high prices for works by the Group of Seven.

1. Stage an art exhibition. Find and display reproductions of paintings by the Group of Seven.
2. How do you think the Group of Seven's paintings created a national style or identity for Canadian art in the 1920s? To answer this question, describe the subjects of the paintings and the moods they create. How did the artists use colour?
3. Make a list of the subjects that you would paint to depict Canada today.
4. Imagine a Group of Seven painting is the opening scene in a movie. Write a paragraph to describe what happens next.
5. Do some further research on one of the members of the Group of Seven. Create a small portfolio of the artist's work, including a short biography and summary of his or her accomplishments on the first page of the portfolio.

A Haida Village
by Emily Carr.

was understood that both of these legal arrangements would be ended when Canadians agreed on powers to be held by the provincial and federal governments. Except for these two minor details, Canada had achieved full independence.

Women and the Persons Case

Women in Canada had won the right to vote in federal elections by 1918, but still did not enjoy all the privileges men had. The famous **Persons Case** underlined the inequality women still faced. Emily Murphy was the first woman judge appointed to a court to hear cases involving women. A lawyer in her Alberta courtroom challenged her right to judge any case because she was a woman. He said that no woman was a "person" in the eyes of the law. Emily Murphy was supported by the Supreme Court of Alberta, which said that a woman had every right to be a judge. This should have settled the matter, but it did not.

Women's groups asked the prime minister to appoint a woman to the Senate. The British North America Act stated that qualified "persons" could receive appointments. Again the question was raised: Was a woman a "person" in the eyes of the law? Was a woman qualified for an appointment to the Senate?

In August 1927, Emily Murphy and four other women decided to petition the prime minister. Besides Judge Murphy, the group of women included Nellie McClung, Louise McKinney, Henrietta Edwards, and Irene Parlby. They asked, "Does the word 'persons' in Section 24 of the British North America Act include female 'persons'?" In April 1928, the Supreme Court of Canada decided that women were not "persons" qualified for appointment to the Canadian Senate.

Judge Murphy and her supporters, nicknamed the **"Famous Five,"** were discouraged, but not defeated. They decided to appeal their case to the Privy Council in Britain. After three months of consideration, the judges of the Privy Council announced their decision. They declared that the word "persons" referred to men and women. Women were indeed qualified to sit in the Senate of Canada. Emily Murphy won her fight.

Many of her friends thought that Emily Murphy deserved to be the first woman appointed to the Senate. However, it was two more years before the first woman was named to a Senate seat. When it did happen it was not Emily Murphy, but Cairine Wilson, who received this honour. Senator Wilson of Montreal had worked as an organizer and president of the National Federation of Liberal Women.

Struggles of Native Peoples

Throughout the 1920s and 1930s, Native peoples struggled to keep their culture and heritage. Government policy during this period was for assimilation. That is, the government wanted Native people to give up their traditional ways and be absorbed into Canadian culture—which was predominantly "white" culture. Traditional Native ceremonies such as the Sun Dance and potlatch were banned. Native children were sent to special residential schools where they were forbidden from learning about their own cultures.

At the same time, Native people who tried to live off reserves in Canadian towns and cities faced discrimination and prejudice. They were given few opportunities to find good jobs and make a living. Many faced poverty and despair. They were caught between two worlds. The timeline below records some of the major events in Native affairs in the 1920s and 1930s. Native peoples were beginning to form organizations to fight for their rights.

1920

Fred Loft, a Mohawk veteran from World War I, organized the **League of Indians**. He wanted to draw attention to the economic and social problems facing his people. The League demanded that Native persons should have the right to vote without giving up their special status.

1921

Some West coast Native people were thrown into jail for taking part in a secret potlatch ceremony. In 1884, the Canadian Government had banned the potlatch. Now the police seized masks and other sacred objects.

1931

A Haida, Alfred Adams, founded the Native Brotherhood of British Columbia. The organization's goal was to defend Native people's lands as well as their hunting and fishing rights.

1920–1980s

Native children continued to be forced to attend government-run residential boarding schools. These schools were often hundreds of kilometres from the students' homes. Children were far away from their families for months at a time. Schools taught nothing about Native culture and students were forbidden to speak their Native languages. Often students lost touch with their traditions and families. The practice of placing Native children in residential schools continued into the 1980s.

Native youths in a residential school.

ACTIVITIES

Check Your Understanding

1. Add the following new terms to your *Factfile*.

    Prohibition   Commonwealth
    rumrunners   Statute of Westminster
    Winnipeg General Strike   Group of Seven
    Bloody Saturday   Persons Case
    branch plants   Famous Five
    Labrador dispute   League of Indians

2. a) Why was Prohibition introduced in Canada?
   b) Describe the ways in which Canadians profited from Prohibition in the United States. Locate on a map of Canada those areas where it would be easy to run liquor into the United States.

3. a) Describe the problems returning soldiers faced after the war.
   b) What problems did Canadian workers face in the early 1920s? How did they attempt to solve these problems?

4. a) Give reasons why Americans invested in Canada in the 1920s.
   b) Correctly use the following terms in a sentence: branch plant, tariff barrier, parent company.

5. a) How did the Statute of Westminster grant Canada fuller independence?
   b) What ties did Canada still have with Britain?

6. On cue cards, write one or two sentences describing the importance of the following people in the 1920s. Using the cards, challenge a partner to correctly identify

the people. Add others if you wish.

Emily Murphy   Alfred Adams
Fred Loft   Arthur Meighen
Rocco Perri   W. L. Mackenzie King
Bessie Starkman   Emily Carr
Cairine Wilson   Joseph-Armand Bombardier

Confirm Your Learning

7. Working with a partner, stage a dialogue between a supporter and an opponent of Prohibition. Prepare by noting arguments that might be used by the side you are representing. Who has the stronger arguments? Why?

8. Create a timeline outlining the major events in Canada's growth as a nation. Start your timeline at Confederation and include major cultural and social landmarks, as well as political changes. Add illustrations, pictures, and symbols. Present your timeline to a partner or group.

9. Create a map entitled "The Economic Development of Canada in the 1920s." Devise symbols to represent the major industries that developed in the 1920s and place them in the appropriate regions on the map. Include short notes explaining how and why the industries developed in these regions.

10. Why were the 1920s not the prosperous "Roaring Twenties" for the following groups? Explain.
    a) Native peoples
    b) people in the Maritime provinces
    c) western farmers

Challenge Your Mind

11.a) Do you think the Prohibition experiment worked? Why or why not?
   b) Someone remarked about the Prohibition experiment that "the cure was worse than the disease!" What does this mean?

12. Canadian economic nationalists oppose American investment in this country. The defenders of US investment claim that American capital is vital to the Canadian economy. Complete a pros and cons organizer like the one below and come to your own decision on the issue. Then take a class survey. Class members may wish to create buttons showing which side they stand on.

American investment in Canada	
Pros	Cons

13. Write a dialogue in which a modern feminist explains to Emily Murphy and Nellie McClung the problems facing women in Canada today. Include information on what gains Canadian women have made since their time. What would the suffragists' reactions be to the changes in the position of Canadian women?

14. Research the backgrounds of the "Famous Five." Each of the other four women was chosen by Emily Murphy to join her in signing the petition requesting the Supreme Court to declare that women are "persons." Try to decide why Murphy chose each one.

15. Name some modern Canadian women who you think should be appointed to the Senate. Give reasons for your choices.

16. Residential schools existed in Canada for Native children until the 1980s. Many people believe that they were harmful. Residential schools divided families and separated children from their culture. In what ways may the residential schools be responsible for some of the social problems Native people have experienced in the twentieth century?

17. Research some important traditions of particular Native nations, such as the potlatch of West coast peoples or the Sun Dance of the Siksika (Blackfoot) nation. Find out how these traditions are celebrated today. What effects would the banning of these traditions have had on the people in the 1920s? To help you understand the effects, think of an important tradition or celebration in your culture and imagine that it were banned.

CHAPTER 9

Life in the Roaring Twenties

"SMARTEST STYLES, NEWEST MATERIALS"

In the 1920s, it must have seemed that the world was suddenly smaller for many people. New inventions such as the radio, talking films, mass produced automobiles, and air travel meant that people in the remotest areas of the country were no longer as isolated. They could share in common forms of entertainment, travel to other regions, and tune in to the latest news broadcasts. While not everyone could afford the new fads and inventions, they moved to within the reach of more than just the wealthy. More and more Canadians were moving into the "modern age."

This is the great picture upon which the famous comedian has worked a whole year.

6 reels of Joy.

Charles Chaplin in "THE KID"

Written and directed by Charles Chaplin

A First National Attraction

Overland

rost is on the Punkin"
l Want this Sedan

OVERLAND, INC., TOLEDO, OHIO.

Radiola
Super Hetrodyne
(Second Harmonic)

Music from Across the Continent without the Aid of Aerials or Wires

Fads and Fashions

Fads swept the country during the "Roaring Twenties." No one can explain exactly how fads catch on, but suddenly many people become interested in a dance, fashion, game, sport, or other activity and take it up with great enthusiasm. Usually the craze does not last long. Fads are dropped as quickly as they are taken up.

One of the first fads of the 1920s was the ancient Chinese game of *mahjong*. *Mahjong* is a combination of dice and dominoes. The game caught on quickly across North America. In homes everywhere people were shouting *pungt* and *chowl* and other Oriental words connected with the game. *Mahjong* parties became the rage and people even imported Chinese robes, furniture, and decorative objects to add to the atmosphere. But by 1927, the novelty had worn off. It was time for a new fad.

The new fad was the crossword puzzle. Two young American publishers, Simon and Schuster, brought out a book of crossword puzzles with a pencil attached. Suddenly, everyone was crazy about crosswords. Dictionary sales soared. Some railways even provided dictionaries to help travellers solve crossword puzzles.

Long races and contests of every kind also became immensely popular. Non-stop talking, kissing, eating, drinking, flagpole sitting, and rocking-chair marathons were some of the contests in which people tried to establish records.

Of all the marathons, dancing was the real rage. Dancers competed for prizes of thousands of dollars. Couples dragged themselves around the dance floor with blistered feet and aching backs. One man dropped dead on the dance floor after 87 hours of continuous dancing. Some con-

Flappers in 1928. How did the style suggest the outrageous?

testants kept themselves awake with smelling salts and ice packs. Mary "Hercules" Promitis of Pittsburgh took a tip from bare-knuckle prizefighters and soaked her feet in vinegar and brine for three weeks before a 1928 marathon. Her feet were so pickled that she felt no pain at all!

Fads also swept the world of fashion. For young women, the "flapper look" was in. A **flapper** was a young woman who dressed outrageously. In winter, she wore galoshes with buckles unfastened to create the greatest possible flap. Hemlines rose above the knees and silk stockings were rolled down. Long hair was cut and set in a short "bobbed" style. Fashions for a young man were often as outrageous. He sported baggy pants or knickers, a bright snappy hat, and a bow tie. His hair was greased down and parted in the middle to imitate the popular movie idols of the day.

Inventions Bring Change

The Radio

Radio was the great invention of the 1920s. Voices, news, and music could now be broadcast across the country using radio signals. It was the invention of the radio that helped shrink Canada's vast size.

SOCIETY AND SOCIAL CHANGE

Slang of the Twenties

Every generation seems to have its own characteristic expressions or slang. "Cool," "awesome," and "Yuppie" are just some of the slang words we use today. Slang refers to informal words or phrases. The expressions are often associated with a particular group and represent certain feelings or attitudes. When these feelings and attitudes change, slang expressions may pass out of use. Our language is always changing. Sometimes slang words become part of common usage and are entered into our formal dictionaries. Do you recognize any of these expressions from the 1920s?

Expression	Meaning	Expression	Meaning
all wet	wrong, mistaken	high hat	snobbish
baloney	nonsense	hooch	bootleg liquor
bee's knees	a wonderful person or thing	hoofer	chorus girl
big cheese	very important person	kiddo	friendly form of address
bump off	to murder	kisser	lips
bunk	nonsense	a line	insincere flattery
carry a torch	to be hopelessly in love	ossified	drunk
cat's meow	superb, wonderful	ritzy, swanky	elegant
cheaters	eyeglasses	real McCoy	genuine article
crush	falling in love	runaround	delaying action
dogs	human feet	scram	to leave quickly
flat tire	boring person	speakeasy	a bar selling illegal liquor
gate crasher	an uninvited guest	spiffy	fashionable
giggle water	alcohol	swell	marvellous
gyp	cheat	whoopee	a wild time
hip	up-to-date		

1. Are any expressions in the list above still used today? Which? Why do you think they have survived?
2. Create a conversation between two students using the above expressions. Role play the conversation for the class or other pairs.
3. In groups, develop your own list of 1990s teenage slang expressions. Which modern expressions have similar meanings to those listed above? What does this suggest?
4. Canadian English is different from American or British English. Make a list of words or expressions that can be considered "Canadianisms."

People living in isolated rural parts of the country were brought in touch with the cities of the nation. It became possible for a farmer living far from the city to twist the dials on the battery set and listen to a hockey game from Montreal. In 1923, the famous Canadian broadcaster Foster Hewitt gave his first play-by-play of a hockey game from Toronto. Radio provided inexpensive entertainment in people's homes.

The earliest home sets had no tubes, but used a crystal (a thin piece of quartz). Listeners tuned in a signal by moving a fine wire "whisker" over the surface of the crystal. Sounds from **crystal radios** were never very loud, so earphones were often needed. Several pairs of earphones were provided when neighbours came to visit and "listen in." A person could take a crystal set on a picnic, hang the antenna on a tree, and sit back and listen through the headphones.

Before long, improved and expensive radio sets appeared in the stores. These were built in elaborate wooden cabinets. Tubes replaced the crystal and whisker, and speakers replaced earphones. The radios operated by large batteries that had to be recharged frequently. In 1925, a brilliant young Canadian inventor, Edward "Ted" S. Rogers, discovered a way of plugging the radio directly into household electrical current. His invention was the world's first battery-less radio. It sold for approximately $150. In 1919, Guglielmo Marconi, the inventor of the first wireless radio, had set up the first commercial radio station in Montreal. In February 1927, Ted Rogers set up his own radio station in Toronto. His station's call letters—CFRB—continue today to stand for his invention (R for Rogers and B for Battery-less).

The Automobile

One of the most obvious signs of prosperity in the 1920s was the growth of the automobile industry. Henry Ford dreamed of making an inexpensive car that almost anyone could afford to buy. Ford decided to apply to car manufacturing a method of **mass production** that was being used in some other industries.

Ford set up an **assembly line** that ran from one end of a building to another. At one end of the line were the frames of the cars. At first, the line did not move. The

CNR parlour car with radios.

workers walked along it adding parts to the automobiles. Later, Ford had the line itself move like a conveyor belt. As the line moved, new parts were added to the frame by workers who remained in one place. By the time a car reached the end of the line, it had been assembled and was ready to be driven.

Each worker on the assembly line had a separate job. Some added parts, while others secured the parts in place. This was called the division of labour. Ford also used standard parts for his cars, which meant that wheels, engines, and bodies were exactly alike for each car. As a result, Ford was able to produce the famous, practical **"Model T"** at a price that average North Americans could afford. The "Tin Lizzy," as the Model T was affectionately called, had a simple box-like design. But in 1924, it could be purchased for around $395.

The automobile has probably done more than any other machine to change our way of living. It put North Americans on wheels. It brought all parts of the country together. On Sunday, a family with a car could call on relatives 15 or 20 km away and still be home in time for supper. New industries sprang to life because of the car: gasoline, rubber, glass, and paint to name a few. New jobs were created in service stations, parking lots, and repair shops. The family car made it possible to have a summer cottage and to travel longer distances for summer vacations. Along the major roads, tourist cabins and hotels developed to house the increasing number of travellers. More trucks were used for hauling freight from factories and food from farms.

Governments spent increasing amounts of money on highways. Main roads were paved and some country roads were given a surface of gravel. A crank and a tow rope were standard equipment in every automobile. The crank was needed to get the engine started. A tow rope was required because motorists never knew when they might get stuck in mud or snow. More than one pleasant Sunday drive was spoiled when the family car became mired in mud. Most motorists did not attempt to drive in the winter at all. They put their car up on blocks because the engines tended to seize up with the cold.

The age of the automobile had arrived. Model T Fords roll along the assembly line.

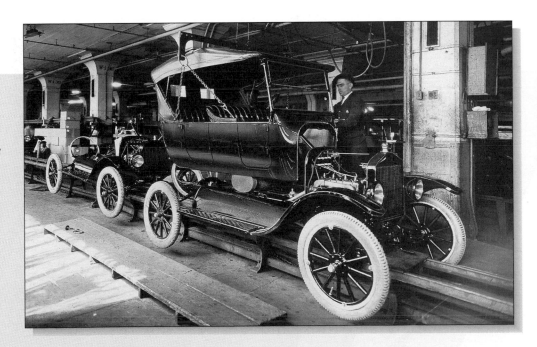

The car also made it possible for people to live farther from their place of work. People sought open green spaces for their houses, so suburbs started to sprawl on the outskirts of many cities. It became increasingly difficult to sell a house without a garage and a driveway.

However, the automobile created problems as well. No one knew that this great invention would pollute the air, cause incredible traffic jams, and bring death to thousands of people each year. Criminals also made use of the automobile. Vancouver police reported at least six robberies a night in which the thieves made their getaway in a car. Police departments were soon forced to buy automobiles themselves.

Motor Vehicle Registration in Canada	
1903	220
1911	22 000
1921	465 000
1931	1 201 000

Entertainment

For flappers, only one kind of music would do and that was jazz. **Jazz** moved north from New Orleans in the United States and was made popular by such musicians as Duke Ellington and Louis Armstrong. Out of African American culture also emerged the dance of the decade—the **Charleston**. Its fast and wild pace quickly caught on with the high-spirited younger generation. Members of the Boston City Council tried to have the dance banned, but the Charleston was here to stay. It became the emblem of the roaring "Jazz Age."

Barnstorming

Stunt flyers and air travel were also part of this high-stepping decade. Canadian aces, who returned from World War I, bought war surplus biplanes and "barnstormed" across the country. These aces would perform daring stunts over country fairs. As onlookers below gasped in horror, they would dive and loop-the-loop, and even hang from the wings of their flimsy craft. For "two bucks a flip," they would take the adventuresome for an airplane ride.

Eventually, the public and government began to see the possibilities of air travel. Bush pilots helped to open northern frontiers of Canada by flying prospectors and supplies into mineral-rich areas. In 1927, the post office hired pilots to fly mail into remote communities within Canada.

In the same year, a young American airmail pilot, Charles A. Lindbergh, completed the first non-stop transatlantic flight

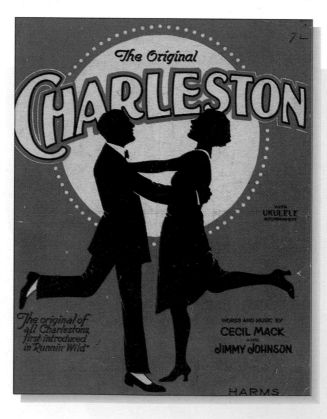

Dancing the Charleston.

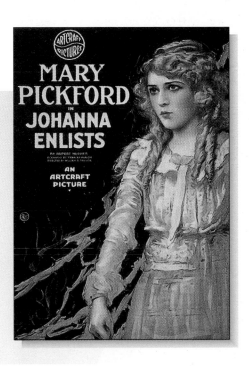

Mary Pickford was a major Hollywood star and went on to found United Artists with Douglas Fairbanks, Charlie Chaplin, and D. W. Griffith.

the decade, films were silent. The stars of the silent screen were idolized by the Canadian public. They provided excitement that ordinary people sometimes lacked in their daily lives. Charlie Chaplin, affectionately called the "Little Tramp," needed no words to get across his hilarious comic routines. Rudolph Valentino and Greta Garbo were other great stars on the silver screen. When Valentino died in 1926, police had to be called in to control the screaming mob.

The Canadian-born star, Mary Pickford, was often called "America's Sweetheart." Born in Toronto in 1893, she started on the stage at the age of five. At the height of her career, she was earning $10 000 a week. As her popularity soared, Mary Pickford came to represent the luxury and wealth the film industry brought to its stars. When she retired from the screen, she bought the rights to all of her old silent movies and refused to release them. Not until after her death in 1979 were her films re-released.

Movie-going became part of life for many people. By the end of the decade, there were more than 900 movie houses across Canada. Every kid wanted to spend Saturday afternoon at the show, and for many adults Hollywood movies were the most popular entertainment.

from New York to Paris. This important event signalled the possibility of long-distance air travel. Suddenly the world seemed smaller!

The Silver Screen

Talking films were another amazing invention of the 1920s. But **"talkies"** did not arrive in Canada until 1927. For most of

Sprinter Percy Williams is congratulated for his victory at the Amsterdam Olympics in 1928. He was one of the sports sensations in the "Roaring Twenties."

Sports

The 1920s were also a golden age of sport in Canada. The sports heroes of the decade were amateurs. They seemed to come out of nowhere to grab the headlines and establish world records. Percy Williams is an example. This 20-year-old sprinter, almost unknown in Canada, stunned onlookers at the 1928 Amsterdam Olympics. In the 100 and 200 metre sprints, he won a sensational double gold victory. Competing athletes acknowledged him as "the greatest sprinter the world has ever seen."

Canada's most famous male athlete of the first half-century was Lionel Conacher. He piled up trophies and medals in wrestling, boxing, lacrosse, hockey, football, and baseball. One day in 1922, Conacher starred in championship games in two different sports. He hit a triple in the last inning to give Toronto Hillcrest the city baseball championship. Then he drove across town to play in the Ontario Lacrosse Championship. In this game, he scored four times. Conacher also excelled in football. In the 1922 Grey Cup game, he scored 15 points leading the Toronto Argonauts to a 23-0 win over the Edmonton Eskimos.

Women also enjoyed a golden age in sport. Before World War I, the sports considered "proper" for women included croquet, skating, fencing, cycling, and lawn tennis. Women participated in many other sports, but it was not until the 1920s that it was socially acceptable for women to play body-contact sports. Women began to compete more actively in a wide range of organized team sports.

In the early part of the twentieth century, basketball became popular and was one of the first sports played by women on the world circuit. The Edmonton Commercial Grads dominated women's basketball for over 20 years. From 1915 to 1940, the team played 522 games and lost only 20. The Edmonton Grads represented Canada at four Olympics between 1924 and 1936 and won 27 consecutive games. Their conditioning and quick-passing teamwork made the Grads the undisputed world champions of women's basketball. Dr. James Naismith, the Canadian-born inventor of basketball, proclaimed the Edmonton Grads the greatest basketball team that ever stepped out on a floor.

Among individual Canadian female athletes, Fanny "Bobbie" Rosenfeld was one of the best. She excelled in so many sports during her athletic career that she was called the "best woman athlete of the half-century." She was a star at basketball, hockey, softball, and tennis, but her greatest triumphs came in track and field. During the Amsterdam Olympics of 1928,

The 1920s were a golden age of women's sports. The Edmonton Commercial Grads dominated the world of women's basketball for over 20 years.

Rosenfeld won a silver medal in the 100 metre dash and a gold medal in the women's 400 metre relay. High-jumper Ethel Catherwood from Saskatoon also won a gold medal at the Amsterdam Olympics.

Unfortunately, this era of prominence for women's sports did not last. By the mid-1930s, many educators and medical doctors argued that girls and women were "biologically unfit" for competitive athletics. Competitive sports were considered "unfeminine." Not until the 1960s did Canadian women have the opportunity to regain the glory they won in the 1920s in a wide range of sports.

DEVELOPING SKILLS: PRESENTATIONS USING DIFFERENT MEDIA

We sometimes think that the only way to communicate history is to write about it. But there are many different ways to present information and ideas about the past. A museum, for example, can mount exhibits or displays on particular periods or themes, such as African Canadian history or the building of the Canadian Pacific Railway. The curator, a historian who manages a museum's collection, gathers photographs, models, costumes, artifacts, and primary source documents. These items are then organized, carefully labelled, and exhibited so that the story unfolds before the eyes of the museum visitors. Sometimes audiotapes are prepared for people or a tour guide presents the exhibit.

Other people interested in history use film as their medium. Films can feature people reminiscing about what happened to them in the past and how world events affected their lives. Films can also be re-enactments of historical events. Sometimes they include actual footage of past events, carefully edited with voice-overs filling in the story.

Another creative way of communicating history is with a time capsule. A time capsule is a collection of objects representing everyday life, usually placed in the cornerstone of a public building. The idea is that a future generation can open the time capsule and discover what was important to people from another generation.

Suppose you want to show what life was like in Canada during a decade like the "Roaring Twenties."

■ Step 1

Divide the class into groups. Each group chooses a decade from Canadian history, e.g., the 1920s, the 1950s, or the 1990s to present.

■ Step 2

Each group should select a different way of presenting its decade. Use the list below for ideas and remember that you can also combine a number of these suggestions in your presentation.

■ Step 3

Research information on life in your decade. Besides written work, look for some or all of the following: music, pictures, artifacts, recorded

exhibit or display	video	time capsule
bulletin board mural	photo essay	scrapbook
timeline mural	collection of artifacts	cartoon or comic strip
performance	news program	vertical file
computer program	demonstration	artistic creation
poster	advertisement	brochure/pamphlets
costumes	simulation game	skit
puppet show	slide show	maps
models	learning centre	docudrama
overheads	project cube	book or magazine covers

interviews, models, charts, and graphs. Organize your materials into sub-topics so that they tell a complete story. Accompany your visuals with brief written comments and notes. The emphasis of the presentation, though, should be on the visual and not the written.

■ **Step 4**

Each group can set up its presentation at a different station in the classroom. Groups can take turns touring the room.

■ **Step 5**

Develop 15 questions for the other groups about your decade. Give other groups time to visit your display and answer the questions about it. Encourage them to ask questions as well.

■ **Step 6**

Have others evaluate how useful your visual presentation was in helping them learn about life in Canada during that decade.

ACTIVITIES

Check Your Understanding

1. Add the following new terms to your *Factfile*.
   flapper   jazz
   crystal radio   Charleston
   mass production   talkies
   assembly line
   Model T Ford

2. Explain how flappers reflected the mood of the 1920s.

3. a) Imagine that you are living on a homestead in Alberta during the early 1920s. Your farm is a long way from urban centres. Your nearest neighbours are located a few kilometres away. What difference would a radio make to your family's life?
   b) What other inventions of the 1920s affected people's lives in a similar way?

4. List 10 jobs that were created as a result of the automobile.

5. Quiz a partner on the major sports figures of the 1920s. Describe each athlete's achievements and have your partner tell you who it is.

Confirm Your Learning

6. Create a chart outlining the benefits and problems that have resulted from the invention of the automobile.

7. Since crossword puzzles were a great fad of the 1920s, try making some. Use a sheet of graph paper. The answers should all be words associated with the 1920s. Write clues to help your classmates solve the crosswords.

8. Make models or bulletin board displays for a crystal radio, battery-less radio, Model T Ford, or other early car models. Include labels and short notes on how these new inventions worked and the effects they had. Or, create a timeline mural

showing the development of radios, automobiles, or telephones from their invention to the present.

9. Create posters, stamps, or sports cards to celebrate great Canadian athletes of the 1920s.

Challenge Your Mind

10. Listen to some music of the 1920s. Describe the mood, rhythms, use of lyrics, and major instruments used. Compare them with a form of music of your choice from today.

11. How has the car affected Canadian life? Would urban sprawl be a problem if the car had not been invented? Justify your answer.

12. In your opinion, who is the best male athlete in Canada today? Who is the best female athlete? Give reasons for your opinions.

13. Research a Canadian woman athlete who has made a significant contribution to sport. Or, compare a female athlete of the 1920s with one who has distinguished herself today. What effects did the social and political climate of the times have on these athletes?

Female athletes of the 1920s	**Modern female athletes**
Ada Mackenzie — golf	Dawn Coe Jones — golf
Jean Wilson — speedskating	Susan Auch — speedskating
Gladys Robinson — speedskating	Netty Kim — figure skating
Myrtle Cook — track and field	Myriam Bédard — biathlon
Florence Bell — track and field	Sylvie Frechette — synchronized swimming
Bobbie Rosenfeld — track and field	Silken Laumann — rowing
Ethel Catherwood — high jump	Manon Rhéaume — hockey
Edmonton Grads Basketball team	Canadian Women's Hockey team

14. Gather recent issues of the following magazines: *Chatelaine*, *Popular Science*, *Maclean's*, *Sports Illustrated*, *Canadian Living*, and *Consumer's Report*. Imagine these magazines were published in the 1920s. In groups, prepare an article for one of these magazines based on some aspect of life in the 1920s that you have read about in this chapter. For example, you could develop a profile of a prominent athlete for *Sports Illustrated* or report on the latest radio design for *Popular Science*. Include photos, illustrations, or cartoons in your articles.

CHAPTER 10

The Great Crash

DIARY FROM THE DEPRESSION YEARS

I was always sick two Fridays of every school year, that is when I was in grades 10 and 11. The first Friday was in early October and the second was late in June.

Those two days were when the school had its big dances, the two of the year. Sure, I got asked. But I always had the flu, which translated means I didn't have any clothes. At school we wore a sort of black uniform, all the girls, so that's how I got by there, but at a dance, no way.

Kinda sad, isn't it? I might have met my one true love at one of those affairs.

A painting by Nathan Petroff entitled Modern Times *(1937) captures the mood of the Depression years.*

Though not everyone shared in the prosperity of the 1920s, there was a general mood of optimism in the country. But this mood changed drastically in the early 1930s. Canada was plunged into the **Great Depression**—the worst economic downturn the country has ever faced. How could prosperity turn to poverty for so many so quickly? What caused the Great Depression?

Many people would say that the Depression was caused by the stock market crash of 1929. However, the stock market crash was not the *cause* of the Great Depression. It was only a *symptom*. It was a sign that the economy of North America was very sick. To understand the Depression, it helps to understand a little about how our economy works and what was happening in the 1920s.

The Business Cycle

Economic conditions are constantly changing. There are good times when the economy is on the upswing, and bad times when business declines. Economists who chart the upswings and downswings of the economy over a period of years call these ups and downs the **business cycle**. The business cycle includes four basic stages: Prosperity, Recession, Trough or Depression, and Recovery.

The economy of North America in the late 1920s is a good example of the **prosperity** stage in the business cycle. In this stage, prices and wages are high. Few people are unemployed. Businesses are making high profits and production is booming. The general mood is optimistic and people are willing to take risks.

When a **recession** sets in, business begins to slow down. Companies that have produced too many goods begin to realize they cannot sell everything. Therefore, they lay off some workers and cut production. Unemployment rises. Workers who have been laid off have less money to spend. Others who still have jobs are more careful about how they spend or invest their money. Sales begin to fall.

If the recession continues and becomes very serious and widespread, it is known as a **depression**. Businesses are forced to lay off many more employees. Unemployment reaches very high levels. Many businesses go bankrupt. Stock markets crash. The economy does not always fall into a depression. Sometimes it just hits a low point known as the **trough**, and then slowly begins to recover. A depression is the worst case scenario.

The Business Cycle

Recession
Sales–Declining
Wages–Falling
Prices–Falling
Production–Declining
Business profits–Decreasing
Business failures–Increasing
Demand for goods–Declining
(Buyers' market)
Labour unrest–High
(Many strikes)
Unemployment–Increasing

Trough or Depression
Sales–Low
Wages–Low
Prices–Low
Production–Low
Business profits–Low
Business failures–High
Demand for goods–Low
Labour unrest–Low
(Few strikes)
Unemployment–Very high

Prosperity
Sales–High
Wages–High
Prices–High
Production–High
Business profits–High
Business failures–Low
Demand for goods–High
(Sellers' market)
Labour unrest–High
(Many strikes)
Unemployment–Low

Recovery
Sales–Rising
Wages–Rising
Prices–Rising
Production–Increasing
Business profits–Increasing
Business failures–Decreasing
Demand for goods–Increasing
Labour unrest–Low
(Few strikes)
Unemployment–Falling

The Economy

As T.C. Douglas, the first leader of the New Democratic Party once said:

A recession is when a neighbour has to tighten his belt. A depression is when you have to tighten your own belt. And a panic is when you have no belt to tighten and your pants fall down.

The economy goes into the **recovery** stage of the business cycle when a shortage of consumer goods develops because of the cutbacks in production. People want and need more goods than are being produced. To meet the demand, businesses begin to increase production again and to call back workers. Wage earners now have more money to spend. Eventually prosperity returns.

The Great Crash

"Black Tuesday"—the day the stock market crashed in October 1929—was one of the most dramatic events signalling the Depression. In the 1920s, it seemed as if almost everyone played the stock market. People dreamed of getting rich overnight. How do people make a fortune on the stock market? The answer is simple: buy plenty of stocks when their price is low and sell those stocks when their price is high. It sounds easy, but a great deal of knowledge, skill, and good luck are needed to make a fortune! Many people who invested in the stock market lost everything in the crash.

24 October 1929

Stock speculators shaken in wild day of panic

29 October 1929

New York stock market crashes

30 October 1929

Greatest collapse ever witnessed in Canada

1933

One in five Canadian workers have no job

Panic on Wall Street outside the New York stock exchange in 1929. The panic quickly spread to Canada.

SOCIETY AND SOCIAL CHANGE

Understanding the Stock Market—A Case Scenario

How does the stock market work and what happened in the 1920s? Suppose it is 1929. A group of friends want to form a new company to produce racoon coats which are very fashionable at this time. They need to buy furs, rent a factory, pay furriers, hire a sales staff, and pay for advertising. They estimate that they need $100 000 to start the company.

How could they raise the money? They could use all of their savings, borrow the money from the bank, or raise money by selling stocks in the company. In this last case, they get people to invest in the company by buying stocks. If they sold 10 000 stocks at $10, they would have the $100 000 necessary to start their company. Each **stock** represents a share of the business. The stockholder, therefore, owns part of the business and shares in the company's success or failure. As proof of his or her investment in the business, the stockholder is given a paper called a **stock certificate**.

Suppose you decide the Canuck Racoon Coat Company is going to be vastly successful and you decide to buy stocks in it. First, you would visit a **stockbroker** whose job it is to buy and sell stocks in a kind of marketplace known as the **stock exchange**. (Both the act of buying and selling stocks, and the place in which this is done, are called the stock market.) The stockbroker places your order and carries out the details of your transaction.

The stocks represent your share in the ownership of the company. If there are 10 000 shares in the Canuck Racoon Coat Company and you own 1 of them, you own 1/10 000 of the company's shares. If you own 10 shares, then you own 1/1000 of the company's shares.

People buy shares in companies to make money. Suppose you buy 100 shares in Canuck Racoon Coat Company. You pay $25 per share. Your total investment is $2500. A few months later, the value of the stocks rises to $35 per share. Business is booming. Racoon coats are the latest fad. At this point, you sell your 100 stocks at $35 per share. You paid $2500, but get back $3500. The difference of $1000 is called a **profit** or **capital gain**. Whether you buy or sell, you pay your stockbroker a small fee for handling the business for you.

Stocks can also make money for you in another way. Companies usually divide some of the profits among the shareholders. These payments to shareholders are called **dividends**. Since you own 1/100 of the stocks in the Canuck Racoon Coat Company, you are entitled to receive 1/100 of the amount the company pays out in dividends.

The prices of stocks go up and down almost every day. There are many complicated reasons for this. One important reason is demand. If people wish to buy a certain stock, prices will go up because they are willing to pay the price. If nobody wants a particular stock, or if several people wish to sell it, the price on the market will probably fall.

Stocks have been in high demand in the 1920s. Many people are buying on the stock market. Then it's 1929 and stock prices are dropping. What is going on? You aren't really alarmed at first. On October 29, you open the morning paper and read the headlines. The stock market has crashed! You've lost everything.

1. Create a mini glossary of terms associated with the stock market in your notebook. Include all the words in boldface on the previous page.
2. Consult the stock market pages in a newspaper to find an example of each term.

DEVELOPING SKILLS: USING SIMULATION GAMES

What was "Black Tuesday" really like? How did the investors, stockbrokers, and company owners react when the stock market crashed?

One way to gain insight into the past is through historical simulation games. A simulation is a situation game. It involves you in a real life situation and you must decide how you will act. The Stock Market Game outlined below gives you a chance to experience the thrills and defeats of the stock market in the late 1920s.

The debriefing process is crucial to any simulation game. A simulation helps you to think critically and to make judgements. Debriefing means that at each stage of the game, you stop and think. Why did you act as you did? What prompted you to make certain decisions?

It doesn't matter if the game doesn't duplicate exactly what happened in reality. What matters is that it helps you to understand the complexity of events in the past, why people acted as they did, and the decisions they faced. After the game, you can compare what happened in the game to actual historical events.

The Stock Market Game

1. Choose three or four class members to be stockbrokers. The brokers set up their offices in the corners of the classroom. Brokers are given a supply of stock certificates and a stock record page.

2. The rest of the class are investors. Each investor keeps an expense sheet.

3. The purpose of the game is to gain experience in playing the stock market. Your aim as investors is to make as much money as possible. You start with $5000 that has been left to you as an inheritance in your grandmother's will. You may invest any amount of money in one company or all three. For the purpose of the game, you cannot sell your stock during the first three stages. Investors must carefully record each purchase on their expense sheets.

Stage 1—Year 1925

Stocks for the following three companies are for sale:

Consolidated Mining and Smelting of Canada	at $50 a share
Atlantic Electric Light	at $30 a share
International Nickel	at $25 a share

Investors are given time to visit the stockbrokers, make their purchases, and record their investments.

Stage 2—Year 1927

Two years have passed. The economy of the country has been strong and the stocks have increased in value. Each investor calculates the profits made on these stocks if they had been sold in 1927. Your teacher will tell you the amount of the increase.

Stage—3 September 1929

Each investor calculates the profits made on the stocks if they had been sold in 1929.

Debriefing
a) If this were real life, how would you feel?
b) What would investors do with their profits?
c) What would companies probably do with their profits?

Stage 4—29 October 1929 ("Black Tuesday")

Each investor calculates the losses on these stocks. Investors should be given an opportunity to sell stocks to the teacher if they wish.

Debriefing
a) How do you feel about your losses?
b) What would you do if this were real life?
c) How would your actions affect the economy of the country?
d) How would companies suffer?

Stage 5—Year 1932

Investors who have held onto their stocks must calculate their losses.

Debriefing
a) What alternatives are open to investors?
b) Who would be buying stocks in 1932?

Causes of the Great Depression

What really caused the Great Depression? There seem to be as many explanations as there are experts to diagnose the illness. However, some of the major causes are as follows.

1 Over-Production and Over-Expansion

During the prosperous 1920s, agriculture and industry reached high levels of production. Almost every industry was expanding. Large amounts of profits were spent adding to factories or building new ones. Huge supplies of food, newsprint, minerals, and manufactured goods were produced and simply stockpiled. Automobile centres such as Oshawa and Windsor manufactured 400 000 cars in 1930. Canadians already owned over a million cars and in the best year ever had purchased only 260 000.

Even in the general prosperity of the 1920s, Canadians could afford to buy only so many goods. As a result, large stocks of newsprint, radios, shirts, shoes, and cars piled up unsold in warehouses. Soon factory owners began to panic and slowed down their production. They laid off workers. Laid-off workers and their families had even less money to spend on goods. Sales slowed down even more.

Industrialists seemed to have forgotten a basic lesson in economics: produce only as many items as you can sell. In the 1920s, wages were simply not high enough for people to buy all the products turned out by the factories.

2 Canada's Dependence on a Few Primary Products

Canada's economy depended heavily on a few primary or basic products, known as **staples**. These included wheat, fish, minerals, and pulp and paper. These goods were Canada's most important exports. As long as world demand for these products was strong, Canada would prosper. However, if there was a surplus of these goods on the world market, or if foreign countries stopped buying from Canada, our economy would be in serious trouble.

Regions which depended largely on one primary product found themselves in deep economic trouble during the Depression. The Depression had hit countries around the world and demand for Canada's products fell. The Maritimes, which depended heavily on fish, and the West, which was geared toward wheat production, were especially hard hit.

In the late 1920s, for example, Canada faced growing competition from other wheat-exporting countries including Argentina and Australia. With a surplus on the world market, the price of wheat began to fall. To add to the problem, western farmers were faced with terrible droughts in the summers of 1929, 1931, and 1933-1937. Without adequate rainfall, crops failed. With little income, farmers could not purchase machinery and manufactured goods from eastern Canada. Many could not afford to pay the mortgages on their farms.

With no wheat to be shipped and no flour to be ground, railways and flour mills began to feel the pinch. Secondary industries such as flour mills, which process primary products, also suffer from any slowdown in production. The farmers' problems had caused a chain reaction in many parts of the Canadian economy and society.

3 Canada's Dependence on the United States

The economy of Canada in the 1920s was closely linked with that of the United States. In those years, we bought 65 percent of our imports from the Americans. Forty percent of our exports were sent to the United States. The United States was our most important trading partner. It had replaced Britain as the largest buyer of Canadian products and the most important supplier of investment funds for Canadian industries. It was not surprising that when the American economy got sick, Canada also suffered. One comedian said, "When the United States sneezed, the rest of the world got pneumonia."

When the Depression hit the United States, banks closed. Industries collapsed and people were out of work as factories shut down. No longer did Americans need to buy our lumber, paper, wheat, and minerals. It was inevitable that Canada's economy would suffer too.

4 High Tariffs Choked Off International Trade

In the 1920s, Europe was recovering from a devastating war. Europeans needed many of the surplus manufactured goods that the United States and Canada produced. Unfortunately, European countries were heavily in debt from the war and often could not afford to buy the goods they needed.

At the same time, many countries adopted a policy known as protective tariffs. To protect their home industries from foreign competition, they placed high tariffs on foreign imports. Country X, for example, would find that its goods were being kept out of country Y by high tariffs. Soon country X placed high tariffs on imports from country Y. Thus trade between nations began to slow down around the world.

5 Too Much Credit Buying

All through the 1920s, Canadians were encouraged by advertising to "buy now, pay later." A famous comedian, Will Rogers, said that the way to solve the traffic problem was to remove from highways all cars that hadn't been paid for. He meant that so many cars were bought on credit, very few would actually remain on the road. Will Rogers was only joking, but his remark points out that by 1929, credit buying was a well-established custom. Why wait to buy a washing machine or a phonograph or a tractor when you could have it immediately with only a small down payment?

Many families got themselves hopelessly into debt with credit buying. The piano that cost $445 cash was purchased with $15 down and $12 a month for the next four or five years. With the interest payments, it ended up costing far more than it was worth. Sometimes by the time the purchases were paid for, they were ready for the junk pile. One radio comedian joked that he had said to his wife, "One more payment and the furniture is ours." To this she replied, "Good, then we can throw it out and get some new stuff!"

If the wage earner became sick or was laid off work, it was often impossible to keep up the payments. If you fell behind in your payments, the person who sold you the goods had the right to repossess them. As the Depression worsened, many people lost everything. Their refrigerators, stoves, washing machines, cars, and even their homes were repossessed by their creditors.

6 Too Much Credit Buying of Stocks

For many people in the 1920s, the stock market seemed an easy way to get rich quickly. People in all walks of life gambled on the stock market. Rich business tycoons invested in shares, but so did their chauffeurs and the typists in their offices. Feelings of confidence were at an all-time high.

It was not even necessary to have a lot of money to play the stock market. You could buy stocks on credit just as you could buy a phonograph or a washing machine. All that was needed was a small cash down payment, usually about 10 percent. The broker loaned you the rest of the money at a high interest rate, of course! To buy $1000 worth of stock you needed only $100 cash. The idea was that as soon as your stocks went up in value, you could sell them. Then you paid back your loan to your broker and pocketed the profits. This risky process was called "buying on margin."

Buying stocks on margin did not require a large outlay of cash if stocks kept rising quickly in value. But what if your stocks didn't go up? Or, worse still, what if they went down? How would you pay back your loans? You would have to sell your stocks or risk financial ruin.

This is exactly what happened in October 1929. When the value of stocks started to drop, people panicked. They decided to sell and get out of the market. Prices fell even lower as more and more stocks were dumped. The market was like a giant roller coaster racing downhill. Nothing could stop it. In a few hours on 29 October 1929, the value of most stocks on the Toronto and Montreal Stock Exchanges nosedived by more than 50 percent. Shareholders lost millions. Many big and small investors were wiped out in a few hours.

At first, few people imagined that the devastating economic times were around the corner. But slowly, it began to dawn on people that hard times were upon them. The Great Depression had begun.

Tenants are evicted from their home in Montreal.

What does this cartoon suggest about playing the stock market?

ACTIVITIES

Check Your Understanding

1. Add these new terms to your *Factfile*.

Great Depression	trough
business cycle	recovery
prosperity	"Black Tuesday"
recession	staples
depression	

2. a) Explain how over-production led to factory slowdowns in the 1930s.
   b) Why did Canadian families stop buying as many products?

3. a) Give examples of primary industries.
   b) Name four secondary industries that would suffer if farmers could not sell their wheat or had no wheat to sell.

4. Why did a Depression in the United States have such serious repercussions in Canada in the 1930s?

5. a) Why do countries put high tariffs on foreign goods? Who benefits from high tariffs? Who suffers?
   b) Why was international trade important to Canada in the 1920s and 1930s?

Confirm Your Learning

6. a) Create an advertisement that could have been in a 1920s newspaper encouraging people to "buy now, pay later."
   b) How did too much credit buying lead to problems for many people in the late 1920s?

    c) Explain "buying on margin." Give an example to show that you understand how it works.

7. a) Is it ever wiser to buy on credit rather than with cash? If so, when?
    b) Why do many people prefer to pay cash while others use credit? Which way seems best to you?

8. a) How does a person gamble when playing the stock market?
    b) Why did investors panic in October 1929?
    c) As more and more investors tried to sell out, why did prices decline even more rapidly?

9. To help you understand the effects of the Depression, identify a major industry in your area and assume it goes out of business. List all the secondary industries related to that industry. How will they be affected by the shutdown?

10. Suppose world sales of Canadian wheat decline. Create a flow chart to illustrate the chain reaction affecting Canadians and Canadian industries.

11. Develop a mind map outlining the major causes of the Great Depression. Remember that a mind map shows the connections between ideas and their importance in relation to one another.

12. Analyze the cartoon on page 168. Refer back to the "Developing Skills" section on pages 69 and 70 for key questions to guide you.

Challenge Your Mind

13. Invite a local stockbroker to visit your classroom. Ask questions about how the stock market works. Also ask her or him to explain the changes in regulations that would prevent the stock market from crashing today as it did in 1929.

14.a) In groups of four, create the front page of a newspaper published on October 29, 1929. Give the paper a name and brainstorm a number of headlines for the lead story.
    b) Assign various tasks to group members.
- The editor oversees the whole process and writes a short editorial presenting his or her view on the events.
- The staff writer writes the short lead article to accompany the headline the group decides to use.
- A cartoonist creates a cartoon illustrating the effects of the stock market crash on investors.
- The art director decides on the design and layout of the page and carefully pastes down all of the elements to create the final product.

    c) Display the finished pages in the classroom.

15. What do you think governments could have done in the 1920s to prevent a depression? Justify your answers.

16. Compare the economic conditions of the late 1920s with those of today. Check the business sections of newspapers to get an indication of the current health of the economy. Some key indicators are the unemployment rate and total production (called Gross Domestic Product or GDP). Speculate about the possibility of a depression occurring again.

CHAPTER 11

Life in the Dirty Thirties

WINDOWS ON LIFE IN THE THIRTIES

In the memory of living Canadians, nothing like the Great Depression had ever happened before. What was it like? The pictures and memories presented below will give you an insight into some of the social conditions. The memories have been collected from interviews with people who remember those times. As you look at each picture and read the text, consider the following questions.

Why did people ride the rails across the country?

What were conditions like on the prairies?

What help was available for people?

How did they feel about accepting government help? Why?

In what ways did they try to help themselves?

A PHOTO STORY

Many unemployed people drifted from town to town across Canada looking for jobs. They rode "free" on the railways by hiding in boxcars, perching on their roofs, or riding the rods underneath the trains.

Nature added to the problems of the West by turning off the tap. The resulting drought meant that large sections of the prairie topsoil just blew away during the "Dirty Thirties." Black blizzards of dust buried fences and drifted up to eaves of houses. In some places the dust drifts were so deep that highways had to be closed. Railway crews used steam shovels to clear dust from the tracks near Grainger, Alberta.

Another disaster to hit the West was grasshopper plagues. The insects ate the crops as soon as they popped out of the ground. They even ate clothes hung out to dry on the line.

In the 1930s, the Saskatchewan government paid children a penny for each gopher tail they turned in. It was an attempt to save the parched wheat from the hungry rodents.

Many penniless prairie families simply gave up in despair and abandoned their farms. The desperation and poverty can be seen on the faces of this family who are heading for the Peace River country. Between 1931 and 1937, 66 000 people left Saskatchewan, 34 000 left Manitoba, and 21 000 left Alberta.

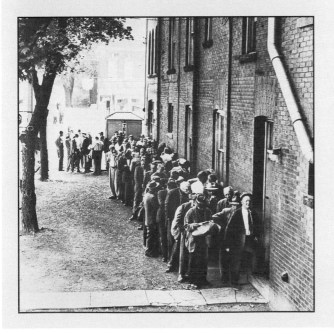

This photo shows a soup kitchen line-up in Toronto. There was no unemployment insurance, no family allowance, and no government medical care. The only help available was government relief. **Relief** was emergency financial assistance to some of the unemployed to keep them from starving. There was no uniform system of relief across the country. The federal government gave sums of money to local municipalities who administered the relief in their own way. Many municipalities demanded that people be resident there for a period of time before they could collect relief.

The unemployed were never given cash, but only vouchers. The vouchers could be exchanged for food, rent, and other necessities. **"Pogey"** was hobo slang for food, clothing, and shelter provided by public relief agencies. A Manitoba judge, George Stubbs, observed of relief, "It's not quite enough to live on, and a little too much to die on."

Applying for relief was the most humiliating thing a person had to do. When you were on relief, the fact was clearly advertised to the world. Merchandise acquired by voucher was seldom wrapped. Merchants did not feel obliged to wrap shoe boxes or clothing when the customer was in no position to complain about it.

"You asked me what a **Bennett Buggy** was? In the twenties, farmers bought automobiles... Chevs, Fords, Overlands, Reos, the Hupmobile, oh,... a lot that they don't even make any more. Then came the crash and the drought and nobody had any money for gasoline, let alone repairs... A car that wouldn't run.

Somebody got the idea of lifting out the engine and taking out the windshield and sticking a tongue onto the chassis... and that's where old Dobbin and Dolly got back to work again. Two horsepower. Eight kilometres an hour, but those oat burners got you there. Then somebody got the idea, the country was full of wits, to call these contraptions Bennett Buggies. Poor old R.B. Bennett. All over... there were these carved up cars, named after him, and a constant reminder that he'd been prime minister when the disaster struck."

In 1932 the federal government began to finance a system of **relief camps** for single unemployed men. Many of the camps were in isolated areas of British Columbia. The men

worked eight hours a day cutting brush, moving rocks, and building roads. In return they were fed and sheltered and paid 20¢ a day. The camps, however, became a source of great discontent. The wage of 20¢ a day was considered little better than slave labour. In June 1935 thousands of men, fed up with life in the BC relief camps, boarded freight trains bound for Ottawa to protest to the government. This was known as the **On to Ottawa Trek**. The men got as far as Regina, where they were stopped by the Mounted Police.

The Worst Years

Few people were prepared for the conditions they faced in the worst years of the Depression. By 1933, almost a third of all Canadians were out of work. People roamed the country, hitching rides on trains, trying to find odd jobs wherever they could. With no income from jobs, there was often no money for food, clothing, and other necessities. Many people lived near starvation and suffered from malnutrition.

Not everyone was in such dire straits. Those with jobs and the wealthy lived quite comfortably, especially since prices of goods were low. But for many others, the only prospect of help was government relief. People found ingenious ways to cope with the shortages. The Bennett Buggy is an example. People also remade old clothes and helped each other when they could. Having to go on relief was often a last resort.

Governments in the 1930s seemed to believe that the best way to deal with the Depression was to wait it out and hope things would get better. When the stock market crashed in 1929, William Lyon Mackenzie King was prime minister. In 1930, King made what many people believe was the biggest political mistake of his career. Providing relief was the responsibility of the provinces and King said that he would not give a "five-cent piece" to any province that did not have a Liberal government.

In the election of 1930, those words kept coming back to haunt him. The voters refused to forget King's **"five-cent piece" speech**. The Liberals were voted out of office, and the Conservative party came into power. The prime minister who replaced Mackenzie King was Richard Bedford Bennett. Bennett was a multimillionaire lawyer from Calgary who believed that governments should not interfere in economic affairs.

During the election campaign Bennett had promised, "I will end unemployment or perish in the attempt." When he came to power, however, his policies did little to ease the economic crisis. Bennett gave emergency funds to the provinces for relief. Military-style relief camps were set up for jobless single men in isolated parts of the country. The highest tariff in Canadian history was introduced to protect Canadian businesses from foreign competition. Unfortunately, none of these acts had any great impact on the Depression. These measures were like first-aid treatment, but they could not cure the Depression.

As times became more difficult, people began to blame Bennett for their problems. Cars that could not run for lack of gas were hitched up to farm animals and called "Bennett buggies." The shacks where the unemployed camped around cities were called "Bennett boroughs." "Bennett coffee," made from roasted wheat or barley, was a cheap substitute for the real thing. Newspapers used as covers by homeless people on park benches were known as "Bennett blankets." A "Bennett barnyard" was an abandoned farm. The

R.B. Bennett was Canada's prime minister during the Depression years.

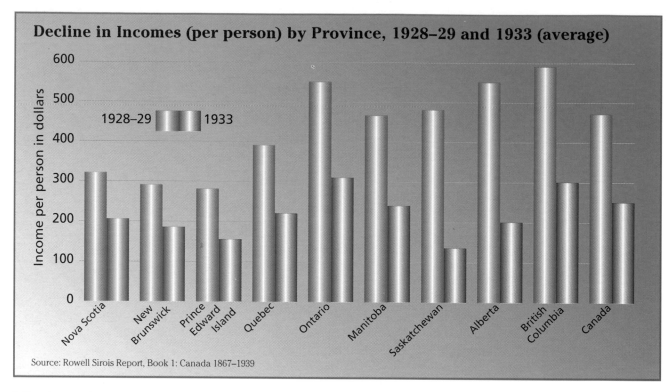

Decline in Incomes (per person) by Province, 1928–29 and 1933 (average)

Source: Rowell Sirois Report, Book 1: Canada 1867–1939

following testimonies express some of the hardships.

Did you have a job during the Depression?

No, but my brothers in Kingston worked for 15¢ a day by driving tractors. I was on relief. They gave us prunes to eat and a pair of boots once a year. We got pants but no suits—just salvage, surplus clothes. I once asked Mayor Kaiser for food but he said no. That guy the mayor had butter on his table. Everyone else had fatty, lardy margarine. To get my relief, I killed rats in the dump on Gibb Street and dug sewers and ditches.

What was life like for you during the Depression? Did your husband have a job?

I remember my husband was very sick for the first few years of the Depression. He worked for a farmer and got $19 a month. We had to try to get by on it, but if his parents hadn't helped us, I don't know what we would have done. The doctor in Beaverton was really good and I remember he operated on my husband right on our kitchen table. He was really sick for a while there, but the doctor had us pay him only $100. We owed him well over $500, but he told us he would wipe his books clean of what we owed him.*

Where did you get your clothes?

Mother made all the clothes for us from old clothes that had been given to us. I remember she knitted wool stockings because it was so cold. Mother's relatives would send us old clothes and many of these had moth holes in them. I was embarrassed to wear the old clothes. It seemed mine were the worst of all the kids in the school.

How did you feel about the railroad riders?

A lot of them came to our place asking for food. We gave them meals, but we made sure they washed first because they were all so dirty. We couldn't turn away these hobos since we had something to eat ourselves.

Which areas of Canada suffered most during the Depression?

What was Christmas like?

Mother and Papa always made sure we would get something for Christmas. Once they bought us a box of chocolates and that was a real treat. In our stockings we would get some apples, an orange, and some candies. We couldn't afford to spend a lot on gifts. I remember giving a towel to my mother-in-law one Christmas. We gave little things like that.

How did your family make a living? What was life like for you during the Depression?

All during the twenties my father was a bricklayer in Toronto, but by mid-1930 he no longer had a job... My parents figured that the only solution was to go and live on a farm where we could get enough to eat. As a result, my family sold our home in Toronto and moved to a farm near Ashburn, Ontario, in the fall of 1930. There was an apple orchard and we raised various farm animals such as cows, chickens, and pigs. To earn money for our family, my parents travelled to Toronto in their old Durant [a make of car] and sold the farm goods there. We only had the car for a few years because it broke down and we could not afford to have it repaired. My parents went from house to house trying to sell apples and eggs. They did not make much money selling their farm produce because few people would buy, or could afford to buy, the goods.

The reason people wouldn't admit poverty was because they were too proud. I remember people brought coal sacks uptown to get relief. It was very humiliating for people to be seen with these. Not everyone got relief though, because there wasn't enough to go around.

Typical Prices in 1932	
Milk	10¢ a quart
Cheese	33¢ a kilogram
Bread	6¢ a loaf
Rolled oats	11¢ a kilogram
Flour	11¢ a kilogram
Rice	16¢ a kilogram
Tomatoes	6¢ a tin
Potatoes	2¢ a kilogram
Carrots, turnips	9¢ a kilogram
Onions	9¢ a kilogram
Cabbage	5¢ a kilogram
Dried beans	4¢ a package
Prunes	12¢ a package
Chuck roast	29¢ a kilogram
Beef liver	35¢ a kilogram
Butter	57¢ a kilogram
Peanut Butter	35¢ a kilogram
Shortening	35¢ a kilogram
Sugar	11¢ a kilogram

Source: *Historical Atlas of Canada, Vol. III.*

Relief provided barely enough to live on. Payments were kept very low to discourage people from applying for them. In 1932, relief payments for a family of five were $6.93 a week. In Montreal, relief was $4.58 a week. In Newfoundland, it was 42¢ a week.

Conditions were worst on the prairies because of the severe droughts, and in the Maritimes. In Newfoundland, still an independent dominion within the British Commonwealth, conditions were so bad that the economy almost collapsed. The Newfoundland government was deeply in debt and could borrow no more. A British commission took over the government to help Newfoundland through the worst period.

SOCIETY AND SOCIAL CHANGE

Letters from the Depression

During the Depression, many people wrote letters to Prime Minister Bennett asking for help. The letters express some of the shame and despair people felt.

Ottawa
March the 4th 1932
Dear Sir,

I am just writing a few lines to you to see what can be done for us young men of Canada. We are the growing generation of Canada, but with no hopes of a future. Please tell me why is it a single man always gets a refusal when he looks for a job. A married man gets work, & if he does not get work, he gets relief. Yesterday I got a glimpse of a lot of the unemployed. It just made me feel downhearted, to think there is no work for them, or in the future, & also no work for myself. Last year I was out of work three months. I received work with a local farm. I was told in the fall I could have the job for the winter; I was then a stable man. Now I am slacked off on account of no snow this winter. Now I am wandering the streets like a beggar, with no future ahead. There are lots of single men in Ottawa, who would rather walk the streets, & starve, than work on a farm. That is a true statement. Myself I work wherever I can get work, & get a good name wherever I go. There are plenty of young men like myself, who are in the same plight. I say again whats to be done for us single men? do we have to starve? or do we have to go round with our faces full of shame, to beg at the doors of the well to do citizen. I suppose you will say the married men come first; I certainly agree with you there. But have you a word or two to cheer us single men up a bit? The married man got word he was going to get relief. That took the weight of worry off his mind quite a bit. Did the single man here anything, how he was going to pull through? Did you ever feel the pangs of hunger? My idea is we shall all starve. I suppose you will say I cant help it, or I cant make things better. You have the power to make things better or worse. When you entered as Premier you promised a lot of things, you was going to do for the country. I am waiting patiently to see the results. Will look for my answer in the paper.
Yours Truly
R.D. Ottawa

May 30/31
Mr. Bennette

Since you have been elected, work has been impossible to get. We have decided that in a month from this date, if thing's are the same, We'll skin you alive, the first chance we get.

Sudbury Starving Unemployed

Passman, Sask.
16 Oct. 1933
Dear Sir,
I am a girl thirteen years old and I have to go to school every day its very cold now already and I haven't got a coat to put on. My parents can't afford to buy me anything for this winter. I have to walk to school four and a half mile every morning and night and I'm awfully cold every day. Would you be so kind to sent me enough money so that I could get one.
My name is
Edwina Abbott
[Reply: $5.00]

Craven, Alberta
Feb 11-1935
Dear Sir,
Please don't think I'm crazy for writing you this letter, but I've got three little children, and they are all in need of shoes as well as underwear but shoe's are the most needed as two of them go to school and its cold, my husband has not had a crop for 8 years only enough for seed and some food, and I don't know what to do. I hate to ask for help. I never have before and we are staying off relief if possible. What I wanted was $3.00 if I could possible get it or even some old cloths to make over but if you don't want to do this please don't mention it over radios as every one knows me around here and I'm well liked, so I beg of you not to mention my name. I've never asked anyone around here for help or cloths as I know them to well.
Yours Sincerly
Mrs. P.E. Bottle
[Reply: $5.00]

Murray Harbour, P.E.I.
March 24 1935

Premier Bennett:

Dear Sir:

I am writing you to see if their is any help I could get. As I have a baby thirteen days old that only weighs One Pound and I have to keep it in Cotton Wool & Olive Oil, and I havent the money to buy it, the people bought it so far and fed me when I was in Bed. if their is any help I could get I would like to get it as soon as possible. their is five of a family, Counting the baby. their will be two votes for you next Election Hoping too hear from you soon.

Yours Truly.
Mrs. Jack O'Hannon

[Reply: $5.00]

1. These letters contain some grammatical and spelling errors. Suggest why.
2. Who are the authors of the letters? What does your answer suggest about the types of people who were most affected by the Depression?
3. a) What kinds of problems did people write about to Prime Minister Bennett?
   b) What emotions are expressed in the letters?
   c) What solutions were available to solve the problems? What did Prime Minister Bennett do?
4. What were the special problems faced by the number of young single men? Was it right that married men got work or relief while single men did not? Why did the government give special preference to married men?
5. Why would a woman who wrote to Bennett beg him not to mention her name?
6. What help would be available today for a woman who gave birth to a one pound (450 gram) baby? What help was available to her in 1935? Do you think it was the duty of the government to help her? Why?
7. Imagine you were living through the Depression. Write your own letter to Prime Minister Bennett.

The Great Escape

Faced with a daily struggle to survive and little hope for the near future, many people looked for a way to forget their hardships. The 1930s were the "golden age" of Hollywood. For the price of a 25¢ ticket, people could forget the dust storms and relief vouchers and enter the make-believe world of the Hollywood stars. The films, radio shows, songs, and magazines of those days provided a brief escape from reality.

Great film extravaganzas such as "Gone With the Wind" and Walt Disney's "Mickey Mouse" were popular box office attractions. Though all the films came from Hollywood, at least a dozen stars were Canadians. These included Beatrice Lillie, Marie Dressler, Norma Shearer, Deanna Durbin, Raymond Massey, and Walter Huston, who became famous international stars.

Shirley Temple was one of the most loved Hollywood child stars of the 1930s. She made her first film in 1934 at the age of four, and for the next four years was Hollywood's top box office attraction. Her golden ringlets endeared her to millions as she sang and danced. Miss Temple's $300 000 yearly salary was boosted by the sale of Shirley Temple dolls, doll clothes, soaps, books, and ribbons. Many little girls in this decade were called Shirley and had their hair done up in ringlets.

The radio also provided a vital escape from the dreariness of ordinary life. In the 1930s, people gathered around the radio in their living rooms to listen to the popular programs. In these days before television broadcasting, families depended on the radio for home entertainment.

Canadian Nell Shipman was one of the writers and stars of films in the 1930s.

Shirley Temple dolls.

The Dionne quintuplets captured the spotlight when they were born in 1934, but their lives in the public eye were difficult.

The most popular radio shows came from the United States. They included "Jack Benny," "George Burns and Gracie Allen," "The Lone Ranger," and "The Inner Sanctum." Because Canadian airwaves were being filled with American radio shows, Prime Minister Bennett felt something had to be done. The **Canadian Radio Broadcasting Commission (CRBC)** was started in 1932 to counteract American influence. The government built more stations across the country to improve the quality of Canadian broadcasting. In 1936, the Commission became the **Canadian Broadcasting Corporation (CBC)**. In 1939, the CBC covered the royal tour to Canada by the new king, George VI, and Queen Elizabeth. The first visit of a reigning monarch to Canada was carried by radio to even the most remote areas. The CBC was proving that it could be a powerful force in establishing a sense of national unity across Canada.

Newspapers of the 1930s downplayed the harsh conditions of the Depression because people became tired of reading bad news. Instead, newspapers gave a great deal of space to human interest stories. One of the most spectacular was the birth of the Dionne quintuplets to a family in Corbeil, Ontario, in 1934. Annette, Emilie, Yvonne, Cecile, and Marie were the world's first quintuplets to survive. The Dionnes became a major tourist attraction, and millions of Canadians flocked to look at the babies through a special one-way screen.

Throughout the 1930s, daily life in Canada was growing more like daily life in the United States. People were so preoccupied worrying about money and trying to escape from the Depression that there was not much concern about this situation. The influence of the United States on Canada through films, radio, magazines, and fads did not become an important political issue until the 1960s.

DEVELOPING SKILLS: ROLE PLAYING

Role playing can help to make the past come alive. You can travel back in time and participate in the events. Role playing is like being an actor in a movie or television show. You need to research your role and prepare for it by imagining what it would have been like to live in that time and at that place. Put yourself in the place of your character. Imagine you really are that person. What would life be like in those circumstances? What choices would you have to make?

■ Step 1

Take time to think about your role and research your character. On a role card, write answers to these questions.
- When did this person live?
- What were the circumstances of his or her life?
- What is the situation of the role play? What problems or decisions is the character facing?

■ Step 2

Add notes on how your character would be feeling in the role play situation. How might he or she act? Why? Refer to these notes if you need them as you present your character.

■ Step 3

Gather props such as a hat or a costume. Props will help you look and feel more like the person you are playing.

■ Step 4

In a role play, you can improvise—reacting to the situation as it unfolds and saying what comes to mind without a set script. Or, you can write a script. With either method, you should take some time to prepare. If you will be improvising, imagine yourself in your role and how you would react to different situations. If you have written a script, rehearse it until you are comfortable.

■ Step 5

Present your role play. Aim for realism, fluency (avoid awkward pauses), and a lively presentation that will hold your audience's attention. Afterwards, classmates can ask questions which you must answer in your role.

■ Step 6

Hold a class discussion or a debriefing about the role play experience.
- Were the characters realistic?
- Are there suggestions for a better representation of the roles?
- How did you feel in your role? Why did you feel that way?
- What did you discover about your character?

■ Step 7

Generalize from the role playing experience. What new insights about the past did you gain from role playing? What solutions did you find? How did your solutions differ from those in the past?

Try It!

In groups of three or four, prepare and present a role play for one of the following. The time is the 1930s, at the height of the Great Depression.
- a family discussing the fact that they must go on relief
- people in a boxcar riding the rails in search of work
- a group of young mothers gathered together to write a letter to Prime Minister Bennett
- a group of single men in a relief camp
- western farmers and workers at a community meeting
- a group of wealthy business owners discussing the economic situation

The Search for Solutions

Prime Minister R. B. Bennett knew that Canadians were growing increasingly angry with the government. The Depression was dragging on and conditions were getting no better. The government seemed to be doing nothing. In 1935, just before an election, Bennett introduced radical reforms. He wanted to establish unemployment and social insurance, set minimum wages, limit the hours of work, guarantee the fair treatment of employees, and control prices so that businesses could not make unfair profits.

The people called this Bennett's **"New Deal."** The program was similar to one introduced in the United States by President Roosevelt. Roosevelt's idea was to use all the government's resources to get the economy going. Large-scale federal public works projects such as road building were funded to provide jobs.

Most people were startled by Bennett's radical new ideas. His political opponents suggested that the New Deal was nothing more than a plot to win votes in the forthcoming election. They felt that Bennett had left his reforms too late to do any good. In the election of 1935, King and the Liberals swept back to power in a landslide victory.

New Political Parties

During the "Dirty Thirties," people had become increasingly dissatisfied with the two main political parties—the Conservatives and the Liberals. The old parties seemed to have no new, fresh ideas for solving the country's economic troubles. New political parties were formed. They promised to take more drastic action to eliminate the problems of the Great Depression.

One new party was the **Co-operative Commonwealth Federation (CCF)**, founded in Calgary in 1932. It was formed by farm and labour groups who wanted social and economic reforms to end the human suffering caused by the Great Depression. The party's first leader was J.S. Woodsworth, a member of parliament in Manitoba. The CCF supported the idea of both nationalized and private industries and wanted Canadians to have pensions, health and welfare insurance, family allowances, unemployment insurance, and compensation for injured workers. By 1961, the CCF had evolved into the New Democratic Party (NDP). The Liberals and the Conservatives have adopted some of the policies first put forth by the Co-operative Commonwealth Federation.

J.S. Woodsworth was the first leader of the Co-operative Commonwealth Federation (CCF) political party.

In 1935, the **Social Credit party** formed the government in Alberta. Its leader was William Aberhart. Aberhart wanted to give a "social credit" of $25 a month to every adult. He believed that by putting purchasing power in the hands of citizens, they would begin to spend money again. Businesses would then increase production. In this way, the Depression could be stopped and prosperity would return. The prosperity certificates of $25 a month were often called "funny money" because they were declared illegal and never paid out. However, the party remained in power in Alberta for many years. The Social Credit party eventually became a federal party and won support in Alberta and Quebec in a number of federal elections.

The **Union Nationale** party was founded in Quebec in 1935. It was a coalition party that began as a protest against the high unemployment and severe economic hardship of the Depression. Its members wanted social, economic, and political reform in Canada. In 1936, under Maurice Duplessis, the Union Nationale became the government of Quebec and governed until 1939.

It was during the Depression that the idea of the **welfare state** took root in Canada. This was the belief that society should support its citizens to prevent extreme economic hardships. Today, there is unemployment insurance so that no one suffers severe hardship because a job is not available. People over 65 years of age are provided with pensions and injured workers receive compensation.

But in the 1930s, these reforms had not yet taken hold and political solutions were not enough to end the Depression. The Depression was ended by World War II. The outbreak of war in 1939 provided jobs for many in the armed forces and in the factories producing war munitions.

DEVELOPING SKILLS: INTERPRETING GRAPHS IN HISTORY

Newspapers, magazines, and atlases frequently present information using graphs. A graph can make information clear that would take many words to explain. Graphs are visual pictures or summaries of key information. You are probably already familiar with various types of graphs, such as bar, pie, and pictographs from your math, science, and geography classes. Graphs are useful in history too. Each type of graph is especially useful for presenting a particular kind of information.

Line graphs are useful when you want to see how something changes under certain measurable conditions, such as over time. Line graphs are also useful to show the development of similar items, so that you can compare them. In the line graph on the next page, for instance, you can see how the number of unemployed and the number of people on direct relief changed over a period of time. The line graph also makes it easy to compare the two.

Follow these steps to analyze information in a line graph.

■ Step 1

Read the title of the graph to find out exactly what information is being presented. The line graph at the top of the next page, for example, illustrates the number of people unemployed and the number on direct relief over several years—from 1926-1940. From what you have learned in this chapter, you know that these years cover the Great Depression.

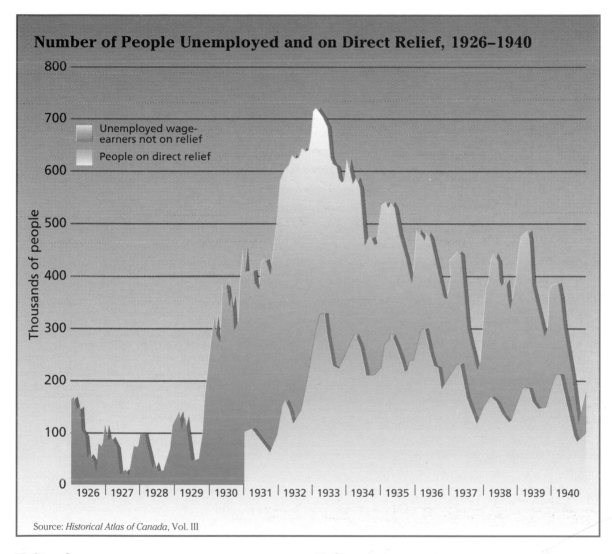

Number of People Unemployed and on Direct Relief, 1926–1940

Legend:
- Unemployed wage-earners not on relief
- People on direct relief

Y-axis: Thousands of people (0 to 800)

X-axis: 1926 1927 1928 1929 1930 1931 1932 1933 1934 1935 1936 1937 1938 1939 1940

Source: *Historical Atlas of Canada*, Vol. III

■ Step 2

Check the legend. A legend tells what the lines, colours, symbols, or other elements in a graph mean or represent. In this graph, the blue line shows the number of unemployed and the gold shows the number of people receiving direct relief.

■ Step 3

Read the numbers along the bottom of the graph. In this graph, they tell you the years being reported. The numbers along the side of the graph represent the number of people and are shown in thousands. The numbers go from zero at the bottom to 800 000 at the top.

■ Step 4

Study the graph. What can it tell you? What conclusions can you draw? Consider the following questions.

a) When was unemployment at its highest level? When was unemployment at its lowest level?

b) What were the levels of unemployment at the end of the 1920s in Canada? What happened to the level of unemployment after the Stock Market crashed?

c) In which year did direct relief begin?

d) Which number is always larger, the number of people on direct relief or the number of unemployed?

e) Hypothesize. From the information you have

read in this chapter and found on this graph, suggest some reasons for your answer in d).

Practise It Further!

Use the data in the table to the right to draw a line graph. Gross National Product or GNP represents the total value of all goods and services produced in Canada in a year. When you have completed your graph, answer these questions.

a) What pattern or trend does the graph show in Canada's total production from 1926 to 1939?

b) In which year was total production lowest? What can you note about the number of unemployed in this year from the line graph on the previous page?

Total Production (Gross National Product) in Canada, 1926-1939

Year	Total Production (billions of dollars)
1926	5.1
1927	5.6
1928	6.1
1929	6.1
1930	5.7
1931	4.7
1932	3.8
1933	3.5
1934	4.0
1935	4.3
1936	4.6
1937	5.2
1938	5.3
1939	5.6

Source: Statistics Canada, Cat. 13-531, 13-201.

ACTIVITIES

Check Your Understanding

1. Add these new terms to your *Factfile*.

relief	Canadian Radio Broadcasting Commission (CRBC)
"pogey"	Canadian Broadcasting Corporation (CBC)
Bennett buggy	Bennett's New Deal
relief camps	Co-operative Commonwealth Federation (CCF)
On to Ottawa Trek	Social Credit party
"five-cent piece" speech	Union Nationale
	welfare state

2. Which regions of Canada were hardest hit by the Depression? Provide evidence for your answers.

3. a) Why were relief vouchers for food and rent given out during the Depression instead of cash?
   b) Do you think vouchers were a good or bad idea? Why?

4. a) Many forms of entertainment in the 1930s were "escapist." Define escapism and give examples.

b) Why did people choose these forms of entertainment during the Depression?

5. a) What measures did R.B. Bennett take to combat the Depression?
   b) How effective were these measures?

Confirm Your Learning

6. Imagine that your family's income dropped suddenly because the wage earner was unemployed. Make a list of the possessions you would sell to raise money. Rank the items in order from those you would be most willing to sell to those you would be least willing to sell. How do you think your situation would compare with a family in the 1930s?

7. Use an organizer to compare popular forms of entertainment today with the entertainment of the 1930s. How do you think people will describe this decade 50 years from now?

8. The Great Depression was a turning point in Canadian history. Make a list of present government agencies and services that were not available for Canadians in 1930.

9. Search out other photographs of life during the 1930s. Organize and display the photographs with captions to create your own photo essay on life during the Depression.

10. Imagine you are a family of five on relief in 1932. You are given $6.93 a week. Suppose you can spend $3.00 of that on food. Refer to the list of typical prices for food items on page 175. Buy food for a week from this list with your $3.00. Are you able to buy enough food to feed your family?

Challenge Your Mind

11. Debate one of the following statements.
    a) Any person who is unemployed and receiving relief should be required to work at some project, such as sweeping the streets, to earn the relief money.
    b) The government is expected to provide too many services for Canadians today. People should not expect the government to look after them from the cradle to the grave. People should care for themselves.
    c) Kids today have got it too easy. If they had lived through the Depression, they would have known hard times but would be better for it.

12. Write a human-interest story based on a photograph in this unit or create an illustration of your own to describe your feelings about the Depression.

13. Do some research to gather information on how the rich lived in Canada during the 1930s. Include facts on automobiles, holidays, clothing styles, etc. Write a report or create a bulletin board display on "How the Other Half Lived."

14. a) The jobless rate in Canada fluctuates from year to year and from region to region. Do some research to discover how many people are unemployed in Canada today. Compare this number with the number of jobless people in Canada in 1933.

b) What are the causes of unemployment today? Which regions suffer most? Is there a difference between the unemployment problem today and the one during the Depression?

c) What measures are taken to deal with unemployment?

15. In the spring of 1935, thousands of men left relief camps in the West and headed out on a protest demonstration to Ottawa. Do some research on this On to Ottawa Trek. What were the demands of the protesters? Find out what happened when the marchers confronted the police in Regina. What was the outcome of the trek?

16. A famous author, Caroline Bird, said that everybody who lived through the Depression carried a permanent invisible scar on their minds. What she meant is illustrated in the comment of a teenager who lived through the Depression:

I would never again like to live through a depression. It makes a person want to cry remembering how horrible life was back then. My parents had to work so hard and they suffered a great deal. Me, I never buy a thing on credit. I always wait until I can afford to pay for everything in cash. We hang on to our money because in 1929 everyone was in the stock market and everybody lost. I want to have some money to put away for a rainy day.

Do you think all survivors of the Depression would feel the same way? Why or why not? Would their children and grandchildren feel the same? Explain your views.

Canada and World War II

1939–1945

TIMELINE

1933 — Hitler becomes Germany's Chancellor

1939 — Outbreak of World War II

1940 — Hitler moves into France; evacuation at Dunkirk
The Blitz begins

1941 — Germany invades the USSR
Japanese attack Pearl Harbor
United States joins the war

1942 — Conscription plebiscite
Internment of Japanese Canadians
Dieppe raid
Hitler decides on the "Final Solution"

1943 — Soviets gradually push Germans back

1944 — D-Day
Liberation of Europe begins
Conscription crisis

1945 — Germany surrenders on VE Day
Death of Hitler
Atomic bombs dropped on Japan
Japan surrenders

If you had been living in Canada in 1939, this newspaper headline would have greeted you at breakfast on Monday, 11 September.

Ten days earlier, the German leader Adolf Hitler had launched an all out attack on Poland. Britain and France demanded the withdrawal of German forces. When Hitler refused, Britain and France declared war on Germany on 3 September. World War II had begun. One week later, Canada declared war on Germany. Canada would stand with Britain and France in the fight against Hitler.

Newspapers were soon filled with pictures of the horrors of modern war. There were pictures of bombed cities, crowds of homeless people, and refugees flooding the roads trying to flee from the enemy. Poland was just the first of many countries to be attacked. For the next six years, the lives of people all over the world were dominated by this war. It was a war in which millions of people would lose their lives.

World War II broke out only 20 years after World War I had ended. The horrors of that first great war were still fresh in the minds of Canadians. Many had lost children, husbands, and other family members. While Canadians again stepped in to make a major contribution to the war, many greeted it with a heavy heart.

LEARNING OUTCOMES

By the end of this unit, you will be able to:

- analyze why World War II occurred
- evaluate the role of Adolf Hitler in causing the war
- recognize anti-Semitism and the horrors of the Holocaust
- describe the major events of the war
- demonstrate Canada's contribution to the war
- evaluate the effects of the war on Canadians at home
- assess the treatment of Japanese, German, Italian, and Jewish people in Canada during the war
- practise effective debating skills
- use maps as visual organizers of information
- recognize and analyze bias in propaganda

KEY THEMES

Social Issues

- internment of Japanese Canadians
- conscription issue
- anti-Semitism and the Nazi Death Camps
- dropping of the atomic bomb on Japanese cities
- changes in the role of women
- wartime propaganda

The Economy

- economic crisis in Germany
- wartime economic boom in Canada
- women in the workforce

French-English Relations

- conscription issue
- treatment and training of French Canadian soldiers

Canadian-American Relations

- United States enters the war on the side of the Allies in 1941
- wartime trade between Canada and the United States

Canada and the World

- Allies' reactions to Nazi advances
- contribution of Canadian troops, navy, and airforce in World War II
- Canada emerges as an important middle power

National Growth and Identity

- economic and industrial development
- Canada establishes itself as an important middle power

Regional Development

- Maritime provinces are major shipping and naval centre
- industrial and agricultural development across the country

Citizenship, Government, and Law

- government control over the economy
- wage and price controls
- leadership of Mackenzie King as prime minister

Technological Change

- radar, medical advances, missiles
- development of the atomic bomb

The Arts

- Canadian war art
- posters
- literature about the war (diaries, memoirs, fiction, etc.)

CHAPTER 12

The Rise of the Nazi Dictator

A Wartime Diary

On 4 August 1944, Nazi soldiers burst into an attic over a warehouse in Amsterdam. An informer had told them that eight Jewish people were hiding there. The Nazis found the Frank family and four other Jews. They had hidden in these cramped quarters for two years. While searching the attic, the sergeant picked up Mr. Frank's briefcase and asked if there were any jewels in it. Mr. Frank said that it contained only papers. Disappointed, the Nazi soldier threw the papers onto the floor. The little group that had spent 25 months in that attic was sent off to concentration camps.

However, there remained on the floor of the attic the diary of a 13-year-old girl, Anne Frank. All the time she and her family were in hiding, Anne had been describing the isolation and constant fear in which they lived. Though Anne died at the age of 15 in a concentration camp, her diary was later discovered and published. It is the remarkable story of one young Jewish girl and her will to survive the Nazi persecutions. The following two passages from her diary tell part of Anne's ordeal.

Anne Frank

20 June 1942

After May 1940 good times rapidly fled; first the war, then the surrender of Holland, followed by the arrival of the Germans which is when the suffering of us Jews really began. Anti-Jewish decrees followed each other in quick succession. Jews must wear a yellow star, Jews must hand in their bicycles, Jews are banned from trains and are forbidden to drive. Jews are only allowed to do their shopping between 3 and 5 o'clock, and then only in shops that bear the placard 'Jewish shop.' Jews must be indoors by 8 o'clock and cannot even sit in their own gardens after that hour. Jews are forbidden to enter theatres, cinemas, and other places of entertainment. Jews may not take part in public sports. Swimming baths, tennis courts, hockey fields and other sports grounds were also prohibited to them. Jews must go to Jewish school and many more restrictions of a similar kind.

9 October 1942

Our many Jewish friends are being taken away by the dozen. These people are treated by the SS [Nazi secret police] without a shred of decency, being loaded into cattle trucks and sent to Westerbork, the big Jewish camp. Westerbork sounds terrible: only one washing cubicle for a hundred people and not nearly enough lavatories... It is impossible to escape; most of the people in the camp are branded by their shaved heads... We assume that most of them are murdered. The English radio speaks of their being gassed.

Anne Frank was just one of the 6 million Jews who died in the horrible concentration camps of Nazi Germany. Another 24 million soldiers and civilians from all sides—Canadian, British, French, Soviet, Dutch, German, Italian, Japanese, American, and others—brought the staggering loss to 30 million casualties in World War II. What caused the world to erupt into the second major conflict of this century?

Case Study: Germany After World War I

To analyze why World War II broke out, it helps to understand the conditions in Germany between 1918 and 1932. Why did the German people turn to the Nazi leader, Adolf Hitler? Why were Jewish people, such as Anne Frank, so harshly treated? With the following case study, you can analyze key problems that contributed to the outbreak of the war.

1 Economic Problems: Inflation

Instead of taxing its people to finance World War I, Germany had borrowed the money. As a result, the country was burdened with a huge debt. To pay off this debt, the German government simply printed more paper money. The money was printed even though Germany's industry, agriculture, and commerce were not ex-

There were often long line-ups outside grocery stores in Germany in 1923. Prices had soared and many goods were scarce.

panding. Instead of going into the economy, all of the country's wealth was going to pay off the debt and the heavy reparations after World War I. The rapid printing of marks (the basic unit of German currency) was not supported by real economic value, and this caused severe inflation. Prices for goods and services rose astronomically.

In the spring of 1922, about 300 marks could buy an American dollar. By early 1923, it took 50 000 marks to buy an American dollar. Soon Germans needed billions of marks to pay for a postage stamp. It took a shopping bag full of marks to pay the fare on a streetcar. Wages were often carried home in wheelbarrows full of almost worthless paper money. A lifetime's savings could become valueless in a matter of weeks. People began to barter or trade goods and services rather than use money. Workers were paid daily and spent their pay at once while it was still worth something. People who ordered a drink in a café paid for it when it arrived. If they left it until later, the price might have gone up. As the paper money dropped in value, the government kept 300 paper mills working 24 hours a day to churn out more currency.

1. Define inflation.
2. What was the major economic problem Germany faced after the war and why did it arise?
3. How did the German government attempt to solve the economic crisis?
4. Who would suffer the most from inflation? Why?
5. Who might benefit from the inflation? Why?

2 Political Instability

After World War I, Germany had more than a dozen major political parties. No party was strong enough to undertake the huge task of rebuilding a war-torn country. The main political parties fell into three general groups as shown in the chart on the next page.

Advertisements from a Berlin paper for Schmidt's Delikatessen		
	1918 Prices	**1923 Prices**
Cabbage	4.50 marks per kg	13 million marks per kg
Dill Pickles	2.80 marks per kg	12.7 million marks per kg
Wieners	6.60 marks per kg	15.4 million marks per kg

Communists	Social Democrats	National Socialists (Nazis)
Beliefs:	**Beliefs:**	**Beliefs:**
• government should be run by councils of workers • industries and agriculture should be owned by the government rather than private individuals • the power of the military should be reduced • workers should be powerful and protected	• government should be run by elected representatives from all parties • a few key industries, such as railroads, should be owned by the government • the terms of the Treaty of Versailles, which limited the army to 100 000, should be honoured • the Constitution must guarantee the rights of minorities and workers • there should be freedom of worship and freedom of the press	• government should be run by the army and the wealthy • industry should be privately owned • power of the military should be increased • democratic government should be outlawed • activities of Jews and foreigners should be severely restricted (because the Nazis believed these two groups were responsible for Germany's economic problems)
Supporters:	**Supporters:**	**Supporters:**
• factory and agricultural workers • some teachers and professors • pacifists (those opposed to any form of fighting)	• some workers • some professional and business people • Roman Catholics	• the army • unemployed people • big business • land owners • aristocrats

1. What were the positions of the major political parties in Germany toward:
   a) the military
   b) industry
   c) who should run the government?
2. Which party or parties would likely support the Treaty of Versailles?
3. Why would owners of big businesses and the wealthy be willing to support the **National Socialists** and Hitler?
4. If you were a Jewish citizen living in Germany, which political party would you support? Why?

3 The Treaty of Versailles

The people of Germany were humiliated by the harsh terms of the Treaty of Versailles.

They considered the new boundaries and reparation payments to be unjust. The War Guilt Clause was seen as a stain on the honour of all Germans. On the morning of the Treaty's signing, the *Deutsche Zeitung* (German News) called for vengeance.

Vengeance!

Today in Versailles the disgraceful Treaty is being signed. Do not forget it! The German people will, with unceasing labour, press forward to reconquer the place among the nations to which we are entitled! Then will come vengeance for the shame of 1919!

1. Review the main terms of the Treaty of Versailles listed under A below. Decide which groups of people listed under B would be opposed to each term. Why?

A

a) The French took rich prizes of German territory west of the Rhine—the Saar Valley with its coal fields and the provinces of Alsace and Lorraine.

b) The German army was limited to 100 000. Germany could have no submarines, aircraft, or heavy artillery.

c) Germany was required to pay $5 billion in reparations.

d) Germany's colonies were parcelled out to France, Britain, and Japan.

e) Germany had to admit that it was totally to blame for all the losses and damages of the war (War Guilt Clause).

B

i) The military
ii) Big business owners
iii) The middle class
iv) Working people
v) All German people
vi) Nationalists

2. To which groups listed under B was Hitler appealing when he promised to:
a) rearm Germany
b) get revenge on Germany's enemies
c) cancel the Treaty of Versailles
d) expand the army
e) restore German honour
f) win back by force all German territory?

4 Depression and Unemployment

In the United States in 1929, the stock market crashed. This marked the beginning of a worldwide depression. Americans could no longer afford to buy German manufactured goods. American banks could no longer lend money to the German government and German businesses to rebuild after World War I. Many German businesses went bankrupt and people lost their jobs. Germany had very little money and could not make its reparation payments. The shock waves of the depression hit Germany full force.

Germans who still had jobs saw their scanty wages fall steadily from month to month. Unemployed miners spent the winter in unheated rooms. Sometimes, in desperation, they broke through fences at the mines to steal a few lumps of coal. In the woods around Berlin, families pitched tents or lived in packing crates. They couldn't afford to pay rents in the city. In the country, farmers stood with loaded rifles to protect their crops and gardens. Starving people came from the city to try to scrounge food for their families. Many people were reduced to begging in the streets.

News item: **Berlin 1932**

Unemployment has now reached 6 million, half of Germany's labour force! People are deliberately seeking arrest in order to receive free food in

Hitler saw his chance. To Germans who were bitter about inflation and economic troubles, Hitler and the Nazi party said:

Believe me, our misery will increase! The government itself is the biggest swindler and crook. People are starving on millions of marks! We will no longer submit! We want a dictatorship.

1. Why would the American depression have an effect on the German economy?
2. What could Hitler and the Nazis promise the unemployed to win them over to the Nazi party?
3. What did Hitler say was the cause of Germany's economic problems? What did Hitler promise to do about the situation?

Hitler Comes to Power

In 1919, Adolf Hitler joined a small political group that was to become the Nazi party. Within a short time, he took over leadership of the party and began to shape it to reflect his own ideas.

Hitler promised the German people he would get back the land lost during World War I. He promised to restore Germany to world leadership. He pronounced that Aryans (Caucasians not of Jewish descent and, for Hitler, particularly people of pure German descent) were the **"master race."** He stated that Aryans deserved to rule the world. Based on this belief, Hitler promised to "deal" with the Jews. He blamed the Jewish people for Germany's defeat in World War I and for the economic hard times that followed.

Hitler was obsessed by hatred of Jews (**anti-Semitism**). In the early 1920s, he wrote a book called *Mein Kampf*, meaning "My Struggle." In *Mein Kampf*, Hitler's anti-Semitic views were there for the world to see. He described Jews as "deadly poison" and "vermin."

In Canada in the 1930s, as almost everywhere, there was massive unemployment. In the United States and Britain, millions were unemployed and on relief. In these countries, there appeared to be no easy cure to the economic troubles. But in Germany, Hitler had persuaded millions of people that their problems would be solved if they followed him.

Hitler and the Nazi party gained control of the German parliament in 1933. Hitler's rise to power meant the end of democracy in Germany. Germans pledged absolute obedience to their leader, *der Führer*. Hitler became a **dictator**, outlawing all other po-

Adolf Hitler. What impressions does this photo give you of the German Nazi leader?

litical parties and using force to keep control. Anyone who opposed him was rounded up by secret police. Hitler had set up an armed force within the party called **Stormtroopers** or SA. They forcibly broke up meetings of other political parties. Opponents were thrown into prison or concentration camps.

Newspapers and radio were also strictly controlled by the Nazi party. The German people read and heard only what their leaders wanted them to read and hear. Books containing ideas that did not please Hitler were burned in huge public bonfires. Teachers were required to be members of the Nazi party. Students were recruited to join the **Hitler Youth Movement**, where they could learn Nazi ideas. Priests and clergy who dared to protest Hitler's methods were thrown in prison. Nazi Germany became a **totalitarian state** in which everything was controlled by the government.

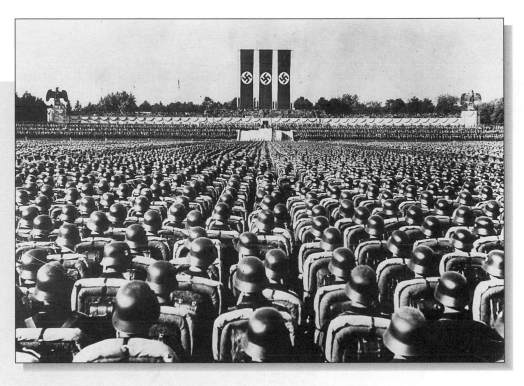

A Nazi rally in Nuremburg, 1937. The swastika symbol is prominent. The colours of the flag were red, white, and black. Red was for Socialism, white for Nationalism, and black the symbol for the struggle of the Aryan victory.

Anti-Semitism

Once in power, Hitler and the Nazi party began the widespread persecution (harsh treatment) of the Jewish people. Jews were banned from all government jobs, as well as jobs in teaching, broadcasting, newspapers, and entertainment. Jews were not allowed to marry non-Jews. Jews were banned from many shops and public buildings. Nazis stood outside Jewish-owned stores and threatened customers who wanted to enter. By 1936, most Jews in Germany found it almost impossible to earn a living. Those who could escaped from Germany in this early period. Among those who left was the famous scientist, Albert Einstein, who later worked on the atomic bomb.

Just before the war broke out, Hitler began a systematic rounding up of Jewish people, placing them in ghettos and concentration camps. When a German embassy official in Paris was shot by a young Jew in November 1938, a brutal attack on German Jews followed. A huge fine was forced on the Jewish population. Seven thousand Jewish shops were looted and 20 000 Jews were arrested. Many were savagely beaten. Later, after the war when Allied troops moved into Germany, the horrors of the concentration camps would become shockingly clear to the world.

An SA guard stands outside a Jewish shop marked by boycott posters.

SOCIETY AND SOCIAL CHANGE

The St. Louis

As life turned worse for Jews in Europe in the late 1930s, thousands attempted to flee from their European homelands. Many of these Jewish refugees had difficulty finding new homes. Countries were alarmed by the flood of Jewish refugees and many did not open their doors. Canada accepted fewer than 4000 Jewish immigrants before the outbreak of the war. On the other hand, the United States accepted 240 000 and Britain 85 000.

Jewish refugees aboard the St. Louis *were refused entry into Latin American countries and Canada.*

In June 1939, the liner ***St. Louis*** arrived off Canada's east coast carrying 907 Jews, including 400 women and children. These refugees had already been denied entrance to Cuba and other Latin American countries. In desperation, they turned to Canada hoping to find a safe haven. The Canadian Immigration Branch of the government refused to allow the passengers on the *St. Louis* to enter Canada. The ship was forced to return to Europe. Many of the Jews on board eventually died in Nazi concentration camps.

1. Canada has not always been open to accepting refugees. Find out more about Canada's immigration policy just before World War II. Why were the Jewish refugees sent back?
2. What is your reaction to the *St. Louis* incident?

The Steps to War

Hitler had promised to return Germany to world power and to take back lands lost by the Treaty of Versailles. One of his first steps was to strengthen the army and the air force. A new German army was created under the slogan, "Today Germany. Tomorrow the world!" Weapons of war started to pour out of German factories. Germany was rearming itself swiftly. Nazi Storm-troopers were wiping out all opposition to the new Nazi regime.

Occupation of the Rhineland

In March 1936, Hitler made his move. German troops marched back into the Rhineland. By the Treaty of Versailles, German troops were forbidden from moving within 50 km of the Rhine River to keep them away from France. But no one stopped the German advance. The Rhineland was Hitler's

Hitler enters Austria triumphant.

test to see if Britain and France would act. Now Hitler knew the answer. This was an important test, because Hitler had plans that went far beyond the Rhineland.

The Takeover of Austria and Czechoslovakia

Hitler wanted all Germans to live within the new German state (the **Reich**). This policy was known as **Anschluss** (union). Hitler himself was an Austrian by birth, so he was very keen to have Austria joined to Germany. In March 1938, Nazi soldiers crossed the frontier into Austria. Hitler argued that Austria should be a part of Germany because many Germans lived there.

Hitler rode in triumph at the head of his army through the streets of Vienna, the capital of Austria. He frightened the Austrians with the threat of a Communist takeover of their country. Only he and the Nazi army could protect them. Without firing a shot, Hitler made Austria part of the German Reich. The other nations of the world did not attempt to stop Hitler from taking Austria because no one wanted to risk another world war.

Czechoslovakia was next on Hitler's list.

Within a short time after seizing Austria, Hitler had a new demand. He wanted the northwestern part of Czechoslovakia known as the Sudetenland. This territory was near the German border and about 3 million German-speaking people lived there. It also contained heavy industry and the main Czech defences.

The Czechs were ready to fight Hitler, but France and Britain were not willing to help them. British Prime Minister Neville Chamberlain and Premier Daladier of France met with Hitler in Munich. In the **Munich Agreement** signed in September 1938, they allowed Germany to have the Sudetenland. Britain and France believed this would save the world from war. Canadian Prime Minister Mackenzie King also supported the Munich Agreement. In June 1937, King had met Hitler in Berlin and was convinced Hitler did not want to start a war. Germany had been treated unjustly after World War I and should be given some concessions.

The Czechs were not consulted in the Munich Agreement. Many were furious about being sold out by their allies. But they were helpless to resist. Though Chamberlain said the Munich Agreement meant "peace in our time," many people disagreed.

Winston Churchill, who was to follow Chamberlain as the British prime minister, called the agreement "appeasement." **Appeasement** means giving in to the demands of a potential enemy. He argued that Hitler should be stopped immediately, at all costs.

Though Hitler had promised at Munich that he would make no new demands for territory, he soon broke that pledge. Six months later, in March 1939, Germany occupied all of Czechoslovakia. Once again, Britain and France did not act. Then, in August of the same year, Germany shocked the world by signing a pact with the Soviet Union. The pact was a shock because Hitler opposed communism and the Communist government in the Soviet Union. But these countries promised that if war came, they would not fight each other. They also secretly agreed to divide Poland between them. Hitler was now free to plan his moves against France and Britain in the west. He no longer had to fear an attack from the Soviet Union on the east.

The Invasion of Poland

Next, Hitler demanded that the Polish Corridor be handed back to Germany. This was the territory awarded to Poland by the Treaty of Versailles. Poland refused. On 1 September 1939, the German army drove over the borders into Poland. The Poles were helpless to defend themselves against the Germans' new style of warfare, called **Blitzkrieg** or "lightning warfare." Blitzkrieg used strategies of surprise, force, boldness, and close co-operation among the air force, tanks, artillery, and infantry.

In the Blitzkrieg, the German Luftwaffe (air force) bombed enemy aircraft on the ground, army barracks, headquarters, bridges, and railways. After the air attacks, the Nazis raced ahead in tanks and armoured cars, moving deep into enemy territory. In the face of this concentrated attack, the Poles were overwhelmed.

The situation was now so dangerous that Britain and France realized they would have to rush to the defence of Poland. There could be no more appeasement. Two days later, on 3 September 1939, Britain and France declared war on Germany. World War II had begun.

Canada Declares War!

Canadians were shocked by the news. There was not the enthusiasm that marked the beginning of World War I, but most Canadians were ready to do what they could to help Britain. However, in September 1939, Canada's entry into the war was not automatic, as it had been in 1914. Canada was no longer a colony bound to follow Britain into warfare. In the years following World War I, Canada had become an independent nation.

Prime Minister Mackenzie King quickly summoned the Canadian Parliament to discuss Canada's involvement in the war. One week later, Canada declared war on Germany. It was a momentous occasion. It was the first time that Canada had declared war on its own behalf. Though Canada was getting ready to fight, it had only about 10 000 soldiers in its armed forces. The Canadian army possessed only 14 tanks, 29 Bren guns, 23 anti-tank rifles, and 5 small mortar guns. The Canadian navy had exactly 10 operational vessels. It would be some time before Canada's armed forces reached an effective size. But by the end of the war, Canada had made a significant contribution in both armaments and battle forces.

Hitler Moves Into France

Within the first four weeks of action, Hitler's modern army crushed the old-fashioned Polish defences. Next, the powerful German forces overran Denmark, Norway, Belgium, and the Netherlands. Then, Hitler

Canadian soldiers march off to war. What was the mood in Canada when war was declared?

turned against France. For the second time in 25 years, German troops poured across the French border.

Thousands of British troops had rushed across the English Channel to help defend France. However, the Germans advanced rapidly and the British and French were trapped. In May 1940, they had to retreat to the seaport town of **Dunkirk** on the French coast. The British hastily collected a fleet of all available boats including pleasure boats and fishing vessels to get their soldiers home. Three hundred thousand soldiers were evacuated safely to Britain, but most of the heavy British war equipment had to be abandoned on the beaches of France. It was a terrible defeat for the Allies. France had fallen in six weeks and Paris was now occupied by the Nazis. A

new French army known as the **Free French**, led by General Charles de Gaulle, was set up in England. The Free French army vowed to continue the fight against the Nazis.

Mussolini, the Italian dictator, at this moment decided to enter the war on the side of Germany. Mussolini and Hitler had signed an agreement in 1936 known as the **Rome-Berlin Axis**. Mussolini had agreed to allow Hitler to take Austria and other territories in northern and central Europe. Hitler had promised to allow Mussolini to take over southern Europe. Now, Mussolini was joining Hitler in the war. Almost all of Europe was in the hands of the Axis powers, Germany and Italy. Only Britain and its Commonwealth allies remained outside their grasp of power.

DEVELOPING SKILLS: USING MAPS AS VISUAL ORGANIZERS

Suppose you need directions to a friend's home for a party. You can ask for verbal directions—whether to go north, south, east, or west, where to turn, or what landmarks to look out for. But if the way is complicated, it will help to have a sketch map. A map is a way of visually presenting or organizing information.

You've just read about Hitler's advances in Europe. How far did Hitler's empire extend by 1939? You could give an accurate picture of the Nazi empire by recording and summarizing information on a map. Every map must have the following four important elements to be complete. Without these, it would be difficult for anyone to use the map.

■ **1.** *Title.*

A map's title should describe the area the map covers and accurately summarize the information it is presenting. If you were describing Hitler's conquests in Europe, why would "Europe, 1935-1939" be a poor title? Why would "Nazi Advancements in Europe, 1935-1939" be a better title?

■ **2.** *Direction.*

Direction is indicated by a compass. Most maps are drawn with north at the top. If north is at the top of the map, then you know south is in the opposite direction, east is to the right, and west is to the left.

Try this quiz. Name three countries located to the west of Germany. Name two countries located to the east of the German border.

■ **3.** *Scale.*

The scale tells distance and size represented on the map compared with distance and size represented on the earth's surface. When you use the scale on a map, you can measure the approximate distance between two places or the rough size of a country.

Look at a political map of Europe. Use the scale to determine the approximate distance from the German-Danish border in the north to the German-Austrian border in the south.

■ **4.** *Key or Legend.*

Information can be placed on maps using symbols. A symbol represents or stands for an idea, person, group, or thing. What symbol could you use on a map to stand for Hitler and the Nazi party? Colours are also often used to represent important information on a map. On a political map, for example, colour can be used to indicate different provinces, states, regions, or countries.

Mapping Nazi Advancements, 1935–1939

1. Start with an outline map of Europe. Give your map a title and be sure that it includes direction and a scale.
2. Locate the borders of Germany in 1935. Label Germany and choose an appropriate colour and symbol to indicate Nazi control of the country. Be sure you identify these in your legend or key.
3. What territory did Hitler take back in 1936? Label that territory on the map, mark out its borders, and record the year of its occupation. Use your colour or symbol to show it is under Nazi control.
4. Which country did Hitler take over in March 1938? Add the name of this country and the date of occupation to the map.
5. Label and date the territory gained by Nazi Germany with the Munich Agreement. What additional territory did Hitler seize six months later in March 1939? Add this information to your map.
6. Indicate the country seized by the armies of the Third Reich in September 1939.
7. As you read through the following chapters, keep your map up-to-date by showing the countries that the Nazis occupied in the rest of Europe.
8. Review your map. Have you included the most important information? People should have a clear picture of Nazi advancements from your map. Exchange your map with a classmate and have your partner check that your map is clear, accurate, and complete.

ACTIVITIES

Check Your Understanding

1. Add these new terms to your *Factfile*.

   National Socialist Party   Reich
   "master race"   Anschluss
   anti-Semitism   Munich Agreement
   dictator   appeasement
   Stormtroopers   Blitzkrieg
   Hitler Youth Movement   Dunkirk
   totalitarian state   Free French
   St. Louis   Rome-Berlin Axis

2. On a timeline, arrange the following steps to war in chronological order.

   Munich Agreement *67*
   Treaty of Versailles *1*
   Hitler demands Sudetenland *6*
   Hitler becomes Chancellor of Germany *2*
   Germany invades Poland *7 8*
   Germany begins to rearm *3*
   Britain and France declare war on Germany *10*
   Hitler invades Austria *4*
   German troops march into the Rhineland *5*
   Germany signs pact with the Soviet Union *9*
   Canada declares war on Germany *11*

3. Decide whether each of the following statements is true or false and explain why.
   a) A dictator depends on force to stay in power.
   b) France and Britain gave in to Hitler at Munich because Germany had promised to pay reparations.
   c) Britain and France approved of Hitler's actions when he seized other countries.
   d) France and Britain declared war on Germany when Austria was taken over.
   e) When Britain declared war on Germany, Canada was also automatically at war.

4. Decide whether each of the following statements is fact or opinion. Explain.
   a) Hitler caused World War II.
   b) Inflation and unemployment were serious problems in Germany in the late 1920s and early 1930s.
   c) Prime Minister Mackenzie King should not have agreed to the appeasement of Germany.
   d) Canada was not ready to enter a war with Germany in 1939.

Confirm Your Learning

5. *On the evening when Hitler was appointed Chancellor, huge crowds joined a torchlight parade. Hundreds of thousands shouted "Heil! Sieg Heil!" as they marched past the Chancellory building. Hitler stood on the balcony taking the*

salute. He must have felt like the hour for which he had been waiting for so long had finally come. That same evening, many other Berliners stayed in their homes, depressed, anxious, and frightened about the future.

   a) Why would hundreds of thousands welcome Hitler as the new leader of Germany?

   b) Explain why Hitler would feel like "the hour for which he had been waiting for so long" had finally come.

   c) Which Berliners would be staying in their homes that night? Why?

6. a) Describe the methods Hitler and the Nazis used to secure power.

   b) Why was influencing the young a vital part of Hitler's plan?

7. a) List the actions mentioned in this chapter that the Nazis took against the Jewish people.

   b) Write the letter "P" beside those actions that would have political consequences. Write the letter "E" beside those that would have economic consequences. Explain your choices.

8. a) Define racism and explain why the Nazi actions were racist.

   b) What fundamental human and civil rights were denied the Jewish people and other non-Aryans?

9. In groups, write a script for the morning news that would be broadcast on Monday, 11 September 1939—the day Canada declared war on Germany. Role play the news broadcast for the class or record it on audiotape. You could include reports from foreign correspondents.

Challenge Your Mind

10. Many people have commented on the power and magnetism Hitler seemed to have. Examine photographs of Hitler and view film footage of him, including some of his speeches. Do you agree that he was a powerful presence? Explain. Describe what you see as his major characteristics based on the visual resources you investigate.

11. Read the following secondary sources.

   The first step was to design an emblem, a party flag, and here Hitler could use his artistic talent. After many attempts he produced a black crooked cross on a red background. It was an ancient symbol known as the swastika.

   Source: From B. J. Elliott, *Hitler and Germany*, 1966.

   In Mein Kampf, *Hitler pretended the swastika flag was his invention. In fact, one of the party members, the dentist Friedrich Krohn, had designed it for a local party group in May 1920.*

   Source: From Joachim Fest, *Hitler*, 1974.

   a) What two interpretations of the swastika's origin are described in the above quotations? How do they disagree?

   b) Can both sources be correct? Explain your answer. Which explanation seems more likely? Why?

   c) Why would Hitler want people to believe that he invented the swastika symbol?

12. The following reasons have been given for why western countries did not act to
stop Hitler before 1939.
    a) No one wanted to go to war.
    b) Britain and France were too weak to fight because of the worldwide depression.
    c) Some people in Britain thought the Treaty of Versailles had been too harsh.
    d) Some people thought these territories rightfully belonged to Germany.
    e) Appeasement was a sacrifice worth making for peace.
    f) Hitler would stop the Communists.
    Discuss the meaning of each statement. Decide which are most reasonable and
    justify your choices.

13. When the French were forced to surrender to the Germans in 1940, Hitler insisted
that the surrender be signed in the same railway carriage that had been used when
the Germans surrendered in 1918. Suggest Hitler's reasons for insisting on this.

14. Write a journal entry from the point of view of one of the following.
    a) Adolf Hitler shortly after one of the major advances of his troops in Europe
    b) a member of a Jewish family hiding from the Nazis
    c) a German teen recruited into the Hitler Youth Movement
    d) a Canadian teen after hearing a news broadcast about Hitler's invasions of
       European nations and Canada's declaration of war

CHAPTER 13

The War in Europe and the Pacific

THE BATTLE OF BRITAIN BEGINS!

Before German troops could invade Britain, Hitler had to destroy the Royal Air Force. In August 1940, the Luftwaffe (German airforce) began attacking southern England and London. Night after night, wave upon wave of bombers struck at British targets. The Nazis called it a war of terror. The British called it "the **Blitz**," short for Blitzkrieg (lightning warfare).

The nightly attacks were designed to destroy the British will to resist.

Though thousands were killed and houses and property were destroyed, the British refused to give up. Londoners grew used to spending their nights in air raid shelters or underground subway stations. To the amazement of all, the greatly outnumbered Royal Air Force shot almost 3000 Nazi planes out of the skies in two months. Speaking of the defence of the country provided by the Royal Air Force, Prime Minister Churchill said, "Never was so much owed by so many to so few." The Germans temporarily gave up the idea of trying to bomb Britain out of the war.

As the war went on, air attacks escalated and cities on both sides were bombed. Aircraft most often attacked in the cover of darkness. Canadian artist Miller Brittain captures the haunting image of searchlights scanning the skies for the deadly planes in this painting entitled *Night Target, Germany*.

The War Accelerates

The **Battle of Britain**, fought from August to October 1940, marked the beginning of the long struggle against the Nazi aggression in Europe which was to continue until 1945. Canadian pilots in the Royal Canadian Air Force fought alongside other Allied pilots in the air. Canadian troops also played a major role in the battles at Dieppe, in the Italian campaign, and on the beaches of Normandy on D-Day. At sea, Canadian ships helped to ensure that vital supplies crossed the Atlantic. Canadian troops were instrumental in liberating the Netherlands from the Nazis, an event still remembered by the people of the Netherlands to this day.

Once again, though Canada started with only a small fighting force, Canadians made a major contribution to the war effort and gained international prestige. You will read more about Canada's role as you follow the events of World War II outlined below.

1941 Germany Advances on the Soviet Union

In June 1941, Hitler decided he could not defeat Britain from the air, so he turned eastward. He attacked his own ally, the Soviet Union (USSR). Hitler wanted to seize the natural resources of that vast country—grain, coal, iron, and oil. Three million German troops moved into the Soviet Union. At first, German armies scored tremendous successes. In just three months they reached the outskirts of Moscow and Leningrad, the two most important Soviet cities. But the Soviet Union would soon prove to be too much for Hitler's armies.

1941 Attack on Pearl Harbor—The United States Enters the War

From 1939 to 1941, the United States remained neutral. It was not directly involved in the fighting. After the fall of France, President Roosevelt urged his country to become a great producer of ammunition to help protect democracy. The Americans introduced a lend-lease policy. By this policy, the Allies did not need to pay for war supplies from the United States until later. The reason for the American generosity was that the president considered the defence of Britain important to the security of the United States.

Meanwhile, Hitler's ally in the East, Japan, had been expanding. Japan had signed an agreement with Germany in 1936 and become one of the Axis Powers. When war began, Japan saw a

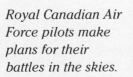

Royal Canadian Air Force pilots make plans for their battles in the skies.

chance to attack British and other colonies in the Pacific. On 7 December 1941, Japanese planes came without warning and bombed the American naval base at **Pearl Harbor**, Hawaii. The attack left half the American fleet crippled or sunk. Americans were shocked.

The attack brought the United States into the war. On 8 December 1941, the United States declared war on Japan. Three days later Germany and Italy, Japan's allies, also declared war on the United States. It was now truly a world war.

1942 Axis Powers Gain Momentum

By 1942, the Japanese had engulfed all of the Philippines. A Canadian force had been captured at Hong Kong, and the British colonies at Singapore, Malaya, Burma, and southeast Asia were controlled by the Japanese.

It seemed that victory for the Axis powers was close at hand. In Europe, Hitler's troops occupied almost every capital from Oslo in Norway to Athens in Greece. In the Pacific, Japan had a stranglehold on southeast Asia. It appeared just a matter of time before Japan and Germany took control of the remaining areas.

Hitler was now in a position to proclaim to his followers that the Nazi empire in Europe would last for a thousand years. The Germans, according to their Führer, were destined to be the "master race." Nazi leaders were already sentencing millions of Europeans, mostly Jews, to slave labour and concentration camps.

1942 Canadians and the Dieppe Raid

By August 1942, the Allies had a plan. It was to send Canadian and British troops, restless for action, to test the German forces along the French coast at Dieppe. This would relieve some of the German pressure on the Soviets in the east.

The raid at **Dieppe** was planned to be a quick punch at the German stronghold. The Allies hoped to worry the Nazis, gather crucial information about their coastal defences, and then return safely to Britain. Dieppe would be a dress rehearsal for the full-scale Allied invasion of Europe to follow.

The dead lay scattered on the beach at Dieppe. Two-thirds of the attacking force were killed, wounded, or captured—many of them Canadians. The raid was a disaster.

At 4:50 on the morning of 19 August 1942, 5000 Canadians began to land on the beaches at Dieppe. However, the German forces were ready for the attack. German artillery on the cliffs mowed down the soldiers as they left the landing crafts and tried to run for cover. By early afternoon, nearly 900 of the Canadian troops were dead or dying. Over 1000 were wounded. Nineteen hundred prisoners of war were taken by the Germans and only 2200 of those who landed that morning returned to Britain.

A French Canadian who fought with the Fusiliers Mont-Royal recalled his experience at Dieppe:

... the wounded and dead lay scattered on the beach. Some of the wounded were trying to swim out to the boats [and] many were bleeding heavily, reddening the water around them. [Once ashore] ... mortar bombs are bursting on the shingle and making little clouds which seem to punctuate the deafening din... close to me badly mutilated bodies lie here and there. The wounded scream, the blood flows from their wounds... For myself, I am absolutely astounded to have reached the shelter of a building. I was certain that my last hour had arrived.

There was a horrible loss of life at Dieppe. It was a major disaster. Today, people still argue over whether the raid had been properly planned. Could some of the terrible losses have been avoided? Was Dieppe another Passchendaele?

Important military lessons were learned, however. When the decisive invasion of Europe finally came two years later, the Allies remembered their Dieppe experience. This time, fire support by sea and air would be overwhelming, and a way would be found to land large numbers of troops and equipment safely on the beaches of France.

1942 The Convoy System

In 1942, the island of Britain was in deadly danger. Fifty million people could not live or fight without food and supplies from outside. Britain depended on a life line of supplies from North America. It was the job of Britain's navy and air division to make sure the precious cargoes got through safely.

This was not an easy task. German U-boats (submarines)

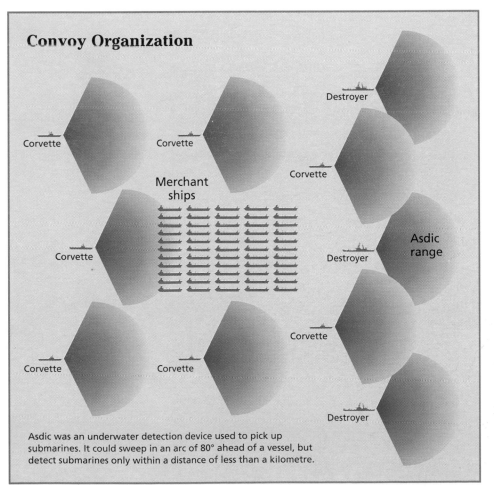

Convoy Organization

Corvette

Corvette

Destroyer

Corvette

Merchant ships

Corvette

Destroyer

Asdic range

Corvette

Corvette

Corvette

Corvette

Destroyer

Asdic was an underwater detection device used to pick up submarines. It could sweep in an arc of 80° ahead of a vessel, but detect submarines only within a distance of less than a kilometre.

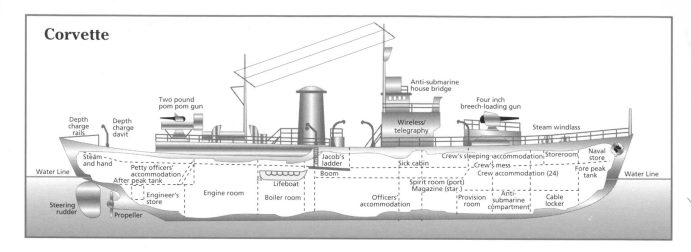

Corvette

Two pound pom pom gun

Anti-submarine house bridge

Four inch breech-loading gun

Depth charge rails

Depth charge davit

Wireless/ telegraphy

Steam windlass

Steam and hand

Jacob's ladder

Crew's sleeping accommodation

Storeroom

Naval store

Water Line

Petty officers' accommodation

Sick cabin

Crew's mess

Fore peak tank

Water Line

After peak tank

Boom

Crew accommodation (24)

Engineer's store

Engine room

Lifeboat

Boiler room

Spirit room (port) Magazine (star.)

Officers' accommodation

Provision room

Anti-submarine compartment

Cable locker

Steering rudder

Propeller

lurked in the dark waters of the Atlantic Ocean. The submarines blasted helpless merchant ships from the United States and Canada as they steamed toward British ports. Winston Churchill said later, "The only thing that ever really frightened me during the war was the U-boat peril." During the day, the U-boats hid under water. At night they surfaced. The merchant ships were sitting ducks for their attacks. Cargo vessels were being sunk at the rate of 20 a week, and the Germans were busy building eight U-boats for every one they lost.

In response, the Allies improved their antisubmarine measures. The Canadian Navy played an important role in escorting groups of supply ships across the Atlantic. Fifty or sixty supply ships would travel as a group. This was known as the **convoy system**. Most convoys were escorted by three or four corvettes. The corvette was a small, fast naval vessel that accompanied the larger supply ships.

A Canadian who sailed on a corvette describes the role these sailors played.

Convoy duty, that was quite a job. Very much like a cowboy herding his cattle. Keeping them together and keeping the wolves away. Sometimes they would get scattered for one reason or another and we would have to get them back on station. If one got hit, all hell would break loose. Some of the escort ships would be

The cover illustration of Star Weekly *in 1943 shows Allied battleships sinking a Nazi raider. Convoys were getting through.*

dispatched to find the sub. Others were on the lookout for survivors and keeping the convoy together.

Improvements in radar for underwater detection of submarines and the protection provided by patrol aircraft eventually helped to make sure more supply ships got through to Britain. By the end of the war, nearly 800 German U-boats had been sunk.

With an adequate supply of food and ammunition, the Allies could face the Nazis on an equal basis. Events were turning in favour of the Allies. British and American soldiers were on the offensive in the deserts of North Africa. American GIs (enlisted soldiers) advanced against the Japanese, island by island, in the steaming jungles of the Pacific.

1942 The Allies' Bombing Campaign

Meanwhile, the systematic bombing of cities in Germany by the Allies had begun. At first, the aim was to destroy German industries, railways, highways, bridges, and oil refineries. However in 1942, Allied air chiefs decided to try to destroy the German fighting spirit by mercilessly pounding cities from the air. On the night of 30 May, a thousand bombers raided the city of Cologne. From 24 to 31 July, Hamburg was attacked eight times. Sixty percent of that city was destroyed by fire bombs and 80 000 civilians were killed. Later in the war cities such as Dresden and Berlin were subjected to wave upon wave of British and American bombers. However, the bombing did not destroy the German will to continue fighting.

1943 Canadians and the Italian Campaign

In 1943, Canadian, American, and British troops advanced on Italy. Their aim was to stop German forces from escaping into that country. Canadian troops were sent to Sicily, the island at the southern tip of Italy. They surprised the Italian forces and took the island easily.

Next, they pushed up into the Italian mainland. There, the battles were much tougher. German forces had established positions throughout the mainland. The Allied forces pushed toward Rome. In the **Battle of Ortona**, an Edmonton regiment succeeded in defeating a first-class German force, but the losses were heavy. Canadian forces continued to hammer away at the German

Before and after photos of a bombed German city.

defences. Eventually, in June 1944, the Allies took Rome. Canadian forces stayed in Italy until early 1945.

1943 The Battle at Stalingrad

Towards the end of 1942, the Nazis had fought a savage battle to gain control over the city of Stalingrad in the Soviet Union. Stalingrad, now called Volgograd, was an important industrial city which controlled rich oil fields. Freezing temperatures to −38°C took a toll on the German troops. Hitler refused to allow a retreat, so German troops fought on during a bitterly cold winter.

By Christmas, the German army was cooking its horses for food. By January 1943, two vast Soviet armies had completely surrounded and trapped more than 250 000 Germans. In February 1943, the German commander disobeyed Hitler and surrendered to the Soviets. Only 91 000 Germans had survived.

Many said that the Soviet victory in the **Battle of Stalingrad** was the turning point of the war. This was the farthest point of the Nazi advance into the Soviet Union. It was the greatest defeat Germany had yet suffered. The Soviets now started to push the Germans back toward Berlin.

1944 D-Day— Day of Deliverance

"OK, we'll go!" With these words, General Eisenhower, commander-in-chief of the Allied Forces, announced the beginning of the long-awaited invasion of Europe. Since the disaster at Dieppe, the Allies had been carefully planning. This time they would be ready. The Normandy

German survivors of an Allied bombing attack. Civilians suffered on both sides as the bombings escalated.

beaches of northern France were selected as the site of the invasion. Normandy was close to Britain and the invading army, supply ships, and reinforcements would not have far to travel.

A huge army gathered in the south of England. American troops numbering 1.25 million joined a similar number of British and Commonwealth troops, including 30 000 Canadians. Four thousand landing craft, 700 war ships, and 11 000 planes were ready.

The Germans had 60 divisions in northern France and the Netherlands under the command of Field Marshall Rommel. In the spring of 1944, Allied bombers started attacking and destroying Nazi military sites in northern France. The idea was to soften the enemy defences.

D-Day was fixed for 5 June 1944, but had to be postponed because of bad weather.

Troops battle their way from landing ships to the beaches of Normandy on D-Day, 6 June 1944.

At 2:00 a.m. on 6 June, paratroopers were dropped to protect the landing forces. Seventy-five minutes later, 2000 bombers began to pound the German defences on the beaches. At 5:30 a.m., the air raids were joined by the guns of the Allied warships. Then at precisely 6:30 a.m., the first waves of Canadian, British, and American troops poured onto the beaches of France.

The Canadians landed at Juno Beach. They faced underwater obstacles, land mines, barbed wire, and heavy machine-gun fire from the Germans. But this time, the invaders kept coming. Within a week, the Allies had 300 000 troops safely on shore. Within a month, 1 million Allies had landed with 200 000 military vehicles. Though the Nazi forces fought hard, Hitler was now caught with war on two fronts, east and west.

This is what Anne Frank wrote in her diary on 6 June 1944.

'This is D-Day,' came the announcement over the British Radio and quite rightly, 'This is the day'. The invasion has begun! It seems too wonderful, too much like a fairy tale. Could we be granted victory this year, 1944?

I have the feeling that friends are approaching. We have been oppressed by those terrible Germans for so long that the thought of friends and delivery fills us with confidence!

SCIENCE AND TECHNOLOGY

Technology and War

Scientists were as important in World War II as soldiers. Both Allied and Nazi researchers were applying scientific techniques to try to win the war.

Radar

The British made important advances in the development and use of radar during the war. Radar uses electromagnetic waves reflected from ships, aircraft, coasts, and other objects. These electromagnetic waves are beamed out, reflected from the target, and picked up by the radar unit. The signals are then converted into images on the radar screen. Radar provided an early warning system of approaching hostile aircraft and ships. After 1943, radar was mounted in Allied planes. The reflected radio waves produced a map-like image of the target below. This made it possible to carry out strategic bombing in darkness and heavy clouds.

Medicine

Great advances were made in medical technology. Improved surgical and medical techniques, such as the invention of the kidney machine, helped to save the lives of wounded soldiers. New drugs were discovered to fight such diseases as malaria. To the troops fighting in the jungles of the Pacific, malaria was a constant threat.

Code-breaking and Camp X

Code-breakers, spies, and sabotage experts were key players in the war. **Camp X**, on the shores of Lake Ontario near Oshawa, was a top-secret training post for many of these experts. Camp X was directed by a Canadian, William Stephenson, whose code name was "Intrepid." At Camp X, technicians provided secret agents with false passports and other documents for use behind enemy lines. Costume experts produced European-style wartime clothing, eyeglasses, soap and toothpaste, and battered suitcases. In case of arrest or interrogation, everything an agent carried had to look right to enemy eyes.

Jets and Rockets

Hitler's scientists developed the first jet airplane that could fly at speeds faster than propeller-driven aircraft. These would have given Germany air superiority if they had been used as fighter planes. But Hitler's demand that the jet plane be adapted for bombing held up production until late 1944.

Nazi scientists were also busy developing two terrifying "vengeance" weapons. The first, the **V-1**, was a pilotless monoplane that carried an explosive warhead. Almost 10 000 were fired at British cities in late 1944. They were nicknamed "buzz-bombs" by the British because of the noise they made.

The **V-2** rocket was even more deadly. It flew at supersonic speed and gave no warning or opportunity for defence. British Intelligence was able to discover and bomb the launching sites, delaying the program for several months.

A V-2 rocket blasts off in northeast Germany. These remote controlled rockets travelled at speeds faster than sound and were almost undetectable.

Wernher von Braun was the German rocket scientist who developed the V-2. After the war, he surrendered to the Americans. He eventually worked for the Americans in the development of intercontinental ballistic missiles and spacecraft for NASA.

The Atomic Bomb

American and German scientists were both working on top-secret projects to produce an atomic bomb. Robert Oppenheimer led a group of American and Allied scientists in developing the bomb. It was known as the **Manhattan Project**. Canadian uranium fueled the laboratories of atomic bomb technology in the United States.

The Americans won the desperate race and successfully tested the bomb in New Mexico in July 1945. The United States then dropped two atomic bombs on the Japanese cities of Hiroshima and Nagasaki. The bombs were small by today's standards, but they brought World War II to a sudden end and marked the beginning of the Atomic Age.

1. a) Which of the above scientific advancements do you consider the most positive and long-lasting? Why?
   b) Which were the most negative? Why?
   c) How are these advancements being used today?
2. It has been said that wars encourage technological improvements for society. Do you agree with this statement? Explain your point of view and support it with facts.

Canadian soldiers are surrounded by Dutch civilians as they march in to liberate the Netherlands.

1944-45 The Liberation of Europe Begins

Other Allied forces invaded Europe from the south through Italy and France. These troops marched north to join those who landed at Normandy. Hitler struck back by unleashing his secret weapons, the flying bomb V-1 and the deadly, faster-than-sound rocket V-2, at war-weary Britain. These missiles were aimed at British cities. But as the Allied invading forces swept north through Belgium, they overran the rocket launching sites. As the Nazis retreated from Holland, they flooded the lowlands.

As often happens in war, the innocent civilian population suffered the most. Homes were destroyed and children suffered malnutrition. Until the Allies could bring in food supplies, some Dutch people had nothing to eat but tulip bulbs.

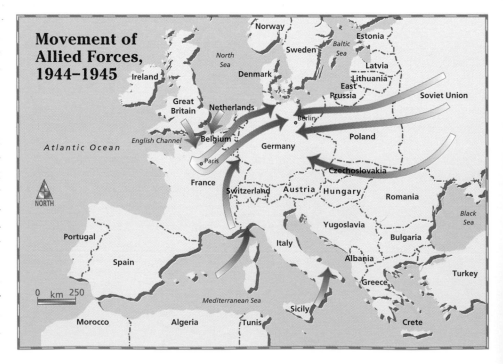

Movement of Allied Forces, 1944–1945

Norway
Sweden
Estonia
Baltic Sea
North Sea
Denmark
Latvia
Lithuania
East Prussia
Soviet Union
Ireland
Great Britain
Netherlands
Berlin
Poland
Atlantic Ocean
English Channel
Belgium
Germany
Paris
Czechoslovakia
France
Switzerland
Austria
Hungary
Romania
Black Sea
Yugoslavia
Bulgaria
Portugal
Italy
Albania
Spain
Turkey
Greece
0 km 250
Mediterranean Sea
Sicily
Crete
Morocco
Algeria
Tunis

NORTH

The troops were not the only ones fighting the war. Thousands of people in Europe joined in the battle against the Axis powers. These civilians were known as "the underground." They struck at the Nazis in any way they could. They blew up railroads, factories, and bridges. They reported on Nazi troop movements and often helped to rescue Allied pilots shot down in German-occupied territory. Without the help of these undercover agents, the liberation (freeing from German occupation) of Europe probably would have taken much longer.

As Allied armies pressed toward Germany, Hitler called upon his soldiers to fight even more fiercely. He warned that whoever gave up a centimetre of German territory while still alive was a traitor. In a last desperate move, Hitler ordered his reserves and 3000 tanks against the Allies in western Europe. Eventually, the Allies broke through and the German retreat began.

Meanwhile, the Soviets were advancing on Berlin from the east. Although the Germans resisted fiercely, they could not hold back the attack that was coming on all sides. By April 1945, Soviet troops were in Berlin. Berliners fought heroically to defend their city, even using veterans and school boys to try and prevent the inevitable. But it was too late. The diary of a captured officer records the plight of Berlin in the last days:

27 April
Continuous attack throughout the night... Telephone cables are shot to pieces. Physical conditions are indescribable. No rest, no relief. No regular food, hardly any bread. We get water from the tunnels and filter it... Masses of damaged vehicles... ambulances with the wounded still in them. Dead people everywhere, many of them frightfully cut up.

The end could not long be delayed. By 8 May 1945, the fighting in Europe was over.

1945 Death of the Dictators

In the last days of the war, Hitler shut himself off from the truth. He had retreated into his bomb-proof bunker deep in the earth below the Chancellory building in Berlin. When Soviet troops were only a few blocks from the bunker, Hitler realized it was all over. He married his companion Eva Braun, and then dictated his will to his secretary. It was said that he had never wanted a war; it was all the fault of the Jews, he believed. He ordered the Germans to fight on and accused his generals of deserting him.

Hitler learned that the Italian dictator, Mussolini, had been captured and killed. Mussolini's body had been strung up by the heels in a public square in Milan. Hitler planned to kill himself rather than suffer the same fate. On 30 April 1945, Hitler shot himself. Eva Braun took poison. Their bodies were carried out of the bunker, soaked in gasoline, and set on fire. For the next several hours, their bodies burned until they were reduced to unrecognizable remains. The next day, Goebbels announced Hitler's death on the radio. He said that Hitler had died a hero's death leading his troops.

1945 VE Day

On 8 May 1945, Nazi Germany ceased to exist. **VE Day**, Victory in Europe Day, had arrived. The long struggle in Europe was over.

Millions of people did not live to enjoy peacetime. One of them was the young Jewish girl, Anne Frank. She had spent much of the war hiding from the Nazis. In August 1944, they caught up with her. She died in the Belsen concentration camp in March 1945, just a month before the camp was liberated by the Allies.

SOCIETY AND SOCIAL CHANGE

The Nazi Death Camps

Months before Hitler died, Allied armies had been making horrifying discoveries in Europe. They had come across the concentration camps. The Nazis had set up concentration camps run by the SS (one of Hitler's special police forces). Most prisoners were there because they were Jews. Others were political prisoners who had dared to speak out against the Nazis.

In 1942, the Nazis had devised one of the most outrageous schemes in human history. They had decided that every Jewish man, woman, and child would be transported to concentration camps and exterminated. Hitler called this the "**final solution**" to the "Jewish problem" in Europe.

Dachau and Bergen-Belsen were typical of the camps in Germany. Here all prisoners were put to work for the Nazi war effort. At least 5 million slaves were working in the German camps. In some places, medical experiments were carried out on helpless human beings who were used as guinea pigs.

Jewish prisoners stand behind barbed wire in a Nazi concentration camp.

At places like Treblinka, Sobibor, and Maidanek in Poland, hanging, shooting, torturing, and overwork were all used to kill Jewish people. At Auschwitz, victims were crowded into gas chambers disguised as showers. The shower rooms were sealed and Zyklon B gas was dropped into the chambers through a small opening in the ceiling. It took from three to fifteen minutes to kill all those confined within the chamber. The bodies were then removed by a special detachment of prisoners. Gold fillings from the teeth of the victims were melted down and made into gold bars. Other valuables such as watches, bracelets, and rings were also deposited in secret bank vaults for future use. Then the corpses were placed in ovens for cremation. Six thousand could be gassed in a day at Auschwitz.

Some of the most moving stories of bravery and heroism have come out of the death camps. At Auschwitz there was an 18-year-old girl, Rosa Robota. Rosa and many of her friends were forced to work for the Nazis in a gunpowder factory. They planned to steal enough gunpowder to blow up the crematorium and the gas chambers. Every day, a dozen girls smuggled out small quantities of explosives hidden in the hems of their dresses. The explosives were buried around the camp until there was a sizeable stockpile.

On the afternoon of 7 October 1944, they successfully blew up Number 3 Crematorium. The Gestapo were enraged by this act of sabotage. An investigation was begun and Rosa and the girls were arrested. Every day Rosa was beaten, and after four days of torture the Nazis hanged her.

Hours before her death Rosa Robota managed to smuggle out a message from the death cell. It read, "Be strong and brave." The message helped give strength to others in Auschwitz who would become victims of Hitler's "final solution."

By the end of the war, Hitler had destroyed over one-third of the Jews in Europe. It is estimated that 6 million people, among whom Anne Frank was one, were put to death. Their only crime was that they were not members of the "master race."

Before the war ended, orders went out from Berlin to destroy the camps to keep them secret. But time ran out. The Allies decided that parts of some camps should be preserved. They would be a permanent reminder of the **Holocaust**, the Nazis' systematic destruction of millions of Jewish people.

1. Define racism. Give some examples. Why is racism harmful?
2. People have described the Holocaust as one of the most horrific examples of racism. Why?
3. a) What is a scapegoat? Describe a situation in which a person or group is made a scapegoat.

   b) Do you think Hitler used the Jewish people as a scapegoat for Germany's problems? Explain.
4. Do you agree that some concentration camps should be preserved as a reminder? Why or why not?
5. What do you think can be done to prevent a disaster such as the Holocaust from ever happening again?

War in the Pacific Continues

On 8 May 1945, the victory in Europe was celebrated. But World War II was not yet over. Fighting was still going on in the Pacific between the Allies and the Japanese.

Since the summer of 1942, the United States had been on the offensive in the Pacific. Their plan was to push the Japanese out of all the islands they had conquered, beginning with Guadalcanal. This was just the first of a long series of bitter battles. One by one the Americans captured islands before finally attacking Japan itself.

In October 1944, American and Japanese navies fought the Battle of Leyte Gulf. It was a decisive naval battle and most of the Japanese fleet was destroyed. But Japan had still not been defeated. Japanese pilots were flying suicide missions against Allied forces. These fliers were known as **kamikaze** pilots. They purposely crashed their planes onto the decks of Allied aircraft carriers and battleships. They hoped the explosives in the plane would seriously damage the ship. To be a *kamikaze* pilot was seen by the Japanese as an honourable way to die. One pilot who made a direct hit could kill many Allied sailors and pilots.

The British and Canadians were also fighting the Japanese in the Pacific. Captured Canadian soldiers were badly treated in prisoner of war camps. Thousands were poorly fed and overworked. Some were tortured and badly beaten. During World War II, prisoners of war were treated with particular brutality on both sides.

The Philippines fell to the Allies in 1945. By then, the American troops knew what a bitter battle they had on their hands. The

Song sung by kamikaze pilots before taking off:

After the battle, our corpses will be strewn

On the green mountain slopes,

Our corpses will rest at the bottom of the sea.

We shall give our lives for His Majesty,

We shall die without regrets.

closer the Americans got to Japan, the more fierce the fighting became. The two islands closest to Japan were Iwo Jima and Okinawa. About 4000 US troops died at Iwo Jima and another 12 000 died at Okinawa. Thousands of Japanese were also killed.

In July 1945, President Truman, who had become president upon Roosevelt's death in April, warned the Japanese to surrender or risk being totally destroyed. The Japanese refused to surrender.

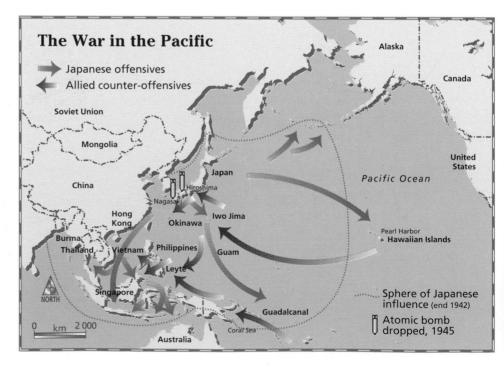

The atomic bomb dropped over Nagasaki, Japan, explodes in a huge mushroom cloud.

The Americans had a powerful new weapon—the atomic bomb. On 6 August 1945, an American bomber appeared in the sky above Hiroshima. The Americans had chosen Hiroshima because it was a major port and an army headquarters. The bomber carried a package about a metre long that would change the nature of war forever. The bomber was the **Enola Gay** and it carried a single atomic bomb. In a few seconds, the city of Hiroshima was covered by a giant mushroom cloud of smoke and dust. A lightning-like flash covered the whole sky. Sixty percent of the city's developed area was destroyed by the blast and the resulting fires. Seventy-one thousand people were dead or missing and 68 000 were injured. Nearly all buildings within 1 km of the blast had been flattened.

The atomic bomb left Nagasaki a wasteland.

All around, I found dead and wounded. Some were bloated and scorched—such an awesome sight, their legs and bodies stripped of clothes and burned with a huge blister. All green vegetation, from grasses to trees, perished in that period.

Still the Japanese did not surrender. Three days later, a second atomic bomb was dropped on the city of Nagasaki. Another 35 000 Japanese were killed and 60 000 were injured. Within a few days, a new kind of death appeared. Survivors developed fever and burns. Others found their hair falling out, their gums bleeding, and their skin just rotting away. They did not know what was happening to their bodies. Today, we know that these illnesses were caused by massive amounts of radiation.

By then, the Japanese were ready to end the war. Officially, Japan surrendered on 2 September 1945 to General Douglas MacArthur, the American commander in the Pacific. The formal surrender took place on the decks of the giant US battleship *Missouri*.

On the slate grey battleship, American admirals and generals, and British, Soviet, French, and Chinese military officials gath-

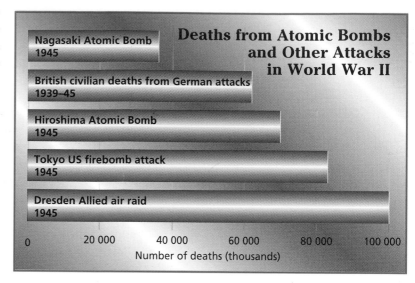

Deaths from Atomic Bombs and Other Attacks in World War II

Nagasaki Atomic Bomb 1945	
British civilian deaths from German attacks 1939–45	
Hiroshima Atomic Bomb 1945	
Tokyo US firebomb attack 1945	
Dresden Allied air raid 1945	

Number of deaths (thousands): 0, 20 000, 40 000, 60 000, 80 000, 100 000

ered for the signing ceremony. The Japanese foreign minister and the chief of the Imperial Staff were ushered on board. After a short speech by General MacArthur, they were led to a table to sign the terms of surrender. With expressionless faces, they put their signatures on the document. General MacArthur then took the fountain pen from his pocket and placed his signature on behalf of the United States. MacArthur hesitated a moment, and then he stepped forward: "Let us pray that peace be now restored to the world..."

World War II was finally over.

The Japanese prepare to formally surrender to General MacArthur aboard the Missouri 2 September 1945. World War II was over.

DEVELOPING SKILLS: DEBATING

Do you ever get involved in heated arguments with your family or friends? Are you determined to convince them that your point of view is right? Then you will enjoy debating. A debate is a formal discussion during which points of view for and against an issue are presented. You probably debate more often than you think, although usually informally. Can you remember your last discussion with your parents over whether or not you should be grounded? What arguments were presented on both sides?

You have probably also seen formal debates between politicians or journalists on television. Members of Parliament in government also debate key issues every day they are in session before any bill is passed. Lawyers use debating skills in the courtroom. But in almost any career or occupation, you can benefit from knowing how to prepare an argument and how to present it effectively.

Most formal debates begin with a presentation of the issue in the form of a clear statement. For example, "The United States was not justified in dropping the atomic bomb on Japan." Two teams are then set up. One team, the "pro" side, presents arguments in favour of the statement. The other team, the "con" side, presents arguments against the statement. Counter-arguments are then heard. The goal is to reach a decision on the issue after careful consideration of all arguments and counter-arguments on both sides.

There are many issues related to World War II that have sparked heated debate over the years. In your class, decide on one of the following issues to debate.

- "The raid on Dieppe was a military disaster that should never have been allowed to happen."
- "The United States was not justified in dropping the atomic bomb on Japan."
- "The decision to attack the Soviet Union was Hitler's biggest mistake."

■ Step I *Preparation*

1. Divide the class into two groups. One group represents the pro side and the other the con side.

2. Research your topic thoroughly. Make sure you separate facts from opinions.
3. Organize your information so that you have reasoned arguments to support your side in the debate. Support your opinions with facts. Use statements by experts on your topic.
4. With your teammates, develop a game plan so that everyone knows his or her role. Remember that every team member must prepare and participate equally.
5. Practise your delivery at home or with other members of your team. Have your teammates suggest ways to improve your presentation.
6. Try to anticipate the arguments of your opponents. Have some counter-arguments prepared.

■ Step II *Process*

7. When you are ready for the debate, choose three people to speak for your side. One student in the class acts as the moderator. The moderator's job is to ensure that the debate flows smoothly and that emotions don't get out of control.
8. The speakers for the two teams then present their arguments in turn, beginning, for example, with the leader of the pro team followed by the leader of the con team and so on. Each speaker adds arguments for his or her side and attempts to counter the arguments of the previous speaker from the opposing side.
9. The concluding speaker for each side should summarize the major arguments for his or her team.

■ Step III *Follow-up*

10. After the debate, have a class vote on which team had the most convincing arguments. Vote based on the debaters' skills, not on whether you agree with their position. Follow up with a class discussion on why the arguments were strong or weak. Class members may suggest arguments that were left out in the debate or refute points raised by either team.

ACTIVITIES

Check Your Understanding

1. Add these new terms to your *Factfile*.

"the Blitz"	V-1 V-2
Battle of Britain	Manhattan Project
Pearl Harbor	VE Day
Dieppe	Hitler's "final solution"
convoy system	Holocaust
Battle of Ortona	*kamikaze* pilots
Battle of Stalingrad	*Enola Gay*
D-Day	
Camp X	

2. Why did the Luftwaffe bomb London and southern England? How successful were these raids?

3. How did the lend-lease policy work? Why was the American president willing to set up a lend-lease policy?

4. How and why did the Germans attack merchant ships in the Atlantic? What measures were used to counter the German threat and how successful were they?

5. a) Why was the attack at Dieppe launched?
    b) What new tactics did the Allies use in the D-Day invasion that were not used at Dieppe?

6. Put the following events related to American involvement in World War II in chronological order on a timeline.

    • the bombing of Hiroshima
    • the attack on Pearl Harbor
    • the lend-lease policy
    • the battle at Iwo Jima
    • the US declares war on Japan
    • the bombing of Nagasaki
    • the Japanese surrender to General MacArthur

Confirm Your Learning

7. Describe the treatment of Jews and others at the Nazi concentration camps. Why were these people treated in this way?

8. What effects did the dropping of the atomic bombs on Hiroshima and Nagasaki have both on the events of the war and on the people of Japan?

9. a) What is meant by the "turning point of a war?"
    b) Where do you think the turning point came in World War II for Hitler? for the Allies? Explain your reasoning.

10. Create a bulletin board display on Canada's involvement in World War II. You could divide your display into Canada's contributions in the air, at sea, and on land. Include photos or illustrations, descriptions, maps, and notes on the major battles and other events. You could also research memoirs or eyewitness reports.

11. "Hitler was too ambitious when he invaded the Soviet Union." Present two arguments to support this statement and two arguments against it. What is your view?

Challenge Your Mind

12. a) The year 1995 marks the 50th anniversary of the end of World War II. What ceremonies and events were held to mark the anniversary? What do you think should be especially remembered about the war? Why?
    b) What do you think should be done to keep the memories of the war always in people's minds?

13. In World War II, many reporters travelled with the Allied armies. Research and write brief articles as "on-the-spot" reporters. Your articles can be organized into a class newspaper on the war years. Here are some events that you can investigate:
    a) the bombing of German cities
    b) life as a crew member on a large bomber
    c) living in a prisoner-of-war camp
    d) the D-Day invasion
    e) sailing with a convoy across the North Atlantic
    f) life as an undercover agent behind enemy lines
    g) the announcement of the German surrender.

14. As in World War I, Canadian artists also went overseas in World War II to record images of the war. Research some Canadian war art. For two pieces of art that most strike you, write your own description of the picture and what it suggests to you.

15. Write a poem or short story about one of the following topics related to World War II or another topic of your choice.
    a) the experiences of Jewish people during the Holocaust
    b) the experience of Canadian soldiers at Dieppe
    c) the experience of Japanese victims of the atomic bombings
    d) the celebrations on VE Day

Total War

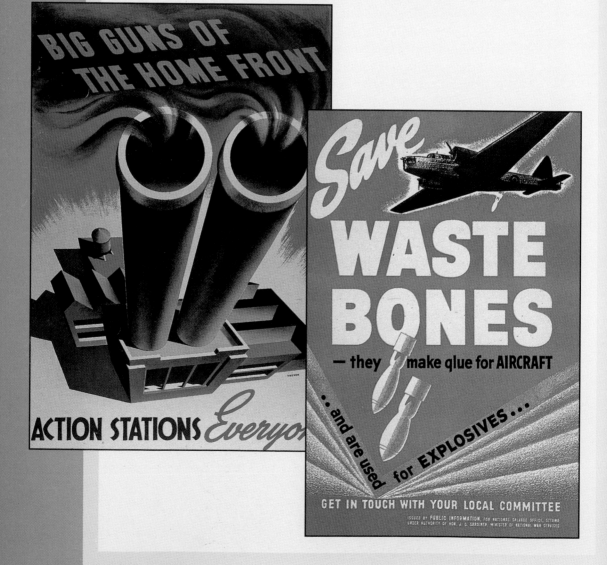

Total War

While war was raging in Europe and the Pacific, important developments were taking place back home in Canada. By 1942, Canada was committed to a policy of "total war." **Total war** meant that all industries, materials, and people were put to work for the war effort. The war affected everyone in Canada.

People were encouraged not to hoard (store away) food, and to stretch their supplies as far as they would go. Some goods became scarce because they were needed for the war. **Ration cards** became necessary for buying gasoline, butter, sugar, meat, tea, and coffee. Rationing means that the government limited the amount a person could buy.

Rubber tires, tubes, and antifreeze were very scarce. A family was limited to 545 litres of gasoline a year for its car. Liquor and silk stockings became luxury items. Silk stockings were hard to find because the silk was needed to make parachutes. For most people in Canada, rationing caused little real hardship. They realized that they were lucky not to be in Europe where the real war was being fought and where the hardship was much worse.

People tried to "do their bit." In many kitchens, bacon fat and bones were saved to provide glycerine for explosives and glue for aircraft. People also gave up buying new aluminum pots and pans and new stoves so that more airplanes could be built. Children became scrap gatherers. Scrap metal, rags, paper, rubber, foil, and wire coat hangers—anything that could be salvaged for the war effort was collected. Posters urged the whole family to help win the war.

One woman recalled how the newspapers were always urging readers to "do their bit" for the war effort.

*The newspapers, they were just **propaganda** sheets. My goodness, on the front pages, war, war, war, and in the insides, how to cook cheaper, how to do Victory Gardens, why we should have car pools, buy Victory Bonds and tell our friends they were traitors if they didn't load up on them too...*

You remember those Sunday sections. They were jammed with war stuff. How to cook cabbage, make cabbage rolls, and then drink the cabbage juice. Did they think we didn't know that stuff, like how to make a dollar do the price of ten? You'd think the idiots in their big offices in Toronto and Ottawa didn't know about the Depression we just went through—ten years of nothing.

Rationing of goods was common during the war years. All necessary resources were directed toward the war effort.

Loyal citizens do not hoard.

RATIONED
SUGAR ½ lb. a week PER PERSON
TEA ½ of the usual PURCHASE
COFFEE ¾ of the USUAL PURCHASE

Canada's Economic Miracle

Before the war, Canada was mainly a supplier of raw materials such as fish, wheat, and metal ores. During the war, Canada became an industrial power. Canadian munitions factories turned out bombs, shells, and bullets for small arms. Shipyards worked full blast building cargo ships, trawlers, mine sweepers, and landing craft. Shipbuilding became the second largest employer in the country. Aircraft manufacturers, such as De Havilland, produced everything from training planes to fighting craft.

In 1942, the government turned all automobile plants over to the production of war vehicles. The plants produced trucks, jeeps, Bren gun carriers, and artillery tractors. It has been calculated that half of the vehicles used by the British in the North African campaign were stamped "Made in Canada." The Nazi general Rommel gave orders to his troops to capture Canadian-made jeeps because they did not get stuck in the sand as the German ones did. Other industries were also switched over to produce war materials.

All kinds of military vehicles, tanks, radar equipment, and penicillin were produced in large amounts. Steel output doubled, while aluminum production increased six times. Canadian farms and fisheries provided astonishingly large amounts of wheat, flour, cheese, canned salmon, fish oil, bacon, ham, canned meat, and dried eggs for Britain and the Allies. Canadian industries also produced engines, synthetic rubber, electronic equipment, and other goods they had not manufactured before. Many of these industries remained an important part of the Canadian economy after the war.

With the commitment to "total war," the government also took control over many aspects of the economy. It geared the country's industries to war production and reduced the number of luxury goods that could be manufactured. It also froze prices, wages, and rents to keep the cost of living down. The government was afraid that with the high demand for scarce goods, prices might skyrocket.

To raise money for the war, income taxes were raised and Canadians were urged to buy Victory Bonds. The government's efforts were largely successful. A great deal of money was raised for the war effort, people had jobs, and the economy was booming.

The Canadian Car and Foundry plant in Amherst, Nova Scotia, was converted to producing aircraft in 1942. Many Canadian plants were turned over to producing munitions and other supplies for the war.

Conscription Again!

Conscription raised its ugly head again in World War II. Prime Minister Mackenzie King was determined that this time conscription would not tear the country apart as it had during World War I.

At the beginning of the war, Mackenzie King had promised that no one would be forced to fight overseas. The Liberals made this pledge primarily to French Canadians. They were determined to avoid the split between French and English Canadians that had occurred in 1917.

However, as the war went on and Hitler's forces scored major victories, the pressure to send more soldiers mounted. Prime Minister King found himself in a corner. Many English Canadians began to call for compulsory military service. Britain had introduced conscription from the start of the war. When the United States entered the war, it too brought in full conscription. Many Canadians whose relatives were voluntarily fighting overseas resented the fact that some Canadians were escaping wartime service.

In 1942, King decided to hold a plebiscite. In a **plebiscite**, all citizens have a direct vote on an issue of major national importance. Canadians were asked if they were in favour of releasing the government from its pledge that it would not introduce conscription for overseas service. Nine of the ten provinces answered with an overwhelming 80 percent "Yes." But 72 percent in the province of Quebec said "No."

English Canadians were reassured by the vote. To satisfy French Canadians, Mackenzie King emphasized that conscription was not yet necessary. He promised that it would be introduced only as a last resort. His famous statement about the policy was purposefully vague. It could be taken favourably by either side. King said, "Not necessarily conscription, but conscription if necessary."

For these Vancouver students, the threat of the war was very real as Japanese submarines were sailing off Canada's west coast. The students went through air raid drills and strapped on gas masks in preparation for a gas attack.

SOCIETY AND SOCIAL CHANGE

The War Effort Across the Country

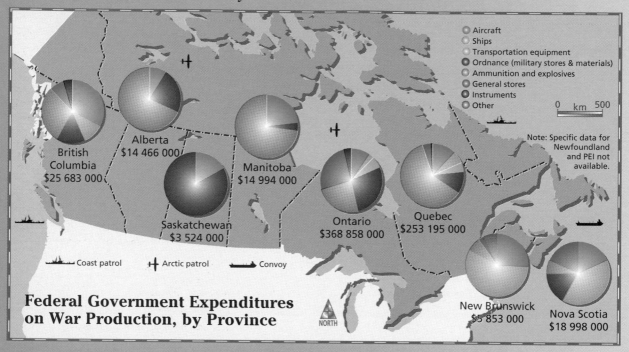

Federal Government Expenditures on War Production, by Province

British Columbia $25 683 000
Alberta $14 466 000
Manitoba $14 994 000
Saskatchewan $3 524 000
Ontario $368 858 000
Quebec $253 195 000
New Brunswick $5 853 000
Nova Scotia $18 998 000

Aircraft
Ships
Transportation equipment
Ordnance (military stores & materials)
Ammunition and explosives
General stores
Instruments
Other

0 km 500

Note: Specific data for Newfoundland and PEI not available.

Coast patrol — Arctic patrol — Convoy

NORTH

British Columbia

The products of BC's forests and rivers were turned to the war effort. The entire 1942 salmon catch was shipped to Britain. Pacific ports vied with Atlantic ports in shipbuilding.

The Pacific Coast Militia Rangers was formed when Japan entered the war. Japanese forces took the Aleutian Islands off Alaska in 1942, but were later pushed out by a joint Canadian-American force. No further attacks were made on the west coast.

The Prairies

The industrial resources of towns and cities on the Prairies were working hard for the war effort. They were turning out guns, locomotives, ammunition, and uniforms. Farmers were harvesting bumper crops of wheat and producing food goods such as pork, beef, dairy products, flax, and oil seeds to meet the demand. Many world famous pilots of the RAF and the RCAF were trained on the Prairies.

Ontario

Ontario's car and farm implement factories were manufacturing armoured vehicles, guns, and planes for the war. Many new plants were also established and were producing shells, explosives, and small arms.

Quebec

Quebec produced 75 percent of the asbestos used by the Allies during the war. The province was a new source of strategic war metals and minerals. Aircraft, tanks, guns, shells, warships, and merchant vessels were produced in its industrial centres.

Maritimes

Thirteen thousand vessels carrying 70 million tonnes of cargo sailed from Canada's eastern ports to Britain in 1943. Ninety-nine percent of this tonnage reached Britain even though hundreds of ships were destroyed by German U-boats. Some U-boats made it up the St. Lawrence River.

Halifax was Canada's major shipping and naval centre during the war. Ships and soldiers from all parts of the Commonwealth stopped at Halifax. Convoys of ships set out with vital war materials across the Atlantic.

Newfoundland and Labrador

During World War II, Newfoundland and Labrador were not part of Canada. The region was being run for a time by a British commission because of its financial problems during the Depression. However, large numbers of Newfoundlanders joined the Canadian or British forces. Important American and Allied air bases were located on Newfoundland and many Newfoundlanders worked on the bases to keep the planes flying. The Royal Navy bases on the island were crucial in the defence of the north Atlantic and in keeping the supply lines open. Many Newfoundlanders experienced at sea helped to keep the convoys of ships sailing to Britain.

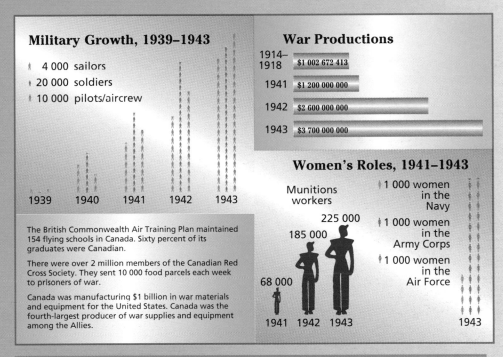

Military Growth, 1939–1943

- 4 000 sailors
- 20 000 soldiers
- 10 000 pilots/aircrew

1939   1940   1941   1942   1943

The British Commonwealth Air Training Plan maintained 154 flying schools in Canada. Sixty percent of its graduates were Canadian.

There were over 2 million members of the Canadian Red Cross Society. They sent 10 000 food parcels each week to prisoners of war.

Canada was manufacturing $1 billion in war materials and equipment for the United States. Canada was the fourth-largest producer of war supplies and equipment among the Allies.

War Productions

1914–1918	$1 002 672 413
1941	$1 200 000 000
1942	$2 600 000 000
1943	$3 700 000 000

Women's Roles, 1941–1943

Munitions workers

225 000
185 000
68 000

1941 1942 1943

1 000 women in the Navy

1 000 women in the Army Corps

1 000 women in the Air Force

1943

1. a) How much did Canada's war production increase from 1941 to 1943?
   b) How does this figure compare with the country's war production during World War I from 1914 to 1918?
   c) What does this comparison suggest about the growth of Canada's economy during the two world wars?

2. How do the graphs above help to illustrate the contribution of women to the war effort and their changing roles?

3. During the war, Canada's production of steel doubled and its production of aluminum increased six times. Suggest why. How were these materials used?

By 1944, the pressure to introduce conscription had increased even further. The army was desperately short of troops. Soldiers who had been wounded two or three times were being sent back to the front lines. King turned to Louis St. Laurent, the leading Cabinet minister from Quebec. With St. Laurent's co-operation, the prime minister announced that a total of 16 000 conscripted soldiers would be sent overseas, but no more for the time being.

The motion to send 16 000 conscripts overseas passed in the House of Commons by a majority vote of 143 to 70. Only one minister from Quebec resigned from the Cabinet. He protested that the government had broken its pledge to French Canadians. There was some rioting in Quebec City and Montreal. However, the response from French Canadians was not nearly as violent as it had been in 1917.

Mackenzie King had won a victory for unity. Most French Canadians acknowledged that King had tried to prevent conscription. He had paid attention to French Canadian opinion. Although many French Canadians were unhappy about conscrip-

How does this cartoon depict Prime Minister King's dilemma over conscription?

tion, they gave Mackenzie King credit for doing his best.

Mackenzie King's conscription policy was probably one of his greatest political achievements. He had remembered and learned from the tragic experience of 1917. This time conscription did not tear apart the Liberal party or the country.

DEVELOPING SKILLS: ANALYZING WARTIME PROPAGANDA

Propaganda is the spreading of particular ideas and beliefs to control people's thoughts and feelings, and to make them act in a particular way. In other words, propaganda is a publicity (public information) campaign to manipulate public opinion and attitudes.

During World War II, both sides used propaganda as part of their military strategy. It was often called "psychological warfare." For the people at home, propaganda was used to instill pride and confidence in the country, to inspire sacrifice, and to show the consequences of defeat. Propaganda also boosted military morale. It convinced soldiers that though they may have lost the battle, the war was being won.

Nazi Germany's propaganda minister was Joseph Goebbels. He had complete control over German radio, films, and newspapers. Papers printed what he wanted them to print. Theatres screened the films he wanted people to see. Goebbels' use of mass meetings, parades, and demonstrations to stir up support for the Nazi cause was brilliant.

Hitler and Mussolini were also masters of propaganda. In their speeches, they used their public speaking skills to convince citizens that their country's mission was just.

The Allies also established a Psychological

Target	Message
The enemy	Eventual defeat
The Allies	Unity, loyalty, and victory
Neutral countries	The rightness of the cause
Home front	The need for effort and sacrifice to be victorious

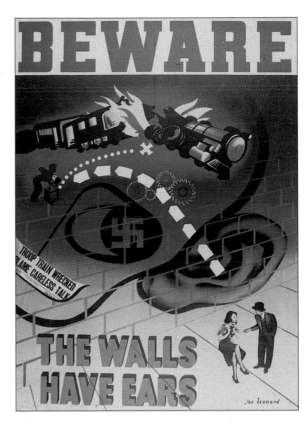

Warfare Division. In Canada, the Wartime Information Board was responsible for propaganda. The propaganda generally appealed to people's emotions. Symbols, such as the flag, and images of the family, the homeland, and the evil nature of the enemy were often used to influence people's behaviour. It was believed that a picture was worth a thousand words. Therefore, posters were a popular form of propaganda.

Wartime propaganda was aimed at four main targets: the enemy, the Allies, neutral countries, and the home front. For each of these targets, a specific message was emphasized.

Below are six questions to ask when analyzing any examples of wartime propaganda. Examine the poster on this page to discover how these questions can be answered.

Question	Answer
1. Who is the intended **target**?	men and women on the streets, therefore the target is the home front
2. Who is the **sender** of the message?	probably the government, which wants everyone on the home front to get this message
3. What is the **message** of the poster?	careless talk could be overheard by enemy spies and could end up costing the lives of our soldiers or civilians
4. What is the **purpose** of the poster?	to warn the general population to be very careful in any conversation because they may be giving away information to the enemy
5. **How** is the message **relayed**?	the face of the dreaded enemy is skillfully drawn as a shadow on the wall with the thoughts of sabotage, and at the same time the viewer is reminded that the walls have ears
6. What is the **effect** of the poster?	clever, ominous; the conversation on the street seems harmless but the dominant image on the wall and several other small symbols contribute to the message that the walls have the ears of the enemy and careless talk can cost lives

Try It!

1. Using the model presented above, analyze each of the posters below.
2. Can you think of any examples of propaganda today? Who are the targets and what are the messages?
3. Do you think propaganda should be used in wartime? Why or why not?
4. In groups, try making propaganda posters. Here are some target suggestions.

   • Allies — Britain or France
   • neutrals — the United States before 1941
   • the home front — the conscription issue

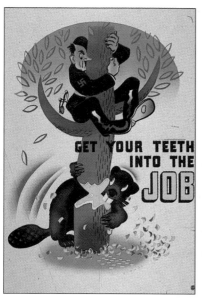

Women Roll Up Their Sleeves for Victory

In World War I, women had served as nurses behind the front lines and made a major contribution to the war industry at home. In World War II, they again did the same, but they also became an active part of the armed forces for the first time. Women pushed to be accepted into official military service. In 1941, the Canadian army, air force, and navy each created a women's division—the Canadian Women's Army Corps (CWAC), the Canadian Women's Auxiliary Air Force (CWAAF), and the Women's Royal Canadian Naval Service (WRCNS). By the end of the war, Canadian women in uniform numbered 50 000. Another 4500 women were in the medical services.

Women were not sent into front-line combat, but they did essential work behind the lines. Some worked as radio operators, guiding back planes and ships from battle missions. Others were mechanics, welders, armourers, or workers in armed forces headquarters. In first-aid posts and in hospitals in Europe and Britain, nurses and Red Cross workers treated the wounded and dying.

A woman who served near the front recalled her wartime experiences:

I was a Red Cross worker. We had to do all we could to help. Some men were cheery, asking for a cigarette, joking. Some were in shock through loss of blood and just torn-up bodies, and some of these were the ones who were dying. You got to know. They had this look about them, a whiteness, a look in their eyes. Some would die while you sat beside them. One did once, a young boy from Ontario, and he died as I was reading the last letter he got from his mother. He let out this kind of sigh and his head fell down a bit and I knew he was gone. He had a lot of steel in his chest. I suppose he never had much of a chance.

It was a time when you could work twelve hours a day and another four if you wanted to, and you'd crawl into the tent just dead. The bombing didn't bother us. The shelling. Sometimes it sounded like thunder rolling across the lake, just like at home at the cottage.

Women also played a vital role in war industries at home. The war once again proved that women could perform jobs in industries and services as well as men. In 1939, there were 638 000 women in the workforce in Canada. By 1944, there were 1 077 000. Traditionally, only unmarried women worked. But during World War II, it became patriotic for all women to help "fight Hitler at home."

Women in overalls and a bandanna on posters everywhere became a symbol of service to Canada. By the thousands, women operated riveting machines in shipyards, welded parts in airplane factories, and worked on assembly lines in munitions plants. In rural areas, they ran farms while men were away fighting. Jobs that had traditionally been done by men were now done effectively by women. These included work in lumber mills and as streetcar and bus drivers.

In Ontario and Quebec, the government established child care centres for women working in war industries. Married women were temporarily allowed to earn more money without their husbands having to pay higher income tax. Salaries for women rose significantly during this time. Women in the aircraft industry received an average

Thousands of Canadian women served overseas as nurses and in the women's divisions of the army, navy, and air force.

weekly wage of $31. This was more than double what women had earned before the war.

Many women who could not serve in uniform or work in war industries contributed as volunteers. They packed parcels for prisoners of war and knitted sweaters and socks for the fighting soldiers overseas. They worked in service clubs and canteens serving coffee and sandwiches to Canadians in uniform and Allied soldiers training in Canada.

In some ways, women's contributions to the labour force during World War II helped to expand the traditional roles of women in Canadian society. But for many women the new freedoms and opportunities were only temporary. Following the war, women often lost their jobs. Men returned from the war and were given their old jobs back. The tax breaks given to married women earning a wage were eliminated. The government-sponsored child care centres were discontinued. The women's service corps were disbanded. Women were expected to return to working at home or to traditional female occupations such as teaching, nursing, or domestic service.

The Internment of Japanese Canadians

One of the most significant events in the war at home was the internment of Japanese Canadians and other "enemy aliens." Shock and anger gripped many Canadians when they heard that the Japanese had attacked Pearl Harbor. That same night the Royal Canadian Mounted Police swept through the Japanese community in British Columbia and began to make arrests. In the next few days, 38 Japanese Canadians judged to be "dangerous individuals" and "troublemakers" were rounded up.

In the months that followed, all Japanese nationals (people born in Japan but living in Canada) and Canadian citizens of Japanese descent were imprisoned under the **War Measures Act**. This act gave the Canadian Cabinet the power to make any

This painting by Canadian artist Paraskeva Clark entitled Maintenance Jobs in the Hangar *shows one aspect of women's contribution to the war effort and symbolizes a change in women's traditional roles.*

decisions during the emergency of wartime without debate in the House of Commons. Japanese were taken from their homes, packed into trains, and sent to **internment camps** in the interior of British Columbia. Some men were assigned to work on road construction in northern British Columbia and Ontario. Others were used as farm labourers in the sugar beet fields of Alberta and Manitoba. Men who resisted were separated from their families and sent to a prisoner-of-war camp in Angler, Ontario.

At first, only Japanese men without Canadian citizenship were held. But later it did not seem to matter whether the people were born in Japan or Canada. In fact, more than 14 000 were second-generation Japanese Canadians born in this country. Another 3000 were Japanese who had become Canadian citizens. It didn't seem to matter that 200 Japanese Canadians had fought in the Canadian army in World War I. Canada and Japan were at war, and all Japanese Canadians were considered to be potentially dangerous. One Japanese

Canadian woman told how on the day the war broke out a man approached her on the street and spat in her face.

Most people of Japanese descent in Canada lived in British Columbia. The first Japanese immigrants had come to work on the railroads, in mines, and in lumber camps in the late 1800s and early 1900s. Later, they established permanent homes and businesses in Canada. Many owned small boats and fished for salmon along the British Columbia coast. Others worked in fish canneries or owned small plots of land where they grew fruit and vegetables for the Vancouver market. Others owned shops, restaurants, and other small businesses. During their internment, their property was taken away and their businesses were ruined.

Japanese in the fishing industry were the first group to be evacuated. There were rumours that Canada would be attacked at any minute and that the Japanese were navy officers sent to spy on British Columbia waters. About 1200 fishing boats belonging to Japanese Canadians were

Japanese Canadians are rounded up and sent to internment camps.

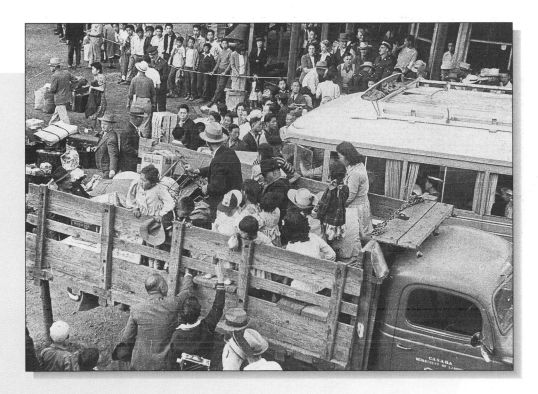

seized by the Canadian government. Their owners were sent to the interior of British Columbia. One person remembered:

To this day I don't know what they thought about these small fishing boats. They were our living. They were small boats made of wood. We had no radar, no radio, no echo sounder. Just tiny little vessels with their chuggy little motors and space for the fish we caught… And they said we were charting the coast and waterways… Why, we could go into Vancouver any time and buy British Admiralty charts of every single kilometre of the coast. But try and convince people that we were not spies, that we were not spying… But oh no, no way.

The Canadian navy saw no further security problem once Japanese Canadians had been removed from the coast. Still, demands continued for the internment of all Japanese Canadians. People were nervous. Japanese forces had swept across the Pacific, occupying Indonesia, parts of China, the Philippines, Malaya, Burma, and Singapore. People feared British Columbia might be next. Feelings against Japanese Canadians ran high.

In February 1942, the Canadian government decided to move all Japanese Canadians away from the coast to inland centres. The government said there were two reasons for doing this: to prevent spying which could lead to an enemy invasion, and to protect Japanese Canadians from being harmed in anti-Japanese riots.

Most Japanese Canadians were sent on special trains to six ghost towns in the interior of British Columbia. They were allowed to take 68 kg of clothing, bedding, and cooking utensils for each adult. They were housed in crude huts. Two bedrooms and a kitchen had to be shared by two families. Until 1943, there was no electricity or running water. Living conditions were so bad that food packages from Japan were sent through the Red Cross to interned Canadians in British Columbia. In these remote communities, they were kept under constant surveillance by the RCMP. World War I veterans were paid to

An RCMP constable checks the documents of Japanese Canadian evacuees at Slocan City, British Columbia.

watch over the settlements and report anything out of the ordinary.

When Japan surrendered, the Canadian government considered sending all Japanese Canadians back to Japan. This would have included many who had been born in Canada and who had never been to Japan. The deportation never took place. A number of Canadian citizens protested that this would be dishonourable and unfair to the Japanese Canadians. However, about 4000 returned to Japan in 1946.

Those who remained in Canada did not have an easy time in the post-war years. Only a few went back to British Columbia. Instead, they spread out across the country. Citizens of Japanese descent were not given the right to vote in federal elections until June 1948. They did not have the right to vote in British Columbia elections until 1949.

After the war, many Japanese Canadians were bitter when they found out that their possessions had been sold, often at a fraction of their value. They had been told the government would hold their belongings in trust.

*When we left we had to turn over our property to the **Custodian of Enemy Property** for safekeeping. Now that meant to us that when the war business was over we'd get our property back.*

It was a terrible shock when we learned that this safekeeping business meant nothing, that all of our stuff had been sold at auction. People would get a cheque or a credit saying so much was due to them, but there were some people who got no money at all. Now that wasn't right. That safekeeping thing caused a lot of bitterness. People would say, "That's all we had and now we've got nothing." It made a lot of people pretty mad. First they take us from our homes and stick us in a dump, and now this.

One family's house sold for $50 at a government auction, and its contents for $8.50. One fishing boat sold for $150, a fraction of what it was worth. Most people felt that they received from the government between 5 and 10 percent of the real value of their property and possessions.

In 1946, a **Japanese Property Claims Commission** was set up by the Canadian government. It was to review the claims of those who felt they had not been treated fairly. Although in some cases additional money was made available, it never fully compensated for what had been lost. It was not until 1988 that the Canadian government formally apologized to Japanese Canadians and offered $20 000 to every survivor of the internment.

The Effects of World War II on Canada

In 1939, Canada was unprepared for war. Nevertheless, the country made a vital contribution to the war effort. By 1945, Canada emerged with an important place in world affairs.

British envoy Athlone, President Roosevelt of the United States, Prime Minister Churchill of Britain, and Prime Minister Mackenzie King meet at the ramparts of Quebec City. Canada emerged from World War II as a significant middle power.

First, Canada made a major contribution in people, munitions, food supplies, and raw materials. In 1939, Canada's three military services had just over 10 000 people. By 1945, over 1 million Canadians had worn a uniform, and 50 000 were women. Fatal casualties numbered 22 964 for the army, 17 047 for the air force, and 1981 for the navy. In a nation with a population of just over 11 million at the end of the war, these figures represent a great loss.

Similarly, in terms of war production, Canadians worked miracles. Starting from almost nothing, Canadian plants turned out 800 000 motor vehicles, 16 000 aircraft, 900 000 rifles, 200 000 machine guns, 6500 tanks, over 400 cargo vessels, and nearly 500 escort vessels and mine sweepers.

Second, as in World War I, Canada's economy was strengthened by the war. In 1939, Canada still suffered the effects of the Depression. Unemployment was widespread and the economy was just beginning to recover. By 1945, the Canadian economy was booming. The gross national production of goods tripled. Materials such as asbestos, aluminum, coal, manganese, chemicals, and paper all contributed to the war effort and Canada's industries expanded rapidly. The increased production of vital agricultural goods such as wheat, flour, bacon, ham, eggs, canned meat, and fish also contributed to the economic boom.

Third, Canada gained new international status. Canada came out of the war respected by other world nations. At the same time, Canada was prepared to accept new responsibilities in maintaining world peace. In a very real sense, Canada grew up as a result of the war. The war had helped Canada establish its place as an important **"middle power"** among nations.

SOCIETY AND SOCIAL CHANGE

Life in an Internment Camp

A Child in Prison Camp by Shizuye Takashima is the true story of a young Japanese Canadian girl's experience in an internment camp during World War II. "Shichan," as she was known to her friends, kept a written record of the three years during which she and her family were isolated in a camp. In the spring of 1944, she recorded a discussion her family had. They were trying to decide whether they should stay in Canada or go back to Japan.

Spring 1944

The war with Japan is getting very bad. I can feel my parents growing anxious. There is a lot of tension in the camp; rumours of being moved again, of everyone having to return to Japan. Kazuo and his family leave for Japan. Many are angry they have left us. Some call them cowards, others call them brave! I only feel sad, for I liked Kazuo so much, so very much.

Father shouts at mother, "We return to Japan!" "But what are we going to do? You have your brothers and sisters there. I have no one. Besides the children..." "Never mind the children," father answers. "They'll adjust. I'm tired of being treated as a spy, a prisoner. Do what you like; I'm returning!"

I can see Mrs. Kono looks confused. "My husband is talking of returning to Japan, too. I think it's the best thing. All of our relatives are still there. We have nothing here." Yuki stares at her. "It's all right for you, Mrs. Kono, you were born there, but we weren't. I'm not going. That's all!" And she walks out of the house.

Mother gets very upset. I know she wants to cry. "I don't want to go to Japan, either!" I say. "They're short of food and clothing there. They haven't enough for their own people. They won't want us back."

All of a sudden I hate that country for having started the war. I say aloud, "Damn Japs! Why don't they stop fighting?" Father glares. "What do you mean 'Japs'? You think you're not a Jap? If I hear you say that again I'll throttle you." I see anger and hatred in his eyes. I leave the room, go out of the house. I hear him say loudly to mother, "It's all your fault. You poison our children's minds by saying we're better off here."

And another argument starts. I am getting tired of it, and confused. I feel so helpless, and wish again I were older, then maybe I could go somewhere… But I do not hate the people in Japan. I know Yuki doesn't hate them either, really. It's all so senseless. Really, maybe children should rule the world! Yuki tells me it is wrong for father, because of his anger at the wrong done towards him and us, to expect us to return to his country: "Sure, we're Japanese. But we think like Canadians. We won't be accepted in Japan if we go there."

Source: From *A Child in Prison Camp* © 1971, Shizuye Takashima, published by Tundra Books.

1. a) What problems do Shichan's family face?
   b) Describe what each member of the family would like to do.
2. a) Describe the behaviour of each member of the family. How does their behaviour relate to their feelings about what is important to them?
   b) Point out the ways in which the beliefs of mother, father, and Shichan are similar and different.
   c) Suggest reasons why each person feels the way he or she does.
3. a) What alternatives are available to the family?
   b) Name some possible consequences for the family if they stay in Canada, and if they go to Japan.
4. a) Imagine you are each of the people mentioned in the excerpt. What would you do about this situation?
   b) Why did you decide on this course of action, and what might be some of the consequences you would have to face?
5. What do you think Shichan meant when she said, "Really, maybe children should rule the world!"

ACTIVITIES

Check Your Understanding

1. Add these new terms to your *Factfile*.

   "total war"   internment camps
   ration cards   Custodian of Enemy Property
   propaganda   Japanese Property Claims Commission
   conscription plebiscite   middle power
   War Measures Act

2. Describe how people and families at home contributed to the war effort.

3. Canada's accomplishments in turning its industries to wartime production during World War II have been called "an industrial miracle." Provide three points of evidence to support this statement.

4. Explain each of the following in a sentence.
   a) Why many English Canadians wanted to have compulsory military service during World War II.
   b) Why many French Canadians did not want to have compulsory military service during World War II.
   c) Why the Liberals did not want to introduce conscription.
   d) What the plebiscite told the government.
   e) What the government decided to do about conscription in 1944.

5. Describe the role of women in World War II.

6. Where were most people of Japanese descent living in Canada in 1941? What occupations did they hold? Describe what happened to them and their property after Japan bombed Pearl Harbor.

Confirm Your Learning

7. a) Rationing is often introduced in times of war or severe economic hardship. Make a list of the "luxury" items you would have to give up if Canada were at war. Do you think it would be easier or more difficult for you to give up these goods than it was for Canadians in World War II? Why or why not?
   b) Which household items do you think you would be able to reuse or recycle? Explain.
   c) If your family's food needs had to be reduced to a minimum, how much bread, milk, sugar, flour, apples, potatoes or rice, meat, and cereal do you think your family would need for one week? Create ration cards showing the minimum amounts. Explain your decisions.

8. Twice in the twentieth century the issue of conscription nearly tore the Canadian nation apart. Use an organizer like the one on the next page to compare the two situations. Account for the different outcome in 1944.

Conscription Issue	World War I	World War II
Party that introduced conscription		
Reasons for introducing conscription		
Groups who supported conscription		
Groups who opposed conscription		
How the decision was reached		
Efforts to accommodate opposition of French Canadians		
Reaction in Quebec		
Effects of decision on national unity		

9. a) What were the effects of the war effort on women's roles in society?
   b) How were these roles similar to or different from the roles women played in World War I?
   c) What changes came about at the end of the war? Did these changes improve or hinder women's struggle for equality?

10. It was once reported in the press that a Chinese woman living in Vancouver wore a sign around her neck that said, "Please don't pick on me. I'm Chinese, not a Jap." Why would this woman wear this sign? What does it suggest about the situation in Vancouver at this time?

11. a) People said that Canada had developed as a nation by the end of World War II. What did they mean?
    b) Are there any areas in which you think Canada still had some "growing up" to do? Explain.

Challenge Your Mind

12. a) During the war the government established a daycare program for children whose mothers were working in war industries. How important do you think this program was in getting women involved in the war effort?
    b) Today, there are over a half million children under the age of six whose mothers work. What community services do you think should be offered to assist working mothers? Can society afford these services that allow women to work?

c) Are these services seen as important priorities in your community?

13. Role play a meeting in which some or all of the following people discuss whether or not Japanese Canadians should be interned during World War II.
   a) Prime Minister Mackenzie King
   b) an officer of the RCMP
   c) a British Columbia politician
   d) a Canadian-born leader of the Japanese community
   e) a non-Japanese fisherman or woman on the British Columbian coast
   f) a representative of a British Columbia labour union
   g) a lawyer interested in civil rights disputes
   h) a person with a son in a Japanese prisoner-of-war camp overseas
   i) a citizen of British Columbia fearful of a Japanese attack

14. a) Should the internment of Japanese Canadians have occurred? Why or why not? Who was responsible?
   b) What does this episode teach us about Canadian society? Do you think a minority group could be interned today? Why or why not?
   c) Why do you think Japanese Canadians were interned, but not German Canadians?
   d) Do you think the Canadian government has made up for the wrongs against Japanese Canadians? Explain.

15. Though they were not interned, German and Italian people in Canada were also treated harshly during the war. They have not received an official apology or financial compensation from the government. Do you think they should? Explain your point of view.

Unit 6

Canada in the Post-War Era 1946–1969

TIMELINE

1945	Igor Gouzenko exposes spy ring; Cold War begins United Nations formed
1948	Louis St. Laurent becomes prime minister Berlin blockade, 1948–1949
1949	Formation of NATO Newfoundland and Labrador join Confederation
1950	Canadian troops fight alongside other UN troops in Korea, 1950–1953
1952	CBC's first television broadcast
1955	Warsaw Pact formed
1956	Canadian peacekeepers in the Suez, Egypt
1957	NORAD agreement Diefenbaker wins landslide election Canada Council established
1960	Quiet Revolution starts in Quebec Native people win right to vote
1963	Lester Pearson becomes prime minister
1964	Beatlemania hits the world Canada gets a new flag
1967	Canada celebrates its Centennial
1968	Trudeaumania; Pierre Trudeau is elected prime minister

World War II was hardly over before the Cold War began. Two new superpowers had emerged from World War II—the United States and the Soviet Union. Countries began to line themselves up with one or the other.

Canada came out of World War II as a respected "middle power." On the international stage, Canada worked for world peace and provided social and economic assistance to war-torn countries. In the Cold War, Canada stood by the United States and joined defensive organizations such as the North Atlantic Treaty Organization (NATO) and the North American Air Defence Command (NORAD).

At home, World War II had completed Canada's transformation from a rural to a mainly urban society. It also set off one of the greatest economic booms in Canadian history. People were ready to raise families in these peaceful and prosperous times. Over 4 million babies were born in Canada during the 1950s. By 1960, 2 million new Canadians had also arrived from all parts of the world. A tenth province, Newfoundland and Labrador, was welcomed into Confederation in 1949.

In the 1960s, the "baby boomers" born in the 1950s were jean-clad teenagers. It was a decade of youth. Young people flocked to rock 'n' roll concerts and went to coffee houses to hear protest songs of stars such as Gordon Lightfoot, Joni Mitchell, and Neil Young. Young people protested against American influences in Canada, nuclear weapons, war, and social injustices.

Political protest also arose in Quebec in the 1960s with the Quiet Revolution. French-speaking Quebeckers declared that they wanted to control the affairs in their own province.

By the late 1960s, Canada was nearing its 100th birthday. In 1967, Centennial celebrations swept the nation. There were 20 million Canadians by this time and a poll showed that 85 percent thought Canada was the best country in the world.

At the end of this unit, you will be able to:

- demonstrate an understanding of the main events in the Cold War
- recognize Canada's foreign policy goals and its role in the United Nations
- explain the population explosion and economic boom in the post-war years
- accurately describe aspects of life and culture in the 1950s and 1960s
- analyze Canadian-American relations in the 1950s and 1960s
- demonstrate an understanding of the Quiet Revolution in Quebec
- practise effective oral presentation skills
- analyze statistics in tables
- demonstrate and apply interviewing skills

KEY THEMES

Social Issues
- post-war immigration and the "baby boom"
- counterculture in the 1960s
- Women's Liberation Movement
- Trudeaumania
- Native issues

The Economy
- post-war economic prosperity; new resource industries
- American investment

French-English Relations
- Quiet Revolution in Quebec
- Quebec separatist movement
- Royal Commission on Bilingualism and Biculturalism
- Official Languages Act 1969

Canadian-American Relations
- co-operation in continental defence with NATO and NORAD
- strained relations over Cuban Missile Crisis
- debate over American influence on Canadian economy and culture

Canada and the World
- the Gouzenko Affair and Canada's role in the Cold War
- role in the United Nations as a "middle power"
- new role in the Commonwealth

National Growth and Identity
- post-war prosperity and population explosion
- Newfoundland and Labrador becomes tenth province 1949
- new flag 1964
- Centennial celebrations and Expo 67

Regional Development
- oil and gas boom in Alberta; potash development in Saskatchewan
- mining and hydroelectric power development in Ontario, Quebec, BC
- Diefenbaker government builds "roads to resources" in North
- St. Lawrence Seaway opens 1959

Citizenship, Government, and Law
- Supreme Court of Canada established 1949
- New Democratic Party formed 1961
- Canadian Bill of Rights passed 1960
- Official Languages Act 1969

Technological Change
- television arrives in homes
- space age begins

The Arts
- Canada Council established 1957
- new theatres, ballet companies, artists, and writers emerge
- rock 'n' roll arrives

CHAPTER 15

Canada on the World Stage

SOVIET SPIES IN OTTAWA!

On the evening of 5 September 1945, an international drama was unfolding in Ottawa. Igor Gouzenko was a young clerk in Ottawa's Soviet embassy. He decided to defect. He wanted to break his ties with the Soviet Union and live permanently in Canada. Gouzenko smuggled 109 top-secret documents out of the embassy under his shirt. His idea was to turn the secrets over to authorities in return for protection and a new life in Canada.

For 36 hours, no one took Gouzenko seriously. A member of Prime Minister King's staff even suggested that he return to the Soviet embassy and replace the documents. By this time, Gouzenko was desperate. The theft had been discovered. Soviet embassy officials broke into Gouzenko's apartment. A neighbour called the Ottawa police and they arrived just as Gouzenko was being hustled away by Soviet officials. Finally, the RCMP were convinced that Gouzenko was telling the truth.

The documents Igor Gouzenko turned over contained shocking information. A massive spy ring was operating out of the Soviet embassy in Ottawa. The police discovered several Soviet agents working in Canada, the United States, and Britain. In Canada, the agents included high ranking military officials, a member of Parliament, and clerks in government offices. In the United States and Britain, the trail led to scientists who had worked on the first atomic bomb.

Igor Gouzenko after he exposed the spy ring operating out of Ottawa. Why is his identity hidden?

Canadians were shocked by the news of the **"Gouzenko Affair."** It was less than a month since the end of World War II. Now they were astounded to learn that the Soviet Union, a former wartime ally, had spies in Canada. But nations that are allies during a war often quarrel when the war is over. This was certainly true after World War II. Canada came to play a crucial role both in peacekeeping and in the new conflicts of the post-war era.

Canada's Foreign Policy

World War II had given a tremendous boost to the Canadian economy. Our prosperity meant that we were one of the few nations that could help the war-shattered world. There was a marked change in **Canada's foreign policy** following World War II. A country's foreign policy is its action plan for handling its relations with other countries. It covers such areas as trade, defence, foreign aid, and immigration.

Following the war, Canada showed a new willingness to play an active part in events on the world scene. Obviously, Canada could not influence international affairs as much as the world powers—the United States, Soviet Union, Britain, France, and China. But neither was Canada a small, weak, or unimportant country. With its abundant natural resources, new military might, size, and political stability, Canada was an important "middle power." Prime Minister King was determined to use this power to advantage.

Canada's foreign policy from 1945 to 1959 was based on four major areas of concern:

1. support of the United Nations to promote world peace
2. co-operation with the United States in continental defence
3. support of the North Atlantic Treaty Organization for defence
4. co-operation within a strong Commonwealth.

Formation of the United Nations

Even before the war ended, the Allies started making plans for peace. They agreed that the old League of Nations formed after World War I had to be replaced. It had failed to prevent another world war. A new organization was needed, with real power. President Roosevelt of the United States, Prime Minister Churchill of Britain, and later General Secretary Stalin of the Soviet Union were determined to set up an international organization that could settle differences among nations before they led to war.

From April to June 1945, representatives of 50 nations, including Canada, met at San Francisco. They signed a charter which established the **United Nations (UN)**. The opening words of the charter read: "We, the peoples of the United Nations, determined to save succeeding generations from the scourge of war, which twice in our lifetimes has brought untold sorrow … do hereby establish an international organization to be known as the United Nations." The charter said that the UN's aims were:

- to band together to avoid war (collective security)
- to encourage nations to co-operate
- to promote better standards of living
- to ensure that everyone enjoys basic human rights.

Canada strongly supported the United Nations and the idea of collective security. Two world wars had emphasized the need for nations to stand together against aggression. By signing the charter, Canada offered money and support for world peace.

The major nations were anxious that the United Nations should succeed. The old

League of Nations had used sanctions (economic and political penalties) to try to stop countries from fighting. That policy had not worked, so it was agreed that the United Nations should have an army. Member countries would contribute troops whenever they were needed. Sometimes the UN forces would be posted between enemy sides to keep peace. At other times, soldiers would work as observers.

The League of Nations had also been weak because some important countries, such as the United States, had not joined. President Roosevelt was determined that the United States would be a full member of the UN. The permanent headquarters of the organization were built in New York City. All the major powers in 1945 had a key role in the United Nations. Since that time, other nations have also joined.

The United Nations at Work

The United Nations established a **Security Council** which was to meet in cases of international emergency. Today there are five permanent members—Russia, the United States, Britain, France, and China. They are often referred to as the "Big Five." Ten other members are elected for two-year terms. Canada has served several times. The Security Council can ask countries to use sanctions to stop fighting, or it can send in a UN peacekeeping force.

The "Big Five" must approve all major decisions of the Security Council. When the UN Charter was signed, these powerful nations demanded a veto right. In other words, if one of them did not agree with a policy, it could block the action. The veto was not intended to be used often. However, both the United States and the former Soviet Union have used the veto to protect their interests. Many people think this veto power is a serious weakness in a crisis. It has at times prevented the UN from taking decisive action.

When the Charter was signed, Canada's Prime Minister Mackenzie King also spoke out for the smaller nations. He wanted to make sure that they could not be dragged into conflicts by the larger powers. He worked to ensure that if a country is to contribute troops or funds to a UN operation, it must be consulted about the action first.

The **General Assembly** of the United Nations meets once a year. Every member country can send representatives, but every country, large or small, has just one

This mural hangs in the Security Council chambers at the United Nations. It was a gift from Norway and is by artist Per Krohg.

vote. In 1993, the General Assembly had 180 member countries. Each member pays a share of the United Nations' costs, depending on its ability to pay. The General Assembly discusses and debates such problems as aid to developing countries and international use of the sea. It suggests ways of settling disputes that arise in various parts of the world. The diagram below shows the other councils and committees which are part of the UN and outlines their major functions.

A great strength of the United Nations was its recognition that world peace depended on more than taking united action against aggression. For this reason the Economic and Social Council, with its many agencies, set out to attack the problems that could lead to war: poverty, disease, energy needs, food and water shortages, pollution, and unemployment.

In 1948, the United Nations also agreed on a Universal Declaration of Human Rights. These were its key points:

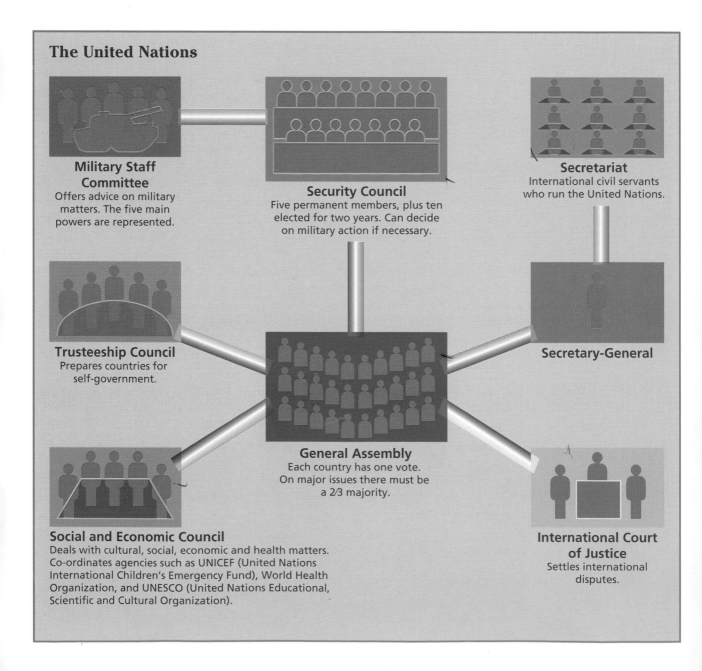

The United Nations

Military Staff Committee
Offers advice on military matters. The five main powers are represented.

Security Council
Five permanent members, plus ten elected for two years. Can decide on military action if necessary.

Secretariat
International civil servants who run the United Nations.

Trusteeship Council
Prepares countries for self-government.

Secretary-General

Social and Economic Council
Deals with cultural, social, economic and health matters. Co-ordinates agencies such as UNICEF (United Nations International Children's Emergency Fund), World Health Organization, and UNESCO (United Nations Educational, Scientific and Cultural Organization).

General Assembly
Each country has one vote. On major issues there must be a 2/3 majority.

International Court of Justice
Settles international disputes.

- right to life and liberty
- freedom from slavery and torture
- right to privacy
- freedom of movement and assembly
- freedom of conscience and religion
- equal protection under the law
- right to take part in government
- right to work, rest, and recreation
- right to adequate health and living standards.

Rise of the Superpowers

While the United Nations was working for peace, other tensions were brewing. Both the United States and the Soviet Union came out of World War II as superpowers, stronger than all other nations. Their large populations, massive wealth in land and resources, and great military might made them world powers. They could be expected to compete to establish influence over defeated countries.

Though the United States and the Soviet Union had fought as allies against Hitler, there were basic differences between them. The Soviet Union was a communist nation. The government controlled most of the property and businesses. It also controlled the individual freedoms of the people, including where they lived, worked, and travelled. On the other hand, the United States was a democracy. Democratic nations are based on the protection of individual rights and freedoms set out in their constitutions. With such basic differences in outlook, it became clear that a lasting friendship between the former allies would be difficult.

During the war, the huge Soviet army had poured into eastern Europe. By the end of the war, it had engulfed Poland, East Germany, Czechoslovakia, Hungary, Romania, Bulgaria, and Albania. The Soviet leader, Stalin, had promised to withdraw his troops from these countries once the war was over. But he refused to keep this promise when Hitler had been defeated.

"The Iron Curtain"

In February 1945, when it was clear that Germany would be defeated, Allied leaders met at Yalta to decide what should happen when the war ended. The most important decision was what to do with the lands they had captured from Germany.

First, there was Germany itself. The Allies agreed that Germany would be divided into four zones. Each zone would be occupied by one of the Allies: Britain, France, the Soviet Union, and the United States. Germany's capital, Berlin, was located entirely within the Soviet zone. However, it was decided that the city would also be divided into four sectors.

Then there was Poland. The Soviet army had entered Poland in March 1944. Stalin did not intend to give up the Polish land he had gained by his agreement with Hitler. In return for this territory, Poland was given German land to the west.

Stalin wanted the Germans to pay reparations. The other leaders, remembering the Treaty of Versailles, did not. In the end, Stalin had his way. Machines were stripped from German factories in the Soviet zone and taken to the Soviet Union.

The Allies agreed that each country freed after the war would be able to choose its form of government. However, both Churchill and Roosevelt knew that the eastern European countries would have no choice. The Soviet Union was in a powerful position. Stalin could use his army to force these nations to adopt communism.

The Soviet Union took complete control of the countries of eastern Europe. They became known as Soviet "satellite states." Like satellites that revolve around the Earth, life and government in these countries revolved around the Soviet Union. These countries were ultimately controlled by orders from Moscow, the Soviet capital.

A communist government was set up in each country which Stalin controlled. Soviet advisers moved in. Anti-communists

SOCIETY AND SOCIAL CHANGE

War Refugees

The United Nations' major aim was to keep peace. But in 1945, the people of Europe were faced with other urgent problems. About 20 million people were without a home. Families were walking the streets carrying everything they owned tied up in bundles. Some of these refugees left their homes to avoid the fighting; others left to escape the Nazis. A third group was leaving lands that were being taken over by communist troops. Many simply didn't have a home any more. Millions of houses had been damaged or destroyed.

The United Nations and the Red Cross set out to help the refugees. Much of the money for their work came from the United States. Canada also made a significant contribution. The UN and Red Cross took over old military barracks and prisoner-of-war camps to provide shelter for the refugees. Some Jewish refugees did not want to return to their former towns and villages. Many chose to go to the state of Israel when it was founded in 1948.

Most countries in the world put a limit on the number of refugees they would accept. Often elderly or sick people were not admitted. Many families had to decide whether to stay in a refugee camp as a family, or to leave behind a sick or elderly grandparent. Canada, however, accepted over 186 000 war refugees between 1947 and 1952.

One woman described her experience in a refugee camp in 1945:

We were put in a camp, a refugee camp. It was fine there. We had pillows, blankets, food, and clothes. There was a cupboard there, toothpaste, and a toothbrush! My God, we hadn't seen one for years. Or soap. We got packets from the Red Cross. I always give something now to the Red Cross when people are collecting. No more lice. I was free!

A family huddles on the street in Warsaw, Poland, after the war. Many people were homeless and famine-stricken.

---

1. a) Why were there so many refugees in Europe following the war?
   b) Why was it important for countries such as the United States and Canada, and for the United Nations, to help?
2. There are still many people alive who came to Canada as refugees after World War II. Interview some of these people. Ask them why they chose Canada. How did they get to this country? What experiences did they have on their arrival?
3. Many of the war refugees, known as "displaced persons" or DPs, faced difficulties being accepted in Canada and adjusting to a new life. What difficulties do you think they would have faced? Why?

were sent to labour camps. Stalin was creating a buffer zone to protect the Soviet Union. He was determined that it would never again be attacked from the west.

The Soviet satellite nations were sealed off from contact with non-communist countries. Travel was restricted and trade was cut off. News from outside was not allowed to enter these countries. Other nations watched as eastern Europe became communist. Fear grew in the United States, Canada, and western European countries that communism would take over the world, just as Hitler and the Nazis had tried to do.

In 1946, British Prime Minister Churchill gave a speech in the United States. He told Americans that "an **iron curtain** has descended across the continent." On one side were the democratic countries of western Europe. On the other side were the communist countries controlled by Stalin. Of course, there was no real iron curtain. But there were minefields to stop people fleeing to the west. There were armed soldiers ready to shoot anyone attempting to escape. And in 1961, the Communists built the **Berlin Wall**, an actual wall separating the western and communist eastern sections of the city.

DEVELOPING SKILLS: MAKING ORAL PRESENTATIONS

Are you someone who prefers to talk about a subject rather than write about it? Oral presentations can allow you to use your skills. Even if you feel nervous about talking, especially in front of a group, some basic steps can help you feel comfortable and set you on the road to presenting an interesting and informative talk.

Oral presentations are an important skill. In many careers and occupations, you will need to give informed talks on some aspect of your work. Lawyers, salespeople, journalists, sportscasters, tradespeople, teachers, artists, and many others use speaking skills everyday. You probably already use speaking skills more often than you think. When you talk about your hobbies, help friends with homework, or explain a new computer game, you are using some oral presentation skills.

The key to good oral presentations is practice. The more often you do them, the more comfortable you feel and the better your presentations become. Don't worry about making mistakes or sounding foolish. If you are prepared and enthusiastic, you deserve your audience's attention. Here are some helpful steps.

■ **Step I** *Plan*
1. Make sure you understand the topic. Ask questions if there is anything you aren't sure about. Know when you will present and how much time you have.
2. Make a written plan of the full presentation just as you would do for a written report. Put the main ideas and sub-points in your own words.

The presentation should have:

a) an introduction which states the main theme, issue, or purpose of the presentation. Try to make the opening powerful to catch the attention and interest of your audience. Consider using a personal reference, a thoughtful question, a startling statistic, a quotation, or a visual such as a slide or picture.

For example, one student started a presentation this way:

My grandmother arrived in Halifax in 1946 as a war refugee. She was one of thousands who came to Canada after World War II. All she had with her was a small bundle of clothes and very little money.

b) content which includes ideas and facts to support your main theme.

c) illustrations to clarify ideas and support your arguments. Your audience will find your presentation more interesting if you use examples and visuals to prove your points. You could use charts, pictures, slides, video clips, short tape recordings, or quotes.

d) a clear, logical organization. Follow a written plan. Deal with one sub-topic at a time. Arrange your ideas in a logical sequence. This will help your audience focus on your theme and follow your thinking.

For example, an oral presentation on war refugees could ask and then answer each of the following questions:

Who were the war refugees?
Why did they come to Canada?
What were some of the problems they had in adjusting to their new lives?

e) a summary which reinforces your message and sums up what you have been showing. You may wish to end with a powerful anecdote, quotation, or even a thought-provoking question.

A sample summary might be:

Some refugees had trouble adjusting to Canadian life. They were not always treated kindly. Many, however, like my grandmother, really did build a new life and grew to love their adopted country. They had families and friends, new and old. My grandmother told me she still keeps in touch with some of the others you came over on the ship with her to Halifax so many years ago.

■ **Step II** *Rehearse*

3. Practise from your script but try not to read your notes.

4. Rehearse out loud in front of a mirror. Use gestures that come to you naturally as you talk and try to keep eye contact with your audience.

5. Vary the volume and pace of your presentation, just as you would in a conversation about something that interests you. Using visuals at key points in your presentation can help vary the pace. Listen to yourself on tape.

6. Rehearse over and over until you are comfortable with your materials and don't have to read from your notes.

7. Time your practice. Be sure to leave time for questions and discussion. Be ready for questions.

■ **Step III** *Deliver*

8. Sit or stand straight and keep eye contact with your audience so that they feel you are talking to them personally.

9. Show enthusiasm for your topic. If you enjoy it, your audience will too.

10. Have members of the class make notes during the presentation. This encourages them to listen carefully. Check with your teacher about this.

11. Have an outline or brief notes to refer to occasionally, but don't read from your notes. Mark off new points with a pause or vocal change. Repeat key points for emphasis but avoid repetition of certain words or phrases. Use simple language and explain difficult terms. Use language your audience understands.

12. Speak clearly and distinctly and make sure you can be heard. The presentation will lose a lot of its appeal if you cannot be heard or understood.

Now that you know the steps, practise them. Research and prepare an oral presentation on one of the following topics:

- war refugees in Canada
- the Gouzenko Affair
- a Canadian peacekeeping operation
- a Canadian foreign aid program
- Canadian space technology
- the nuclear arms race
- CUSO (Canadian Universities Service Overseas) programs or a similar program for students or young people overseas

The Cold War

So while World War II had ended, the **Cold War** had begun. The term "Cold War" originally meant that the two superpowers would try to defeat each other by any means short of actual fighting. The Gouzenko Affair played out in Canada was one of the early dramatic events in the Cold War. The Cold War would be fought with espionage (spying), propaganda, and political pressures, not guns. Yet it still frightened people. Above all, everyone feared the use of atomic bombs. The Cold War involved a terrifying **nuclear arms race**. Although there was never a declaration of war between the United States and the Soviet Union, there were several conflicts.

The first open clash in the Cold War was in 1947. It was caused by events in Greece and Turkey. In Greece, political confusion followed World War II. Greek communists were struggling against supporters of the Greek king for control of the government. The Soviet Union was helping the Greek communists. At the same time, Stalin was trying to seize oil-rich lands on the Black Sea in Turkey.

President Harry Truman announced in 1947 that the United States would help Greece and Turkey and any other nation threatened by communism. The United States would follow a policy of "containment." It would try to "contain" or stop the spread of communism anywhere in the world. This policy became known as the **Truman Doctrine**. With American military and economic help, Greece and Turkey were both able to resist communist pressures at this time.

The Marshall Plan

There were, however, serious problems in other parts of Europe as well. Much of Europe lay in ruins after World War II. President Truman believed that people struck by poverty and upheaval were more likely to support communism. Therefore, the United States was determined to help rebuild Europe and stop the influence of the Soviet Union.

The American Secretary of State, George C. Marshall, announced the European Recovery Plan, or the **Marshall Plan** as it is now known. This was a huge self-help program of American economic aid for Europe. Vast amounts of machinery, raw materials, food, and building supplies were sent to help Europe recover from the war.

Canada was already giving aid to Europe, but welcomed the opportunity to help with the Marshall Plan. In the first year of the Plan, 1948, Canada shipped $706 million in goods to war-torn countries. During the five years of the plan, $13.5 billion of supplies were sent to 16 European nations by the United States and Canada. European countries made remarkable progress. The Soviet Union never extended its influence over western Europe.

The Berlin Blockade

A major confrontation, however, took place in 1948 with the **Berlin Blockade**. The city of Berlin was situated deep inside the Soviet controlled area of East Germany. The Soviets cut off all rail and highway access into the British, French, and American zones of Berlin (West Berlin). The United States government was determined that West Berlin should not fall to communism. It began a massive airlift of food and supplies into Berlin. The airlift took Stalin by surprise, and eventually led to the abandonment of the blockade.

Canada and NATO

The year 1948 was a crucial one in the Cold War. The Soviet Union was continuing to expand its powers. First, it tried to take control of the city of Berlin. Then, Soviet troops moved into position to seize control of Czechoslovakia. Czechoslovakia was taken over in 1949. In 1949, the Soviet Union also exploded its first atomic bomb, four years after the United States had dropped its atomic bomb on Japan. The United States, Canada, and other western powers viewed this expansion and development with alarm. They decided to take joint action.

On 4 April 1949, the **North Atlantic Treaty Organization (NATO)** was formed. Twelve nations signed the treaty. They were Belgium, Britain, Canada, Denmark, France, Iceland, Italy, Luxembourg, the Netherlands, Norway, Portugal, and the United States. By 1955, these countries had been joined by Greece, Turkey, and West Germany.

Canada's Prime Minister Louis St. Laurent, who became Canada's leader after Mackenzie King's retirement in 1948, was a strong supporter of a defence alliance. St. Laurent realized that the weakness of the United Nations was that it had no permanent armed force of its own. The United Nations was not able to defend Canada against a possible Soviet threat. St. Laurent said in the House of Commons, "We are fully aware of the inadequacy of the United Nations at the present moment to provide the nations of the world with the security which they require."

The NATO alliance committed its members to collective security. This meant a kind of safety in numbers. All members banded together and promised to defend each other in the event of an attack. An attack on one member was considered an attack against all. It was hoped that the combined strength of the NATO alliance would discourage the Soviet Union from taking any hostile action against NATO members.

The Soviet Union responded in 1955 by forming its own military alliance, the **Warsaw Pact**. Its members were the Soviet Union, Albania, Bulgaria, Czechoslovakia,

Both Mackenzie King (right) and his successor, Louis St. Laurent, were determined that Canada should take an active role in world affairs after World War II.

Post-World War II Europe

NATO

Warsaw Pact

Norway, Sweden, Finland, Denmark, Baltic Sea, North Sea, Soviet Union, Ireland, Great Britain, Nether-lands, East Germany, Poland, West Germany, Belgium, Czechoslovakia, English Channel, Luxembourg, Atlantic Ocean, France, Switzerland, Austria, Hungary, Romania, Bay of Biscay, NORTH, Yugoslavia, Black Sea, Portugal, Italy, Bulgaria, Adriatic Sea, Albania, Spain, Tyrrhenian Sea, Greece, Turkey, 0 km 250, Ionian Sea, Mediterranean Sea, Sicily, Crete, Morocco, Algeria, Tunis

East Germany, Hungary, Poland, and Romania. Thus in 1955, just 10 years after World War II, Europe was once again divided into two hostile camps—the NATO and Warsaw Pact countries.

Canada and the Korean War

In 1950, the outbreak of the **Korean War** opened another chapter in the Cold War. The crisis was also the first real test of the UN's peacekeeping ability. Canada's involvement showed that it was willing to take action in support of the United Nations and world peace.

The Koreans had been an independent people for centuries, but in the early 1900s they had been taken over by Japan. After World War II, Japan lost control of Korea. The Soviet army occupied the northern half of the country and a communist government was established there. American troops occupied the southern half. The 38°N parallel was the border. The United Nations had been trying to reunite the Koreas with no success.

Then, in June 1950, a powerful North Korean army invaded South Korea. It seemed likely that the heavily armed North Koreans would take over the entire country. The matter was brought to an emergency meeting of the UN Security Council. At that moment, the Soviet delegate was boycotting (refusing to attend) the Security Council. The Soviet Union was, therefore, not able to exercise its veto power. The Security Council agreed to take action. It ordered North Korea to withdraw its forces. It called on members to send military forces to Korea. The American general, Douglas MacArthur, was appointed to command these UN troops. Most troops were from the United States, but other nations, including Canada, contributed to the peacekeeping effort.

Canada sent one infantry brigade, three naval destroyers, an air transport squadron, and about 8000 soldiers in all. In April 1951, the Princess Patricia's Light Infantry won praise at the **Battle of Kapyong** in central Korea. The "Princess Pats," although outnumbered eight to one, dug in to defend Hill 677. They spent three days in terrifying hand-to-hand fighting. But the Canadians held on, saved by an air drop of food and ammunition. The Canadian victory at Kapyong probably prevented Seoul, the South Korean capital, from falling to the North Koreans.

Four hundred and six Canadians were killed in the Korean War, and over one thousand were wounded. Canada had shown the world that it was prepared to take a responsible role in the actions of the United Nations.

The Korean War ended in 1953 with a truce. Both sides agreed to stop fighting. However, the war did not succeed in uniting the two Koreas. The border between North and South Korea was back to approximately where it had been when the war started in 1950.

The Suez Crisis

In 1956, a situation arose which could easily have developed into a major war between the superpowers. Egypt's head of state, President Nasser, decided to take over the Suez Canal from British and French control. The canal was a vital trade route in the East. Ships could travel from the Mediterranean Sea to the Red Sea and the Indian Ocean through the Suez Canal without sailing around Africa.

The Egyptian action greatly alarmed Israel, Britain, and France. These nations responded by attacking Egypt. The Soviet Union threatened to send missiles to support Egypt. The United States warned that it would step in if the Soviet Union interfered. An explosive situation was building.

Frantic activity took place at the United Nations. Members desperately looked for a way to reduce the tension. Lester B. Pearson was at that time Canadian Secretary of State for External Affairs. Pearson persuaded the General Assembly to order all

War artist Edward Zuber painted scenes of battle involving Canadian troops in the Korean War. This painting is entitled Contact.

foreign troops out of Egypt. He convinced the UN to set up a **United Nations Emergency Force (UNEF)**. This would be an international police force. It would keep peace between the rival armies until a settlement could be worked out.

The UNEF was Pearson's brainchild. Its members would be drawn from middle powers who had no individual interest in the dispute. The force would not fight unless attacked. Instead, it would observe, investigate, mediate, and report back to the UN General Assembly. The force would be composed of 6000 soldiers. One thousand were Canadians. Major-General E.L.M. Burns of Canada commanded the UN force.

In the days that followed, Egypt, Israel, Britain, and France obeyed the ceasefire. The UNEF succeeded in bringing peace to the region. Much credit for this success must be given to Lester Pearson. For this achievement, Pearson was the first Canadian to be awarded the Nobel Peace Prize in 1957. It was a great honour for him and for Canada. In his Nobel address, Pearson said:"In the end, the whole problem always returns to people … to one person and his own individual response to the challenge that confronts him."

Canada, the United States, and the Nuclear Arms Race

By the mid-1950s, both the United States and the Soviet Union had nuclear missiles. Atomic bombs had been followed in the 1950s by hydrogen bombs (H-bombs). The United States exploded its first hydrogen bomb in 1952. The Soviet Union exploded its H-bomb in 1953. Hydrogen bombs were 40 times more powerful than the atomic bomb dropped on Hiroshima. The nuclear warheads were capable of wiping out a large city.

Canada was in a crucial position located between the Soviet Union and the United States. Missiles fired at the United States would probably come across the North Pole. They could reach their targets in a matter of hours. A means of early detection had to be found. Suddenly, the Canadian Arctic became of immense strategic importance.

Three chains of radar stations were built to detect an air invasion of North America. The Pinetree Radar System was built along the Canadian-American border. The Mid-Canada line ran along the 55°N parallel, and the Distant Early Warning Line (DEW Line) was situated along the Arctic coastline. Ships and aircraft provided radar surveillance on both the Atlantic and Pacific coasts.

This defence co-operation between Canada and the United States increased in 1957 when the **North American Air Defence Command (NORAD)** was set up. NORAD brought the air defence of the

Lester and Maryon Pearson with the Nobel Peace Prize in December 1957. Why was this a momentous event for Canada?

Drop in the Bucket

"Doesn't it seem kind of academic to be debating whether we should have nuclear weapons?"

What view does this cartoon present of Canada's position in the nuclear arms race?

two countries under a fully-integrated joint command. The commander was an American; the deputy-commander was a Canadian.

The main operation centre for NORAD was built deep within the Cheyenne Mountain in Colorado. A NORAD centre was also constructed at North Bay, Ontario. If there was a nuclear attack, the defence of North America would be directed from NORAD headquarters. From there, nuclear missiles could be fired against the Soviet Union. It was hoped that the NORAD defences would stop the Soviet Union from striking at North America.

Some people criticized the plan. They felt Canada was giving up too much control of its defences to the United States. The arms build-up and threat of nuclear war also made people very nervous. Many were not convinced that gathering bigger

and more destructive weapons would keep peace by deterring or stopping others from attacking. A nuclear war could mean complete and utter destruction. Anti-nuclear protesters demonstrated across the country. Over the next decades, people lived with the threat of nuclear war over their heads.

Canada in the Commonwealth

In the post World War II years, Canada also forged a new role for itself within the Commonwealth. All members acknowledged the British monarch as head of the Commonwealth. However, the Queen was not necessarily the head of state for all member countries. Some countries, like Canada, kept the Queen as the head of state.

SCIENCE AND TECHNOLOGY

The Space Age

The space age began in 1957. In that year, the Soviet Union launched the first satellite into space—*Sputnik*. The world was astonished! *Sputnik* captured people's imagination. The Soviet success was followed a month later with *Sputnik II*, which carried a small dog into orbit. United States' scientists scrambled to keep pace with the Soviets. The United States launched its first satellite, *Vanguard I*, a few months later. The launch failed as the rocket carrying the satellite exploded seconds after takeoff. In 1958, the United States successfully sent the *Explorer I* satellite into orbit. The space race was on!

By the early 1960s, both superpowers had long-range missiles called Intercontinental Ballistic Missiles (ICBMs). These missiles were rockets with hydrogen warheads. An ICBM launched from the Soviet Union could destroy targets in Canada within half an hour. The space race was not only about exploration. As long as the Cold War continued, it was also about military power.

Canada has played a major role in space research. Canada was the third nation in space after the Soviet Union and the United States, and has become a world leader in satellite and aerospace technology.

In 1962, the Canadian-built Alouette *satellite was launched into space. It was the beginning of Canada's major contribution to space exploration and research.*

1. Do further research to find out more about the major developments in space exploration. Create a timeline to record and illustrate the events from 1957 to the present. Be sure to include Canadian achievements.
2. a) What were some of the positive aspects of the space race? What were some negative aspects?
   b) If you were living in Canada in the early 1960s, how would you have felt about the development of nuclear missiles?

Others established their own monarchs or became republics with no monarchs. Countries of many different languages, religions, races, and cultures share membership in the Commonwealth.

Canadians have one of the highest standards of living of all the Commonwealth countries. Since 1945, Canada has given economic aid to many other members. In 1950, Canada was a major supporter of the **Colombo Plan**. This plan was set up to give technical and financial support to developing countries in Asia. In the first year, $25 million was pledged for factories and equipment. Canadians helped to establish a nuclear generating plant in India, a cement factory in Pakistan, and irrigation and transportation systems in several Asian countries.

Under the plan, students from developing countries could also attend Canadian universities, and work with Canadian governments and industries. Thousands of young people have studied medicine, forestry, education, agriculture, and administration. By 1973, Canada had contributed $2 billion to the Colombo Plan. Since then, Canada has continued to provide foreign aid to developing countries through a variety of programs.

ACTIVITIES

Check Your Understanding

1. Add these new terms to your *Factfile*.

Gouzenko Affair	Marshall Plan
Canada's post-war foreign policy	Berlin Blockade
United Nations	North Atlantic Treaty Organization (NATO)
UN Security Council	Warsaw Pact
UN General Assembly	Korean War
iron curtain	Battle of Kapyong
Berlin Wall	Suez Crisis
Cold War	United Nations Emergency Force (UNEF)
nuclear arms race	NORAD
Truman Doctrine	Colombo Plan

2. a) Copy the organizational chart on page 252. Underline in red the parts of the United Nations organization that are connected with keeping peace. Underline in blue those that are directly concerned with helping people. Explain your choices.

   b) How does the United Nations differ from the old League of Nations? Why were these changes made?

3. a) Explain why the Soviet Union and the United States emerged as superpowers after World War II.

   b) Why was Canada considered a "middle power?" What were some advantages and disadvantages of this position?

4. Describe the Gouzenko Affair. How was it a signal that the Cold War was on?

5.a) What were the goals of the Truman Doctrine and the Marshall Plan? How successful were these policies?

b) Describe Canada's role in these measures.

Confirm Your Learning

6. Develop a mind map to illustrate the major aspects of Canada's foreign policy after World War II. Consider Canada's involvement in:

a) the United Nations

b) NATO

c) NORAD

d) the Commonwealth

7. Germany was defeated and heavily damaged at the end of World War II. Were Canada and the United States wise to help rebuild Germany and make it an ally? Explain your point of view.

8. Why was the Korean War called an international police action? Did its outcome strengthen or weaken the security of the world? Explain your answer.

9. Canada is a member of both the United Nations and NATO. What are the arguments for and against our memberships in these organizations?

10. Are there any advantages in having the United States responsible for Canada's defence? What are the disadvantages?

11. Create a poster, cartoon, button, song, or poem to show your point of view on the nuclear arms race if you had been living in Canada in the 1950s.

12. In groups, script and present a short TV or radio spot to report on one of the significant events described in this chapter. Your spots could include short interviews with some of the key people involved or people on the street. Consider the following events.

a) the Gouzenko Affair

b) presentation of the Nobel Peace Prize to Lester Pearson

c) the launch of Sputnik

d) the formation of NORAD

Challenge Your Mind

13. To broaden your understanding of Canada's role as a peacekeeper, investigate one or more of the operations in which Canada played a part. Summarize your research in an organizer with the following headings.

a) causes

b) Canada's role

c) Canada's impact during the crisis

d) significance for Canada

14. Discuss how Canada's foreign policy between 1945 and 1959 might have affected the attitudes of people in other countries to Canadians.

15. Canada's contribution to NATO has cost hundreds of millions of dollars in armed forces and military equipment. Do you think this cost has been worth it for Canadians? Poll the class, then ask for explanations.

16. Debate: Canada should help the poor in our own country instead of sending foreign aid to other countries.

17. Select a United Nations agency (such as UNESCO, UNICEF, or WHO) and research its work. You may wish to write to the Information Division of the United Nations, New York City, for particular details. Present a short report to your class describing the agency's activities and evaluating its achievements.

CHAPTER 16

The Fabulous Fifties

HERE COME THE BRIDES

The band played "Here Comes the Bride" as the *Aquitania* steamed into Halifax harbour. It was carrying more than a thousand **war brides** of Canadian soldiers. One in five Canadian soldiers who went overseas as a bachelor came home married. More than 40 000 war brides and 20 000 children arrived in Canada after World War II. Brochures were distributed and a Canadian Wives' Bureau was set up in London, England, to prepare many new brides for their life in Canada. They were given information on everything from shopping with mail-order catalogues to sleeping arrangements on Canadian trains. But all the help in the world could not prepare some of them for what they found upon arriving in Canada. Some found themselves alone on isolated farms with no modern conveniences. Others had to live with in-laws who were complete strangers until their soldier-husbands returned from Europe. A few were so homesick and discouraged that they went back to their own countries. However, most stayed, adjusted, and started new lives in Canada.

Two war brides remember their first impressions of Canada.

I really hadn't the slightest idea what to expect when I arrived in Quebec. We stayed three months in St. Jean and then moved to Drummondville where we settled. Of course, I'd known that my husband was a French-speaking Canadian, but it was quite a shock to find that his relatives spoke no English at all. Although his family was a bit put out that he'd married une Anglaise (and a Protestant one at that), they were very good to me.

My husband and I had two great days in Saskatoon when I arrived. We'd never had a real honeymoon in England, and those two days were all we could afford. Then we took the train to his home town, Birsay, Saskatchewan. At that time it was an all-day trip to cover the 160 km. What a welcome awaited us at Birsay station. I felt like the Queen of England! All the people of the village and surrounding farm area were there to welcome me. I met my in-laws, two lovely people who still had their Yorkshire accents.

New Canadians

The war brides were the first of a great wave of new immigrants who came to Canada following the war. All through the 1930s and early 1940s, Canada's immigration policy had been very restrictive. That is, Canada had only been accepting people from the so-called "white" Commonwealth countries. When only 7576 immigrants came to Canada in 1942, it marked the lowest number to arrive since 1860.

But with the end of World War II, Canada returned to an open door policy. The country needed trained people for postwar development. But the policy was also changed for humanitarian reasons. The suffering of so many war refugees could not be allowed to continue. Starting slowly with war brides and "displaced persons" (European refugees who had no homes),

the number of immigrants to Canada increased through the 1950s. In 1948, 50 000 people immigrated to Canada. In 1957, the number reached 282 164, the highest total since 1913. The largest group came from Great Britain, followed by Italy, the United States, Germany, Greece, Portugal, Poland, and the Netherlands.

People from Poland and the Netherlands were particularly attracted to Canada because of wartime connections. The Polish army had fought alongside Canadian troops in northwest Europe and Italy. Polish fliers had trained in Canada, and after the war, many Polish people decided to make Canada their home. Doctors, lawyers, engineers, and highly trained technical people were among the Polish immigrants. Many, however, had to take jobs below their skill levels to get established.

The Dutch also had a soft spot in their hearts for Canada. Canadians had helped

Tulips blooming on Parliament Hill are the legacy of a thank-you gift from the Dutch royal family for Canada's hospitality to the family during the war years.

to liberate the Netherlands from the Nazis. After the war, 30 000 Dutch—mostly farmers—arrived in Canada. Crown Princess Juliana of the Netherlands had lived in Ottawa during the war. A room in the Ottawa Civic Hospital had been declared Dutch territory so that her third daughter could be born on "Dutch soil." The Netherlands expressed its gratitude to Canada with an annual gift of tulip bulbs which bloom each spring in Ottawa's parks.

There were two major differences between the immigrants of Laurier's time and those who came after World War II. In Laurier's day, most new Canadians headed to farms in western Canada. After World War II, most immigrants tended to settle in cities and towns. The other important difference was that most immigrants in the early 1900s had been farmers or labourers. The immigrant of the post-war period was often a skilled worker or professional.

On 5 December 1960, Canada welcomed its two-millionth immigrant since the end of World War II. A 16-year-old Danish girl, Anette Toft, landed at Quebec City. Anette was one of the two million immigrants who came to Canada between 1945 and 1960. These 15 years brought the

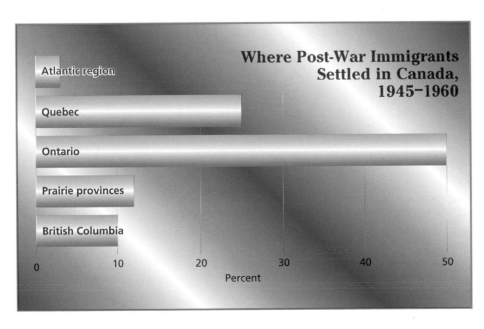

Where Post-War Immigrants Settled in Canada, 1945–1960

- Atlantic region
- Quebec
- Ontario
- Prairie provinces
- British Columbia

Percent
0   10   20   30   40   50

greatest wave of immigration to Canada since the early days of the century.

A New Prime Minister: Louis St. Laurent

Mackenzie King had led Canada through World War II. In fact, he had been prime minister longer than anyone. When he retired in 1948, he had been succeeded by Louis St. Laurent.

St. Laurent was the second French Canadian prime minister in Canadian history. He had been a prominent corporate lawyer in Quebec City. St. Laurent had come to Ottawa and entered politics out of a wartime sense of duty. He was fluently bilingual and his popularity in Quebec had helped Prime Minister King and the Liberals carry that province during the conscription crisis in 1944.

During the federal election campaign of 1949, St. Laurent spent so much time patting the heads of small children and kissing babies that a reporter had nicknamed him "Uncle Louis." The nickname stuck with St. Laurent and conveyed the image of a kindly, elderly gentleman. The Canada that St. Laurent took over as prime minister was a country of booming prosperity and growing confidence.

Under St. Laurent and the Liberals, Canada took further steps toward becoming a completely independent nation. The **Supreme Court of Canada** was set up in 1949 as the final court of appeal for Canadians. No longer would Canadians have to appeal the decisions of their court cases to the Privy Council in Britain.

In 1952, Vincent Massey became the first Canadian-born governor general of Canada. In his years as governor general, 1952 to 1959, Vincent Massey travelled throughout Canada. He wanted to give Canadians a sense of pride in their country and a sense of national identity.

Newfoundland and Labrador Joins Confederation

Canada was also still growing. On 1 April 1949, Newfoundland and Labrador became Canada's tenth province. Feelings about joining Confederation in the new province were mixed. Some people hung black flags out their windows and wore black armbands in protest. Others gathered in community halls to celebrate becoming Canadians.

Newfoundland had flatly rejected Confederation in 1867, preferring to keep its historic ties with Britain. Sir John A. Macdonald was disappointed when the colony rejected Confederation. He had once remarked, "The Dominion cannot be considered complete without Newfoundland. It has the key to our front door."

Since 1855, Newfoundland and Labrador had been self-governing. The worldwide depression of the 1930s, however, had hit Newfoundland and Labrador very hard. The government went broke and had to accept British administration and assistance. After World War II, Joseph R. Smallwood and others began to urge fellow Newfoundlanders and Labradorians to join Canada. Smallwood, a former organizer of a fishing union, publisher, and radio personality, became the driving force behind joining Confederation.

It was a tough fight. Anti-Confederationists warned that joining Canada would mean the loss of local power, identity, and values. People were very proud of their historic ties with Britain and the fact that Newfoundland was Britain's first overseas colony. They argued that Confederation would also bring economic ruin. Goods from Canada would be so cheap that Newfoundland products would not sell. The Canadian government would probably tax their boats, fish, and fishing tackle. The Roman Catholic

Church feared that Confederation would mean the end of the Roman Catholic school system.

Jocy Smallwood was convinced that Newfoundland and Labrador had to join Canada to move into the modern era. Belonging to Canada would provide much needed money to build schools, hospitals, and roads. It would also provide jobs for the people and other important government benefits. The "baby bonus," a monthly allowance from the Canadian government for each child, could provide extra money for the many large families. A family of nine or ten was not uncommon. The excerpt below from *The Confederate* in 1948 is an example of some pro-Confederation propaganda.

Fierce debates over Confederation kept people glued to their radios. Referendums (direct public votes) were held on whether to join Canada. In the first direct public vote on the issue, there was no clear decision. In the second referendum, the people

Are You in This List?

To All Mothers: Confederation would mean that never again would there be a hungry child in Newfoundland. If you have children under the age of 16, you will receive every month a cash allowance for every child you have or may have.

To All War Veterans: Canada treats her Veterans better than any other country in the world. She has just increased their War Pensions 25 percent. Under Confederation you will be better treated than under any other form of government.

To All Wage-Workers: All wage-workers will be protected by Unemployment Insurance. Newfoundland, under Confederation, will be opened up and developed. Your country will be prosperous. Your condition will be better.

To All Over 65: You would have something to look forward to at the age of 70. The Old Age Pension of $30 a month for yourself, and $30 a month for your wife will protect you against need in your old age.

To All Railroaders: You will become employees of the biggest railway in the world, the CNR. You will have security and stability as CNR employees. Your wages and working conditions will be the same as on the CNR. Under any other government you face sure and certain wage-cuts and lay-offs. You, your wives and sons and daughters and other relatives should flock out on June 3 and vote for Confederation.

To All Building Workers: Under Confederation Newfoundland will share fully in the Canadian Government Housing Plan, under which cities and towns are financed to build houses. 1000 new homes will be built in St. John's under this plan.

To All Light Keepers: You will become employees of the Government of Canada. Your wages and working conditions will be greatly improved.

To All Postal-Telegraph Workers: You will all become employees of the Government of Canada, at higher salaries and much better working conditions.

To All Fishermen: The cost of living will come down. The cost of producing fish will come down. The Government of Canada will stand back of our fisheries. The Fish Prices Support Board of Canada, backed by Canada's millions, will protect the price of your fish.

To All Newfoundlanders: The cost of living will come down. The 120 000 children in our country will live better. The 10 000 Senior Citizens of our country will be protected in their old age. Newfoundland will be linked up with a strong, rich British nation. Newfoundland will go ahead with Canada.

The Confederate, May 31, 1948

voted by a narrow majority—52 percent to 48 percent—to join Canada. Smallwood, a new Father of Confederation, became the province's premier. By the terms of union, Newfoundland and Labrador received the same financial benefits as other provinces. It also got special assistance because of its uncertain economy and relatively low standard of public services. The federal government took over the province's public debt and the operation of the Newfoundland Railway.

The New Prosperity

A tall pillar of flame and smoke shot up into the Alberta winter sky. The crowd of oil workers, geologists, and officials let out a whoop and a cheer. It was 13 February 1947 and the fabulous **Leduc Number 1 oil well** near Edmonton had just come in. That day marked a new stage in Alberta's oil and gas boom.

Oil company crews had been exploring intensively in Canada's West since 1913. But until the Leduc strike, about 90 percent of Canada's total output was coming from the Turner Valley near Calgary and Norman Wells in the Northwest Territories. By 1947, Turner Valley production was falling off by about 10 percent a year. When Leduc Number 1 started pumping, oil hysteria swept the country again. Almost overnight sleepy little towns near Edmonton became boom towns. Soon more than 1200 wells were steadily producing in the Leduc area.

In a sense, the Leduc oil strike marked the beginning of the post-war economic boom in Canada. But oil was just one of the natural resources that fuelled the dynamic growth of Canada's economy after 1945.

In every area of economic activity, new production records were set. At no time before had Canada experienced such tremendous expansion. The Ford Motor

Carving Newfoundland's arms at the Parliament Buildings in Ottawa. Newfoundland and Labrador became Canada's tenth province in 1949.

Company opened a huge automobile plant near Oakville, Ontario, and General Motors built a plant in Ste-Thérèse, Quebec. North Star aircraft were being manufactured in Montreal, and Hamilton steel mills were rolling out steel for Alberta oil pipelines.

New mining operations also multiplied across the country. When the Ungava Peninsula in northern Quebec became the centre of high-grade iron ore mining operations, tent cities sprang up in the bush. A great aluminum smelter was built at Kitimat far up the British Columbia coast. Construction began on a railway to Great Slave Lake to help develop mining resources in the Northwest Territories. Uranium from northern Saskatchewan and from Elliot Lake and Bancroft in Ontario went into the production of new American nuclear weapons. Britain and the United States contracted to buy as much uranium as Canada could produce.

Potash development in Saskatchewan did much to improve the economy of that province in the 1950s. The construction of refineries, processing plants, and the world's

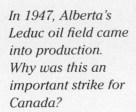

In 1947, Alberta's Leduc oil field came into production. Why was this an important strike for Canada?

longest oil and gas pipeline added to the prosperity of the West. The prairie provinces were finally able to shake off the 20 terrible years of dustbowl and depression.

New products and resources became the driving force behind Canada's economy. For a long time, wheat had been Canada's leading export. Now wheat stood in third place in Canada's trade list. Newsprint and lumber moved into first and second place. Next came resources that were unknown or reasonably unimportant exports before World War II—aluminum, uranium, asbestos, oil and natural gas, iron ore, and chemical products. With the development of these new resources, Canada's economy became more diversified.

The Atlantic provinces, however, did not share in the new prosperity. With the falling demand for coal, fish, and farm produce, many people found themselves out of work or making only a meagre living. The region had few other natural resources to develop. Many people were forced to move to other areas of Canada.

The St. Lawrence Seaway

More than any other project of the 1950s, the construction of the **St. Lawrence Seaway** illustrates Canada's spectacular industrial growth. Jacques Cartier had tried to sail up the St. Lawrence River in 1535. He found when he got to Montreal (Hochelaga) that he could go no farther. Ahead lay the roaring white water of the Lachine rapids. More than 400 years later, North Americans could still not travel on ocean-going ships all the way up the St.

Lawrence River into the Great Lakes.

For years, Canadian and American officials had talked of expanding this great inland waterway so that ocean-going ships could travel as far as the western end of Lake Superior. They also hoped to harness the rapids on the St. Lawrence River for hydroelectric power. Both Ontario and New York State desperately needed the extra power that this project could produce.

Although the joint plan had been discussed thoroughly, American officials hesitated. American railroad companies were afraid they would lose business if ocean vessels could sail directly to cities such as Detroit and Chicago. In 1951, Canada decided to go ahead with the construction of the St. Lawrence Seaway on its own. Only at the last minute did the Americans decide to join in. The United States may have realized that, once built, the Seaway would be entirely within Canadian territory and control unless the project was a joint agreement.

The planning and design of the Seaway, and most of the construction, were carried out by Canadians. The control dam required by the power project flooded a large area between Cornwall and Iroquois in Ontario. Entire towns and villages had to be relocated and new homes were built for 6500 people. Sixty-five kilometres of the CNR were rerouted and Highway 2 was relocated. The St. Lawrence Seaway was officially opened on 26 June 1959 by Queen Elizabeth II, representing Canada, and President Eisenhower, representing the United States. The project was an example of the strong ties binding the Canadian and American economies.

The Debate Over American Investment

Before World War II, Canada's exports went mostly to Britain and our imports came mostly from the United States. During the war, Canada's trade with Europe declined because of the U-boat menace. As a result, trade with the United States increased. In the post-war years, the United States became Canada's chief customer.

The American economy was booming after the war and the United States was the fastest-growing market for goods in the world. As its close northern neighbour, Canada was in a position to take advantage of this huge market. Canada also had most of the resources the United States needed and wanted. The trade friendship between these two countries was strengthened by the tremendous flow of American capital (money and machinery) into Canada. American capital and technical expertise poured in to advance the large-scale development of Canada's natural resources.

Many Canadians thought that American trade and investment was a positive development. Huge American markets for Canadian goods meant more jobs for Canadians and a high standard of living. Heavy American investment in Canada was helping to develop our resources and finance major industrial projects.

However, some Canadians warned that American domination of the Canadian economy was a serious threat. There was a real danger that some major industries such as oil, minerals, and paper could some day be completely owned by Americans. Canadian nationalists were alarmed by the growing trade imbalance: Canada was importing more goods from the United States than it was exporting across the border. As early as 1957, a Royal Commission on Canada's economic prospects, headed by Walter Gordon, warned of the danger of too much foreign ownership in the Canadian economy. It strongly advised the Canadian government to make policy decisions about this important issue.

DEVELOPING SKILLS: INTERPRETING DATA IN TABLES

You have probably come across tables of data in magazines, newspapers, and in your science, math, and geography classes. Tables are also useful in history. Tables are just a short-form way of communicating information. It would probably take several paragraphs to describe in sentences all the information you can present in a simple table. The secret to using tables effectively is to recognize their main features and understand how they present information.

Helpful Hints

1. Read the title. The title tells you the main purpose of the table. Why was it prepared? What is it about? What are the limits of its contents?

2. Note the units. What are the actual units that the numbers represent? The units are usually given in the title, in the columns or rows, or in the footnotes.

3. Scan the format. Tables are set up in columns, which present information vertically (up and down), and rows, which present information across the page. In the table below, for example, the first column tells the year. The

top row gives the Canadian export figures for three parts of the world in 1901.

4. Interpret the data. To determine any changes, increases, or decreases from the data in the table, you have to make comparisons. The table below is organized chronologically from 1901 to 1961. To see a pattern or trend in exports to each part of the world, you would have to read down the columns. But if you want to see which part of the world received most Canadian exports in 1901, you have to read across the top row.

   If you want to know which area received the most exports at any time covered by the table, you have to use information from both columns and rows.

5. Note the source of the data. Knowing who compiled the data helps you to assess the accuracy of the information. Is it a reliable and unbiased source? The *Historical Atlas of Canada* is considered accurate and reliable.

Practise It!

Examine the information in Table 1 below. What conclusions can you draw from the data? Use the following questions as a guide.

Table 1
Canadian Commodity Exports, Selected Years, 1901-1961
(in millions of dollars)

	Column 1	Column 2	Column 3	Column 4
	Year	**Canadian Exports to Britain and the Commonwealth**	**Canadian Exports to the United States**	**Canadian Exports to Other Countries**
Row 1	1901	101	68	26
Row 2	1911	149	104	37
Row 3	1921	403	542	265
Row 4	1931	220	240	140
Row 5	1941	879	600	161
Row 6	1951	891	2 298	774
Row 7	1961	1 238	3 107	1 550

Source: *Historical Atlas of Canada, Volume III.*

1. In a sentence, state the purpose of the table and the years covered.

2. What are the two units used in the table?

3. a) In a sentence, explain what Column 3 tells you.
   b) Explain what Row 2 tells you.
   c) What does the figure in Column 3, Row 4 tell you?

4. a) What general trend or pattern over time do the data reveal about Canadian exports to Britain from 1901 to 1961?
   b) What is the general trend in exports to the United States over the same period?
   c) What is the general trend in Canadian exports to the rest of the world over the same period?

5. Which area of the world received the most Canadian exports in 1911? in 1951? in 1961?

6. Which part of the world received the most Canadian exports between 1941 and 1961? In which year did this occur?

7. Suggest reasons why exports fell off in 1931. Why were exports to Britain in 1941 higher than exports to the United States?

8. Who was Canada's best customer in 1901? Who was Canada's best customer in 1951?

9. Examine Tables 2 and 3 below. State two conclusions you can draw from each table.

Table 2
Canadian Commodity Imports, Selected Years, 1901-1961
(in millions of dollars)

Year	Imports from Britain and the Commonwealth	Imports from the United States	Imports from Other Countries
1901	47	107	24
1911	129	276	48
1921	266	856	118
1931	152	394	82
1941	360	1 004	85
1951	727	2 813	545
1961	910	3 864	995

Source: *Historical Atlas of Canada, Volume III.*

Table 3
Percentage of Foreign Ownership in Canada, Selected Years, 1900-1960

Year	Percentage of British Ownership	Percentage of American Ownership	Percentage of Other Foreign Ownership
1900	85	14	1
1910	77	19	4
1920	53	44	3
1930	36	61	3
1945	25	70	5
1950	20	76	4
1960	15	75	10

Source: *Historical Atlas of Canada, Volume III.*

The Trans-Canada Pipeline Debate

A wild and bitter debate over American control of the economy broke out in Parliament in 1956. The Liberals had decided to finance the building of a **trans-Canada pipeline**. The pipeline would carry natural gas from its source in Alberta to markets in Ontario, Quebec, and the United States. In Parliament, the opposition asked pointed questions. Why was the government loaning $118 million to a pipeline company that was 83 percent American-owned? How much of the natural gas would end up in the United States? Was the Trans-Canada Pipeline Company getting too generous a deal from the Canadian taxpayer?

C.D. Howe, the cabinet minister in charge of the pipeline, was impatient to get construction started. He did not want to sit around the House of Commons debating the issue. The government forced the bill through Parliament using closure. Closure is a special rule limiting the amount of time that a bill may be discussed in Parliament. The opposition raised a storm of protest, but the bill was passed by the Liberal majority.

Forcing the pipeline bill through Parliament hurt the St. Laurent government. Now John G. Diefenbaker, leader of the Conservatives, had a major issue on which to fight the next election. Diefenbaker claimed that, by using closure, the Liberals had trampled on the rights of Parliament. He thundered that this was one more example of the American takeover of the Canadian economy. Above all, Diefenbaker argued that the Liberals had been in power too long and had lost touch with the people. The debate about American investment was not over.

The Diefenbaker Era

In the election of June 1957, 112 Conservatives were elected to 105 Liberals. It was a minority government, but John Diefenbaker became prime minister. There was another election the following year. Lester B. Pearson had become the leader of the Liberal party. In the 1958 election, there was a Conservative landslide in Canada. The Conservative party won the largest majority of any party since Confederation. For the first time since the days of John A. Macdonald, the Conservatives won a large number of seats in Quebec (50 of 75).

In a speech in 1958, Diefenbaker presented his "vision" of Canada. He saw great promise in Canada's North. "Roads to resources" would be built to open the northland to development, settlement, and prosperity. Oil and mineral exploration would be increased. A great irrigation and power project was begun on the South Saskatchewan River. Federal money helped construct the Trans-Canada Highway.

Diefenbaker also pronounced that all Canadians and all regions of the country would share equally in the new prosperity. The new prime minister was seen as a champion of ordinary people. Money was poured into badly needed housing and into job creation projects in the Atlantic provinces. In the field of radio and television, the government set up the Board of Broadcast Governors to supervise the quality of broadcasting. Native people were given voting rights equal to those of all other Canadians.

Perhaps of all the programs, the one that gave Diefenbaker the greatest sense of accomplishment was the **Canadian Bill of Rights**. Most countries have a constitution that guarantees the rights of its citizens. In Canada, these rights had been upheld by custom and tradition rather than by law. In 1960, an act of Parliament was passed guaranteeing Canadians the traditional freedoms by law.

- Freedom of speech (right to state an opinion without being afraid of government or law).
- Freedom of assembly and association

PROFILES

A Tale of Two Prime Ministers

John Diefenbaker: The Man from Prince Albert

Early one morning in 1909, a 14-year-old newsboy talked to Sir Wilfrid Laurier. The boy resolved then and there that one day he too would be prime minister. By 1958, John George Diefenbaker had reached his goal. He was the prime minister and leader of the party with the greatest majority in Parliament in Canadian history.

The road to political power had not been easy for John Diefenbaker. He was born in rural Ontario near Owen Sound, but his family settled on a homestead in northern Saskatchewan in 1903. He spent one summer as a travelling bookseller and slept "in almost every haystack in Saskatchewan." In 1919, he graduated with a law degree from the University of Saskatchewan.

In his early career, Diefenbaker suffered many defeats. Four times he was defeated in provincial and federal elections before he won a seat in the House of Commons in 1940. Twice he was rejected by the Conservative party for the leadership before they turned to him in 1956.

John Diefenbaker was known as a fiery speaker. He won the support of a large majority of Canadians.

Diefenbaker was the first prime minister of Canada of neither British nor French heritage. He was intensely proud of his German background and was conscious that he represented a large number of Canadians who were neither British nor French. He brought into politics the sort of people who had not been there before: a Chinese Canadian member of Parliament and a Ukrainian Canadian minister of labour. He appointed James Gladstone as the first Native senator in 1959. For the first time a woman, Ellen Fairclough, was named to the federal Cabinet. Fairclough's appointment as Secretary of State represented a breakthrough in public service for all women. Diefenbaker chose Georges Vanier to be the first French Canadian governor general.

Diefenbaker was also proud that he had come from a homesteading family in the West. He saw himself as the champion of the common person. Indeed, he had the tremendous ability to appeal to Canadians and win their devotion. Experience as a criminal lawyer had made him a dynamic and persuasive speaker. On stage or before television cameras, he revealed a kind of political charisma. By the strength of his personality and his spellbinding oratory, he was able to stir many Canadians and win their support.

Lester Pearson: The Quiet Diplomat

Lester Pearson became leader of the Liberal party when Louis St. Laurent retired in 1958. When Pearson was only 17, he interrupted his education to serve overseas in World War I. He enlisted in the army, but transferred to the Royal Flying Corps. An officer said to him, "Lester is not a very belligerent name for a man who wants to be a fighter pilot. We'll call you 'Mike.'" The name stuck.

After the war, "Mike" Pearson taught at the University of Toronto. In 1948, he joined the Department of External Affairs. Pearson enjoyed a successful diplomatic career, which included being Canada's ambassador to the United States. He was also active in the establishment of the United Nations. He was actually nominated as the first Secretary General of the UN, but the Soviet Union would not accept a Canadian in that post. The Soviets believed that a Canadian would tend to take the side of the United States. Pearson did serve as President of the UN General Assembly in 1952-1953.

Pearson gained international respect for helping create the UN Emergency Force in the Suez crisis of 1956. His friendly and modest manner and skillful powers of persuasion made him a major force in international affairs. For his contribution to world peace, he received the Nobel Prize for peace in 1957.

Lester Pearson flies a plane over Vimy, France (site of the famous World War I battle) in 1964. He was an accomplished pilot.

Unlike Diefenbaker, Pearson was soft-spoken and never really seemed at home in the give-and-take of the Parliamentary debates. He was known in later life to sneak out of Cabinet meetings to watch World Series baseball games on television in a nearby room.

Pearson became Canada's prime minister in 1963. During his term, the government pushed forward reforms in many fields. A medical insurance plan and a Canada pension plan were set up. The Company of Young Canadians was established to help Native people and the urban and rural poor. Even after his retirement in 1968, honours continued to come Pearson's way.

1. Lester Pearson held at least six major jobs in his lifetime: wartime pilot, university professor, ambassador, politician, secretary of state for external affairs, and prime minister. What skills do you think Pearson must have had for these jobs?
2. What skills and characteristics did John Diefenbaker have that qualified him as prime minister?
3. Compare the leadership qualities of the two prime ministers. How were they similar and different?

(right to hold meetings, parades, and join clubs).

- Freedom of religion (right to worship as you please).
- Freedom of the press (right to publish opinions without fear of the government or law).
- Right of the individual to equality before the law (right to a fair trial, legal council, and protection against unfair imprisonment).

Another success of the Diefenbaker government was a series of massive wheat deals. In the 1950s, granaries, port terminals, and prairie grain elevators were jammed with wheat which farmers were unable to sell. Diefenbaker understood the desperate economic situation of the farmers. He succeeded in arranging huge wheat sales to the People's Republic of China and other communist nations. Almost 20 million tons of wheat were exported and Diefenbaker won the unending political support of prairie farmers.

In spite of these successes, Diefenbaker's appeal to Canadians began to fade. In 1959, both Canada and the United States went through an economic slowdown. Oil and mineral exploration in the North produced few results and not all of the government's projects had succeeded. By 1962, unemployment figures in Canada had climbed higher than in any year since the Great Depression.

Life in the Fabulous Fifties

Suburbs and Urbanization

In the 1950s, the population of Canada exploded. Hard times and the war had kept people from having big families in the 1930s and 1940s. But in the 1950s, the future looked promising again. People were ready to have children. Four million Canadian babies were born in the 1950s. It was a baby boom!

Families needed new homes. Many people had been too poor in the 1930s to build or buy new homes. During the war, there had been a shortage of building materials. In the 1950s, Canadians went on a home-building spree. **Suburbs** mushroomed around the major cities. Developers began to build planned communities using the neighbourhood plazas or schools as their focus. People flocked to new bungalows with big picture windows, spacious lawns front and back, and an attached garage or carport. New fads in home design and decorating took hold. Inside, white woodwork was popular and the living room featured three walls painted one colour, and the fourth covered with wallpaper.

As the city spread to the suburbs, more people needed cars. Canadians bought

EXCITING ESCAPE !

Cars in the 1950s were large, long, and low with distinctive tail fins. They were a symbol of the post-war prosperity.

over 3.5 million passenger cars in the 1950s. Each year's model seemed to grow longer, lower, and wider. North Americans believed that "bigger was better," so enormous V8 engines and power steering were added. Two-tone colours, plenty of chrome, and outlandish tail fins became the fad of the 1957 and 1958 models.

Gas was cheap and Canadians seemed to drive everywhere. Instead of shopping downtown or on Main Street, Canadians headed for the shopping centres. Shopping malls were another new invention of the 1950s. Plazas were designed to serve suburbia and the automobile. Rows of stores faced a parking lot where customers could drive in for one-stop shopping convenience.

Television

Canadians had money to spend and Canada became a consumer society. The appliance that everyone wanted first was a television set. TV did not become widespread in Canada until the 1950s. The screens were small and the picture was in black and white, often lost in a snowstorm of dots. But television caught on quickly. CBC television went on the air in 1952. Even then, stations were few and far between. Television was not available in the less populated regions of Canada until years later.

Soon television completely revolutionized Canadian life. Eating habits changed when families bought TV tables so they could eat their meals in front of the set. Children were watching so much television that homework suffered. Children's viewing habits became an urgent topic at hundreds of parent-teacher association meetings.

If your family was the first on the block to have a set, you invited the neighbours in to watch. They were motioned to sit down and be quiet. There was no time for conversation. Family life underwent great changes because of television. Families that used to go to church on Sunday evening, play games, or visit relatives, suddenly found themselves watching the "Ed Sullivan Show."

Among the favourite Canadian shows and entertainers were comedians Wayne and Shuster, Tommy Hunter on "Country Hoedown," "Front Page Challenge," and "Hockey Night in Canada."

In the 1950s, there was no fad quite like hula-hooping. The idea was supposed to have come from Australia.

Rock 'n' roll and Elvis

It all began in 1954 when Elvis Presley wrote and recorded a couple of lively tunes for his mother's birthday. The recording engineer liked what he heard, and called Elvis back in a couple of months to cut a single called "That's All Right, Mama." A Memphis disc jockey started to give it some air play on the radio, and orders poured in. It seemed that Elvis had something special. Elvis was not sure what it was, but later remarked, "I don't want it ever to end." It was star quality, youth, sex appeal, and a dynamic singing style.

Many teenagers considered Elvis Presley the "King of rock 'n' roll." When he visited Toronto, 24 000 teenagers packed Maple Leaf Gardens for two shows. He gyrated through his hits "Love Me Tender," "Hound Dog," and "Heartbreak Hotel." The show ended with Elvis flinging himself to his knees, sweat pouring down his face, and people screaming and crying for more.

What made **rock 'n' roll** so popular with the teenagers of the Fifties? For one thing, it was a way for them to express themselves against the adult world. It seemed to deal with the feelings and concerns of youth. Teenagers in the 1950s had money to buy records and record players. Disc jockeys began to feature the new music on their radio shows.

Elvis died at his estate, Graceland, in August 1977. Hundreds of thousands of fans still pay their respects to the "King" who gave rock 'n' roll its style in the 1950s.

Canadian Culture and the Canada Council

In the 1950s, radio, films, books, television, art, music, and even sports in Canada were all in danger of being swamped by American influences. In 1951, Vincent Massey, who was to become Canada's governor general, chaired a commission that investigated the problem of American influence on Canadian culture. The Massey Report suggested one solution would be to set up an organization to promote the Canadian arts. The **Canada Council** was established in 1957. In the late 1950s and early 1960s, there was a great outburst in the Canadian

Elvis Presley became the "King" of rock 'n' roll. Why did rock 'n' roll have such wide appeal for young people in the 1950s?

arts, though the debate over American influence continued. Canada Council money still helps to encourage and support artists, scholars, musicians, and writers.

Stratford and Theatre

In the sleepy little town of Stratford, Ontario, Tom Patterson had an idea. He persuaded Tyrone Guthrie, a famous director, to produce a Shakespearian festival at Stratford. In a tent beside the Avon River, the Stratford Shakespearian Festival held its first season with a production of *Richard III* in 1953. Opening night was hailed by the drama critic of *The Globe and Mail* as "the most exciting night in the history of Canadian theatre." Year after year the crowds continued to come and the festival outgrew the tent. A permanent theatre was constructed.

Stratford's success became an inspiration for theatres across the country. Drama lovers built the Neptune Theatre in Halifax, the Manitoba Theatre Centre in Winnipeg, Theatre New Brunswick in Fredericton, and similar theatres in many other centres across Canada. Thanks to Stratford and these other theatres, Canadian actors have become internationally known. These include Kate Reid, Jessica Tandy, Lorne Greene, Margot Kidder, William Shatner, Kate Nelligan, Christopher Plummer, Donald Sutherland, Brent Carver, Richard Monette, and Gordon Pinsent. Though some of these performers went to the United States or Europe to establish their reputations, many got their start in Canadian theatres such as Stratford.

Ballet

In 1951, a 29-year-old ballerina named Celia Franca founded the National Ballet of Canada. Franca and Betty Oliphant travelled more than 8000 km across Canada in search of talent. Three hundred auditions were held in schools and public halls. Twenty-eight dancers were chosen. The company could only afford to pay the dancers $25 per week, and $5 more for performances. But they opened their company that year to rave reviews from audiences wherever they danced. Similar companies, such as the Royal Winnipeg Ballet and Les Grands Ballets Canadiens in Montreal, have also won an important place in the hearts of Canadians.

The Stratford Theatre opened in 1953. Many of Canada's most talented actors got their start at Stratford.

ACTIVITIES

Check Your Understanding

1. Add these new terms to your *Factfile*.

   war brides   Canadian Bill of Rights
   Supreme Court of Canada   suburbs
   Leduc oil well   rock 'n' roll
   St. Lawrence Seaway   Canada Council
   trans-Canada pipeline

2. Make a two-column chart. In the left column, list the factors that were pushing people out of Europe after World War II. In the right column, list the factors that were pulling people to Canada.

3. How did Canada's trade pattern change after World War II? Explain why.

4. a) Why do governments in Canada change hands? List as many reasons as you can.
   b) Why did Canadians reject the Liberals in 1957?

Confirm Your Learning

5. Imagine you are a war bride who has just arrived in Canada to join your Canadian husband. Write a letter to your family in Britain. Include in your letter how you feel and some of your first impressions of Canada.

6. a) Review the reasons why Newfoundland rejected Confederation in 1867. (See pages 15 and 16.)
   b) List the factors you think were important in persuading Newfoundlanders and Labradorians to vote for joining Confederation in 1949.

7. How many other provinces joined Confederation after referendums? Why do you think the referendum was important in the case of Newfoundland and Labrador?

8. Create a map entitled "Canadian Economic Development in the 1950s." Start with an outline map of Canada, label the provinces and major cities, and devise symbols to represent the major types of development (mining, for example). Place the symbols in the appropriate areas on the map.

Challenge Your Mind

9. a) Canadians have protested against American influences on the Canadian economy and Canadian culture since Confederation. Why are Canadians uncomfortable with American influences?
   b) Do you think these fears are justified? Provide examples of American influences on Canadian culture in the 1950s and today.
   c) Provide examples of Canadian influences on American culture today.

10. Research some of the most popular television shows of the 1950s. View clips from the shows if possible. Compare television productions from the 1950s with some of those today. Record your observations in an organizer.

11. Compare rock 'n' roll music of the 1950s with rock 'n' roll today. Consider the themes, lyrics, instruments used, and stage presentation styles. Suggest reasons for similarities or differences.

12. a) Science fiction, youthful rebellion, and shock/horror were popular movie themes in the 1950s. Find examples of 1950 movies for each of these themes.
    b) Why do you think these themes were so popular in the 1950s?
    c) What themes are popular in movies today? Provide an example of a contemporary movie for each theme you suggest.

13. Discuss why certain decades in the twentieth century have names such as the "Roaring Twenties," the "Dirty Thirties," and the "Fabulous Fifties." Are these decade labels appropriate? Give reasons for your answer.

14. Prime Minister Diefenbaker's plans to build "roads to resources" in Canada's North had a profound effect on Inuit life. Research how the Inuit were affected and present a short oral report to the class.

CHAPTER 17

The Swinging Sixties

CANADA'S CENTENNIAL

A massive crowd gathered on Parliament Hill to celebrate Canada's Centennial, 1 July 1967.

At 11.50 p.m., the lights of Parliament Hill flickered off. In a few minutes, it would be **1 July 1967**. A crowd of 50 000 people on the lawns of the Parliament Buildings held up sparklers to light the night sky. Suddenly the sky blazed with red, white, blue, and green fireworks. At midnight, the carillon chimed "O Canada" and the huge throng joined in song. As the anthem ended, there was an outburst of cheering, clapping, and horn honking such as Ottawa had not heard in a hundred years. Many of the party-goers broke open champagne and stayed to dance in the streets until the sun dawned on the first day of Canada's second century.

The capital's welcome of Canada's 100th birthday was repeated all across the country. Canada broke into a frenzy of parades, picnics, and pageants. Bells pealed and were answered by hundred-gun salutes. In Edmonton, the Alberta premier cut the first slice of a giant, eight-tier birthday cake for thousands of party-goers. The crews of eight voyageur canoes, who were racing from Alberta to Montreal, stopped to celebrate with 30 000 Winnipeggers at a regatta on the Assiniboine River. At schooner races in Halifax, 20 000 people ate bowls of fish chowder in the Halifax Public Gardens. Students at Kimberley, British Columbia, sewed together 60 bedsheets to make a 610 m maple leaf flag. And St. Paul's, Alberta, a Centennial-mad town, built a UFO landing pad to welcome any little green visitors to the celebrations.

In Prince Edward Island, the premier led a ceremony of rededication to Confederation. It was in Charlottetown in 1864 that the delegates had first met to discuss union. In 19 cities and towns, great-grandchildren of the Fathers of Confederation laid wreaths at the gravesides of their famous relatives.

Canada Begins Its Second Century

The Centennial celebrations in 1967 were the highpoint of the decade for Canada. There was scarcely a city, town, or village in the country that did not dedicate a new park, library, or concert hall to the Centennial. But the crowning achievement of the Centennial celebrations was **Expo 67** in Montreal. This was a world's fair hosted by Canada in a beautiful park on two islands in the St. Lawrence River. Sixty-two nations built pavilions to show the achievements of their artists, engineers, architects, and scientists. Kings and queens, presidents and politicians came to Canada from around the world that summer. The fair attracted over 50 million visitors.

Expo 67 showed Canadians and the world an unforgettable picture of our land and its people. It made Canadians think about all they had accomplished in 100 years. Canadians were a free and prosperous people about to begin their second glorious century. But some Canadians in 1967 did not share this bright outlook for the future. Not every Canadian felt included in the country's good fortune. Native peoples still faced discrimination and were organizing to fight for their rights. People who were poor and people with disabilities were still sometimes overlooked or neglected. Many French Canadians felt there was very little in the country's future for them. The 1960s was also a time of tension and unease in Canada.

Québec Libre!

The visit of France's president, Charles De Gaulle, created an incident that rocked the Centennial celebrations. De Gaulle came to Canada at the invitation of the Quebec government. He was to visit the magnificent site of Expo 67. De Gaulle sailed up

Maurice Duplessis (holding scissors) dominated Quebec politics in the post-war era. Why was his term as premier of Quebec significant?

the St. Lawrence River and was given an enthusiastic welcome at Quebec City. From there, he travelled to Montreal in an open car. All along the route, which was lined with Quebec and French flags, De Gaulle was cheered by the crowds.

At a reception held by the city of Montreal, De Gaulle appeared on a balcony to address a wildly cheering crowd. He told the people that he felt that day as he had on the day France was liberated from the Nazis in 1944. He ended his speech with the resounding cry, *"Vive le Québec libre!"* ("Long live free Quebec!"). ***"Québec libre"*** had been the well-known slogan of Quebec separatists since 1963. De Gaulle seemed to be giving his enthusiastic support to the separatists in their struggle for the "liberation" of Quebec.

Many Canadians watching De Gaulle on television were stunned by his comparison of their government with the Nazis. Prime Minister Pearson was outraged by De Gaulle's interference in Canadian affairs. Pearson issued a sharp statement to the press, labelling as "unacceptable" De Gaulle's encouragement to "the small minority of our population whose aim it is to

destroy Canada." The prime minister went on to say that "The people of Canada are free. Every province in Canada is free. Canadians do not need to be liberated. Indeed, many thousands of Canadians gave their lives in two world wars in the liberation of France."

President De Gaulle cancelled the rest of his trip and returned immediately to France. Until De Gaulle's retirement in 1969, relations between France and Canada continued to be tense because of this affair.

Quebec Before the Quiet Revolution

The separatists were a small group in Quebec in 1967, but feelings of loyalty to French Canadian traditions and values among Quebeckers were strong. Maurice Duplessis was premier of Quebec from 1936 to 1939 and again from 1944 to 1959. He was called *le chef*, the chief, and he dominated his Union Nationale government. Duplessis was determined to stop any federal government interference in Quebec's affairs and to develop Quebec's resources. He refused some federal programs and grants for education and health care that would affect traditional life and values in Quebec. Many schools and hospitals in Quebec were run by the Roman Catholic Church.

Duplessis saw no problem with encouraging English Canadian and American investment in Quebec, however. English-speaking businesspeople established new factories and businesses. Quebec became more urban and industrialized under Duplessis. But the development also came with scandal and accusations of corruption. For almost every bridge, road, or hospital built, Duplessis expected something in return. He demanded political favours, campaign funds, or votes—and he got them.

Although Duplessis was creating a new industrialized Quebec, he emphasized traditional ways and values. Quebec society was largely closed to outside influences. The Roman Catholic Church and the French Canadian ties to the land were supported.

In September 1959, while visiting northern Quebec, Maurice Duplessis died. His iron hand rule was over. Pressures for change were suddenly let loose in Quebec. Reforms began almost immediately. But the real change came when the new Liberal government under Jean Lesage was elected in 1960. It was the beginning of the Quiet Revolution.

The Quiet Revolution

Lesage gathered around him an impressive team of cabinet ministers which included René Lévesque as minister of natural resources. The new government promised to do two main things. One was to improve the economic and social standards of the people of Quebec. The other was to win greater recognition for all French-speaking people and give them greater control over their own futures. These changes under the Lesage government came to be known as the **Quiet Revolution** in Quebec.

One of the government's first moves was to take control of the hydroelectric

A new group of painters in Quebec reflected the wave of change. This painting by Paul-Émile Borduas entitled The Circular Path, Nest of Aeroplanes *represents a move to a more abstract style.*

companies. Control over hydroelectric power would give Quebeckers more say in their economic future. The government also supported the building of the Manicouagan Power Dam, one of the largest in the world. French Canadian engineers from all parts of Canada returned to Quebec to work on the project. The catch phrase was *"on est capable"* or "we can do it!"

Another slogan of the Quiet Revolution was *"Maîtres chez nous,"* meaning "Masters in our own house." The government wanted more control for French Canadians over affairs in Quebec. Many businesses were run by English Canadians and French Canadian workers often earned less than workers in other parts of the country.

Quebeckers of British origin were at the top of the economic ladder. Their average annual wage in 1960 was $4940. Average wages then declined through a number of other largely English-speaking ethnic groups: Scandinavian, Jewish, German, Polish, and Asian. Almost at the bottom of the economic ladder were the French Canadian Quebeckers. Their average annual wage was $3185.

Most top management jobs in the province were held by English-speaking people. Twice as many English as French Canadians held high paying, high status professional and managerial jobs. French-speaking Quebeckers, 80 percent of Quebec's total population, were among the least favoured in their own province.

The Lesage government also began to replace programs previously run by the Church. These included hospital insurance, pension schemes, and the beginnings of medicare. To do this, the Quebec Liberals had to struggle with Ottawa for a larger share of the tax dollar.

One of the most sweeping reforms was the modernization of the school system. In the past, the schools of Quebec had been run by the Church. Priests and nuns provided a good education, but not in business and technology which was what Quebec now needed. Lesage wanted a government-run school system that would equip a modern Quebec with experts in engineering, science, business, and commerce.

The new freedom of expression in Quebec gave rise to a flood of books, plays, art, and music about the French culture in Quebec. Gratien Gélines became one of the most popular contemporary playwrights. New film directors such as Claude Jutra began to emphasize themes drawn from Quebec life in their films. Of all the

Robert Charlebois was one of the Quebec musicians popular in the 1960s.

artists, the singers of Quebec in the 1960s used political themes and messages the most. The song "Mon Pays" by Gilles Vigneault describes his tender feelings toward his "country," Quebec, and his French Canadian heritage.

But all was not well in the province of Quebec. Relations between French- and English-speaking people were tense. Author Hugh Maclennan wrote about the "two solitudes" in Canada. English and French Canadians seemed to live parallel but completely separate lives.

Separatism and the Independence Movement

Some Quebeckers suggested that the only solution to Quebec's problems was **separatism**. Separatism means the desire of a province to break away from the Canadian union. During the Quiet Revolution of the 1960s, a small but influential group began to talk seriously about separation. Separatists demanded immediate independence for Quebec. They argued that as long as Quebec was associated with the rest of Canada, French Canadians would never be treated as equals. The separatist slogan was *"Québec libre"* or "Free Quebec."

The **Front de Libération du Québec (FLQ)**, founded in 1963, was a radical group of separatists. The FLQ had no leader, but was a collection of separate cells or groups. Their idea was to use terrorism as a weapon to achieve independence for Quebec. A number of bombs were exploded, mostly in Montreal, and at least one person was killed.

Another separatist group, the Armée de Liberation du Quebec (ALQ), used even

A mailbox bomb explodes in Montreal. Why did some Quebec separatist groups use these measures?

more violent methods. They robbed banks to get money and raided Canadian Armed Forces depots for ammunition. They set off bombs in letter boxes in the English-speaking districts of Montreal. Between 1963 and 1970, there was a terrorist bombing somewhere in the province almost every ten days.

In the Quebec provincial election of 1966, the Union Nationale party under Daniel Johnson was elected. Their slogan was "Equality or Independence." Johnson warned Ottawa that unless Quebec was given "special status" in Confederation, it would have to go its own way. This demand included control over economics, social welfare, housing, and tax dollars to carry out these responsibilities. Quebec also wanted to deal directly with foreign governments in matters of culture and education.

The independence movement continued to gain momentum. In 1968, René Lévesque formed the **Parti Québécois**. Lévesque was a fiery broadcaster and former politician. He spoke passionately about Quebec's rights and the wrongs that had been done to French Canadians. He was a hero to a new generation who preferred to be called Québécois, not French Canadians.

Lévesque proposed **sovereignty** for Quebec. This means that he believed the future for Quebec was as an independent country, running its own affairs without interference from the rest of Canada. Lévesque always opposed terrorism and insisted on democratic and moderate means for achieving independence.

Responses to the Independence Movement

Many Canadians were alarmed by talk of separatism. The Canadian government realized that Quebec was changing dramat-

ically during the Quiet Revolution. There were new ideas and attitudes in Quebec that had to be addressed by the federal government.

Bi and Bi Commission

In 1963, the Pearson government set up a **Royal Commission on Bilingualism and Biculturalism** (Bi and Bi Commission). It was to examine the relations between French and English Canadians. It was also to consider Quebec's role in Confederation. The Commission studied the issue for several years. It concluded that Canada was passing through its greatest crisis. The Commission warned that unless there was a new and equal partnership between French and English Canadians, a breakup was likely to result. Among the Commission's major recommendations were the following:

i) Canada should be officially declared bilingual by making French and English the official languages of the federal Parliament and courts

ii) New Brunswick and Ontario should officially declare themselves bilingual provinces

iii) provinces where the minority group is more than 10 percent should provide government services in both English and French

iv) the region of Ottawa-Hull should be made a national capital area and should be officially bilingual

v) students in all provinces should be given a chance to study both official languages

vi) more French Canadians should be employed in the federal government

vii) in Quebec, French should be the main language of work, government, and business.

By 1970, many of the major recommendations of the Commission had been carried out.

A New Flag for Canada

The federal Liberals also decided to adopt a new Canadian flag. It would replace Britain's Union Jack or the Red Ensign with its Union Jack in the upper corner and the Canadian Coat of Arms diagonally opposite it. Both the Union Jack and the Red Ensign were disliked by many French Canadians because of their close association with the British Empire and the conquest of New France in 1759. Many other Canadian citizens also thought it was time Canada shed its colonial past and had its own distinctive flag.

The design of the new flag submitted to Parliament by the Liberals purposely avoided British and French symbols—the Union Jack and the fleur-de-lis. Instead, there were three red maple leaves sprouting from a single stem on a white background. At each end of the flag were vertical blue bars to suggest the Atlantic and Pacific.

In Parliament, John Diefenbaker led the opposition to "Pearson's Pennant." Diefenbaker, proud of Canada's British connections, wished to keep the Red Ensign. He was not alone. Many veterans who had fought bravely under the Red Ensign in two world wars did not want to see it replaced.

Months of controversy followed. Finally, an all-party parliamentary committee recommended a new design. It was a single red maple leaf on a white background with red borders at each end. Diefenbaker and some of the opposition hoped to delay the passing of the flag bill by using filibuster. Filibustering means talking on endlessly until the plan has to be dropped so the government can go on with other business.

For 33 days, opposition members stated and restated their reasons for rejecting the new flag. Neither side would give in. Finally, the Liberal government ended the flag debate by using closure. At 2:30 in the morning of 15 December 1964, Canada's new red maple leaf flag was officially passed. It was a scene full of emotion. As the vote was announced (163 for, 78 against), the MPs rose to their feet to sing "O Canada."

Emerging Federal Leaders from Quebec

Many French Canadian nationalists in Quebec were not separatists. They believed French Canadians could play a role in a genuinely bicultural Canada. They believed the answer for Quebec lay in federalism.

The flag in the top right is the Red Ensign, which was replaced by the flag with the single red maple leaf.

The New .. The Old ..

These Also Ran .. Commonwealth?

Prime Minister Pearson was actively looking for well-known Quebeckers to run as candidates for the Liberal party. He wanted to give Quebeckers a strong voice in the federal government. He invited the so-called "Three Wise Men from Quebec," Gerard Pelletier, Jean Marchand, and Pierre Trudeau to run for federal Parliament in the election of 1965. All three were elected. Quebec now had representatives with power and influence in the federal cabinet.

The Official Languages Act 1969

The federal government also took steps to give greater recognition to the French language in the **Official Languages Act** in 1969. The Act declared:

The English and French languages are the official languages of Canada for all purposes of the Parliament and Government of Canada and possess and enjoy equality of status and equal rights and privileges as to their use in all the institutions of the Parliament and Government of Canada.

In other words, the Act guaranteed that both French and English Canadians could deal with the federal government in their own language. All documents, reports, speeches, and pamphlets issued to the public were now to be published in French and English. In parts of Canada where there was a sizable French Canadian minority, government services were to be available in both languages.

Federal funds were provided to the provinces to promote bilingualism. Facilities for French language radio and television in provinces outside Quebec were expanded. Regulations required bilingual labelling on products sold across Canada. The government also pledged to provide more jobs in the federal government for French-speaking citizens. Until that time, only 14 percent of the top government jobs were held by French Canadians, even though they made up 25 percent of the population.

Pierre Trudeau described bilingualism as the most important issue in French-English relations since the Conscription Crisis. However, there was widespread criticism of the Official Languages Act outside Quebec. Many Canadians living in a multicultural Canada felt that the federal government was trying to "ram French down people's throats." The issue of French-English relations in Canada was far from resolved.

Protest and Social Change

In the 1960s not only Quebec, but the whole country seemed eager for change. The decade of the 1960s is sometimes called "The Decade of Protest." Young people in particular were questioning society's values. Protests arose over nuclear armament, war, American interference in Canadian affairs, and rights for social groups including Native peoples and African Canadians.

Canadian-American Relations

In 1957, Canada had signed an agreement with the United States setting up the North American Air Defence Command (NORAD). Despite the agreement, the Diefenbaker government refused to accept nuclear warheads for the Bomarc B, a surface-to-air missile. Diefenbaker felt that arming the Bomarcs with nuclear warheads would set back the hopes for nuclear disarmament in the world. He preferred storing nuclear warheads south of the border until they were needed. His opponents argued that Bomarc missiles without nuclear warheads were useless.

The question became critical during the **Cuban Missile Crisis**. In 1962, the world came dangerously close to nuclear war. The Soviet Union had installed missiles in Cuba. From the Cuban launch sites, missiles could attack most major American and Canadian cities. The United States demanded the Soviet missiles be removed. It blockaded the shipment of Soviet military equipment to Cuba.

The United States asked Canada as its defence partner to put all Canadian forces on alert. Canada hesitated to do this, causing a deep rift between the American and Canadian governments. Canada's Bomarc missiles were still not armed with nuclear warheads. Diefenbaker accused the United States of pressuring Canada. He also accused Liberal leader Pearson of flip-flopping on the issue of nuclear arms. Pearson had opposed nuclear missiles in Canada, but gradually became more accepting of them.

The issue of nuclear weapons and American involvement in Canadian affairs became key election issues in 1963. In April, the pro-nuclear Liberal party won 129 seats in the House of Commons. Diefenbaker and the Conservatives won 95. It was during that election that Lester Pearson became prime minister. The new Liberal government was committed to arming the Bomarcs with nuclear warheads and supporting Canada's NORAD commitment.

The issue also sparked debate and protest across the country. Many people were seriously concerned about a nuclear war. Anti-nuclear demonstrations were held in many areas of Canada. Women's groups, youth groups, members of the CCF (Co-operative Commonwealth Federation), and others raised their voices against "nukes" in Canada.

Canadians also held anti-war demonstrations demanding that the United States remove its forces from the war in **Vietnam**. One of their anti-war slogans was "Make Love — Not War." Young Americans were being drafted into the armed forces to fight in Vietnam. Thousands burned their draft cards and fled to Canada to avoid fighting in a war they did not believe in. They were called draft dodgers.

Native Rights

In Canada, Native leaders such as Harold Cardinal, Howard Adams, and Kahn Tinehta Horn campaigned to protect the rights of their peoples. Native peoples had succeeded in gaining some changes to the Indian Act in 1951. Bans on their ceremonies and dances were lifted, band members no longer needed special permits to sell produce, and the veto right of the Indian Affairs minister over band decisions on reserves was reduced.

But in 1969, the government published

Canadians stage a peace demonstration. What other issues sparked Canadian protests in the 1960s?

THE ARTS

As Native political leaders spoke out for the rights of their peoples in the 1960s, some Native artists were also gaining international recognition. Their work increased awareness of Native cultures. Two prominent artists included Norval Morrisseau and Pitseolak Ashoona.

Norval Morrisseau

In the fall of 1962, the work of a young Ojibwa artist caused excitement in Toronto. The artist was Norval Morrisseau and it was his first exhibit. On opening night, all his paintings were sold. Such success was remarkable.

Morrisseau's paintings represented subjects from the oral tradition of the Ojibwa people. Many showed the Manitous, the spirits of the Ojibwa. For a long time Morrisseau wondered whether it was proper to paint and exhibit these spiritual subjects. Eventually, he had a vision in a dream which told him it was all right to do so.

Morrisseau had no formal art lessons, although his grandfather had showed him how to make pictures on birchbark. His earliest pictures were in black and shades of brown on paper. Later, he began adding brilliant colours and painting on canvas in acrylics.

Morrisseau has created large murals for public buildings and his works now hang in major collections all over Canada. His work has influenced a new generation of Native painters in eastern Canada such as Benjamin Chee-Chee and Carl Ray. Like Morrisseau, they interpret traditional stories of their people.

The Water Spirit, *by Norval Morrisseau.*

Pitseolak Ashoona

Her prints hang in the National Gallery in Ottawa and in museums in Europe and the United States. They show traditional Inuit scenes. Her energetic drawings capture the spirit and the customs of the traditional life on the land. They show families on hunting expeditions, hooded figures in sealskin boats, and little girls learning to catch a goose. But the way of Inuit life the pictures show has largely disappeared in the North.

The artist is Pitseolak. She was born in 1904 on Nottingham Island in the Arctic. For most of her life, she lived a traditional camp life moving with her husband and family in search of good hunting.

After her husband's death, Pitseolak was very poor. In 1957, she heard that Inuit at Cape Dorset were learning to make stone cuts and prints from drawings. Pitseolak decided to try drawing to earn a living. She had never drawn before, but her talents were quickly recognized. Her first drawings were eagerly bought at the Cape Dorset Co-operative. Before she died in 1983, she had created more than 7000 drawings showing the ways of her people. She received many honours for her artistic achievements. In 1977, she was awarded the Order of Canada.

Women Juggling Stones by Pitseolak Ashoona.

1. Today, Native artists, writers, and performers are gaining increasing recognition nationally and internationally in many different fields. Investigate some of these artists. For visual artists, you could create a short portfolio to represent their work. For musicians or others, you could present a short biography and list of achievements or an audiotape. Consider some of the following people and investigate others.

John Kim Bell	Buffy Sainte-Marie	Daniel David Moses
Tantoo Cardinal	Tomson Highway	Thomas King
Graham Greene	Carl Ray	Susan Aglukark
Tom Jackson	Kashtin	Douglas Cardinal
Rita Joe	Ruby Slipperjack	Daphne Odjig

a White Paper (policy paper) on Indian affairs. It recommended that the special status of Indians set out in the Indian Act be gradually eliminated. Prime Minister Trudeau proposed that Native peoples should be given exactly the same rights as all other Canadians and move toward "full social, economic, and political participation in Canadian life."

Many Native people strongly opposed this policy, however. They believed it would result in the loss of their cultures and heritage by absorbing them into mainstream Canadian society. They argued that they should be treated as independent peoples who had negotiated special protection of their lands and special rights through treaties. They also believed in their aboriginal right (rights as the first inhabitants) to lands not covered by treaties.

Some court decisions had come down in their favour. A 1965 ruling in Saskatchewan said that all registered Indians had the right to medical insurance from the government even if they lived off reserves. Treaty No. 6 signed in the 1870s had stated "a medicine chest will be kept at the house of each Indian agent." This was taken to mean that the government had made a commitment to look after the health of the Native people whose ancestors had signed the treaty. The decision implied that treaties must be honoured by the government even within modern times and in modern terms. The federal government changed its policy and established a forum to handle Native land claims.

In 1972 the National Indian Brotherhood had asserted the inherent right of Native peoples to control over their own education in a paper entitled *Indian Control over Indian Education*. The major goals were to reinforce the identity of Native children and encourage parental and local control over Native education. The government accepted the paper in principle, but many questions over rights and claims had still to be resolved.

Youth and "Hippies"

Other social protests in the 1960s centred on university campuses. There were sit-ins and marches as students demanded more say in the running of schools. Students also argued that Canada was too closely allied to the United States. They wanted a country free from foreign control and directing its own destiny. Many young people were idealistic and truly wanted to make a contribution to the world. Canadian Universities Service Overseas (CUSO) sponsored young Canadians who wanted to go abroad to help in developing countries.

Another group rebelled by dropping out of society. They became **"hippies."** Outwardly, they rejected many of society's values. Some went "back to the land" where they tried living in communes and raising organic foods. Many preached international peace and love. They wore their hair long and dressed exotically. Some experimented with drugs, especially marijuana.

The Women's Movement

Like students and workers, many Canadian women in the 1960s were prepared to work for social change. The **Women's Liberation Movement** burst on the scene in the 1960s. Women protested and marched for changes in employment practices. Many jobs held by women were lower paying and had less prestige than jobs held by men. Ninety-five percent of all secretaries were female, but fewer than seven percent of doctors were women. Women still met with discrimination when they tried to move into jobs previously done by men. Women also wanted the chance to combine career and family.

Women in the 1960s also had little voice in politics. There were only a handful of women members of Parliament and just a scattering of women in local and provincial governments. Women's Liberationists wanted equal treatment with men.

But things were starting to change. By 1967, the Women's Movement had pushed

SOCIETY AND SOCIAL CHANGE

A View on the 1960s

Talk like a Hippie: Slang of the Sixties

Slang term	*Meaning*
bread	money
rap	discuss
groovy	really fine
flower child	hippie
far out	great!
out of sight	terrific!
good vibes	positive feelings
psychedelic	pertaining to drugs

1. Listen to music by performers from the 1960s. What major themes are expressed in the songs?
2. Investigate popular fashions and fads of the 1960s. How did they reflect the "Decade of Protest?"
3. What influences from the 1960s can you still see in music and fashions today?

The Beatles burst on the scene in the 1960s. They began a revolution in popular music.

Joni Mitchell was one of the best known Canadian performers of the 1960s. Her expressive, confessional songs caught the imagination of many young people.

the Canadian government into establishing a **Royal Commission on the Status of Women**. It was headed by Florence Bird, a journalist and broadcaster. The Commission's purpose was to recommend steps that could be taken by the government "to ensure for women equal opportunities with men in all aspects of Canadian society."

A New Political Party— The NDP

Many workers, farmers, and intellectuals were also looking for a stronger political voice to represent their views and interests. They felt that the Liberal and Conservative parties tended to reflect the interests of "Big Business." Many dreamed of a new party which would revive the flagging CCF.

In 1961, a political convention was held in Ottawa by the CCF and the Canadian Labour Congress. At that convention, the **New Democratic Party (NDP)** was born. The colourful and energetic premier of Saskatchewan, T.C. "Tommy" Douglas, was elected its leader. People now believed that voters would have a clear alternative to the old-style politics of the Liberal and Conservative parties.

The New Democratic Party stood for full employment, free education, Canadian control of the economy, and public ownership of important natural resources. Perhaps the greatest contribution of the NDP was the idea of universal free medical care. Medicare was first introduced in Saskatchewan in 1962. Today, all provinces have some sort of medical insurance program. All Canadian citizens have access to medical care regardless of their ability to pay for it.

Popular Culture in the Sixties

In the 1960s, the baby boomers were growing up. Youth was in style. Everyone wanted to look young, feel young, and act young. Many young people rejected everything they saw as part of the "establishment"—police, values of parents, government, big business.

The term "counterculture" came into the language. The cultural standards among youth ran counter to the values and materialism of their parents' generation. Miniskirts, long hair, tie-dyed t-shirts, beads, and brightly coloured bell-bottom pants replaced the grey flannel suit look of their parents. Many young people "turned on" to drugs. Marijuana, LSD, amphetamines, and barbiturates were all part of the counterculture. In districts such as Yorkville in Toronto, mobile clinics were set up to rescue young people on "bad trips" from taking drugs. Changes in society seemed to be everywhere, but some of the greatest changes were taking place in music.

Beatlemania

In 1964, teenagers discovered the Beatles! To the shock of adults, young people copied shaggy Beatle haircuts, bought Beatle buttons, watches, wigs, dolls, and wallets, and repeated Beatle lyrics, such as "She loves you, yeah, yeah, yeah." Sociologists called **"Beatlemania"** a form of protest against the adult world. They said it could not last. The experts were wrong. The boys from Liverpool, England, made some of the most important advances in popular music in their era.

The 1960s was the decade of the "British invasion." Groups such as the Rolling Stones, the Dave Clark Five, Herman's Hermits, the Animals, and Peter and Gordon followed the Beatles's popularity in Canada and the United States. The 1950s was the era of the solo singer, but with the popularity of the Beatles, the 1960s saw the growth of musical groups. Songs by American groups such as the Beach Boys, Creedence Clearwater Revival, the Monkees, and Led Zeppelin went to the top of the charts.

Motown music featured singers such as Stevie Wonder, Aretha Franklin, and James Brown. Teenagers loved to dance in the 1960s. The driving music of Janis Joplin,

Jimi Hendrix, Jim Morrison and the Doors, and Pink Floyd got everyone dancing.

Bob Dylan was known as America's foremost folk singer. Many of his songs, such as "Blowing in the Wind," "The Times They Are a'Changing," and "Don't Think Twice, It's All Right," became top 40 hits. As the protest movement gained momentum, Bob Dylan's words and music became the protest movement's anthems. Among the Canadian voices of protest in the 1960s were artists such as Ian and Sylvia Tyson, Gordon Lightfoot, Buffy Sainte-Marie, and Neil Young.

DEVELOPING SKILLS: INTERVIEWING

An interview is a face-to-face meeting between people to talk about a topic or issue. Usually one or both parties want to obtain information. When you go for an interview for a summer job, you want to know about the job and whether you have the skills to do it. The employer wants to know whether you are the right person for the job.

Journalists make their living conducting interviews. Barry Broadfoot is a newspaper reporter and social historian who has collected information through interviews. He travelled across Canada talking to people about their experiences. The interviews are collected in books describing what life was like during the Great Depression and World War II. The books and interviews are an important part of our oral history.

There were three secrets to Broadfoot's success. He went armed with a tape recorder, he did thorough background research, and he went prepared with good questions. You can collect valuable information about the culture of the 1960s by interviewing someone who was a teenager during that decade. Use the questionnaire below or make up one of your own. Share with the class what you discover in the interviews.

Steps for an Effective Interview

■ Step 1
Know your purpose. What information are you after? In this case, you want to know more about teenage culture in the 1960s.

■ Step 2
Prepare well in advance by researching the topic. You need to be well informed to ask intelligent questions. For example, some research will tell you that television did not come into most people's homes until the 1950s. With this knowledge, you can ask whether the person had a television and what shows were popular.

■ Step 3
Write out questions beforehand. The right question is the only way to get the right information. You could decide on key topics you want to cover such as clothing styles, music, etc. These topics will help you focus your questions.

■ Step 4
Be flexible. Think of secondary or follow-up questions to get deeper explanations. Listen actively to what the person is saying and encourage him or her to expand on a topic that may uncover some interesting information.

■ Step 5
Make arrangements with the person to be interviewed at a convenient time and place. Make sure the arrangements are comfortable.

■ Step 6
Write down as much information as you can or take an audio or video recorder. Always get permission to tape the interview from the person you are interviewing and know how the machine operates. Practise before the interview.

■ Step 7
Finish the interview with an open question such as: "Do you have anything else to add?" Valuable information may be overlooked if you use only your directed questions.

■ Step 8
Expand your notes as soon as possible after the interview.

■ **Step 9**

Practise good manners. Be on time. Thank the person at the end of the interview, and send a thank you letter afterwards.

■ **Step 10**

Share the results of your interview with your classmates.

Sample Questionnaire

Subject's Name: _____

Interviewer's Name: _____

Approximate age of the subject during the 1960s: _____

1. Background: When and where did you attend high school? What are your best memories of high school?

2. Fashion: What styles of clothing do you associate with the 1960s? Describe your favourite outfit. Did you wear anything that could be described as outrageous? If so, describe it.

3. Music: What types of music did teenagers listen to in the 1960s? Who were your favourite male and female artists and groups? What were the themes of the popular songs?

4. Movies: Do you recall any movies that you watched during the Sixties? What were the themes of films during this time? Who were your favourite movie stars?

5. Television: Did your family have a television in the Sixties? What were your favourite TV shows?

6. Attitudes: Did you feel there was a generation gap between you and your parents? If so, explain.

7. Protests: What protest movements do you associate with the decade? Were you personally involved in any?

8. What is your happiest memory of being a teenager? Do you have any other memories of the 1960s that you would like to share?

Trudeaumania

The Sixties was a time for youth. Canadians were tired of the same old faces in politics. They wanted someone new. It was in this atmosphere of change and rebellion that Pierre Trudeau became leader of the Liberal party and prime minister in 1968. To many Canadians, Trudeau seemed to be the man of the hour. For one thing, he was a French-speaking Quebecker. Many felt he would be able to address Quebec's concerns. He was also youthful, casual, and stylish. He drove fast sports cars and had been photographed doing jack-knife dives into swimming pools and riding a camel.

As minister of justice, Trudeau had convinced people he was cool under pressure, logical, and scholarly. Above all, on television he showed wit and confidence. His charisma on television and at huge political rallies made him exceptionally popular. Wherever Trudeau appeared to give a speech, it was like a rock concert. Young Liberals screamed themselves hoarse and the crowds swarmed around their hero. During the 1968 election campaign, Trudeau spoke French from Victoria to St. John's. Every speech had some paragraphs in French, and English-speaking audiences cheered, even though they did not understand the language.

Trudeau adopted a whole new campaign style. He arrived in many cities by jet, and then descended into a suburban shopping centre parking lot by helicopter. He mingled with the crowd, shaking hands and accepting kisses from admirers. Trudeau talked to the crowds about building a "just society," in which all Canadians were respected and shared in the country's prosperity. Hecklers were put down easily with quick-witted replies. He ended by challenging Canadians to take a chance on the future and vote for the Liberals. Smiling for the cameras, he then tossed the flower from his buttonhole to the crowd. He stepped back into the helicopter and was whisked away to his next rally. He seemed to be willing to meet the people and discuss the issues with them in plain talk. The crowds loved him. The press called it **Trudeaumania**.

Next to Trudeau, Robert Stanfield, leader of the Conservative party, appeared steady, but dull. He was particularly uneasy in front of news cameras. He once complained, "You walk out of the House of Commons and they shove a bunch of microphones in your face, and in 30 seconds you are expected to produce a profound and intelligent answer to an extremely complicated national issue." Stanfield's answers were thoughtful and honest, but his slow manner of speaking made him seem indecisive and weak. Stanfield never had a chance.

On the eve of the election, 24 June 1968, the St. Jean Baptiste parade was held in Montreal. Trudeau stood on the platform with the special guests. In the crowd were some radical separatists determined to demonstrate against Canadian federalism. The parade turned into a riot. Demonstrators began throwing rocks and bottles. Most of the guests on the platform dashed inside for safety, but Trudeau remained on the platform. The people of Canada, watching on television, saw their next prime minister standing firm against the radical separatists.

Headlines the next day said "Trudeau defies separatists." Citizens read the headlines as they went to the polls to vote. It clinched an already assured victory. Trudeau won a resounding majority in the election. Trudeau's Liberals won 155 seats, the Conservatives 72, and the NDP 22.

The major appeal of Trudeau in 1968 seemed to be that he offered Canadians new hope for a fresh beginning. An editorial in *The Globe and Mail* said of Trudeau:

Trudeau attracted large crowds and gained tremendous popular support in the 1960s. It was Trudeaumania.

The argument most frequently made against Trudeau is that he is unknown, that we have no long-term record of Mr. Trudeau as an administrator, that we can't be certain how he will react in any given situation.

But perhaps it is one of the facts of life in the Sixties that Canada no longer needs the great certainties that are largely born of fear. Canada is willing to adventure. It may be that what Canadians see in Mr. Trudeau is this new side of themselves, a readiness to gamble on the unknown, to move into areas not explored before.

The Globe and Mail

ACTIVITIES

Check Your Understanding

1. Add these new terms to your *Factfile*.

1 July 1967	Cuban Missile Crisis
Expo 67	Vietnam War
"Québec libre"	hippies
Quiet Revolution	Women's Liberation Movement
separatism	Royal Commission on the Status of Women
FLQ	New Democratic Party (NDP)
Parti Québécois	Beatlemania
Quebec sovereignty	Trudeaumania
Bi and Bi Commission	
Official Languages Act	

2. a) What problems did leaders of the Quiet Revolution feel Quebec faced?
   b) Identify the leaders and other personalities who played a role in shaping changes during the Quiet Revolution. What role did each play?

3. Explain briefly the views of each of the following on Quebec in the 1960s.
   a) Daniel Johnson
   b) René Lévesque
   c) Pierre Trudeau
   d) the FLQ

4. Why has the 1960s been called the "Decade of Protest?" Which groups in society pushed for change? Why?

Confirm Your Learning

5. a) In your opinion, what were the most important achievements of the Quiet Revolution? Support your answer.
   b) How did the federal government attempt to resolve the concerns of French Canadians? How successful were these measures?

6. If you were a French Canadian living in Quebec in the 1960s, would you have joined the separatist movement? Why or why not? Use a decision-making organizer in your answer.

7. a) What are the special symbols that represent your school or community? How do you feel when you see these symbols used?

   b) Why are symbols, such as a flag, important to a country? Do you think Canada should have gotten its own flag in 1964? Why would some groups of people be strongly opposed to a new flag?

   c) Identify some other symbols that represent Canada. What aspects of Canada do these symbols emphasize?

8. Why were Canadian voters attracted to Pierre Trudeau in 1968? Ask someone who remembers the election of 1968 what he or she can recall of Trudeaumania.

9. Prepare a time capsule or audio-visual presentation capturing teenage life in the 1960s.

10. Role play a radio or television news broadcast on one of the following events of the 1960s.

    a) a peace demonstration

    b) a bomb blast in Quebec

    c) a speech by Trudeau during the 1968 election campaign

    d) a college or university sit-in

    e) a debate over the flag issue

Challenge Your Mind

11. Debate:"Canada should not have accepted nuclear warheads for the Bomarc missiles in 1963."

12. a) The Bi and Bi Commission challenged both English and French Canadians to make serious changes in their attitudes. Read the quote below from the Royal Commission carefully. Make a two-column chart in your notebook and label the columns "What English Canadians should do" and "What French Canadians should do." Summarize in your own words the recommendations to both cultural groups.

    b) Do you think the recommendations were sound? Explain.

From evidence so far accumulated, it appears to us that English-speaking Canadians as a whole must come to recognize the existence of a vigorous French-speaking society within Canada, and to find out more about the aspirations, frustrations, and achievements of French-speaking Canadians, in Quebec and outside it. They must come to understand what it means to be a member of a minority, or of a smaller partner people, and to be ready to give that minority assurances which are unnecessary for a majority. More than a century ago, Sir John A. Macdonald wrote to an English-speaking friend: 'Treat them as a nation and they will act as a free people generally do—generously. Call them a faction and they become factious! They have to face the fact that, if Canada is to continue to exist, there must be a true partnership, and that the partnership must be worked out as between equals. They must be prepared to discuss in a forthright, open-minded way the practical implications of such a partnership.'

On the same evidence, it seems to us that French-speaking Canadians for their part must be ready to respond positively if there are to be truly significant developments towards a better partnership. It would be necessary for French-speaking Quebeckers to restrain their present tendency to concentrate so intensely on their own affairs and to look so largely inward. Problems affecting all Canada are their problems too. They would need to beware of the kind of thinking that puts 'la nation' above all other considerations and values. They too, like the English-speaking, should forget the conquest and any psychological effects they think it left. They would have to avoid blaming English-speaking Canadians for shortcomings which are their own and, at times, to remember that English-speaking Canadians have their feelings too. They, as well as the English-speaking must remember that, if a partnership works, each party must give as well as get.

13. "Campaign styles are more important than campaign issues." Discuss this statement with respect to Trudeaumania in 1968. Is this statement true of political leaders today? Justify your answer.

Contemporary Canada, 1970–Present

TIMELINE

1970	October Crisis in Quebec
1971	Foreign Investment Review Agency (FIRA) formed
1974	Quebec Official Languages Act (Bill 22) passed
1976	Parti Québécois forms the Quebec government
1977	Bill 101 passed in Quebec
1980	Quebec votes "No" to sovereignty association National Energy Program established
1982	Constitution Act signed by Queen Elizabeth
1985	Arctic sovereignty dispute with the United States
1987	Meech Lake Accord defeated
1989	Free Trade Agreement with the United States
1990	Mohawk stand at Oka, Quebec
1991	Agreement reached on Nunavut
1992	Charlottetown Accord defeated
1994	North American Free Trade Agreement signed
1995	Sovereignty referendum in Quebec

At the end of the 1990s, the world will enter the twenty-first century. Sir Wilfrid Laurier had said that the twentieth century would belong to Canada. You have read about just how much Canada has grown and changed in this century.

Many of the issues that characterize contemporary Canada have been important throughout the century. Relations between French and English Canadians still dominate our national life. Quebec's future relations with Canada remain an open-ended question.

Canada's relationship with the United States and its role in the world have also remained important issues. The Free Trade Agreement and North American Free Trade Agreement have forged stronger economic ties with our neighbours and stirred controversy. Canada is taking a new role in an increasingly global economy. But living next door to a powerful neighbour, we still struggle to maintain our Canadian identity.

Canada has also struggled with its Constitution in the last decades. A constitution describes the way in which the government works and outlines people's rights. In 1982, changes were made to Canada's Constitution, but they did not satisfy all Canadians. Quebec did not sign until five years later. Native peoples, women, and some of the less wealthy provinces struggled to have their rights recognized. Further attempts to find a new constitutional agreement ended in failure.

Canada began the twentieth century with a great immigration boom. Contemporary Canada continues to be enriched by an influx of immigrants from around the world. Unfortunately, recent immigrants are still sometimes treated with prejudice and racism. The challenge in contemporary Canada is to respect the rights of minorities and educate all Canadians about cultures other than their own.

At the end of this unit, you will be able to:

- describe some of the significant changes Canada has undergone in the twentieth century
- analyze the reasons for the growing nationalist movement in Quebec
- explain the issues involved in the debates over the Constitution
- recognize the major issues in Canada's relations with the United States and the world
- understand some of the challenges facing contemporary Canada, such as immigration policy, equality between the sexes, protection of the environment, racial tolerance, Canada's role as a peacekeeper, and the national debt
- demonstrate the skills in preparing a research essay
- conduct a sample of public opinion
- effectively analyze and evaluate news articles

KEY THEMES

Social Issues

- Oka crisis and Native issues
- racism vs tolerance in Canada
- equality between men and women
- protection of the environment

The Economy

- energy crisis of the 1970s and economic nationalism
- Free Trade and North American Free Trade Agreements
- national debt issue

French-English Relations

- October Crisis 1970
- Parti Québécois victory in Quebec 1976 and 1994
- Quebec language bills
- referendums on sovereignty, 1980 and 1995
- rejection of Meech Lake and Charlottetown Accords

Canadian-American Relations

- debate over American influence on Canadian economy and culture
- Arctic sovereignty dispute 1985
- Free Trade and North American Free Trade Agreements
- changing roles in NATO and NORAD

Canada and the World

- foreign aid programs
- changing defence policies
- Canada's peacekeeping role
- trade agreements and Canada's role in the global marketplace

National Growth and Identity

- patriation of the Constitution 1982
- immigration boom and increasing cultural diversity

Regional Development

- crisis in Newfoundland fishery
- establishment of new territory in north, Nunavut
- Quebec sovereignty issue

Citizenship, Government, and Law

- War Measures Act invoked 1970
- Constitution Act 1982 and Canadian Charter of Rights and Freedoms
- constitutional reform issues: Meech Lake and Charlottetown Accords
- new political parties: Reform party and Bloc Québécois
- issue of aboriginal self-government

Technological Change

- nuclear disarmament
- Canada's role in space research and satellite technology

The Arts

- funding for the arts
- blossoming of arts in Quebec
- international success of Canadian artists, musicians, etc.

Canada and Quebec: One Nation or Two?

OCTOBER CRISIS

5 October 1970, 8:15 a.m. – The doorbell rings in the luxurious home of the senior British trade commissioner in Montreal, James R. Cross. Two men carrying a gift-wrapped package tell the person who opens the door that they want to deliver it to Mr. Cross. Inside the house, they pull a rifle from the package and seize James Cross.

11:30 a.m. – A radio station receives ransom demands from the kidnappers. They identify themselves as members of the FLQ and demand the release of 23 "political prisoners" being held for bombings and terrorist activities. They also demand transportation to Cuba or Algeria, $500 000 in gold bars, and publication of the FLQ Manifesto (statement of beliefs). The government has 48 hours to comply or Cross will be killed.

8 October – The government refuses the demands of the kidnappers, but the FLQ Manifesto is read on the radio and television networks of Radio Canada. It calls the people of Quebec to revolution and ends with the words "Long live free Quebec!"

Soldiers stood on the streets of Montreal during the October crisis in 1970.

10 October – Quebec Labour Minister Pierre Laporte is in his front yard tossing a football with his nephew. Suddenly, a blue Chevrolet stops. Four men with machine guns shove Laporte into the back seat and speed away. The No. 2 man in the Quebec government has been kidnapped. The Quebec government now begins to take this crisis very seriously. Premier Bourassa takes refuge in the Queen Elizabeth Hotel surrounded by armed guards. Laporte's kidnappers identify themselves as a second cell of the FLQ.

12 October – In Ottawa, federal troops take up positions around government buildings and provide escorts for important politicians.

16 October, 4:00 a.m. – On the advice of the Quebec government, Prime Minister Trudeau proclaims the **War Measures Act**. It is the first time the act has ever been used in peacetime. The War Measures Act takes away the civil rights of Canadians. It makes membership in the FLQ a criminal offence and bans political rallies. The police anywhere in Canada can hold people without charge for up to 21 days and without trial for up to 90 days. Police and military can arrest people just on the suspicion of belonging to the FLQ.

Trudeau argues that the act is justified because the kidnappings are the beginning of a conspiracy to overthrow the government. Asked by a reporter how far the government will go, Trudeau replies, "Just watch me."

In pre-dawn raids the police round up, among others, 50 members of the Parti Québécois. A total of 465 are eventually arrested.

18 October – In the early hours, the body of Pierre Laporte is found in the trunk of the car used to kidnap him. He had been choked to death with the religious chain he wore around his neck. Amazingly, the car is parked near the armed forces base at St. Hubert.

4 December – Police surround a house in suburban Montreal where James Cross has been held for 59 days. After hours of bargaining, the armed kidnappers and their lawyer drive to the Expo 67 site. The kidnappers surrender Cross, and in exchange, are flown to Cuba.

28 December – Three FLQ members accused of assassinating Laporte crawl out of a tunnel hidden under a farmhouse south of Montreal. They surrender to the police and are charged with murder. The FLQ crisis is over.

Quebec and Canada

The relationship between Canada and Quebec is one of the most fundamental issues facing contemporary Canada. The FLQ crisis in 1970 was one of the most dramatic events in the long-standing tensions. But the end of the FLQ crisis did not end the differences or the turmoil between French and English Canadians. Many Quebeckers supported the steps Ottawa had taken in the heat of the crisis, but the idea that Canadian soldiers had to move in to keep peace in Quebec was disturbing.

In time, the feeling grew that Ottawa had overreacted. Too many questions remained unanswered. Was there really a conspiracy to take over the Quebec government? If the trouble was in Quebec, why did the government take away the civil rights of every Canadian? These questions have never been fully answered. Bitterness still lingers among hundreds of people who were arrested during the crisis for nothing more than their nationalistic beliefs.

The Language Crisis

Quebec was facing another crisis in the 1970s. Before World War II, the birth rate among French Canadians had been the highest in Canada. By 1970, it was the lowest in Canada. At the same time, an increasing number of non-French-speaking immigrants were coming to Quebec. Most of these immigrants settled in the Montreal area and preferred to educate their children in English. Many immigrants believed that if their children spoke English, they could move anywhere in North America and feel at home.

The Quebec Liberal government became increasingly concerned about the survival of French culture in Quebec. They believed protecting the French language was the most important way to keep French culture alive. In 1974, the **Official Languages Act, Bill 22**, was introduced.

It proclaimed French the official language of the civil service in Quebec.

Bill 22 limited immigrant parents' rights to choose the language in which their children would be educated. Only children who passed a test showing that they knew English could attend English schools. All others were required to go to French schools.

The legislation was widely criticized by non-French Quebeckers and recent immigrants. Many Canadians outside Quebec who were struggling to become bilingual also thought the legislation was unfair. Premier Bourassa argued that French-speaking Quebeckers were like a tiny island surrounded by an ocean of English-speakers. Strong measures had to be taken if the French language and culture were to survive. But Quebec nationalist groups and some labour groups felt the bill did not go far enough. It did not make French the only official language in Quebec.

Parti Québécois Victory!

In November 1976, public opinion polls had been saying that René Lévesque and the Parti Québécois could win the provincial election. Outside Quebec, few people wanted to believe that a separatist government could come to power. As the first election results began to pour in, it was clear that "the impossible" was happening.

A huge crowd gathered on the night of 15 November 1976 in the Paul Sauvé arena in Montreal. Over and over they chanted the slogan "Quebec to the Quebeckers." When René Lévesque arrived, a frenzy of cheering broke out. It was a full five minutes before they allowed him to speak. The Parti Québécois had driven the Liberals from office winning 71 of 110 seats. For the first time, Quebeckers had elected a government dedicated to establishing an independent Quebec. In an emotional speech,

SOCIETY AND SOCIAL CHANGE

A Conversation

The FLQ Crisis in Quebec shook Canadians across the country. The following conversation expresses some of the reactions people had. The conversation is between two prominent women, Solange Chaput-Rolland from Quebec and Gertrude Laing from Alberta. It was recorded in 1972 in their book, *Face To Face*.

Solange: It is so difficult to explain how we felt when the army was here.... I felt reassured, and at the same time, I hated the army in Quebec. It was the Redcoats [British soldiers] again! I know that what I am saying will make our readers jump, but to me the army in Quebec means occupation. I know we *asked* the soldiers to come, because at that time we really thought that a lot of people needed to be protected. But while I was physically reassured, at the same time, I was psychologically hurt. The army is in Quebec! Quebec is occupied!

A newspaper headline proclaimed "War Measures Act Invoked." What reactions did this act evoke in and outside of Quebec?

Gertrude: I think I would have felt the same way if they had come to Alberta to protect me from my fellow Albertans.

Solange: You know ... the Patriots and the revolt of 1837 are very much alive today in Quebec. We seem to be re-living history. Some of the FLQ militants in jail are beginning to sound like heroes to some of our youth. I have even heard there are classrooms in Quebec where huge posters of Paul Rose, who is accused of the murder of Pierre Laporte, hang on the walls. This is the part that I despise. But to come back to the army .... The army came once because the government of Quebec asked for protection. Now there are a number of people in Quebec, and I think I am one of them, who believe that if tomorrow we were to vote massively for the independence of Quebec, the Canadian government, backed by nine provinces, would send the army back, not to keep us in Confederation because they want us, but so as not to disrupt the Canadian Confederation.

Gertrude: Some Canadians have said quite openly that they would "send in the troops," but I wonder if they would if the time ever came.

Solange: When the War Measures Act was proclaimed, I was awakened with the words that still haunt me. "Ottawa has declared war on Quebec!" You can imagine how I felt. For about ten minutes I really believed this, until listening to the news, I began to understand that Bourassa had asked the troops to come to Quebec.

There is no doubt that the War Measures Act is a very drastic act. We still don't possess all the facts surrounding the FLQ crisis. But we certainly know now that there was not an armed guerrilla uprising planned, that there was not an "apprehended rebellion," that only 32 guns were found, and so on. I believe that our government overreacted, but I think I would have done the same thing if I had been in their shoes. What I cannot accept is that the government has neither given us the facts, or admitted that it overreacted. As a result, we live in a very uncertain atmosphere.... Are we to suppose that we will once again be occupied if another crisis arises in Quebec?

1. To what event in the past was Solange referring when she said "It was the Redcoats again!"?
2. What did Solange mean when she said she was "psychologically hurt" by seeing the army in Quebec? Suggest why she might have felt this way.
3. Do you think the War Measures Act was too drastic? Why or why not?
4. Do you think the government would send in the army today if Quebec were to separate? Explain your point of view.

Lévesque put forward the challenge, "Now we have to build this country Quebec!"

The Parti Québécois victory sent shockwaves across Canada. For the first time since 1867, Canadian Confederation faced the genuine possibility that one of its largest provinces might separate. For many Quebeckers, however, 15 November 1976 announced the "hour of freedom." Others said, "Quebec is awake now ... We have stood up and we shall not sit down again." The triumphant slogan "Frogs have teeth" was chalked on walls all over Montreal.

Bill 101

One of the first steps the Parti Québécois took was to pass the controversial language bill, known as **Bill 101**, in 1977. This bill went even further than Bourassa's language legislation, Bill 22. More restrictions were placed on the use of languages other than French in Quebec. French was to be used in government, the courts, and business. No business could display a sign in a language other than French.

French also became the language of the workplace. Until this law was passed, an English-speaking business owner could insist on running a factory or office in English, even if all the employees were French-speaking. Now Quebeckers had the right to use French on the job. French-speaking Quebeckers who didn't speak English could enter jobs they had been excluded from before.

Probably the most controversial part of the bill concerned the language of education. Immigrants to Quebec could not send their children to English language state schools. There would still be English language schools, but only for children already enrolled in them or children with at least one parent who had attended an English elementary school.

Some businesses announced that they were having difficulty getting employees with school-aged children to accept transfers to their Montreal offices. Even on a temporary transfer, the employees would have to send their children to French schools.

English-speaking Quebeckers and members of immigrant communities who were outraged by Bill 101 formed a group called **Alliance Quebec**. They tried to challenge the law in the courts. Other English-speaking Quebeckers responded by voting with their feet. In the last half of 1977, 50 000 people left the province. Many English-speaking companies also left Montreal, moving their head offices to cities such as Toronto and Calgary. But other English-speaking Quebeckers stayed and began learning French.

The Parti Québécois leaders explained that they were protecting their language and culture just as the federal government was taking steps to protect Canada from being swamped by American culture. Those businesses that left the province were accused by the PQ of practising economic blackmail.

The Supreme Court of Canada later ruled that Bill 101 violated the Charter of Rights and Freedoms with its restrictions on education and business signs. Thousands of Quebeckers demonstrated in support of the Bill in late 1988 and early 1989. The Quebec government, then with Bourassa as premier, responded by passing Bill 178. It required all *outside* signs to be in French only.

Supporters gather around Parti Québécois leader René Lévesque. What was the PQ's platform for Quebec?

The Referendum of 1980

The Parti Québécois stressed the importance of gaining independence for Quebec. But despite their election victory, polls throughout the 1970s showed that less than 20 percent of Quebeckers favoured independence. They seemed to draw back from a clean break. Some feared they would be swamped economically, culturally, and politically if they had to share the continent with the United States and Canada. However, 84 percent said they wanted some kind of change.

Lévesque promised that his government would hold a referendum before making any move toward independence. He told the Canadian Jewish Congress, "Whatever is going to happen is going to happen as democratically as we have acted in the last ten years…. We will do our best to win the referendum. But, if we lose, it goes without saying that we will respect that decision."

By 1980, the Parti Québécois was ready to give Quebeckers a chance to vote on

The Miracle of Survival

1976: 4.5 million French Canadians in Quebec
1 million English-speaking people in Quebec
1.5 million French-speaking people in the rest of Canada

The 6 million French-speaking Canadians represent about 3 percent of the total English-speaking population of North America. The fact that a small French minority survived and flourished in North America has been called the "Miracle of Survival."

their future. Lévesque knew that only a minority wanted outright independence, so he proposed **sovereignty association**. Quebeckers were asked to vote "oui" or "non" to giving the Quebec government a "mandate to negotiate sovereignty association with Canada."

The referendum campaign was intense. Lévesque and the PQ wanted the vote to be a resounding "oui." A "oui" vote would be an enormous boost for the independence movement and a grave setback for Canadian national unity. The federal government, under Trudeau, and the provincial Liberals in Quebec, under Claude Ryan, were urging the people of Quebec to vote "non!" A resounding "non" vote would derail the independence movement—at least for the time being.

The "oui" and "non" sides placed ads in newspapers, in magazines, on television, and on radio. Quebeckers were bombarded with propaganda.

Thousands of Quebeckers demonstrated in support of Bill 101 and the use of French only on signs inside and outside businesses in 1988.

What does sovereignty association mean?

Sovereignty means that Quebec would be politically independent. It would collect its own taxes and have its own citizenship and immigration laws to protect French culture. No law passed in Ottawa would be binding in Quebec.

Association means that Quebec would still have close economic ties with the rest of Canada. The two "countries" would have the same trade policy with the same tariffs (taxes on imports) and other trade rules. They could share the same money. Quebec was proposing a common market with Canada, along the lines of the common market in Europe.

Mandate to negotiate means that Quebeckers were just giving their government the power to work out a deal with the rest of Canada. The government promised that the people would get another chance to vote on any agreement.

Through it all, they had to decide if sovereignty association would benefit Quebec or not. What would be the losses, especially the economic ones?

Just six days before the referendum, Prime Minister Trudeau stood before 10 000 wildly cheering supporters in Montreal. "I am making a solemn commitment," said Trudeau, "that after a 'non' vote, we are going to set into motion the mechanism of constitutional renewal. We will not stop until it has been achieved!"

"Now I address myself solemnly to Canadians in other provinces!" Trudeau continued. He pointed toward the 73 Quebec members of Parliament surrounding him on the platform. "We in Quebec are putting our heads on the block. When we tell Quebeckers to vote 'non', we are telling you that we will not accept that a 'non' be

"A House Divided." Opinions over the 1980 sovereignty association question were decidedly mixed.

interpreted by you as an indication that everything is fine, that everything can remain the way it was before. We want changes made. We are putting our seats at stake to obtain these changes!"

On 15 May 1980, Canada held its breath as Quebec voted. There was an overwhelming turnout at the polls. Sixty percent voted "non," and forty percent voted "oui." Sovereignty association had been rejected, at least for the time being. But Trudeau had made a promise about constitutional reform to the people of Quebec that he would now have to honour.

Bringing Home the Constitution

The British North America Act, Canada's Constitution, was still a British act. Any changes required the approval of the British government. For years, Canadian governments had considered patriating, or bringing home, the Constitution but no agreement could be reached on the changes. Trudeau decided it was time to act. If a new Canadian Constitution could be worked out, Quebec might be persuaded to remain in Canada. A new federal system would have to recognize French Canadian Quebeckers as equal partners in Confederation. But Quebec was not the only province dissatisfied with the current system. Other provinces also wanted more power to run their own affairs.

Less than a month after the Quebec referendum, Trudeau organized a conference with the provincial premiers. However, the premiers could not agree on how to revise the Constitution. Trudeau then went on national television to tell Canadians that the federal government would act on its own, or unilaterally, to bring home the Constitution.

In early November 1981, Trudeau made one last attempt to involve the provincial premiers in the patriation process. At the last possible moment, a deal was hammered out. All of the provinces (except Quebec) and Ottawa reached an agreement. Quebec was left out of the final meeting. Lévesque said Quebec had been betrayed. The new Constitution was meant to consider the needs of Quebec, but an agreement had been made without Quebec's consent. Lévesque complained that the deal confirmed what he had always suspected, that "Quebec is alone."

Three main points were included in the agreement:
1. the power to amend the Constitution would be brought home from Britain
2. changes to the Constitution could be made if the federal government and seven provinces (representing 50 percent of the population) agreed
3. a Charter of Rights and Freedoms would be added to the Constitution.

On 2 December 1981, Parliament voted in favour of the patriation package. One MP had left his hospital bed to vote. Liberals were all wearing red carnations in their lapels to "reflect the blossoming of a new country, the blooming of a new Canada!" But in Quebec, the PQ government ordered the Quebec flag to be flown at half mast to signify the "insult done to Quebeckers by English Canada."

A Canadian delegation went to London, England, to ask the British Parliament for approval to change the BNA Act and received it on 8 March 1982. It was 115 years to the day since the BNA Act had become law. At last, Canada's status as a fully independent nation was recognized. The BNA Act was officially changed and renamed the **Constitution Act**.

It would take a new government and five years before Quebec would sign the Constitution. In the meantime, there had been many changes. The Parti Québécois was out of power in Quebec and the Liberals were governing in that province under Robert Bourassa. On the federal scene, Pierre Trudeau decided in 1984 to

On 17 April 1982, Queen Elizabeth signed the agreement that brought home Canada's Constitution. Quebec representatives did not participate in the ceremony.

resign from public office and return to private life in Montreal. At the Liberal party convention, delegates elected John Turner as leader. The Conservative party had also changed its leader. Joe Clark had been replaced in a bitterly contested leadership convention by Brian Mulroney, a bilingual Quebecker from Baie-Comeau. When an election was called in 1984, the stage was set for Canadians to choose between two new leaders.

With 95 seats, Quebec held the key to an election victory for the Conservatives. With a native-born Quebecker as its leader, it looked as if the Conservative party might stand a chance of winning in Quebec. On election day, the Conservatives won an overwhelming majority with 211 seats, the largest electoral victory in Canadian history. The Liberals, led by Turner, won only 40 seats. The New Democratic Party, led by Ed Broadbent, won 30 seats.

Meech Lake Accord, 1987

When he came to power in 1984, Brian Mulroney vowed to end the bitterness between Quebec and the rest of Canada over the Constitution. In 1987, he persuaded all the premiers, meeting at Meech Lake, to hammer out a new constitutional agreement.

The major changes proposed by the **Meech Lake Accord** were:

1. Quebec was to be recognized as a "distinct society" within Canada
2. provinces would be allowed to opt out of any new federal programs and still receive money from Ottawa for their own matching programs
3. provinces would be given a say in the appointment of Supreme Court justices and senators; three of the nine Supreme Court judges would be from Quebec

Elijah Harper holds an eagle feather for spiritual strength as he blocked passage of the Meech Lake Accord in the Manitoba Legislature. Why did Native peoples oppose the Accord?

federal government. Many Canadians agreed with Trudeau.

The provinces of Manitoba, New Brunswick, and Newfoundland and Labrador had elected new governments after 1987. Their premiers had not been at the Meech Lake talks and they wanted further changes made to the Accord. As time was running out, Newfoundland and Labrador, and Manitoba, had still not ratified the agreement.

The Accord had ignored the Native peoples, and they too were determined that it must not pass without including them. Manitoba was one of the provinces that had not yet approved the Accord. At the last moment, Elijah Harper, a Native member of the Manitoba Legislature, prevented the legislature from debating and voting on the issue. His objection was that the Accord did not provide special status for the Native peoples as it did for Quebec. On 23 June 1990, time ran out for the Meech Lake Accord.

4. future changes to federal institutions, such as the Senate or the Supreme Court, or the creation of new provinces would require agreement by Ottawa and all 10 provinces, and
5. Quebec would control its own immigration policy.

The federal government and each province had to approve the Meech Lake Accord within three years, by 23 June 1990, or the agreement was dead.

When the details of the Meech Lake Accord were made public, former prime minister Trudeau broke his political silence to denounce the agreement. Trudeau argued that the proposal gave far too much power to the provinces, particularly Quebec. He warned that it would result in a powerless

The Charlottetown Accord

Many Quebeckers interpreted the defeat of the Meech Lake Accord as a rejection of Quebec by the rest of Canada. Polls in Quebec in 1991 showed that two-thirds of Quebeckers now favoured independence. Premier Bourassa decided to put forward Quebec's proposals for constitutional change. If the rest of Canada did not accept Quebec's proposals, or come up with acceptable counter-proposals, he would hold a referendum on independence in October 1992.

DEVELOPING SKILLS: WRITING A RESEARCH ESSAY

"We live in an information age." You've heard this said many times, and it is very true. Our success in and out of school often depends on how well we can find information to answer questions, and how well we can present our point of view. In any occupation or career, you will be called upon to process information, make decisions, and present your ideas clearly. Planning and writing a research essay is excellent practice for the job and life skills you will need in the future.

Earlier, you may have done a research report on a topic related to World War I. A report, however, is different from an essay. In a report, you present facts to describe or explain. For example, you might write a report on what happened during the FLQ crisis in Quebec. In an essay, you present facts to support a particular point of view or argument. For example, you might write an essay to argue that the War Measures Act should not have been introduced during the FLQ crisis. Writing an essay can be fun because it gives you a chance to argue and to persuade other people that your ideas have merit.

Steps in Essay Writing

■ Step 1

Every essay needs a thesis. A thesis tells what you are going to prove in the essay. It clearly states your argument.

How do you formulate a thesis? Suppose your topic is "The introduction of the War Measures Act in 1970." First, do your research. Use books, magazines, films, and computer databases to investigate your topic. Decide on three or four main sub-topics for your research. For example, you need to know what the War Measures Act is, the background to the October crisis, and the results.

Then review all of the information you have collected and let it ferment in your brain. As ideas are twisting and turning through your head, you will be formulating a point of view. For example, you may have found that the War Measures Act took away the civil rights of *all* Canadians. You do not think this was justified since only a small radical group of people were involved in terrorist activities. This is the basis for your thesis.

■ Step 2

State your thesis clearly in a sentence.

Example: The War Measures Act should not have been invoked in 1970 because it violated the rights of all Canadian citizens.

This thesis statement clearly summarizes your point of view or argument.

■ Step 3

Prepare an outline for your essay like the one below. Use this outline to organize your ideas and the facts gathered in your research. Each paragraph should state a main idea to help prove your thesis (argument) and include subpoints (facts) to support the main idea.

For example, the main point in paragraph 2 may be that the War Measures Act is meant to be used only in times of war or grave national crisis. There was no proof that there was a conspiracy to overthrow the Canadian government during the FLQ crisis. Your subpoints should give specific examples and evidence to support this idea.

Outline	
Paragraph 1	Introduce Thesis
Paragraph 2	Main Point
	Subpoint
	Subpoint
	Subpoint
Paragraph 3	Main Point
	Subpoint
	Subpoint
	Subpoint
Paragraph 4	Main Point
	Subpoint
	Subpoint
	Subpoint
Paragraph 5	Summarize and Restate Thesis

■ Step 4

Once you have organized your ideas in your outline, you are ready to write your essay. Concentrate on presenting your ideas clearly and persuasively. Make sure that your facts clearly support your thesis.

■ Step 5

In your concluding paragraph, sum up all your main arguments. Be sure you show how your arguments prove the thesis you stated in the introductory paragraph. As a final point, build on your thesis by restating it in different words.

■ Step 6

Try to allow time to set your essay aside for a few days or a week. Then reread it. You will have a fresh perspective on your work.

Ask yourself the following questions:

- Is my thesis statement clear?
- Do my arguments in each paragraph clearly support my thesis?
- Do the facts I have presented clearly support each argument?
- Is my essay persuasive?
- Can I make it better? Do I need to make any revisions?
- Is it grammatically correct?

Try It!

Write a mini research essay on one of the following topics or another topic of your choice.

- Introduction of the War Measures Act in 1970
- The miracle of French Canadian survival
- Quebec Language Bill 101
- American influences on Canadian culture
- Why worry about the Americanization of Canadian culture?
- The Canadian sporting event of the 1970s
- Canada's foreign aid program in one country
- Equal work for equal pay issue
- Immigration in the 1990s
- Racism in Canada
- An environmental issue

Prime Minister Mulroney believed that the federal government and the provinces had to come up with a proposal acceptable to Quebec. This time the government would open the debate to the public and interest groups. A Citizen's Forum on Canada's Future was formed. It organized hearings throughout the country to listen to the suggestions and complaints of thousands of Canadians. Mulroney appointed a former prime minister, Joe Clark, to head a committee on constitutional reform.

It was not an easy task. Clark had to turn around anti-Quebec feelings among anglophones (English-speakers). At the same time, he had to offer Quebec a deal more appealing than independence. Said Clark, "There is nothing automatic about this country. Canada was not here at the beginning of the last century. There is no logic that says it must be here at the beginning of the next. We have to work to keep it. We always have."

After months of intense work, the premiers of the nine anglophone provinces, Native leaders, and the prime minister met at Charlottetown. The site was symbolic because the Fathers of Confederation had met there in 1864. This time another group of politicians agreed to the **Charlottetown Accord** on 28 August 1992. It included proposals for:

- *Quebec.* Quebec would be recognized as a distinct society with its own language, culture, and civil law tradition.
- *Senate reform.* The Senate would be elected, not appointed.
- *Division of federal and provincial powers.* The provinces would be given power over such areas as tourism, housing, culture, and forestry.
- *Social and economic issues.* There were commitments to preserve such

THE ARTS

Contemporary Quebec Culture

Since the Quiet Revolution in the 1960s, Québécois culture has blossomed and flourished. Today, French Canadian writers, artists, musicians, and performers are gaining increasing recognition in Canada and internationally. They have sparked interest in Québécois culture, and many have been recognized as innovators in their artistic fields.

The Cirque du Soleil was founded by a group of street performers from Montreal in 1984. Today, they have achieved an international reputation for their performances which combine traditional circus arts with theatre. Music, sets, dance, lights, themes, and costumes are combined with clowns, acrobats, and aerialists.

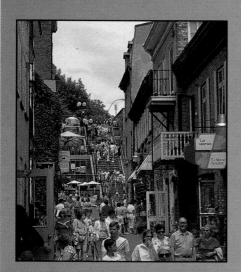

Quebec is one of the oldest parts of Canada. It has a wealth of historic properties dating to the seventeenth and eighteenth centuries. Many heritage buildings are being preserved and restored. The goal is to protect Quebec's architectural heritage and maintain old Quebec City and Montreal as communities where people still live and work.

From her start in Quebec, Céline Dion has gone on to win several music awards—both for her francophone albums and her hit songs in English. She is recognized as an outstanding female vocalist.

Many Québécois writers, playwrights, and filmmakers have won awards in Canada and internationally for their work. Writer Anne Hébert won a Governor General's Literary Award for Best Fiction (French) for her novel *L'enfant charges de songes* (1992). An earlier novel, *Kamouraska* (1970), recounted hardships in early Quebec and was made into a movie by filmmaker, Claude Jutra. Michel Tremblay, Yves Beauchemin, and Roch Carrier are just some of the other writers whose works have come to the forefront.

1. Many Quebec artists have been well received in Europe and even in the United States, yet they sometimes receive less recognition in the rest of Canada. Why? Do you think this situation is changing? Explain.
2. Can you name other prominent Québécois artists and performers? Find out more about them and create a collage with captions.

programs as universal health care and workers' rights.

- *Minorities.* Anglophone communities in Quebec and francophone communities in the rest of Canada would be protected.
- *Aboriginal rights.* The right to Native self-government was accepted. Aboriginal government was recognized as one of the three orders of government along with Ottawa and the provinces.

Mulroney announced that all of Canada would have a chance to vote on the Accord in a national referendum. All three major political parties supported the Charlottetown Accord. Opposition came from a new western political party called the Reform party, the National Action Committee on the Status of Women, the Parti Québécois, and former Prime Minister Trudeau. In the weeks before the referendum, there was growing opposition in the country to the Accord. Almost every section of it came under attack. Many felt that the proposal gave too much to Quebec and too little to other regions of Canada.

On 26 October 1992, Canadians voted in a national referendum on the Charlottetown proposal. Across the nation, 54.4 percent of voters said "No" and 44.6 percent said "Yes."

The collapse of the Charlottetown Accord was a blow for Native peoples. For years they had been negotiating with the government over the right to govern themselves. The proposal for aboriginal self-government in the Charlottetown Accord had been a step forward. Since the collapse of the Accord, Native peoples have continued to work for self-government.

Which Way Are We Going—One Nation or Two?

Shortly after the collapse of the Charlottetown Accord, Brian Mulroney resigned as the leader of the Conservative party. He was succeeded by Kim Campbell, the first female prime minister in Canada's history. Within four months, Kim Campbell announced a federal election, and the Conservative party was almost wiped out in Parliament by the voters. The Liberal party won a large majority government.

The new prime minister was Jean Chrétien, a French-speaking Quebecker. After the election, Chrétien stated that the time had come to leave constitutional quarrels on the back burner. Many Canadians seemed to agree with him. In a Maclean's/Decima poll, two-thirds said that unemployment and the weak economy were the two most important problems facing the nation. But the question of Quebec's future in Canadian Confederation won't go away. The same election that had put Chrétien and the Liberals in power had also elected 54 **Bloc Québécois** members to the federal Parliament. In fact, the Bloc became the official opposition in Ottawa. Like the provincial Parti Québécois, the Bloc was dedicated to achieving sovereignty for Quebec. Their role as the official opposition in Parliament gave them a platform for making Quebec's demands heard across the country.

The emergence of the Bloc Québécois represents a new stage in the movement for Quebec sovereignty. Leader Lucien Bouchard, a former Progressive Conservative member of Parliament, is determined to bring Quebec's concerns to the attention of the House of Commons and all Canadians.

Another new party rose to national importance in the 1993 election. The party that won the third largest number of seats was the western-based **Reform party** under Preston Manning. The Reform party opposes bilingualism and special treatment for Quebec. On the issue of Quebec, Manning stated, "People are saying yes to a fair language policy, but no to forced bilingualism."

The rejection of the Charlottetown Accord left many French Canadians feeling that the rest of Canada was indifferent to the wishes of Quebec and perhaps even hostile to the French culture. On the other hand, some English-speaking Canadians felt that Quebec was demanding too many special rights. The strength of the Bloc Québécois in Quebec and the strength of the Reform party outside Quebec suggested that public opinion was deeply divided between French and English Canadians.

The question of sovereignty for Quebec remains a major national issue. The Parti Québécois under Jacques Parizeau was returned to power in Quebec in 1994. Parizeau promised a referendum on sovereignty in 1995. The results and long-term consequences of that referendum have yet to be seen.

Bloc Québécois leader Lucien Bouchard speaks to the general council of his party. The Bloc became the official opposition in the House of Commons after the 1993 federal election.

Activities

Check Your Understanding

1. Add these new terms to your *Factfile*.

   October Crisis

   War Measures Act

   Quebec Official Languages Act
   (Bill 22)

   Bill 101 (Quebec)

   Alliance Quebec

   1980 Quebec referendum
   sovereignty association

   Constitution Act 1982

   Meech Lake Accord

   Charlottetown Accord

   Bloc Québécois

   Reform party

2. Identify each of the following people and explain their roles in the FLQ crisis.
   a) James Cross
   b) Pierre Laporte
   c) Pierre Trudeau
   d) Robert Bourassa

3. What democratic rights of Canadians were lost when the War Measures Act was introduced?

4. Make a timeline of the events in the campaign for constitutional change from 1982 to 1994.

Confirm Your Learning

5. What effects did the FLQ crisis have on each of the following? Explain your answers.
   a) separatism in Quebec
   b) English minority in Quebec
   c) Prime Minister Trudeau
   d) people living in other parts of Canada
   e) Liberal party in Canada

6. a) Role play a conversation involving the following people just after the introduction of Bill 101 in Quebec.
   i) a francophone Quebecker
   ii) an anglophone Quebecker
   iii) a new immigrant to Quebec of neither English nor French origin
   iv) a Canadian outside Quebec
   b) Hold a debriefing session after the role play. Do you think the Parti Québécois government was justified in introducing the Bill? Explain your point of view.
   c) What long-term effects do you think the Bill has had?

7. a) Which groups opposed the Meech Lake Accord? Why?
   b) Were the concerns of these groups considered in the Charlottetown Accord? If so, how?

c) Suggest reasons for the defeat of the Charlottetown Accord.

Challenge Your Mind

8. a) Is the War Measures Act ever justifiable in peacetime? Explain your answer.
   b) Suggest other ways the government might have handled the October crisis in Quebec.

9. Take a stand. Social protest sometimes involves violence. The FLQ crisis was an example. Do you think violence is ever justified in drawing attention to a group's goals? Explain your reasons.

10. How difficult is it to write a constitution? Try it. Divide the class into two committees. One writes a constitution to govern the running of a classroom. The other writes a constitution for a school club or team. Both constitutions should cover the rights and responsibilities of teachers and students.

11. Prime Minister Mulroney said at the time of the Meech Lake Accord in 1987:

Because Quebec was not a signatory to the Constitution, there were two Canadas emerging when this government took office—those Canadians who had accepted the Constitution and those who had been left out. Now there is one Canada, strong and united.

Explain what the prime minister meant. Do you think he was right? Explain.

12. The following is Pierre Trudeau's comment on the 1987 Meech Lake Accord.

Those Canadians who fought for a single Canada, bilingual and multicultural, can say goodbye to their dream. We are, henceforth, to have two Canadas, each defined in terms of its language. And because the Accord states that 'Quebec constitutes within Canada a distinct society' and that 'the role of the legislature and government is to preserve and promote this distinct identity,' it is easy to predict what future awaits anglophones living in provinces where they are fewer in number than Canadians of Ukrainian or German origin.

a) How does Trudeau's view of Canada differ from Mulroney's view in 1987?
b) What does Trudeau predict will happen to anglophones living in Quebec and in other provinces where they are a minority? Why?
c) Do you agree with Trudeau's view? Explain.

13. Read a short story or poem by a Québécois writer that deals with life in Quebec. Report to the class summarizing the theme of the piece, telling about the author, and describing your impressions.

14. As a class, keep a current events file on relations between Quebec and Canada. Discuss new developments as they happen.

CHAPTER 19

Canada, the United States, and the World

THE BEAVER AND THE ELEPHANT

"Living next door to the United States," said Prime Minister Trudeau, "is like sleeping in the same bed as an elephant. No matter how friendly and even-tempered is the beast, one is affected by every twitch and grunt!" If the elephant rolls over in its sleep, the Canadian "beaver must be ready to jump." Most of the time, the elephant and beaver get along very well. Once in a while, however, the elephant gets a little grumpy, or the beaver feels threatened. When this happens, these oddly matched neighbours sit down and talk about their problems.

In many ways, the comparison made by Trudeau was a good one. The United States is certainly a giant—one of the richest and most powerful nations in the world. It has 10 times our population and economic production. The United States also greatly overshadows Canada as a military power.

Throughout our history, people have been alarmed over the amount of control the American "elephant" has on our lives. Our economy, foreign policy, and culture may all be affected by the twitches and grunts of the elephant.

American Influence on the Canadian Economy

By the early 1970s, several government studies had shown just how much of the Canadian economy was owned by foreign investors, especially Americans. **Economic nationalists** feared that if the trend continued, the United States would take over the Canadian economy. They argued that American investment:

- allowed profits to flow out of Canada to the United States
- meant top management jobs often went to Americans, not Canadians
- took Canada's natural resources out of the country for processing (Canada then had to buy back the resources as expensive manufactured goods)
- made us more "American" in our tastes
- discouraged technological advances in Canada (it was easier to borrow technological advances from the Americans)
- caused key decisions about expanding or shutting down a plant to be made outside the country
- sometimes restricted the trade of Canadian branch plants with countries considered unacceptable by the United States (an example was Cuba)
- brought American-based unions into Canada.

On the other hand, a large number of Canadians favoured American investment in Canada. They argued that American investment:

- created thousands of jobs for Canadians
- provided money to help develop Canadian resources and industries when Canadians were unwilling to take the risks
- helped raise the standard of living in Canada to almost the same high level as that of the United States
- brought advanced technical knowledge and machinery into Canada
- contributed to the growth and welfare of Canada since American owned companies paid taxes to the Canadian government

- increased business for Canadian-owned companies
- profited Canadians who bought shares in American-owned businesses
- provided Canadians with a greater variety and the highest quality of manufactured goods
- made for friendly relations between Canada and the United States.

The long-standing debate over American investment was to continue throughout the next decades. But in the 1970s, it caused particular concern. The federal Liberal government under Trudeau introduced policies to limit foreign investment in the Canadian economy. These initiatives decreased foreign ownership from 36 to 26 percent between 1970 and 1981.

> **In March 1979, economic nationalist Mel Hurtig announced in a speech that foreigners controlled:**
> - 65% of all our combined manufacturing, mining, petroleum, and natural gas
> - 98% of our rubber industry
> - 82% of chemicals
> - 46% of pulp and paper
> - 74% of the electrical apparatus industry
> - 59% of transportation equipment
> - 96% of the automobile and parts industry.

Foreign Investment Review Agency 1971

In 1971, the **Foreign Investment Review Agency (FIRA)** was established. Any takeover of a Canadian company or new foreign-owned business had to be approved by FIRA. The government emphasized that FIRA was not trying to block or discourage foreign investment. Its purpose was to ensure that foreign investment would have significant benefits for Canada.

FIRA was resented by Americans and some Canadian business leaders who believed in economic expansion. They were worried that FIRA might cut off the flow of much needed money for resource industries. They need not have worried. From

What does this cartoon suggest about American influences on Canadians?

The Energy Crisis

In the 1970s, the energy crisis also emphasized the amount of control the United States had on the Canadian economy. Major Arab oil producers had been cutting back their exports and raising prices. People around the world were facing shortages and high prices. Canada had abundant oil and gas resources, but the Canadian industry was mostly foreign-owned. Large amounts of Canadian oil and gas were being shipped to the United States. As a result, Canadians faced the prospect of severe shortages in the near future.

In 1975, the Canadian government responded by establishing an oil company owned by the government—Petro-Canada. Petro-Canada profits, made from the sale of gasoline, would be pumped back into oil and gas exploration to meet the needs of future generations. The government also gradually decreased our oil exports to the United States to 800 000 barrels a day in 1975, 460 000 barrels a day in 1976, and 260 000 barrels a day in 1977. Americans found it hard to adjust to this policy. They were accustomed to importing Canadian oil at low prices.

May 1974 to August 1982, approximately 3865 investment applications were examined. Only 293 applications were rejected.

In 1984 under the Mulroney Conservative government, FIRA was replaced by a new agency called **Investment Canada**. It was designed to be more welcoming to foreign investment, but would still review any takeovers of cultural industries. There is still controversy, however, over how effective the agency really is and just how much foreign ownership should be allowed in Canada.

The National Energy Program

In 1980, the federal government took further steps to ensure Canadian control of energy supplies. It introduced the **National Energy Program (NEP)**, and this made the American "elephant" very grumpy.

The goals of the National Energy Program were to establish 50 percent Canadian ownership of the Canadian oil and gas industry by 1990, to make

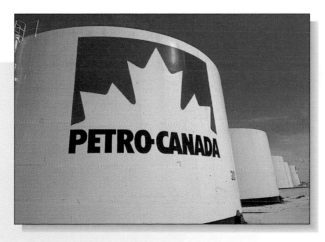

In 1975, the federal Liberal government established Petro-Canada to help ensure Canadian control over oil and gas resources. Later, shares were sold to private interests.

Canada self-sufficient in energy by 1990, and to control oil prices so that Canadians were not at the mercy of fluctuating world oil prices. Oil prices had risen from $3 a barrel in 1973 to over $40 a barrel in 1980.

American oil companies were incensed. In retaliation, they pulled many of their drilling rigs out of Canada. The drop in oil and gas exploration increased unemployment in the Canadian West. Oil-producing provinces in western Canada bitterly opposed the National Energy Program because it threatened their economic survival.

To many Americans, the National Energy Program was the most anti-American initiative introduced by the Canadian government. FIRA and now NEP were seen as unfriendly actions to take against a neighbour and ally. However, an opinion poll in 1981 showed that 84 percent of Canadians supported the goals of the NEP. As oil prices dropped in the 1980s and an economic slowdown increased interest in foreign investment, the NEP was dropped. Shares in Petro-Canada were also sold to private interests. The furor over the energy crisis had faded.

SOCIETY AND SOCIAL CHANGE

How Does the Elephant Affect You?

How does the United States affect your lifestyle? Do you resent this influence, or do you welcome it? Make a profile of your tastes and attitudes by completing the following questionnaire.

Favourite movie of the last year
Favourite actor (male)
Favourite actor (female)
Two favourite television programs
Favourite television news program
Most admired woman
Most admired man
Favourite musical group
Favourite female singer
Favourite male singer
Two favourite magazines
Favourite professional sports team

Favourite professional hockey team
Favourite female athlete
Favourite male athlete
Most admired political figure (living or dead)
TV channel watched most often
Radio station listened to most often
City in North America you would most like to visit
Place you spent your last vacation
Make of family car
Favourite breakfast cereal
Favourite brand of jeans

1. Go through your answers and sort out which are American and which are Canadian.
2. How "American" is your lifestyle? How do you feel about this? Why?
3. What answers reveal you to be "Canadian?" How?
4. How "Americanized" do you think Canadian life is? Support your answer.
5. Do you think the results of your questionnaire will be different 10 years from now? Why or why not?
6. How does Canadian culture influence American life? Brainstorm as many examples as you can.

Americanization of Canadian Culture

In the 1970s, Canadians also expressed concern over the Americanization of Canadian culture. A story circulated of how a Canadian high school student was asked to identify Margaret Laurence and Earle Birney, two of Canada's most popular writers. The student replied, "Never heard of them. They must be Canadian."

In 1968, the government had established the **Canadian Radio-Television and Telecommunications Commission (CRTC)**. The CRTC issued broadcasting licences to Canadian-owned companies. It made sure that 30 percent of the music played on AM stations was Canadian.

Margaret Laurence was one of the writers who flourished in the 1970s with the increased focus on Canadian arts. Her most well-known books included The Stone Angel *(1964) and* The Diviners *(1974).*

Canadians listened to entertainers such as Anne Murray, Bachman-Turner Overdrive, Rush, and Stompin' Tom Connors in addition to popular American artists. The law required that 60 percent of primetime television be "made in Canada." Viewers watched Bruno Gerussi in "The Beachcombers," Al Waxman in "The King of Kensington," and Adrienne Clarkson in "The Fifth Estate." All of these shows featured Canadian actors, writers, and producers.

The Canadian government also spent millions of dollars to build a Canadian film industry. Films made in Quebec promoted French culture and won some major international awards. Claude Jutra won acclaim for his film *Mon Oncle Antoine* (1971) about life in a Quebec asbestos town. In 1975, Michel Brault's film *Les Ordres* won an important award at the Cannes Film Festival. The following year, Jean Beaudin's *J. A. Martin, Photographe* won the award for best Canadian film.

The English language commercial film industry and the National Film Board also produced important Canadian films. These included *Goin' Down the Road* (1970), the story of two Maritimers trying to establish themselves in Toronto, and *Why Shoot the Teacher?* (1977), the story of a young teacher in a one-room school on the prairies in the 1930s.

Canada's performing arts also blossomed, thanks in part to strong government financial support through Arts Councils. Suddenly, a whole group of small Toronto theatres began to flourish. Original Canadian plays were produced and made a stunning impact. David Freeman's *Creeps* on the unlikely subject of cerebral palsy was a hit and went on to New York. David Luscombe's production of *Ten Lost Years* was a moving stage portrayal of Canadian life during the Great Depression.

But the emergence of new Canadian theatre was by no means happening only in Toronto. Michel Tremblay's *Les Belle Soeurs* entertained both French and English language audiences. Talent from the Vancouver East Cultural Centre produced outstanding shows including *Billy Bishop Goes to War* and *Eighteen Wheels*.

Canadian writers also flourished, and the number of Canadian publishing companies almost doubled in the 1970s. Margaret Laurence, Mordecai Richler, Margaret Atwood, Gabrielle Roy, and W. O. Mitchell were just some of the writers gaining recognition.

Trudeau also visited the Soviet Union. He was especially interested in sharing knowledge and experience in northern development. Canada and the Soviet Union signed an agreement to exchange scientific, technical, and cultural information. The hockey games between Team Canada and the Soviet national team were examples of the increasing openness between the two countries. In 1973, the government made a $200 million sale of wheat and barley to the Soviet Union.

Canada and the Pacific

Trudeau also believed that Canada should take advantage of its ringside seat on the Pacific. By 1970, Canada and China (a Communist nation) had exchanged ambassadors, two years before the United

Canada and the Changing World

The Trudeau government also decided on a new path for Canada's foreign policy. Canada would develop trade and friendly relations with other countries to reduce its dependence on the United States. Tensions in the Cold War were thawing and the government felt it could open new relations with Communist and other nations.

Trudeau made frequent trips abroad. In Europe, he tried to promote the sale of Canadian technology, especially nuclear power plants. He also wanted to attract more European investment to Canada. Swedish and French car manufacturers established branch plants in Nova Scotia and Quebec, and several other European nations invested in Canadian real estate and industry.

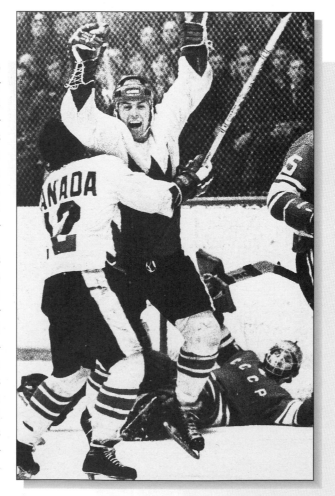

Paul Henderson scored the winning goal in the last 34 seconds of the deciding game in the famous series between Team Canada and the Soviet national team, 28 September 1972.

Prime Minister Trudeau visited China in 1973 to establish diplomatic relations and explore new trade opportunities. How was this visit significant for Canadian-American relations?

Important trading relations were also developed with Japan. The Japanese began to invest heavily in Canadian industries and the development of our natural resources. The United States, however, remained Canada's dominant trading partner and investor. The Canadian and American economies were still very closely linked.

Defence Policy

In the 1970s, Prime Minister Trudeau began to have second thoughts about Canada's role in the defence of Europe. The major nations of Europe had recovered from the effects of World War II and tensions in the Cold War had relaxed. Canada withdrew 50 percent of ground troops from European bases. The defence budget for NATO was frozen at $1.8 billion until 1972, one of the lowest budgets of any NATO member. Canada's forces in NATO would also no longer use nuclear weapons. The government felt that the role of Canada's armed forces should be concentrated on North American defence and the Arctic.

States officially recognized China. Canada strongly supported China's request to join the United Nations. This brought us into conflict with the United States which opposed Communist China being represented at the UN. However, in 1971, due largely to Canada's leadership, China was admitted to the United Nations. Trudeau paid an official visit to China in 1973 and, at that time, China placed a huge order for 5 million tonnes of Canadian wheat.

Students cheer Henderson's winning goal. Schools across the country set up televisions in classrooms and gymnasiums for students to watch the game. Why was this hockey series so significant?

However, pressure from our NATO allies led to a total about-face in Canadian defence policy. Canada reconfirmed its serious commitment to NATO with increases in defence budget spending between 1975 and 1977.

Changes also took place in Canada's role in NORAD. In 1972, the Trudeau government dismantled the two nuclear-armed Bomarc missile bases in Ontario and Quebec. Some critics urged that we abandon NORAD altogether. But Americans felt Canada was taking advantage of US defence while giving nothing in return. After 1975, the Canadian government strongly reconfirmed its commitment to NORAD.

Star Wars 1985

Further change occurred when the Conservatives under Brian Mulroney came to power in 1984. The number one priority of Conservative foreign policy was to establish good relations with the United States, both in trade and defence.

In 1985, President Reagan announced the **Strategic Defense Initiative (SDI)**, more commonly known as **Star Wars**. Reagan proposed to spend billions of dollars on an intercontinental ballistic missile system (ICBM). SDI was a highly sophisticated defence shield to protect the United States against an enemy nuclear attack.

Many Canadian nationalists and peace groups did not want Canada to become involved in new and dangerous American nuclear defence projects. Anti-nuclear groups held demonstrations across the country. Protests were also held when Canada allowed the Americans to test unarmed Cruise missiles over northern Alberta.

The Mulroney government wavered over what action to take. Should Canada participate in Star Wars research? Would a refusal affect friendly relations with the United States? Did our membership in the North American Aerospace Defence Command (formerly NORAD) commit us to participate in SDI?

The issue was resolved when the US government stated it did not expect Canada to participate officially in Star Wars research. However, it was pleased when Mulroney promised that no barriers would be put in the way of private Canadian companies who wanted to bid on SDI contracts.

Arctic Sovereignty Dispute 1985

During the summer of 1985, a US Coast Guard icebreaker called the *Polar Sea* sailed through the Northwest Passage from Greenland to the Beaufort Sea and Alaska. Its mission was unspecified research for the United States Navy.

Canada claimed the Northwest Passage as internal waters. Any nation wishing to sail through this passage needed to have

Prime Minister Mulroney made good relations with the United States a priority. At a meeting with President Reagan at Quebec City in 1985, the leaders announced a number of agreements including defence arrangements and joint ventures in space.

Canadian permission. The American government viewed the passage as an international waterway. It simply informed Canada as a courtesy that American ships would sail through these waters. The Mulroney government took no action against the American ship.

The government was surprised by the outcry from the opposition parties and the public in Canada. Canadians saw the *Polar Sea* incident as a challenge to our sovereignty over Arctic waters. The Mulroney government responded to public pressure. After some hesitation, they warned the Americans that failing to recognize the Arctic as Canadian territory was "an unfriendly act." They promised Canadians that steps would be taken to build the world's most powerful icebreaker, increase aerial patrol flights in the far North, buy nuclear submarines for Arctic patrol duty, and draw new boundary maps that would define Canada's sovereignty in the area more clearly. Neither the icebreaker nor the submarines were ever built.

At a 1987 summit meeting between Mulroney and Reagan, the Americans offered to make a concession to Canada's claim of Arctic sovereignty. The Americans promised to get prior permission every time a government ship or aircraft wanted to cross the Arctic. They would also uphold Canada's ownership of the Northwest Passage against all nations except the United States.

Acid Rain

Another problem between the neighbours in the 1980s concerned acid rain. Acid rain is caused by emissions of sulphur dioxide into the atmosphere from factories, refineries, and other industrial plants. Acid rain devastates the environment by killing the fish in lakes and rivers. The contaminated water also affects birds and other animals who depend on fish to survive. Acid rain causes direct damage to foliage, re-

tards plant growth, and contaminates drinking water.

By 1985, the annual emission of sulphur dioxide in Canada was dangerously high. Some of the acid rain that fell in Canada was produced by our own industries. But, because of the wind patterns, more than half came from the industrial smokestacks of the northeastern and midwestern United States.

Neither the Liberals nor Conservatives had much success in persuading the Americans to do anything about acid rain. In 1982, Canada proposed a 50 percent reduction in sulphur emissions. American companies threatened to close their factories if they were forced to install expensive pollution controls. As a result, the American government would not take steps to reduce sulphur dioxide emissions. They proposed only further research on acid rain.

The Canadian government offered a $150 million program to help Canadian industries clean up their own operations. They also brought in pollution control standards on automobiles beginning with the 1988 models. Environmental lobbyists on both sides of the border continued to pressure the American government to take action. Finally in 1990, the US Congress passed a new law to control acid rain.

Free Trade

In September 1985, Prime Minister Mulroney proposed the most momentous step of the decade in Canadian-American relations—free trade. Free trade became one of the most controversial issues of the 1980s. Groups who favoured the deal included most of Canada's large and small businesses, the Canadian Chamber of Commerce, financial institutions, most of the provincial premiers, the Royal Commission on Economic Union and Development Prospects for Canada, and the Canadian Consumers' Association. The forces against free trade

Free trade	No free trade
Trade is vital to the growth of the Canadian economy.	Free trade benefits only "big business."
United States is our best customer and we should take advantage of increased trade opportunities.	Many Canadian businesses would close down because they could not compete with larger American companies.
We need to overcome US protectionism. (The United States was considering trade barriers to protect its industries from foreign competition. This could be devastating for Canada.)	Jobs would be lost as businesses closed down or moved to the United States.
Free trade would increase productivity because Canadians would have access to a larger market.	Free trade threatens Canadian social programs such as medicare.
It would create jobs.	It threatens Canadian culture.
Consumers would benefit from a greater variety of goods and lower prices.	It threatens Canadian political sovereignty.
Free trade works elsewhere.	Americans would no longer need to invest in Canadian industries if they had open access to our market.
Free trade would encourage foreign investment in new businesses.	

consisted of nationalists, pensioners, unions, churches, women's groups, and many ordinary citizens. Arguments on both sides are outlined in the box above.

January 1988 was the deadline for a free trade deal between the United States and Canada. Minutes before the midnight deadline, it was announced that Canada and the United States had reached an agreement-in-principle.

Some of the major points of the deal were:

- *Elimination of tariffs.* The two countries would eliminate tariffs on goods and services starting 1 January 1989 and have open access to each other's markets.

- *Dispute-settlement mechanism.* A five-member panel, with at least two members from each nation, would discuss any issues causing trade problems between Canada and the US.

A demonstration against the Free Trade Agreement. What do the signs and placards suggest about the reasons for the opposition to free trade?

- *Investment.* Restrictions on American investment in Canada would be reduced, but Canada kept the right to screen and approve takeovers in cultural industries such as publishing and the media.
- *Energy.* Canada cannot restrict sales of energy resources to the United States except during shortages and then must provide Americans with a proportional amount of what is available.
- *Agriculture.* All tariffs on agricultural products and processed foods would be eliminated over a 10-year period.

As soon as the continental trade deal was announced, the debate in Canada heated up. Provincial leaders in Quebec, Saskatchewan, Alberta, and British Columbia were quick to give their support. The agreement opened the door for Quebec to make huge sales of hydroelectric power to the northeastern United States. Western producers of oil, gas, hogs, and cattle welcomed the chance to sell their products freely on the American market.

Provincial premiers in Manitoba, Ontario, and Prince Edward Island voiced opposition to the deal. The premier of Manitoba worried that the deal would permit greater foreign ownership of Canadian resources. Among the potential losers in Ontario were the grape growers and wine makers, the music-recording industry, food processing plants, and the auto parts industry, all of which faced tough competition from US industries. Prime Minister Mulroney promised public hearings and an open debate in Parliament on the free trade proposal.

In many ways, the debate was similar to the one that occurred over Reciprocity in 1911, though the politicians had changed coats. In 1911, the Liberals supported free trade and the Conservatives opposed it—but the arguments are virtually the same. In both eras, people who believed in free trade saw it as the key to Canadian economic prosperity, while opponents warned of possible American takeover. In 1911, opponents advised that Canada should have "no truck or trade with the Yankees." In 1987, Liberal leader John Turner warned that the country was being "sold down river." Ed Broadbent, leader of the NDP, claimed that he "feared for the future of the nation" if this agreement came into place.

Laurier's campaign for free trade was hurt when important Americans fed the fear some Canadians had of the deal. One prominent American politician talked about the day when the American flag would fly over all of North America, including the North Pole. In the 1987 debate, US Trade Representative Clayton Yeutter told Congress that Americans gave very little and gained a lot from the deal. Also, President Reagan predicted an economic boom for the United States. Critics of free trade seized upon these comments as proof that free trade would be dangerous for Canadian economic and political independence.

However, there were important differences in the reciprocity debate of 1911 and the free trade debate in the 1980s. When Canadians rejected reciprocity in 1911, they knew they could rely on the British Empire for trade. But, in 1988, Canadians had almost three times as much trade with the US as with the rest of the world.

Some experts warned that not having a trade deal might be even worse than this deal. They believed that if either Parliament or the United States Congress rejected the deal, a trade war between the two countries would follow. With protectionism being so strong in America, the US would probably erect higher and higher trade barriers, causing Canada to retaliate.

Free trade became the most important issue in the 1988 federal election. When the Conservatives won a majority of the seats in Parliament, the **Free Trade Agreement (FTA)** became law on 1 January 1989.

DEVELOPING SKILLS: SAMPLING PUBLIC OPINION

An opinion survey is an excellent way to discover what people think about an issue, personality, or government. Governments sometimes use polls to decide when to call an election or how to proceed on a sensitive issue such as capital punishment or free trade.

Polls are not completely reliable. They indicate only what people feel at the exact time they are asked the question. Sometimes people give answers that do not truly reflect their opinions. A margin for error must always be considered. If the sample is large enough, however, the poll will be fairly accurate. Official polls are usually accurate to within four percentage points either way.

How could you prepare an effective opinion survey?

■ Step 1

Decide what information you want to collect. Suppose you want to discover whether Canadians agree or disagree with the North American Free Trade Agreement, for example.

■ Step 2

Decide on your target audience and how large a group you would like to survey. Consider this step carefully. In some cases, you might target particular groups. For example, if you wanted to gauge the popularity of your student council, you would restrict your sample to students and teachers in your school. For the free trade issue, you will want a broader but still manageable sample, perhaps including friends and family.

■ Step 3

Prepare your questions. Make sure:
- they will give you the answers you're searching for
- the wording is clear, precise, and simple
- they are arranged in a logical order
- they are worded so that they do not offend anyone (race, religion, or gender)
- they do not "tip" or bias the answer.

■ Step 4

Most opinion surveys use closed questions since these are the simplest to analyze. A closed question gives the survey participants the answers and asks them to choose one. For example: Should Canada have joined the North American Free Trade Agreement?

Yes ☐   No ☐   No opinion ☐

If only presented with the options of "yes" or "no," participants might choose one of them, even though they really don't have an opinion. The third option (don't care, don't know, or no opinion) will make your survey more accurate. If the vast majority of respondents express "no opinion," you will know that the question is not an issue.

■ Step 5

Test your survey to make sure there are no problems. Ask several friends or classmates to answer the questions. Are the questions too long and complicated? Is the survey too long?

■ Step 6

Prepare your final draft. Pay special attention to its overall appearance. It should be typed neatly and well-spaced on the page. Directions should be clear.

■ Step 7

Conduct your opinion survey and tabulate your results. Transfer the information from all answer sheets onto a single tally sheet. Double check your results. Accuracy is essential.

■ Step 8

Prepare a report to summarize and clearly present your information. Your report should state the purpose of your survey, identify your target audience, note the size of your sample, include a blank questionnaire, and present your results. Consider using graphs and tables to show your results. Also state your conclusion and comment on the value of the survey.

Apply Your Knowledge

1. A series of public opinion surveys were carried out on free trade between 1984 and 1986. The results are shown in the table on the right. As a class, update this information by conducting a similar opinion poll. You could also conduct a poll on other recent issues, such as NAFTA, Quebec sovereignty, or party popularity at the time of an election.

   Add other probing questions to your poll if you wish (e.g., concerning loss of jobs, US political takeover of Canada). For example, "Does free trade affect Canada's ability to maintain its independence and identity?"

2. Each year, *Maclean's* magazine publishes a poll indicating what Canadians feel is the most important issue facing the country. Results since 1985 are shown in the graph below.

Free trade			
	For	Against	Uncertain
		(percentage)	
April 1984	78%	17%	5%
June 1985	65	30	5
November 1985	58	31	11
February 1986	54	35	11
June 1986	52	36	12

a) Which issue has been rated as most important most often over the past 10 years? Suggest why.

b) Update this poll by conducting your own survey. Present your results in a similar bar graph. You may wish to suggest other issues to add to the *Maclean's* list.

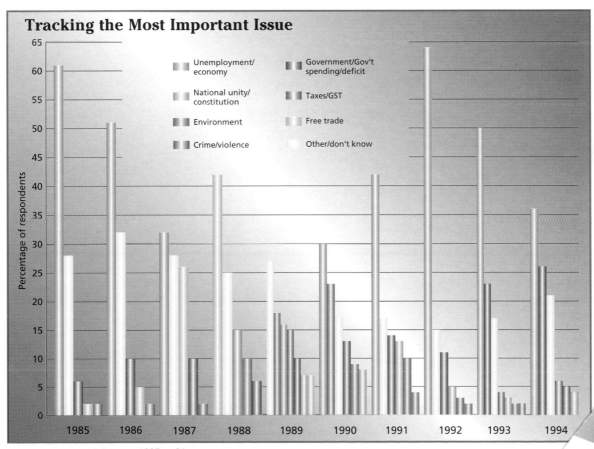

Tracking the Most Important Issue

Legend: Unemployment/economy; Government/Gov't spending/deficit; National unity/constitution; Taxes/GST; Environment; Free trade; Crime/violence; Other/don't know

Source: *Maclean's*, 2 January, 1995, p. 21.

The North American Free Trade Agreement (NAFTA)

Not long after the Free Trade Agreement was signed, Mexico expressed interest in joining the association. Canada entered the **North American Free Trade Agreement (NAFTA)** with the United States and Mexico on 1 January 1994. Canada's trade with Mexico was only $3 billion annually compared with $180 billion with the United States. However, the Canadian government feared that if it remained on the sidelines, it could lose trade with the United States, our best customer. NAFTA created a market which linked almost 370 million North Americans into a single trading region stretching from the Yukon to the Yucatan. By the agreement, Canada, Mexico, and the United States provided open access to each other's markets for most goods.

Those who favoured NAFTA said it would make North America more competitive with Asian and European trading blocs. It could also be a step toward a North and South American free trade area. Canadians had to be prepared to compete in the new global marketplace. Many Canadians, however, worried that the free trade agreement was another step toward complete domination of Canada by the United States. Would Canada, they asked, be able to protect its own steel, textile, and automobile industries in the face of much cheaper production costs in the United States or Mexico? Could Canadians maintain a unique culture while forging closer economic ties with much larger nations?

Shortly after becoming prime minister in 1994, Jean Chrétien and a delegation of Canadian businesspeople travelled to countries in the Pacific Rim and Latin America to forge stronger trade and investment links. Chrétien indicated he supported the expansion of NAFTA to include other Latin American nations. The challenge for Canada in the next decades will be to establish our position in the new global marketplace and spark our lagging economy.

Prime Minister Chrétien reviews the honour guard with Chinese Premier Li Peng during Chrétien's visit to China in 1994.

SCIENCE AND TECHNOLOGY

Canada—A Leader in Satellite Technology

From 800 km above the Earth, it will penetrate the deepest night and sweep the clouds away.

When it's blasted into its low Earth orbit over both poles, Canada's Radarsat satellite will compile the only completely clear picture of the world ever taken as it hurtles around the spinning globe every 110 minutes.

Its night eye technology could have scanned Soviet ship movements from space. Its cloud-piercing radar would have tracked tank columns across stormy Warsaw Pact terrain before superpower tensions subsided.

But Radarsat, whose special radar technology was once used exclusively by the military, is a peaceful bird. Radarsat will scope out an enormous range of Earthly objects for government and business.

'It can tell you how a city is shaping up, it can tell you where ships are no matter what the weather is … or how fish stocks are doing…. It can tell you a lot about what's going on with water flows and help you to predict flood conditions and ice conditions for ship navigation and all sorts of things.'

— *The Toronto Star*, 28 November 1994.

The Radarsat satellite represents a major advance in satellite technology. It will provide the clearest pictures yet of the Earth from space.

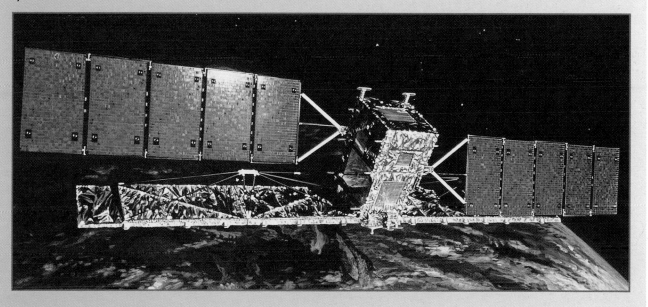

In 1994, Canada was testing its new *Radarsat* satellite—one of the most advanced satellites of its kind. Canada began its ventures into space with the launch of the *Alouette* satellite in 1962. Since then, satellite technology and its applications have become a major industry in Canada. Canada was one of the first countries to receive *Landsat* satellite images of the Earth.

Today, these images are used for resource exploration, mapping, and for monitoring weather systems and the environment. Satellites are also used to detect distress signals from crashed airplanes or sinking ships to help in search and rescue efforts.

The wide range of channels you receive on your TV and cellular telephones are also the results of satellite technology. Canada was the first country to have a domestic satellite communication system. Today, Canadian satellites send television and telephone services across the country and around the world.

Canadians have taken part in many projects with other countries to establish satellite systems.

1. Examine satellite images of the Earth and of Canada. Identify key features shown on the images. How do you think these images can be useful?
2. Why are some of the applications of satellite technology especially useful for a country such as Canada?
3. Canada has made major contributions in other aspects of research and technology, such as with the development of the Canadarm, the CANDU nuclear reactor, and IMAX films. Prepare a research report on another example of Canadian achievements in technology.

Defining a Canadian Identity

There has always been a touch of anti-Americanism in our Canadian identity. Canadians have always worried about American economic control and cultural influence. In the late 1700s, after the American Revolution, many settlers came from the United States to the Maritimes and Ontario. They were known as the United Empire Loyalists because they wished to stay loyal to Britain. They did not want to be Americans. When the Americans briefly invaded Canada during the War of 1812, both English and French fought together to keep their land free of American economic and political control. At the time of Confederation, the Fathers looked closely at the American model of government and decided it was not for Canada. The founders of Canada decided in 1867 to keep the British system of government. Unlike the United States, Canada kept the British monarch as head of the new country. It was a deliberate decision that showed the rest of the world that we were not Americans.

These feelings continue to the present day. In a 1989 poll, 66 percent of Americans favoured a union between Canada and the United States. Eighty-five percent of Canadians, however, still wished to remain independent. Canadians travelling overseas do not like to be mistaken for Americans. We often wear a maple leaf symbol on our jacket or backpack to identify us as Canadians.

Students wave flags in celebration of Canada Day.

What makes Canadians different from Americans? What is the Canadian national identity? Suppose your school was twinned with a school in a newly independent nation in Africa. Your principal asked your class to put together a multimedia presentation about Canada to be sent to the African school. How would your audio-visual presentation describe for the Africans what Canada and Canadians are like? How would you make clear to the African students how Canadians differ from Americans? Consider the following factors that influence the Canadian identity.

The Land

One of the strongest feelings uniting Canadians is the vastness and grandeur of the landscape. Although half of the population live in cities of over 100 000, the land is an inescapable influence. Even the city dweller does not have far to travel to rural areas or the "wilderness." Throughout history, Canadian artists such as the Group of Seven have expressed a sense of belonging to our rugged northern environment.

Compare the coins and paper currency of Canada and the United States. American money pictures national heroes, monuments, or symbols of power and authority, such as the eagle with bolts of lightning in its talons. Canadian money, on the other hand, pictures aspects of the land—prairies, mountains, rivers, moose, beavers, and loons.

Regional Differences

Canada is one of the world's largest countries, but nature has subdivided it into regions. Each region claims unique features and strong loyalties from those who live there. Westerners and Atlantic Canadians see themselves as separate and distinct from people in central Canada. People in northern Ontario feel they have a character different from that in southern Ontario. Quebec is determined to be recognized as a distinct society. Some Westerners have talked about their sense of "alienation" in Canada.

These regional differences, though sometimes the source of conflicts, are nonetheless part of what identifies and distinguishes Canada from other nations. Our particular diversities are part of our nature.

The People

Canada has often been described as a "mosaic." A mosaic is made by placing small pieces of multi-coloured tile or glass in mortar. Canadian society is a mosaic because people from different lands have contributed aspects of their cultural heritages and have kept aspects of their distinct identities. People of different races and customs, with different languages and accents, make up the Canadian mosaic.

Government policy has encouraged immigrants to keep their heritage. Multicultural radio and television stations, ethnic presses, and heritage language programs have contributed to the diversity. Minority communities take pride in their members who achieve in the arts, politics, science, and business. The differences have sometimes led to conflicts and racial tension. Canada's diverse peoples, however, have lived together in relative peace for over 125 years. Debates continue over how to define a Canadian identity, but it can be argued that diversity is an integral part of Canada's character.

The challenge for the 1990s and beyond is to maintain the programs that support and cultivate our culture. Television and radio, literature and magazines, theatre, music, and the other arts all help to express the Canadian identity. Music, for example, has always been part of our identity. We have sung about the life of the *habitant*, the backbreaking toil of railway builders, and the loneliness of pioneer settlers. Popular singers in Quebec have written music and lyrics that keep alive the culture of French Canadians. Contemporary musicians such as k.d. lang, The Tragically Hip, Rush, Bryan Adams, and others have brought Canadian musical styles to the United States and gained international reputations.

However a lagging economy and rising government debts have brought significant cutbacks in arts funding over the late 1980s and 1990s from both government and private sources. National institutions such as the Canada Council, CBC, National Film Board, National Gallery, and smaller arts companies have struggled with cutbacks. Many Canadians are concerned about the future of our arts. Can arts programs and companies survive in Canada with the reductions in funding? What implications will there be for Canadian culture?

Canadian musician Bryan Adams has gained popularity in Canada and the United States. He once stated, however, that requirements for Canadian content in the media and government subsidies for Canadian musicians support mediocrity. What do you think?

ACTIVITIES

Check Your Understanding

1. Add these new terms to your *Factfile*.
   economic nationalists
   Foreign Investment Review Agency (FIRA)
   Investment Canada
   National Energy Program (NEP)
   Canadian Radio-Television and Telecommunications Commission (CRTC)
   Strategic Defense Initiative (SDI)
   Free Trade Agreement (FTA)
   North American Free Trade Agreement (NAFTA)

2. a) Why did Americans complain that FIRA and NEP were unfriendly actions?
   b) How effective were these programs?

3. What steps did the Liberal government in the 1970s and early 1980s take to protect Canadian culture? Describe the results.

4. a) Why did Trudeau attempt to reduce Canada's involvement in NATO and NORAD?
   b) Why did his policy change?

5. Describe the *Polar Sea* incident. How did Canadians react and with what result?

Confirm Your Learning

6. Compare the policies of the Liberal government under Trudeau and the Conservative government under Mulroney using the following organizer. Summarize the similarities and differences and suggest reasons.

Criteria	Liberal government under Trudeau	Conservative government under Mulroney
Economy		
Culture		
Foreign policy		
Defence		

7. Create a cartoon on an issue of your choice from this chapter. Consider the beaver and the elephant, the energy crisis, free trade, or the Canadian identity, for example. Have a partner interpret your cartoon. Collect the cartoons created in your class into a "Cartoon Portfoolio."

8. Calculate the number of hours you spend in one week watching television. How many of these hours are spent watching American television programming? What impact do you think American television has on Canadian life?

9. What impact does American culture have on other countries? Is the Canadian experience unique? Explain.

10. Do you feel that Québécois culture helps to protect the Canadian identity from American influence? Why or why not? Explain.

Challenge Your Mind

11. "This is a paid political announcement." In groups, create TV or radio advertisements paid for by political parties or particular interest groups and aired during the free trade debate. The ads should clearly present the view of the party or group on the issue in 30 seconds. Record your ads on video, if possible. Be creative.

12. a) Some people have suggested that, as a way of strengthening the Canadian economy, individuals and governments should buy Canadian products whenever possible. How would a "Buy Canadian" policy benefit the country?
    b) Examine your own buying pattern over the last year. When faced with the choice of a Canadian-made or foreign-made product, which did you buy?
    c) Plan a "Buy Canadian" project to make your school aware of what you have discovered.

13. It has been said that Canadians dislike being mistaken for Americans, but will defend Americans to the British. Why do Canadians work so hard trying to show the rest of the world that we are not Americans? Why would Canadians defend Americans to other countries of the world?

14. The American humourist Henry Morgan lived for a while in Canada. The biggest difference he noticed between Canada and the United States was the bilingual characteristic. "I have been here for almost ten weeks now and the only difference I've found is that when you pick up a jar that says peanut butter, the other side says 'beurre d'arachides.'" What do you think are the differences between Canadians and Americans?

CHAPTER 20

Canada: A Nation of Diversity and Change

STANDOFF AT OKA

A Mohawk and a Canadian soldier stand face-to-face during the confrontation at Oka in 1990.

"We are prepared to fight … and if necessary, to die … in defence of our land." With these words in the summer of 1990 a small band of Mohawks announced that they had had enough. The town council of Oka, Quebec, wished to expand the golf course. The land they wanted was the ancestral burial grounds considered sacred to the Mohawk people. The courts had rejected the Mohawks' claim to the land. The Mohawks decided not to stand by and allow the land to be taken. They erected a barricade across the road and a 78-day armed standoff began.

On 10 July 1990, about a hundred Quebec provincial police attempted to break through the barricade which was guarded mostly by women and children. Mohawk men, armed with rifles, were off to the side in the woods. Police wore gas masks and carried assault rifles. Overhead a police helicopter hovered, attempting to spot the Mohawks in the brush. A few minutes before 9:00 a.m., an armed conflict broke out. Hundreds of rounds were fired, bullets coming from both sides. A 31-year-old police officer was hit and later died.

Oka and Native Issues

The **Oka standoff** brought concerns of Native peoples to the forefront of national and international attention. Across Canada and internationally, news reports focussed on the events unfolding at Oka. Thirty kilometres to the southeast, the Mohawks of the Kahnawake Reserve were outraged at the police raid on the people at Oka. In their support, the Kahnawake blocked all roads into the reserve. These roads included two major highways as well as the southern tip of the Mercier bridge. The bridge was a vital link between the island of Montreal and several heavily populated suburbs on the south shore of the St. Lawrence River. The Kahnawake Mohawks had a warning: "We'll bring down the bridge if there is another police assault at Oka."

More than a hundred chiefs gathered from across Canada at Kahnawake to discuss solidarity with the Mohawks. They warned the federal government that they would not stand by and watch the Mohawks be assaulted. One chief said his people would bring down the power lines into Edmonton if the police moved against the Mohawks. Others suggested they would block more highways or rail lines. The chiefs

A stuffed poncho on a stick with the painted message "All Native people want peace and sovereignty" stood facing the troops at Oka.

called on the international community to condemn Canada for its handling of the crisis. They asked the United Nations to investigate the Mohawks' complaints that their civil and human rights were being violated.

Meanwhile, no progress was made toward a negotiated settlement. Early in August 1990, Prime Minister Mulroney announced that the Canadian armed forces would be sent to Oka and Kahnawake. They would replace the Quebec police. The decision to send in the army came at the request of Quebec Premier Bourassa.

Approximately 4400 soldiers were moved into Oka and Kahnawake. The troops were backed by armoured personnel carriers and heavy weapons. Military officials said the mission was to remove the barricades peacefully. After tense negotiations, the barricades came down on the Mercier bridge. During the following weeks, negotiations continued. Finally, on 26 September, the 11-week standoff ended.

Most of the Mohawks considered that they had been successful in achieving their goal. The sacred burial grounds had been saved from the developers. As important, the issue of Native rights had been put before the world through the media. But Native peoples in Canada warned that there would be more Okas unless Canada respected their land claims and other rights.

> Ovide Mercredi, then vice-Chief of the Assembly of First Nations, said after Oka that the federal government still hadn't learned the lesson of Oka. "Ottawa is once again announcing what it is going to do for Natives. Canada's 500 000 Status Indians are tired of this treatment. They want meaningful negotiations on problems, not to be told what someone else has decided for them."

Native Rights and Land Claims

The issue of Native rights and land claims is not a new one in Canada, but it has gained increasing attention in the past three decades. In July 1977 at a ceremony marking the hundredth anniversary of the Blackfoot Treaty (Treaty No. 7), a chief told visiting Prince Charles, "Our tribes still suffer from poverty, unemployment, alcoholism, poor health, and lack of good opportunities for education. We have become a forgotten people. We don't want to wait another hundred years before we take our rightful place beside our fellow citizens of Canada."

In August 1973, the Minister of Indian and Northern Affairs had announced that the Canadian government would negotiate land titles with Native groups. For the Native peoples, this was a first step toward recognition of their rights. One of the largest land deals in the 1970s centred around the Quebec government's huge hydroelectric project in the James Bay region. The project would flood the traditional lands of Cree and Inuit. They insisted on receiving a share from the benefits of development based on their aboriginal right. No treaty had been signed in the area and the Cree and Inuit claimed rights to the land as the first inhabitants.

For two years, the project was halted until the land claims were settled. In 1975, the **James Bay Agreement** was signed. In return for 13 844 km² (60 percent of northern Quebec), the Cree and Inuit received land on which to hunt, fish, and trap.

The Cree and Inuit had succeeded in negotiating a land claim with the Quebec government based on their aboriginal right. An important precedent (example) had been set. Native peoples felt that they could now force the federal or provincial governments to the bargaining table. This

Manitoba Grand Chief Phil Fontaine and Indian Affairs Minister Ron Irwin sign the self-government agreement for Manitoba Natives in December 1994.

was especially true where treaties had never been signed or where previous treaties could be challenged.

In 1978, the government agreed to pay $48 million to 2500 Inuit of the western Arctic. In return, the Inuit agreed to give up aboriginal rights to land they had originally used. This was just the beginning of several land claims. Frustrations were also to come, however. Through the 1980s and 1990s, many claims became bogged down in the courts. Native peoples began to look for other means to establish their rights.

The patriation of the Constitution and the passage of the Charter of Rights and Freedoms were thought by many Canadians to be the greatest success stories of the 1980s. But when the Charter was being drafted, there was no mention of aboriginal rights. Many Native people believed it was just another example in a continuing story of neglect. Like women, whose rights had also been left out of the draft, Native people spoke out. Finally, agreement was reached. The rights of both Native peoples

and women would be written into the new Constitution. The revised Charter said that "existing aboriginal and treaty rights" of Native peoples were "recognized and affirmed."

In the negotiations for constitutional reform at Meech Lake, the Native peoples were again left out. Elijah Harper's stand in the Manitoba Legislature made it clear that Native peoples would not be ignored. The Charlottetown Accord recognized the right to aboriginal self-government. Though the Accord was defeated, Native peoples have continued to negotiate for the right to govern their own affairs. A landmark agreement was signed in 1990 to create the new territory of Nunavut with Inuit self-government by 1999. Another landmark agreement was made in 1994 by Manitoba chiefs and the federal Indian Affairs minister. The agreement proposes to dismantle the Department of Indian Affairs in the province and transfer power and funds to the bands.

Major Northern Land Claim Agreements, 1975-1990

Claim	Agreement type and date	Number of persons to benefit	Area in km²	Money paid to First Nations
James Bay Cree	Final 11 Nov. 1975	6 650	5 542	$135 million
Inuit in northern Quebec	Final 11 Nov. 1975	4 390	8 150	$90 million
Naskapis of northeast Quebec	Final 12 Jan. 1978	390	4 145	$9 million
Inuvialuit	Final 5 June 1984	2 500	12 950	$55 million
Yukon Natives	Final 31 Mar. 1990	6 500	41 595	$242.7 million
Dene-Métis of the NWT	Final 9 Apr. 1990	13 000	181 299	$500 million

Note: While the land claims agreements involved a sum of money in each case, First Nations peoples also negotiated hunting, fishing, and sovereignty rights in individual cases.

SOCIETY AND SOCIAL CHANGE

Nunavut

The map of Canada is being redrawn. In May 1992, 52 percent of voters in the Northwest Territories accepted an agreement reached with the Canadian government to split the Territories into two parts. A new eastern Arctic territory extending over 2 million km² was created and named **Nunavut**. Nunavut means "our land"—land of the Inuit who make up the majority of the population. The western Arctic is home of Dene, Métis, and non-Natives.

The new territory comprises a fifth of Canada's land area and has been called the largest peaceful land settlement in history. The Inuit received title to 350 000 km² and $1.15 billion over 14 years. In return, they renounced their claim to another 1 658 000 km² of aboriginal land, possibly rich in oil and gas fields. They will have Inuit-controlled government by 1999 and hunting, trapping, and fishing rights over all of Nunavut.

Inuit leader James Eetoolook noted, "Inuit will have a management role in our own land. This agreement will give us self-determination over our lives in the future." The Inuit believe that when they have control, they will be able to deal with the social problems facing their people—including a high suicide rate and alcoholism.

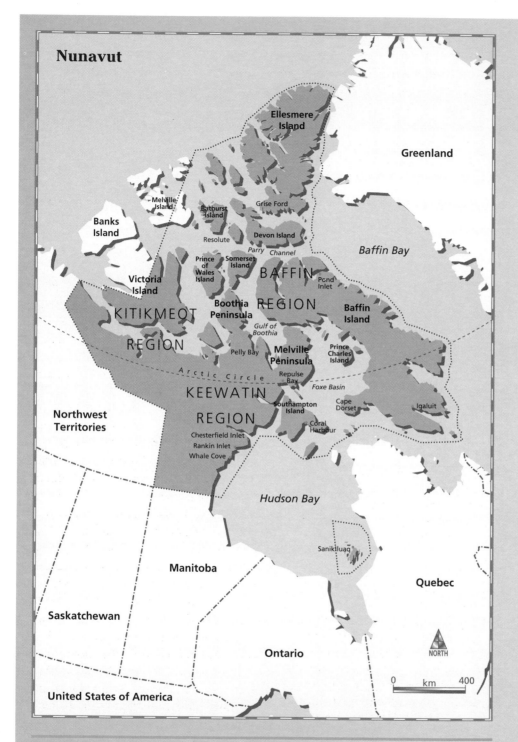

Nunavut

Ellesmere Island

Greenland

Melville Island

Grise Ford

Banks Island

Bathurst Island

Devon Island

Baffin Bay

Resolute

Parry Channel

Prince of Wales Island

Somerset Island

BAFFIN

Victoria Island

Pcnd Inlet

Boothia Peninsula

REGION

Baffin Island

KITIKMEOT

Gulf of Boothia

Melville Peninsula

Prince Charles Island

REGION

Pelly Bay

Arctic Circle

Repulse Bay

Foxe Basin

KEEWATIN

Southampton Island

Cape Dorset

Igaluit

Northwest Territories

REGION

Coral Harbour

Chesterfield Inlet
Rankin Inlet
Whale Cove

Hudson Bay

Sanikiluaq

Manitoba

Quebec

Saskatchewan

Ontario

NORTH

0 km 400

United States of America

1. Why is the creation of Nunavut an important settlement for the Inuit?
2. The agreement officially comes into effect in 1999. What preparations do you think need to be made?
3. Do you think similar land settlements can be made in other areas of Canada? What challenges might there be? Explain.

Immigration in Contemporary Canada

A new wave of immigration flooded into Canada in the 1980s. Rather than coming from Britain, the United States, or European nations, the majority of immigrants now came from a wide range of other nations including the Caribbean, Vietnam, India, Pakistan, and Hong Kong. Between 1980 and 1986, immigrants from Asia, Latin America, and Africa made up 65 percent of the total.

Under the **Immigration Act of 1978**, Canada had set out two major objectives. The first was to attract people who would "promote the domestic and international needs of Canada." They would be assessed according to a point system in which education, training, experience, and personal suitability were the factors that counted. The second goal was to accept "the displaced and the persecuted" for humanitarian reasons.

The Act recognized three classes of immigrants.

- *Family class* were wives or husbands and unmarried children under 21, and parents or grandparents of people who were already citizens or permanent residents of Canada.

- *Independent class* were individuals who had family members in Canada willing to sponsor them and help them get established. They were also people who had $250 000 to invest for three years, or were willing to set up and work in a business. In 1987, the top source countries for business immigrants were Hong Kong, South Korea, Taiwan, the United States, and France. Independent class immigrants could also gain entry on the basis of a point system that awarded certain professions more points than others. For example, nurses and therapists who were urgently needed in Canada got 10 points. Doctors got zero points. Veterinarians got one point.

- *Refugee class* were persons who feared or suffered persecution in their own countries because of their political ideas, religion, race, or nationality. It included the "boat people" from Vietnam and Chileans fleeing from the military dictatorship in their country. Refugees were permitted to apply for immigrant status from within Canada. Others had to apply for entry visas before coming to Canada.

The Refugee Crisis

The refugee class created problems for immigration officials. It was difficult often to tell legitimate refugees from those just claiming to be refugees to get quick admission into Canada. As more and more political refugees arrived in this country, the system got badly backlogged.

In August 1986, 115 Tamils from Sri Lanka without visas were found drifting in lifeboats off the coast of Newfoundland. They asked to be admitted to Canada as refugees fleeing persecution and possible death in their own country. In the following year, 174 East Indians, mostly Sikhs from the Punjab, came ashore in southwest Nova Scotia. They also asked to be granted refugee status. Parliament was recalled from summer recess to pass emergency legislation aimed at halting the flood of people seeking refugee status in Canada.

The crisis sparked angry public debates over immigration policy. The government was pressured to crack down on illegal refugees. Illegal refugees were resented by genuine immigrants and their sponsors. There was also a growing fortune being made in "people-smuggling." Sophisticated criminals were forging documents and smuggling illegal immigrants into the country.

During the 1980s, the Canadian government allowed several groups of special refugees to enter the country for humani-

Number of people in Hong Kong applying for immigration visas to Canada immediately after the Tiananmen Square massacre in Beijing in June 1989:

9000 a day

tarian reasons. But Canadians remained sharply divided on the refugee issue. In a 1987 poll, 45 percent agreed that Canada had a moral obligation to accept those fleeing persecution in their own countries. However, 46 percent disagreed. Many Canadians believed that some refugees were not genuine targets of political persecution. They were victims of economic poverty looking for a better life. Admitting them as refugees was seen as an abuse of the system.

During the recession in the early 1980s, racial tensions had increased. In Toronto, Montreal, and Vancouver, Asian and African Canadians faced job discrimination and racial prejudice. One Montreal taxi company dismissed 24 Haitians on the grounds that customers didn't wish to be driven by a Black driver. On radio talk shows, callers became increasingly negative about "non-white" immigrants.

A study done by the government found a disturbing level of racism in Canada. Most of it was based on the fear that the British and French Canadians were being overwhelmed by immigrants from other cultures. In the Laurier era, 95 percent of Canadians were of British or French descent. By the mid-1980s, the figure was down to just over 68 percent. No other ethnic group made up more than 5 percent of the population.

Disturbed by the reports of racially motivated incidents, the government established a race relations unit. Its aim was to discover the causes of racial tension and to devise ways to reduce it. Schools were encouraged to establish programs to deal with anti-racist attitudes and behaviours. The courts provided protection to victims of racial discrimination. The government gave assistance to immigrant women who, as a group, were often isolated at home with few opportunities to participate in Canadian life. It also continued to fund writing about Canada's ethnic groups and other ethnocultural activities.

Refugees to Canada by Country, 1982–1992

Year	Country of Origin	Number of Refugees
1982–1985	Poland	9 365
1982–1992	Iran	7 604
1982–1992	El Salvador	6 370
1983–1992	Lebanon	12 108
1983–1992	Sri Lanka	10 843
1984–1992	Guatemala	2 405

Source: Immigration Canada

Immigration in the 1990s

In the 1990s, Canada's immigration policy has remained one of the most open in the world. We accepted more immigrants in proportion to our population than any other nation. A total of 252 042 were admitted in 1993, one of the highest totals since World War I. Still, the influx is nothing like the wave of newcomers that arrived in the first two decades of the century. In 1913, 400 000 reached Canadian shores at a time when the total population was only 8 million.

Why are some Canadians concerned about high immigration? Some of the concerns and counterarguments are outlined in the chart on the next page.

The challenge for the 1990s and beyond will be to ease racial tension and promote tolerance. This can be done by laws, but also through ethnocultural education and the media. Festivals such as Caribana, which celebrate customs brought from many homelands, help to break down walls of prejudice and fear.

The Struggle for Equality Between Men and Women

The role of women has changed in Canadian life. The historic battles to win the right to vote and for the freedom to work

Concerns	Counterarguments
Immigration puts a strain on our ailing economy. In the 1993 election campaign, Reform party leader Preston Manning suggested cutting immigration levels by 100 000 to bring them in line with Canada's current economic needs.	Immigration was of net economic benefit to Canada according to a 1991 Economic Council of Canada study. Immigration creates jobs because it makes the population larger, thereby increasing the need for products and services. Experts say the future depends on immigration to replace retiring workers.
Immigrants cause unemployment. An Angus Reid/Southam News poll suggested 47 percent of Canadians believe the country is accepting too many, and one third said they take jobs away from Canadians.	The Demographic Review in 1989 and the Economic Council in 1991 both affirmed that high immigration does not create more unemployment. Between 65 and 70 percent of both immigrants and Canadian-born aged 15 and older were employed in the workforce.
Immigrants put a strain on the welfare system and social service programs. Many abuse these programs.	In the 1991 study, it was shown that immigrants are less likely to be on welfare than Canadian-born adults.
Fifty percent of current immigrants speak neither official language when they arrive. Without language to build on, it is very difficult to get established in the labour market.	English and French language programs are available for immigrants and many of them work hard to learn either language.
Increasing numbers of visible minorities will dramatically alter the traditional face of Canadian society. In a government survey of 2000 adults carried out in 1992, more than half said, "They were really worried that they might become a minority if immigration is unchecked."	This argument is unfounded and based on racial discrimination. In 1986, Canada's non-white population stood at 1 600 000. That figure represented just 6.4 percent of the total population. If 70 percent of all immigrants between 1994 and 2001 are non-white, Canada's total non-white population would not exceed 9.6 percent. However, as a result of the 1992 government survey, tighter immigration regulations were introduced.
As they did in the 1980s, most immigrants in the 1990s will settle in the cities, adding to the pressures that some people feel to move to the suburbs and rural areas. Since most immigrants are settling in Metro Toronto, some fear a major crisis there.	Much of Metro Toronto's recent population growth has been as a result of immigration. The immigrants have brought their skills, talents, and hard work to the economy. Without immigration many of our best scientists, nurses, and other skilled and unskilled workers would not be here. Nor would some of our most successful entrepreneurs, such as Thomas Bata, James Ting, and Frank Stronach.
The immigration system lets in criminals. In 1994, two immigrants were charged with vicious killings in Toronto. There was tremendous media attention given to these crimes.	Immigrants are under-represented in the Canadian prison population according to the report "Canada's Changing Immigrant Population 1994," published by Statistics Canada. The 1993 revisions to the Immigration Act aim to turn away any individual actively involved in organized crime and terrorism.

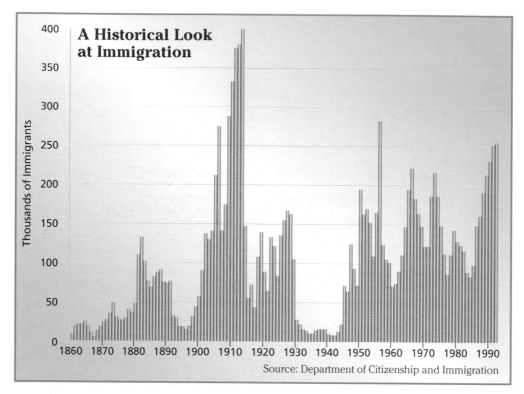

A Historical Look at Immigration

Source: Department of Citizenship and Immigration

outside the home have been won. Today's struggle is to bring about a change in attitudes and greater opportunities for social and economic equality.

The Canadian Human Rights Commission in 1977 outlawed discrimination on the basis of sex and established the principle of **"equal pay for work of equal value."** Men and women doing jobs requiring similar skills and responsibilities were to be paid the same wage. In the 1990s, however, women still face job discrimination and in-

equality in pay and working conditions. The majority of workers in the lowest paying occupations are women.

In lean economic times, dealing with inequities between men and women in the workplace is a challenge. Some businesses argue that raising women's wages to equal those of men can make a business less competitive and profitable. Though progress is slow, government programs have had some effect on pay equity.

Other issues facing women in the 1990s

Revisions to the Immigration Act in the 1990s

1. Only close relations, such as spouses and dependent children, will be allowed into the country under the family classification.

2. Stricter rules have been designed to detect illegal immigrants or people with false travel documents.

3. The selection process will be streamlined. More business immigrants and persons with money to invest will be accepted. The government can tell immigrants who are chosen because of their skills where they must live and for how long. Under the old rules, a physiotherapist who was accepted because his/her skills were needed in Newfoundland could settle in Toronto or Vancouver.

4. As of February 1995, all immigrants are required to pay a $975 tax when they apply for residence in Canada. The government stated that the tax was meant to offset the costs of language and skills training and other social services.

PROFILES

Roberta Bondar

Roberta Bondar is the second Canadian astronaut and first female Canadian astronaut to travel in space. Canada's first space traveller was Marc Garneau, who participated in a mission on the space shuttle *Challenger* in 1984. The preparation and training for a space mission is long and intense, but Roberta Bondar has said that the rewards are immense. The view of Earth from space left her in awe.

Roberta Bondar applied for the Canadian space program in 1983 and was chosen as one of six out of the 4300 applicants. Her opportunity to join a mission did not come until 1992. She was aboard the American space shuttle *Discovery*. As a medical doctor and neurobiologist, her role was to conduct life sciences research including experiments on motion sickness, weightlessness, the ways the human body adapts to space flights, and the amount of energy astronauts use in space.

Following her journey, Roberta became a spokesperson for Canada's space programs: "I have a ... commitment to be seen as a person educated in Canada who has participated at the world level. It is the scientific Olympics. I didn't mess up. I have pride in that and now I want to share the adventure that I've had."

In recognition of her accomplishment as Canada's first woman in space, Roberta Bondar was awarded the Order of Canada in 1992.

1. Roberta Bondar has said that, as a woman, she faced "preconceived ideas of my potential, of my behaviour, of my contribution." What might some of these preconceived ideas have been? How did she overcome them?

2. Prepare a short report on another prominent Canadian woman of the 1990s.

Average Earnings in the 10 Lowest Paying Occupations Full Time, Full Year 1990

Ten lowest paying occupations	No. of male earners	No. of female earners	Average earnings men	Average earnings women
	Total 65 225	Total 170 230	$18 794	$13 673
Livestock farm workers	10 415	5 795	$19 279	$11 788
Sewing machine operators, textiles, and similar materials	2 765	29 370	$22 991	$15 933
Other farming, horticulture, and animal care work	13 860	11 320	$19 537	$12 174
Crop farm workers	6 015	5 780	$19 814	$12 421
Bartenders	6 320	7 440	$18 558	$13 952
Lodging cleaners, except private households	1 060	6 910	$19 238	$15 178
Service station attendants	8 370	2 065	$16 135	$13 359
Housekeepers and related workers	1 145	12 680	$19 210	$14 053
Food and beverage sector	13 845	48 505	$17 822	$13 037
Child care	1 440	40 365	$20 987	$13 252

Source: Statistics Canada

Average Earnings in the 10 Highest Paying Occupations Full Time, Full Year 1990

Ten highest paying occupations	No. of male earners	No. of female earners	Average earnings men	Average earnings women
	Total 214 755	Total 53 460	$79 463	$48 609
Judges and magistrates	1 660	475	$109 313	$79 204
Physicians and surgeons	24 120	7 320	$111 261	$73 071
Dentists	6 015	760	$99 280	$67 997
Lawyers and notaries	30 755	10 430	$86 108	$50 012
General managers and other senior officials	104 645	24 580	$74 425	$40 633
Other managers and administrators of mines, quarries, and oil wells	2 915	950	$73 281	$39 151
Airline pilots, navigators, and flight engineers	7 110	375	$66 087	$31 026
Osteopaths and chiropractors	2 030	440	$68 404	$45 368
Management occupations, natural sciences, and engineering	12 520	1 785	$66 668	$41 800
University teachers	22 985	6 350	$65 671	$49 000

Source: Statistics Canada

Women hold only 20 percent of the positions in the 10 highest paying occupations. Even then, there is a noticeable wage gap for work of equal value between males and females.

In 1977 Sandra Lovelace, a Tobique from New Brunswick, filed a complaint with the United Nations over her loss of her Indian status because she had married a non-status man. According to the Indian Act, a woman who married a non-status man lost her Indian status. She no longer had access to federal programs providing housing, education, and other benefits. Although the United Nations committee supported Sandra Lovelace, it could not help her because the UN does not have any legal power over Canadian laws. In 1985, the Indian Act was changed. Women marrying non-status men and their children could retain their status and privileges.

and beyond include fighting for improved child care facilities and health care, and working to change laws to fight discrimination and sexual harassment in the workplace. Canadians are demanding action from the government and courts to prevent violence against women and children. All of these are crucial hurdles that will have to be cleared before equality between women and men can be established.

Protecting the Environment

Canadians, along with people throughout the world, are beginning to realize the increasing threats an industrialized society poses to life, health, and the environment. In the mid-1980s, Canadians of all ages became more environmentally aware. Many new projects were established to help prevent or ease damage. But with the economic slowdown in the 1990s, less money was available for these projects and some environmental problems reached crisis proportions. Case studies of two recent environmental crises are described below.

The Crisis of the Newfoundland Fishery

When John Cabot visited the Grand Banks off Newfoundland in 1497, he reported the sea was teeming with fish. His sailors could pull up cod and haddock by simply lowering baskets into the water. As recently as the 1960s, Canadian and foreign fleets from West Germany, Spain, and other countries were pulling in as much as 800 000 tonnes of fish annually on the Grand Banks. Today, fish stocks are severely depleted. The federal government announced in 1992 a ban on all northern cod fishing. Some scientists think the fish stocks may not recover until the late 1990s, if at all.

The fishing industry was the backbone of the Newfoundland economy. The ban put more than 25 000 fishery workers out of jobs. The disaster forced Ottawa to set up an $800 million compensation program for unemployed Newfoundland fishery workers. It offers jobless workers re-training courses in different lines of work. But it is difficult to compensate for the loss of a way of life.

Why were the fish stocks so drastically depleted? A number of reasons have been suggested. Abnormally cold currents and colder average water temperatures may have driven the cod to seek warmer spawning grounds. Since 1983, when a ban on seal products was introduced, the seal population has soared. Seals consume large quantities of small fish such as capelin, on which cod also feed.

Many people feel that the most likely cause of the problem, however, is high technology fishing. Large trawlers equipped with funnel-shaped nets drag the sea bottom and scoop up everything in their path. Vessels with these high-tech nets have been operating on the Grand Banks since 1977. The draggers capture large numbers of baby cod which are too small for use and so are dumped back into the ocean.

Fisheries Minister Brian Tobin shows where the Spanish vessel Estai *was seized in 1995 for using illegal nets. Tobin brought international attention to Canada's conservation efforts on the Grand Banks.*

Many of these draggers are foreign-owned. However, Canadian corporations and offshore fishers have also participated in dragging operations. Some experts called dragger fishing the marine equivalent of clear-cut logging.

In 1995, the Canadian government took a strong stand on fish conservation in the Grand Banks. A Spanish trawler, the *Estai*, was seized and charged with overfishing and using illegal nets. The incident gained international attention and was not resolved until an agreement was reached with the European Union on acceptable quotas. Negotiations on how much fish can be caught are likely to continue and the question of whether the fish stocks can recover remains.

The Crisis at Clayoquot Sound

On Canada's West coast, another environmental battle is being waged between loggers and environmentalists. Clayoquot (pronounced KLAK-wut) Sound, on Vancouver Island, is the largest patch of temperate rainforest left in British Columbia.

Towering stands of cedar, hemlock, balsam, and cypress would yield an immensely valuable crop. National and international environmental groups have opposed the clear-cutting of this forest.

The ecologists have argued that logging in Clayoquot would destroy animal, plant, and bird species. It would pollute the streams where the salmon spawn. Logging roads cause erosion and landslides. They compare the destruction of the BC forests with the destruction of the rainforest in the Amazon. Environmental activists have staged demonstrations in Canada and have made their protest international in an anti-logging campaign.

The forest industries have argued that logging provides important jobs, especially in a time of high unemployment. Each logging job also generates employment for others in goods and services. Forest products are among Canada's most important exports. The logging company, Macmillan Bloedel, has agreed to strict guidelines. Only 1000 ha a year will be logged for the next 80 years. No more than 30 ha will be

Several demonstrations were held against logging in Clayoquot Sound. How effective were these campaigns?

clear-cut, and all cut areas must be reforested.

In the summer of 1994, British Columbia Premier Harcourt announced a government plan to reduce logging on Vancouver Island. The government intends to create 23 new parks by designating 13 percent of the island as parkland. The move will eliminate 900 logging jobs over five years. Harcourt said that international pressure and boycott threats left him with little choice. "We have come to the point," he said, "where irresponsible abuse of our forests threatens both our environment and our economy."

In 1995, however, the World Wildlife Fund still gave the federal and many provincial governments a failing grade on their environmental programs.

Canada's Role in World Affairs

Canada has a long history of providing aid to foreign nations, particularly developing countries. The **Canadian International Development Agency (CIDA)** was established in 1968 to co-ordinate all Canadian aid from the Canadian government,

religious organizations, and charities. Major emphasis was placed on helping countries improve food production, public health, education, shelter, and energy. Funds were also provided for emergency food, aid, and disaster relief to stricken areas of the world.

At the end of the 1980s, the shape of global politics changed dramatically. The Cold War was over. Communist governments in eastern Europe collapsed. Even the Soviet Union broke apart into 15 new nations. In 1989 the Berlin Wall, the symbol of a divided Europe, came down. The threat of global nuclear war seemed to fade. Prime Minister Mulroney's government felt that it was important to provide Canadian aid to former Soviet bloc countries to help them get on their feet. He believed that the area was critical to the future stability and prosperity of both developed and developing countries. Therefore, CIDA shifted almost $100 million in aid to the former Communist nations of eastern Europe.

Some critics of the government were angry with this change in direction. To them, it seemed that the government was transferring assistance to nations with export potential rather than helping developing world nations. Critics said that promoting trade and industry was a sound policy, but it should not be considered foreign aid.

Furthermore, while some Canadians believe that assisting developing countries gain self-sufficiency is a moral obligation of a rich nation like Canada, others feel Canadians should come first. The amount spent on foreign aid has been criticized when Canada's economy is struggling, many people are unemployed or on welfare, and Canada has a huge national debt.

Foreign Aid to Africa
1970–1991
(millions of dollars)

Year	1970	1980	1991
Total foreign aid	$37.4	$285.7	$1 109.6
Country receiving the largest amount	Tunisia	Egypt	Ethiopia
Amount received	$7.2	$27.8	$70.4

Foreign Aid to Asia
1970–1991
(millions of dollars)

Year	1970	1980	1991
Total foreign aid	$140.9	$234.6	$822.8
Country receiving the largest amount	India	Pakistan	Bangladesh
Amount received	$88.6	$67.1	$190.4

Foreign Aid to Central and South America and the Caribbean
1970–1991
(millions of dollars)

Year	1970	1980	1991
Total foreign aid	not available	$66.8	$348.5
Country receiving the largest amount	Jamaica	Jamaica	Jamaica
Amount received	$2.7	$7.8	$42.1

Source: Canadian International Development Agency

Peacekeeping

Canada has played a major role in international peacekeeping operations ever since Prime Minister Pearson received the Nobel Peace Prize for his role in creating a formal UN peacekeeping force in 1957. When the Liberals came to power in 1993, they promised to reduce defence spending by 3 percent a year for four years. The government indicated that the high cost of peacekeeping operations may not be affordable in the future. A sweeping Parliamentary inquiry was launched into the future of Canada's $11.3 billion defence effort.

Some defence experts have argued that a portion of Canada's troops should be permanently assigned to peacekeeping duties. A "quick reaction force" should be established to assist in a wide variety of international situations. These troops would be available to go anywhere in the world for the first few weeks or months of a crisis, after which other countries' troops would relieve them.

In the early 1990s, however, a number of incidents have thrown a shadow over Canadian peacekeepers. The Canadian Airborne Regiment was dismantled after videos released to the media and the Defence minister showed questionable initia-

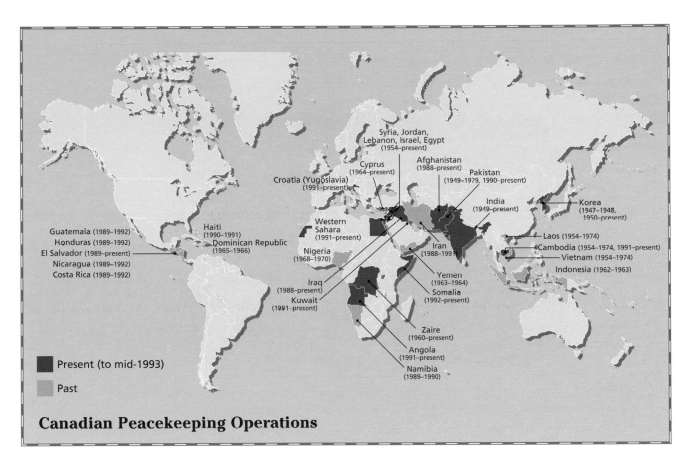

Guatemala (1989–1992)
Honduras (1989–1992)
El Salvador (1989–present)
Nicaragua (1989–1992)
Costa Rica (1989–1992)

Haiti (1990–1991)
Dominican Republic (1965–1966)

Syria, Jordan, Lebanon, Israel, Egypt (1954–present)
Cyprus (1964–present)
Croatia (Yugoslavia) (1991–present)
Afghanistan (1988–present)
Pakistan (1949–1979, 1990–present)
India (1949–present)
Korea (1947–1948, 1950–present)

Western Sahara (1991–present)
Nigeria (1968–1970)
Iran (1988–1991)
Laos (1954–1974)
Cambodia (1954–1974, 1991–present)
Vietnam (1954–1974)
Indonesia (1962–1963)

Iraq (1988–present)
Kuwait (1991–present)
Yemen (1963–1964)
Somalia (1992–present)

Zaire (1960–present)
Angola (1991–present)
Namibia (1989–1990)

■ Present (to mid-1993)

■ Past

Canadian Peacekeeping Operations

tion practices and evidence of racism among members. A few soldiers serving in Somalia have been tried for their involvement in the killing of a Somali citizen.

Some people feel these are isolated incidents that should not reflect on the remarkable record of Canadian peacekeepers over many years. Others feel strong measures need to be taken to counter any racism in the military and ensure Canada continues to play a responsible peacekeeping role.

The National Debt

For many years, Ottawa has spent more money than it has taken in. It wasn't always so. The federal budget was balanced from the 1930s to the 1960s. In the 1970s, new social programs such as unemployment insurance, pensions indexed to inflation, health care, regional development, housing, and foreign aid were introduced. Most Canadians supported these programs. But rather than raising taxes significantly, the government ran deficits to pay for the programs. A deficit is the amount by which spending exceeds income each year.

As government spending grew, deficits rose and the federal debt ballooned. The debt is the accumulation of annual deficits into the total amount that we owe. The Canadian Chamber of Commerce estimated that the federal debt was rising by $76 million a day. When the debts of the provinces were added to what Ottawa owes, the total debt in Canada reached $661 billion in March 1994. Under the Mulroney government, one out of every three tax dollars went to paying the interest on the federal debt. This amount was larger than its spending on health care, pensions, social assistance, and family allowances combined.

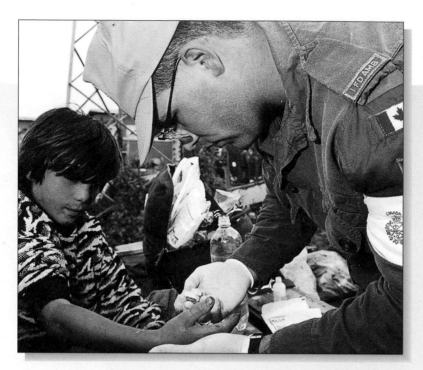

A Canadian peace-keeper helps a child in Sarajevo.

Mulroney argued that, due to the size of the national debt, Canada could no longer afford to pay well-off Canadians pensions or child allowance payments. The government started to tax back social assistance benefits. In 1992, family allowance benefits were replaced with a supplement for low-income families. Many Canadians were unhappy with the cutting of funds to families, pensioners, and the unemployed, especially in a time of high unemployment.

The Liberal party came to power in 1993 with a promise to reduce the federal deficit to 3 percent of the GDP (Gross Domestic Product) by the end of the government's third year in office. This would bring down the annual deficit from $45.7 billion to about $25 billion.

What alternatives were available to reduce the national debt?

- *Pare down the deficit by cutting spending.* This option looks promising, but large savings could only come by wiping out whole government departments. If cuts are deep, unemployment will increase and many citizens will suffer.

- *Pay off the debt with new income.* A booming economy would help to achieve this option because it would raise additional tax revenues. Or, the government could simply raise taxes to pay off the debt, but this would also be extremely unpopular with voters.

- *Ignore the debt and don't worry about paying it back.* This is much like refusing to pay the balance owed on your credit card. If you did this, your credit would be quickly cut off. If a government did this, investors would refuse to risk putting their money into businesses, and the economy would soon collapse.

- *Borrow more and continue to spend.* Individuals and governments eventually reach their credit limit. Borrowing additional money could only be done at sky-high interest rates because of the risk factor.

In his federal budgets, Finance Minister Paul Martin introduced serious spending cuts. Over five years, $7 billion was to be

Developing Skills: Analyzing and Keeping Up With the News

If you're like most Canadians, you keep up with the news by watching it on television. In most cases, the problem with TV is that there are severe time limitations on every story. The journalist has 60 seconds to get the main idea across to viewers. That's often not enough time to examine the issue in depth. So what you get from television is essentially a front-page headline service.

To be informed, you have to get the whole story behind the TV headlines. You need a complete account of the news from a well-edited, well-written newspaper or news magazine. Regular reading of a newspaper will keep you informed about current international, national, and local events.

There are a few things you should know about the setup of a newspaper. The size of the headline will tell you how important the story is. For example, when the Berlin Wall was torn down in 1989, most newspapers proclaimed this in very large, bold type. The less important the story, the smaller is the headline.

The main story of the day is usually the one with the largest headline. But newspaper editors attract your attention to the story by placing it above the fold in the newspaper. So, when you walk by a newspaper box or stand, you'll see the top story.

A good news story provides you with four basic ingredients: information, background, analysis, and interpretation.

■ Information

First, you need basic facts. A news story should report the facts *and* give you a balanced, unbiased view. It should present both sides of an issue, not just one side.

Reporters write a story in a special way. They use what is called the inverted pyramid style. They start with the climax, or the end, of the story first to get the readers' attention. The most important details come next, followed by the less important details. Knowing how a news story is written will help you sift through the facts.

■ Background

A well-reported story will tell you who, what, where, when, and how. The best news stories will also tell you why, and the *why* is often the key ingredient. The best reporters tell you why they are giving you background information. The "why" helps you understand the story and evaluate it for yourself.

■ Analysis

Leading newspapers also offer analysis of the news. Analysis goes beyond reporting of the facts. Newspapers hire columnists, who are usually experts in a particular field, to explain and offer insight into various current events.

■ Interpretation

In a reliable newspaper, interpretation isn't mixed with the news. It is usually reserved for the editorial page. Interpretation goes beyond the news and beyond analysis. It tells you not just what has or will probably happen, but what *should* happen. Editorials offer opinions or personal viewpoints. They express a bias that is designed to stir your thinking about an issue. Do you agree or disagree? What facts are used to support the opinion? Read about the issue, wrestle with different approaches, and come to your own conclusion about the impact of the issue.

Put Your Skills to Work

1. Choose an important television news story from an evening report. Then examine how the story is reported in a reliable newspaper. Continue to follow the story closely on TV and in print. Write a short paragraph or use an organizer to compare the treatment of the story on television and in a newspaper.
2. As a group project, create your own four-page newspaper. Decide on the current events or issues you think should be covered and then assign tasks to individuals in your group. Include an editor, reporters, photographer, columnist, cartoonist, and designer/layout artist. Work together to plan and complete your newspaper.

slashed from the Department of National Defence and 16 500 military and civilian jobs disappeared as bases closed. Prime Minister Chrétien honoured his election promise and cancelled the $5.8 billion order for 50 helicopters that had been placed by the previous Conservative government. Unemployment insurance spending was reduced and benefits lowered. A number of tax loopholes were plugged for better-off citizens. Martin hoped that economic growth and renewal would create jobs, particularly in small business. New jobs would mean that more people were paying taxes and there would be increased revenue for the government.

At the same time, the Liberals promised to protect Canada's social programs. Health care and a welfare system that ensures a minimum standard of living for all Canadians were seen as part of Canada's birthright. Martin's plan was to count on moderate economic growth to reduce the deficit gradually and not have to resort to radical spending cuts that would hurt a lot of Canadians. How successful the government can be with these goals, however, has yet to be seen.

National Debt, 1940-1990

Year	Net Debt (millions $)	Interest on Debt (millions $)
1940	3 271	139
1950	11 645	440
1960	12 089	736
1970	16 943	1 676
1980	72 159	8 494
1990	357 811	38 820

Source: Finance Canada

ACTIVITIES

Check Your Understanding

1. Add the following terms to your *Factfile*.

    Oka standoff
    James Bay Agreement
    Nunavut
    Immigration Act 1978

    Refugee crisis
    Equal pay for work of equal value
    Canadian International Development Agency (CIDA)
    national debt

2. a) What were the reasons for the Mohawk standoff at Oka?
    b) What support did the Mohawks at Oka receive from other Native groups? Why?
    c) Why did most of the Mohawks consider that they had succeeded in their action?

3. a) Define "aboriginal right."
    b) Outline some successes Native peoples have had in asserting their aboriginal right. Also provide evidence of frustrations and obstacles they have encountered.

4. a) Define the term "refugee."
    b) What provisions did the Immigration Act of 1978 make for refugees?

c) Why did the arrival of the Tamil refugees off the coast of Newfoundland in 1986 create a problem?

d) How did the government attempt to deal with the flood of refugees?

5. State three successes women have had in gaining equality with men. State three problems they still face.

6. Provide reasons for the increase in the national debt since 1970.

Confirm Your Learning

7. Refer to the graph "A Historical Look at Immigration to Canada, 1860-1993" on page 358.
   a) In which two decades were immigration levels highest? Explain why.
   b) What differences were there in the origins of immigrants during these two periods?
   c) In which decade was immigration lowest? Why?
   d) How would you describe the immigration levels in the early 1990s compared with other levels throughout Canada's history?
   e) How has Canada's ethnic make-up changed since the turn of the century?

8. Develop a mind map outlining the problems women still face in the struggle for equality with men. Under or beside each problem, suggest a number of solutions. When your mind map is complete, decide on the three most important problems and the best solution for each one. Support your decisions.

9. Fish and forests are renewable resources. What conservation measures should be used to make certain these resources are constantly renewed?

10. In what ways are people in Hamilton and Edmonton affected by the Atlantic fishing disaster? by the clear-cutting of forests in Clayoquot Sound?

11. Some alternatives available to the government to reduce the national debt are outlined on page 366. Place these alternatives in a decision-making organizer and develop criteria to evaluate them. Make your decision on the best option.

12. How could the federal government cut spending? Obtain a list of federal government departments. Which one or two would you eliminate to make big cuts in spending? Explain your answer.

13. Debate: "Foreign aid should benefit Canada as well as the recipient country."

Challenge Your Mind

14. This chapter focussed on two case studies of environmental crises in Canada. Identify others. Check newspapers, newsletters from environmental groups, TV, and radio reports for evidence of problems. In groups, choose one and prepare a short case study. Your case study should clearly identify the problem, suggest reasons for it, outline what has or has not been done, and suggest possible solutions.

15. Do some further research to find out what was happening in 1991 in Jamaica, Bangladesh, and Ethiopia. Suggest possible reasons why these three countries received the largest amounts of Canadian foreign aid that year.

16. Do some research to find out where Native groups in British Columbia stand on the Clayoquot Sound dispute.

17. Some Native communities are conquering successfully the problems of alcoholism, suicide, and school dropouts among their people. Do some research to identify these communities. Describe their programs, and account for their success.

Unit 8

Citizenship, Government, and Law

TIMELINE

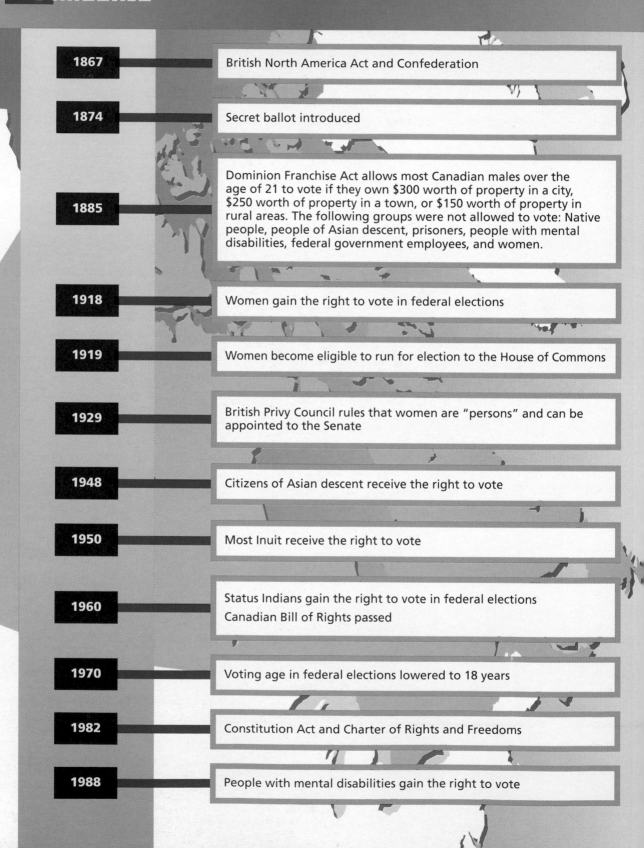

1867 — British North America Act and Confederation

1874 — Secret ballot introduced

1885 — Dominion Franchise Act allows most Canadian males over the age of 21 to vote if they own $300 worth of property in a city, $250 worth of property in a town, or $150 worth of property in rural areas. The following groups were not allowed to vote: Native people, people of Asian descent, prisoners, people with mental disabilities, federal government employees, and women.

1918 — Women gain the right to vote in federal elections

1919 — Women become eligible to run for election to the House of Commons

1929 — British Privy Council rules that women are "persons" and can be appointed to the Senate

1948 — Citizens of Asian descent receive the right to vote

1950 — Most Inuit receive the right to vote

1960 — Status Indians gain the right to vote in federal elections
Canadian Bill of Rights passed

1970 — Voting age in federal elections lowered to 18 years

1982 — Constitution Act and Charter of Rights and Freedoms

1988 — People with mental disabilities gain the right to vote

What would happen if we had no government? Perhaps if you lived alone and produced everything you needed to survive, you would not need governments and laws. You could do whatever you wanted because your actions would not affect anyone else. Since we do not live in isolation, organization and rules are essential. You need rules to know what you can do without harming or limiting the rights of others. These rules also protect you from being harmed or inconvenienced by other people.

Imagine a hockey, basketball, baseball, or any game without rules or officials. It would be chaos. You need rules and a system to which you can appeal any fouls or broken rules. In the same way, society would be in chaos without governments and laws. Governments provide ways for people to live together in an organized and co-operative manner. They try to protect people in a society from danger by making laws that are enforced by police and the courts.

But if people are to live together in an organized and co-operative manner, each person in a society must accept certain responsibilities. So while being a citizen of a society protects our rights, it also brings with it obligations. In Canadian society, some of our responsibilities include respecting the rights of others, obeying the laws, and casting an informed vote in elections. Exercising these responsibilities is as important as knowing our rights.

In this unit, you explore the major features of government, law, and citizenship in Canada. You investigate the type of government we have in Canada, how it works, and what your rights and responsibilities are as a citizen of Canadian society.

At the end of this unit, you will be able to:

- define the system of government in Canada
- recognize the powers of the federal, provincial, and municipal governments
- describe and evaluate the roles of the political parties and other key players in government, including Native organizations
- demonstrate an understanding of the election process
- explain how a law is passed
- determine the differences between criminal and civil law
- effectively analyze a current issue
- practise and appreciate the rights and responsibilities of Canadian citizenship

CHAPTER 21

Government—It's All Around Us

A Scenario

Imagine you are a member of a space crew. You are scheduled to rendezvous with another ship on the lighted surface of the moon. As you are approaching the moon, your ship suddenly loses power. The computer points to a malfunction in the engines, but there is no way to repair it. You are forced to crash land—still about 300 km from the rendezvous point. In the crash, the captain is killed. Much of the equipment aboard is badly damaged. The only supplies left undamaged are: boxes of dehydrated milk; 2 tanks oxygen; solar-powered FM receiver-transmitter; map of moon's surface; matches; life raft; 20 m of nylon rope; first aid kit; portable heating unit; 35 L of water; flares; 2 laser pistols; and food concentrate.

Discuss the problems you face.

1. List at least five decisions you have to make in the first few hours after the disaster.
2. What will you decide about the supplies available?
3. How will you select a new leader?
4. What kind of person would you want as your leader?
5. Make a list of three to five rules that will allow the crew to live in peace and harmony. Who will make these rules?
6. Could you survive without rules? Explain your answer.

What Do Governments Do?

As you reflect on the crash scenario, think about the problems that face any group of people trying to work together. All organizations, groups, and nations must meet the same essential needs. They must establish rules, make decisions, and choose leaders. In other words, they must set up a system of government. The crew members from the crashed space ship need some form of government to make rules and to satisfy their basic needs if they are to survive.

In our more complex society today, we have many different needs and, therefore, many kinds of government activities. If you think about it, you'll recognize many of the services provided by government all around you. In Canada, three different levels of government meet our different needs: local or municipal, provincial, and federal.

Municipal or Local Government

We need our garbage picked up and taken away on a regular basis. We need to know that if our house is on fire, emergency services will arrive to assist us. In winter, the snow on the roads has to be plowed so that we can get to school or work. Our local or municipal government looks after these services. It also takes care of other services that directly affect or benefit our local community, as outlined in the chart on the next page.

Rural municipal governments include village, town, and township councils with reeves or mayors and councillors elected by the people. Urban municipal governments include city and regional councils with elected mayors and councillors. Large Canadian cities, such as Toronto, Montreal, Winnipeg, and Vancouver have metropolitan governments that include the city and the surrounding municipalities. In Toronto, for example, the Metropolitan Toronto (Metro) government includes the cities of Toronto, North York, Scarborough, Etobicoke, York, and the borough of East York.

Emergency firefighters represent one of the essential services provided by local governments.

Powers of the Three Levels of Government

Local	Provincial	Federal
• police protection • fire and ambulance services • public utilities commissions • local schools and libraries • recreation facilities • public transit • water and sewage • local museums • local planning and maintenance of roads, sidewalks, street lights, housing, etc.	• education • direct taxation for provincial purposes • borrowing money for provincial purposes • provincial prisons • hospitals and charities • management of natural resources, e.g., forests, electricity • licences, e.g., for shops, taverns, driving • licensing of companies operating in the province • administration of justice and the courts • supervision of local governments	• defence and foreign policy • regulation of trade and commerce • taxation • borrowing money for government spending • banking, interest rates, and the issuing of money • bankruptcy, patent, and copyright laws • criminal law and penitentiaries • shipping and navigation • seacoast and inland fisheries • international and interprovincial ferries • keeping statistics about Canada • weights and measures • unemployment insurance

Laws passed at the municipal level are called by-laws. They have the same force as federal and provincial laws.

Provincial Government

Some services are needed by all the citizens of the province. We need highways to connect towns and cities, hospitals and schools, power to heat our homes and run our businesses, and rules for protecting our natural resources. These services are provided by the provincial government. In some cases, when services affect both the people in the province and the nation as a whole, powers are shared between the provincial and federal governments. Both levels of government share powers over immigration, the environment, and agriculture, for example.

Federal Government

Matters that affect all people in Canada are the responsibility of the federal government in Ottawa. These include relations with foreign nations, defence, and the country's finances, for example. If the people of Atlantic Canada find foreign boats fishing in Canadian waters, they call the federal government to send in the Navy or the Coast Guard. When you mail a birthday card to a cousin in Alberta, it is the federal postal service that delivers it. When a land claim agreement is settled with the Inuit in the eastern Arctic, it is the federal government that signs the deal. The federal government also has power over all matters not specifically assigned to the provinces.

What Type of Government Does Canada Have?

Canada has what is called a **federal system** of government. Rather than one central government to take care of everything, a federal system divides the powers among several different levels. This system of government and the powers of each level (federal, provincial, and local) are set out in Canada's Constitution. A **constitution** outlines the basic principles on which a government is founded, establishes the organization of government, and may outline the rights of citizens. Canada's Constitution has undergone changes since 1867, including some changes in the powers of the three levels of government and the addition of a Charter of Rights and Freedoms, as you will see later. Government is not set in stone; it changes to meet new needs.

Canada is also a **democracy**. In a democracy, individual people have a voice in government through their elected representatives. All Canadian citizens over the age of 18 may vote for the representative of their choice federally, provincially, and locally. These representatives discuss issues and make decisions on behalf of all Canadians.

All three levels of government work the same way. A candidate is elected to represent everyone in a geographical area. These areas are known by different names: a riding, constituency, ward, or township. Voters cast their ballots for the candidate they think will best represent their wishes. But what happens if the candidate you vote for does not win? Does this mean that you aren't represented in the government? No. The winning candidate must represent all the people, regardless of whether or not they voted for her or him. You are always represented in your government.

However, this does not mean that your representative will vote the way you would like on every issue. Politicians have viewpoints and ideas of their own. But they must always be prepared to listen to the ideas, problems, and complaints of the people they represent.

Our Federal Government— The Three Branches

Our federal government has three major functions, which are carried out by three

different branches—legislative, executive, and judicial. The first job of a government is to make laws and regulations. In Canada, this function is carried out by **Parliament**. Parliament consists of two separate houses. The lower house, which is called the House of Commons, is made up of our elected Members of Parliament. The Senate, also called the upper house, is composed of appointed representatives called senators. The House of Commons and Senate together form the legislative (law-making) branch of government.

Making the laws is just the beginning. Someone must carry out and administer the laws. In Canada, the governor general, prime minister, and members of the Cabinet are responsible for carrying out the laws. To help them, many administrators, executive assistants, ambassadors, scientists, economists, and others are hired. These government employees are known as civil servants. This part of government is the executive branch.

A third branch of government decides what the laws mean and whether a person has broken the law. The courts interpret the laws and settle disputes between individuals and the government. This is the judicial branch.

The Executive Branch

The Monarch and the Governor General

Canadians are sometimes surprised to learn that the prime minister is not the official head of state for Canada. It is the queen or king of Britain, currently Queen Elizabeth II. Her ancestors, such as Elizabeth I (1558-1603), were strong rulers with enormous powers. However, the power of the monarch has gradually decreased. Power has shifted to the people's representatives who sit in the House of Commons.

Today, Canada has a **constitutional monarchy**. This means that the powers of the monarch are limited by the Constitution

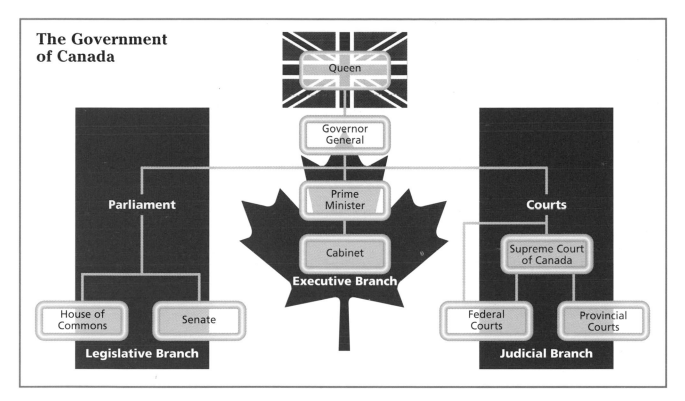

The Government of Canada

Queen

Governor General

Prime Minister

Cabinet

Executive Branch

Parliament

House of Commons

Senate

Legislative Branch

Courts

Supreme Court of Canada

Federal Courts

Provincial Courts

Judicial Branch

and laws of the land. The monarch has little political power in Canada or Britain. The queen's powers are mostly symbolic and ceremonial.

Since Queen Elizabeth II lives in England and visits Canada only occasionally, she is represented in Canada by the **governor general**. The governor general resides at Rideau Hall in Ottawa. Today, the governor general's duties are also mainly ceremonial and symbolic:

- represents the monarch in Canada
- ensures the government carries on its business
- signs all bills before they become law
- opens and closes Parliament
- reads the Speech from the Throne which outlines the government's plans for the next session of Parliament
- performs ceremonial and social duties, such as entertaining foreign leaders and presenting awards and honours
- visits all regions of Canada, meeting with citizens from all walks of life
- offers valuable but impartial advice to the prime minister, but it is the prime minister who actually leads the nation.

Until 1952, the governor general of Canada was always from England. Since then, the governor general has been a Canadian citizen recommended by the prime minister. The usual term of office is five years, but may be extended to seven years. It is a tradition to alternate the honour between French-speaking and English-speaking Canadians.

The Prime Minister in Canada

Real political power in Canada rests with the **prime minister**. The people of Canada do not vote directly for the prime minister. The prime minister is the leader of the political party that wins the most seats in the House of Commons.

If a job advertisement ever appeared in Canada's newspapers requesting applications for the position of prime minister, it might look like the one on the next page.

The Cabinet

The prime minister could not possibly govern the country alone. So, one of the prime minister's first responsibilities is to choose

Position available
Prime Minister of Canada

Duties

- choosing members of the Cabinet
- providing leadership in the Cabinet and the House of Commons
- developing programs, projects, and policies for the country
- keeping his/her political party popular with voters
- representing Canada at international conferences
- providing effective government for all Canadians
- working with the provincial premiers
- appointing Supreme Court judges, senators, ambassadors to foreign countries, and other officials

Qualifications

The successful candidate must be:
- a Canadian citizen over 18 years of age
- the leader of the political party with the most seats in the House of Commons

The successful person should also be:
- fluent in both official languages
- well educated
- experienced in government
- energetic and charismatic
- an excellent public speaker
- well-known and popular in all parts of the country
- knowledgeable about world affairs and world economics
- aware of the problems in all regions of Canada
- supported by a strong political party
- willing to work long hours
- experienced at problem-solving
- able to delegate authority and work well with people
- able to persuade Canadians to work together in harmony
- skillful at working with the media, especially television

Term of employment

- up to five years or as long as the prime minister's party is not defeated in a vote in the House of Commons
- eligible for re-election with the support of the candidate's political party

Remuneration

- annual salary in the range of $134 320 plus tax-free allowance of $21 300
- entertainment allowance
- a large private mansion at 24 Sussex Drive overlooking the Ottawa River
- summer home in the Gatineau Hills outside Ottawa
- private government jet for travelling across Canada and abroad
- chauffeur and limousine
- 24-hour security for prime minister and family
- opportunities for worldwide travel
- opportunities to work with international leaders

*Applications will be reviewed by the voters of Canada
every time there is a federal election.*

ernment policies and make sure those policies are carried out.

Each Cabinet member is put in charge of a government department, or **portfolio**, such as defence, finance, fisheries, immigration, or health. Sometimes, the prime minister wants an MP to be an adviser in the Cabinet, but does not have a portfolio for that person. In this case, the person is made a minister without portfolio and is free to move from one special assignment to another. All members of the Cabinet are called ministers and have the title "The Honourable" before their names for life. The prime minister's title is "The Right Honourable."

Choosing a Cabinet is a juggling act. It's not just a matter of selecting the most competent people for the jobs. The prime minister must ensure that all regions of Canada are represented in the Cabinet. The minister of fisheries usually comes from Atlantic Canada or British Columbia. The agriculture portfolio is often given to someone from western Canada. Women must also be well represented in Cabinet. Popular and experienced members expect to be included too. The multicultural aspect of Canada means the Cabinet should include people of various languages, religions, and ethnic backgrounds.

What does a Cabinet minister do?

- oversees the running of his or her department
- explains policies and answers questions about the department in Parliament and to the media
- discusses general government policy with the prime minister, offers advice, and assists with political decisions

Governor General Romeo LeBlanc inspects his footguards after his swearing in ceremony in Ottawa.

advisors to form a **Cabinet**. Usually about 30 members of Parliament from the governing party are selected for the Cabinet. Prime Minister Chrétien chose 23 MPs for the Cabinet in 1993. Together with the prime minister, Cabinet ministers are the most powerful people in government. They decide on gov-

Prime Minister Jean Chrétien receives a standing ovation from party members and supporters after a speech in the House of Commons.

PROFILES

Ovide Mercredi

Ovide Mercredi is one of the most prominent Native leaders in Canada. In 1991, he was elected National Chief of the Assembly of First Nations and was re-elected in 1993. The Assembly of First Nations is a national political organization representing the status First Nations in Canada. It presents the views of First Nations through their leaders in areas such as aboriginal and treaty rights, the environment, economic development, education, housing, health, social services, land claims, and other issues of common concern. The National Chief is elected every three years by the Chiefs-in-Assembly.

Ovide Mercredi began to take an active political role for his people in the 1960s. He witnessed first-hand the upheaval a massive hydro development project caused in his home community of Grand Rapids, Manitoba. The land where many Crees, including his father, lived and trapped was flooded. After that event, Mercredi said, "I decided that if I ever were to have a position of authority, I would come back and help my people."

Mercredi later became a lawyer, graduating from the University of Manitoba. He entered the university at a time when there were very few Native people on campus. By the time he graduated in 1977, a strong department of Native Studies had been established. This was largely the result of Ovide Mercredi's influence.

As National Chief of the Assembly of First Nations, Mercredi's main message is that Native people, as original inhabitants, have inherent rights to self-government. In his book *In the Rapids*, he wrote:

> *We have never denied ourselves the basic freedom of all human societies, the one that derives from self-determination: the freedom to determine our destiny by the free will of our people. The first peoples of Canada had governments long before the European newcomers....As peoples with distinct cultures, languages, governments, territories, and populations in Canada, we must be recognized as full and equal participants in the Canadian political system.*

1. There are other political organizations representing Inuit and Métis in Canada. Find out more about these organizations, their leaders, and their aims.
2. Ovide Mercredi has said that he has had to work hard to learn what it means to be Cree "because the schools, the churches and the government are all geared to making me erase that part of who I am, and who we are collectively." Why do you think Native people feel control over their own education is especially important?

- presents and guides new laws that affect the operations of the department through Parliament
- interprets and defends government policy to the public
- must also represent the interests of the people in the constituency that elected him or her

Cabinet meetings are always held *in camera*. This Latin term means "behind closed doors." Topics discussed by the Cabinet are secret and may not be discussed outside the meeting. This is to ensure that each Cabinet minister speaks openly and freely. However, once a policy has been decided upon, all ministers are expected to publicly support it. This is called Cabinet solidarity. If a Cabinet minister cannot publicly support government policy, he or she is expected to resign from the Cabinet.

Cabinet ministers may be removed at any time by the prime minister if they are not doing a satisfactory job. Sometimes, the prime minister simply decides to move or "shuffle" cabinet ministers from one job or portfolio to another. A shuffle sometimes gives the Cabinet a new look when a party is not doing well in the public opinion polls. Cabinet ministers receive an allowance in addition to their salary as a member of Parliament.

The Legislative Branch

Members of Parliament

Canada is divided into 295 federal electoral districts called ridings or constituencies. Each riding sends one representative, known as a member of Parliament (MP), to the House of Commons in Ottawa.

MPs have a duty to stay in touch with their ridings and be aware of the problems and issues faced by their constituents. When Parliament is in session, many MPs return to their ridings from Ottawa on weekends, if they live within commuting distance. In their riding, they have a constituency office to help people deal with a wide range of problems. For example, a pensioner whose cheques fail to arrive could seek the assistance of the MP. Constituents who disagree with a government policy can make their views known by visiting or calling the MP at his or her office. MPs often attend social functions in their ridings to keep in touch with what people are thinking and feeling.

In Ottawa, MPs are expected to attend Question Period in the House of Commons and to participate in the debates. On issues of major concern to their constituents, members of Parliament frequently make

Member of Parliament Ethel Blondin Andrew makes a speech in the House of Commons. What other duties do MPs perform?

speeches. MPs also discuss bills, vote on whether or not they will be made law, and work on parliamentary committees studying proposed new laws.

MPs also have responsibilities to their own political party. They must attend weekly **caucus** meetings. The caucus consists of all elected members of the party. In caucus meetings, MPs have a chance to form the policies and discuss the strategies their party will follow in the House of Commons. Each MP of the governing party is bound to support the government's policies. This is known as party loyalty. MPs are also expected to make speeches explaining their party's policies, give interviews to the media, and raise funds for the political party.

The Senate

The other part of the legislative branch of government is the **Senate**. Unlike the House of Commons, its members are appointed. Senators are appointed by the governor general on the recommendation of the prime minister. According to the Constitution, the Senate is to have 104 members representing various regions of Canada (24 from each region defined as the Maritimes,

Number of Senators From Each Province and Territory	
Nova Scotia	10
New Brunswick	10
Prince Edward Island	4
Newfoundland and Labrador	6
Quebec	24
Ontario	24
Manitoba	6
Saskatchewan	6
Alberta	6
British Columbia	6
Northwest Territories	1
Yukon Territory	1

Quebec, Ontario, and the West, plus 6 from Newfoundland and Labrador and one each from the Territories).

Although the Senate can create its own bills, this is rarely done. Usually the senators debate and vote on bills sent to them from the House of Commons. Sir John A. Macdonald's idea was that the Senate would provide "a sober second thought" to any bills being proposed as future laws. The Senate reviews and debates all bills.

The Canadian Senate chambers. What role does the Senate play in Canada's government?

Senators must pass, defeat, or amend a Commons bill before it becomes law. They may make minor changes to clarify the legislation.

Periodically, proposals are put forward to reform the Senate. One criticism is that many senators obtain their seats through patronage. This means that the prime minister usually appoints friends of the political party in power.

What will happen to the Senate? No one person or group has been able to devise reforms acceptable to all involved. Senate reform requires a change to Canada's Constitution, which must be approved by Parliament and at least seven provinces representing 50 percent of Canada's population.

DEVELOPING SKILLS: ANALYZING A CURRENT ISSUE

At various times in Canada's history, the role of the Senate has been questioned. Some people believe the Senate is outdated and undemocratic. One proposal for reform is known as the Triple E Senate. The triple Es stand for elected, equal, and effective. A Triple E Senate would be elected by Canadians, each province would have an equal number of senators, and the senators would exercise real power to pass or reject bills.

Do you think we should abolish the Senate, keep it as it is, or reform it? You can analyze this issue by using an issue analysis organizer.

Steps

■ Step 1
State the issue in the form of a focus question. Example: What should be done with the Senate?

■ Step 2
Identify the possible choices or alternatives and write them across the top of the organizer. In this case they are clear: keep the Senate as it is, abolish it, or reform it.

■ Step 3
Develop a list of criteria by which you can evaluate the alternatives. This is an important step. Ask yourself on what bases or points the Senate should be judged—functions, cost, experience of members? You may want to start by brainstorming possible criteria and then choosing the most important. Example criteria have been set out for you in the organizer on the next page, but you may change them. The criteria are listed down the left column of the organizer.

■ Step 4
Locate as much information as possible on the Senate so that you can evaluate the alternatives effectively. Read what people with differing opinions have written or, if possible, invite local politicians or other speakers into your class to present their views on the issue. Based on the information you collect, fill in the organizer using point form. Consider the positive and negative sides of each alternative using the criteria.

■ Step 5
Synthesize and draw conclusions. Individually or in groups, review all the points under the various alternatives. Which column on the organizer has the strongest points? Make a decision.

■ Step 6
Communicate your conclusion either orally or in writing. Explain why you feel the way you do to an interested group of students, teachers, or parents.

Practise It!
Put this new skill to work by completing the organizer that has been started for you on the next page. Apply the skill to other issues as well, such as the federal gun control legislation or other important government policies. Should or should they not be enacted?

Issue: What should be done with the Senate?

Criteria	Alternatives		
	Keep the Senate as it is	**Reform the Senate**	**Abolish the Senate**
Historical function/purpose	• Senate serves as a useful check on the House of Commons • was meant to take a "sober second look" at all legislation		
Present-day functions	• Senate committees write reports about the issues they investigate and make recommendations for action • quality of work by Senate committees often leads to the creation of new laws		
Cost	• as it now stands, cost of the Senate is a worthwhile government expense		
Age of members	• most senators are experienced politicians, generally in their fifties when appointed • they have valuable contributions to make; it is age discrimination to suggest that people stop being useful members of society when they get older		
Selection process	• one of original purposes of the Senate was to protect the interests of the provinces; smaller provinces have better representation in the Senate than in the House of Commons		
Experience of members	• senators bring many years of knowledge and expertise to their jobs because of their political, business, legal, and administrative experience		

A Working Day in the House of Commons

What happens on a typical day in the House of Commons? The day usually begins at 2:00 p.m. when the Speaker of the House, dressed in the robes of office, enters and takes his or her place on the raised platform at the end of the chamber. The Speaker is a member of Parliament who acts as a sort of referee. It is his or her responsibility to make sure the rules and regulations of parliamentary debate are followed. As the debates can sometimes be heated, the Speaker must keep order. He or she also announces the results of votes in the House. It is considered an honour to be chosen Speaker.

To formally open the day's business, the Sergeant-at-Arms, who is in charge of security, lays the ceremonial mace on a large table in front of the Speaker. The mace is a gold-plated club symbolizing the Speaker's authority over the House.

Members of the government sit to the Speaker's right and opposition MPs to the left. The prime minister and Cabinet members occupy the first few rows of desks on the government side, front and centre. Other seats on the government side are filled by **backbenchers**—government MPs who are not Cabinet members.

Opposition members sit directly across from the governing party. The **official opposition** is the second-largest party in the House of Commons. The leader of the opposition and the shadow cabinet sit opposite the prime minister and the Cabinet. The shadow cabinet is composed of opposition MPs who follow a specific minister's portfolio. They make sure the minister is doing the job satisfactorily. The leaders

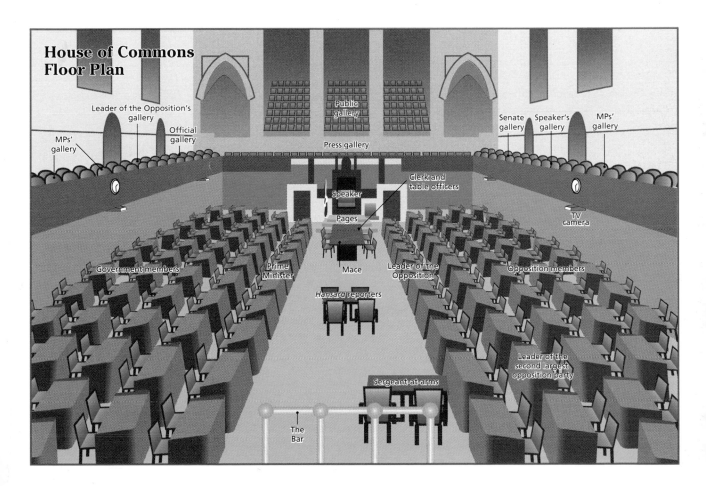

House of Commons Floor Plan

Leader of the Opposition's gallery

MPs' gallery

Official gallery

Public gallery

Press gallery

Senate gallery

Speaker's gallery

MPs' gallery

Clerk and table officers

Speaker

Pages

TV camera

Government members

Prime Minister

Mace

Leader of the Opposition

Opposition members

Hansard reporters

Leader of the second largest opposition party

Sergeant-at-arms

The Bar

of the smaller opposition parties sit in the front row, but farther away from the Speaker. The role of the opposition parties is to constructively criticize government policies, help improve government legislation through questioning and debate, and make sure the government is dealing responsibly with the issues that concern Canadians.

Many other people also ensure that the proceedings in the House run smoothly. Pages, who sit around the Speaker's chair, are young people responsible for delivering messages and running errands for MPs. At a long table in the middle of the House are clerks who keep official records of decisions made by the House. Speeches are also recorded and printed in a daily publication called *Hansard*. All speeches are simultaneously translated into French and English. The proceedings of the House of Commons are also televised. Members of the press and the public can observe the proceedings by sitting in galleries above the floor of the House.

After the Speaker officially declares the day's proceedings open, Question Period begins. Members, mostly from opposition parties, grill the government and its ministers on government policies. Question Period lasts about 45 minutes. The balance of the day is taken up with debate and discussion of bills.

Elections and Political Parties

Governments in Canada are elected in much the same way as your students' council or your class executive. Candidates put forward their names for election. During the campaign, meetings are held, speeches are made, and posters are put up. In a federal election, newspapers and television screens are also filled with political announcements. All the candidates try to convince the voters they are the best people to represent them. Finally, on election day, the people vote for the candidate of their choice. By voting, you have an opportunity to say how you want things run and to choose your leaders.

Getting Ready
In Canada, the law states that a federal election must be held at least every five years. However, the prime minister can decide to call an election earlier. Why would

The House of Commons. Can you identify where the prime minister and the leader of the opposition are seated?

How a Law is Passed

One of the most important functions of the legislative branch of government is to pass laws. Do you have a say in the laws that are made in Canada? Yes. Examine the process outlined below.

A Problem is Identified

Imagine that a number of recent news reports have revealed an increase in incidents of drunk driving. Deaths on the highways caused by drunk drivers are increasing. Concerned people contact their members of Parliament to ask what the government is doing to stop drunk drivers.

Citizens Demand Action

Over the next weeks and months, citizens' groups continue to pressure the government for action. During Question Period in the House of Commons, opposition members demand that the government take action. An important Canadian newspaper conducts a public opinion poll that shows 70 percent of Canadians favour stricter laws against drunk driving.

The House of Commons

The bill must be given three readings in the House of Commons.

First reading: The bill is introduced in the House. There is no discussion or debate.

Second reading: The advantages and disadvantages of the bill are debated and a vote is taken. After the second reading, the bill goes to the legal committee to be studied in detail. The committees are made up of small groups from all parties. Changes or improvements are made in committee.

Third reading: The members of the House accept or reject the bill in its final form. If the bill is accepted, it is sent on to the Senate.

Any member can introduce a bill. These are called private members' bills, rather than government bills. Private members' bills can only be considered during certain hours set aside for this purpose, and speeches are limited. Most private members' bills are introduced in the Senate. Very few ever become law.

The Prime Minister and Cabinet Take Action

The prime minister and the Cabinet direct civil servants to study the problem and suggest solutions. The solutions are presented in the form of a **bill**. The bill is not a new law at this point. It must first be presented and passed in the House of Commons. Because it is sponsored by the governing party, it is called a government bill and must be guided through the House of Commons by the minister in charge of that department.

The Senate

The bill must go through exactly the same steps in the Senate that it did in the House.

First reading: The bill is introduced and there is no debate.

Second reading: The bill is discussed, debated, and a vote is taken. A Senate committee examines the bill phrase-by-phrase.

Third reading: The Senate votes to accept or reject the bill. If the Senate has made any changes in the bill, it must be sent back to the House of Commons for approval. If the Senate approves the bill, it goes directly to the governor general to be signed into law.

Royal Assent

The governor general, as the representative of the monarch, signs the bill. The drunk driving bill is now a law and an act of Parliament. Its provisions are binding on all Canadians.

an election be called early? Governments study public opinion polls closely. They choose a time when they think they are popular with the voters and have a good chance of being re-elected. Therefore an election could be called after only four years, or sooner, in the hopes of winning a new five-year term.

For the purpose of a federal election, the country is divided into 295 ridings. Ridings are often quite different in size and population. For example, the riding of Nunatsiaq in the Arctic covers over 2 million km². The smallest riding in the country is called Rosemont. It covers only 8 km² in Montreal. Attempts are made to keep the population of the ridings approximately the same size, about 100 000. However, in some cases, this is not possible. Nunatsiaq contains only 21 000 people.

As soon as the election is called, the Chief Electoral Officer swings into action. Elections Canada organizes all the details that make an election run smoothly. In every riding a Returning Officer is appointed. One of his or her main functions is to prepare a list of eligible voters. An eligible voter is a Canadian citizen over 18

years of age. Enumerators are hired to go door-to-door to make up the voters' list. If you are not enumerated, you have until the day before the election to get your name on the voters' list.

Soon after the election is called, all political parties are busy nominating candidates. Any Canadian citizen over the age of 18 can try to become the candidate for a political party. A candidate running for office who is not chosen by a political party is called an independent candidate.

The Campaign

Every federal election is approximately 50 days long. During this time, the candidates make speeches to express their views on the issues. They, or their volunteer supporters, visit with people in the riding, give out pamphlets, erect lawn signs, and put up posters. Running an effective campaign is expensive. Candidates depend on contributions from party members within the riding and from national party headquarters. Since 1974, campaign spending has been limited by law and candidates must identify any person or organization who contributes more than $100.

Reform party leader Preston Manning greets supporters in the 1993 federal election campaign.

On a national level, the political parties spend millions of dollars for television, radio, and newspaper advertisements. Often, the leaders of the parties hold nationally televised debates. In this electronic age, political parties, their leaders, and their candidates are judged on their performances during the debates and on nightly news clips covering the campaign. Some people have complained that voters are not seeing the "real" leader. They feel the media often controls how the candidates are presented to the public. Voters may judge the leader of their country based on personality and not on substance.

Election Day

On election day, citizens go to polling stations to vote. Polling stations are often in a school gym or community centre. The polls are open from 9:00 a.m. to 8:00 p.m. so that everyone has a chance to vote. If you suspect you won't be able to vote on election day, you can vote in advance.

Polling stations may be divided into various individual polls. The voter is given a ballot. The ballot lists the names of the candidates in alphabetical order and the party they represent. The voter goes to a polling booth, a screened area, and marks the ballot in private. If the voter does not mark the ballot correctly with an X, or writes any words on the ballot, it is considered a spoiled ballot and will not be counted. The completed ballot is then refolded and the deputy returning officer (poll official) drops it into the ballot box.

A deputy returning officer is in charge of the polling station. Poll clerks check the eligibility of the voter and record who has voted. Scrutineers are assigned by the candidates to observe the procedures and ensure that the vote count is accurate and honest.

On election day, campaign workers do their best to "get out the vote." They try to ensure that every possible supporter has the opportunity to vote. Voters are phoned and reminded to vote. Rides are arranged for people who would have difficulty getting to their polling station.

The Result

The ballots are not counted until after the polls are closed. Many Canadians watch the results come in on television. They want to know who has won in their own riding, and also which political party has won the most seats in the House of Commons.

When one party wins more seats than all the other parties combined, it is a **majority government**. In the 1993 federal election, Jean Chrétien and the federal Liberals won an electoral majority with 177 seats. They could pass bills because they outnumbered the opposition. A majority government has a strong advantage in the House of Commons.

1993 Federal Election Results

Government	Opposition
177 Liberal MPs	54 Bloc Québécois MPs
	52 Reform party MPs
	9 New Democratic Party MPs
	2 Progressive Conservative MPs
	1 Independent MP
Total 177 MPs	Total 118 MPs

Suppose, however, that no political party wins a majority in the House of Commons. That was the situation in 1979. Examine the election results below.

1979 Federal Election Results

Government	Opposition
136 Progressive Conservative MPs	114 Liberal MPs
	26 New Democratic Party MPs
	6 Social Credit MPs
Total 136 MPs	Total 146 MPs

The Progressive Conservative party still formed the government in 1979 since it had elected more members to the Commons than any other party. However, when the seats of all the opposition parties were combined, the opposition outnumbered the Conservatives. This is a **minority government**. A minority government is one that has elected fewer than half of the seats in the Commons.

A Motion of Non-Confidence

In some cases, the opposition parties in the House may try to defeat the government by introducing a **motion of non-confidence**. The motion says that the opposition believes the government has lost the support of the majority of members in the House of Commons. It has therefore lost the right to govern. If the motion passes, the prime minister and the Cabinet must resign, or an election must be held.

If the government has a large majority of seats in the House of Commons, it can usually out-vote a non-confidence motion. A minority government, however, is in a much more difficult position. If the opposition parties unite, a minority government can sometimes be defeated and forced to resign. This is exactly what happened to Prime Minister Joe Clark on 13 December 1979. John Crosbie, Minister of Finance, presented the government's budget to the House of Commons. The budget was unpopular and the opposition held a vote of non-confidence. Clark and the Conservatives were defeated and the government resigned.

Political Parties in Canada

For decades, there were three main federal political parties in Canada: the Liberals, Progressive Conservatives, and New Democratic Party. However, in the election of 1993, the Progressive Conservatives and the

Ballot marked incorrectly

Ballot marked correctly

New Democratic Party were nearly wiped out in the House of Commons. Two new parties had also emerged and won a significant number of seats: the Bloc Québécois and the Reform party.

Every political party develops a **platform**. A platform is a package of ideas or policies based on the party's beliefs. The platform also tells us what the party would do if it formed the government. The party hopes voters will agree with the platform and vote for its candidates. Many voters find that platforms make it easier to decide which party they want to support.

The main goal of politics is to gain power. To win an election, a party must please as many voters as possible. Sometimes, people think one party sounds just like the next one. The differences in the parties are often not in what they stand for, but in how they want to reach their goals. For example, all three main parties stand for full employment. But each has different ideas about how to achieve that goal.

In fact, there is a wide range of viewpoints on political matters. One way to illustrate this is to put differing political viewpoints on an imaginary line called the political spectrum. People or parties with moderate political opinions are situated in the centre. On either side of the centre are positions we call left- and right-wing.

Traditionally, the Liberal and Progressive Conservative parties have vied for the political centre. This is where most of the votes are found in any election. The

The Political Spectrum

	Left	Centre	Right
Change	Unjust conditions must be changed as quickly as possible.	There may be things that are unjust in our society, but change does not happen overnight. We must attack the problems, but realize it may take years to bring about change.	Tend to support the establishment and *status quo* (things as they are). Don't want sweeping changes.
Role of Government in Social Programs	The government has a responsibility to care for all people, especially the less fortunate (e.g., child care programs, medicare, etc.)	Believe in searching for ways to provide for the greatest number of people based on what the country can afford.	The government should not interfere in the lives of individuals. Expensive social programs should be cut.
Government Ownership	The government should own key industries and resources. (e.g., transportation systems, natural resources)	Accepts moderate government management and intervention in the economy.	Business and industry should be kept in private hands and the government should be limited.
Individual Rights	The rights of the individual have high priority.	Believe in law and order, but the rights of the individual come first.	Law and order have high priority.

NDP are often found on the political left. The Reform party would be placed to the right. But parties and views cannot always be so neatly placed. Some party policies may shift on the spectrum depending on the times and the situation.

Any citizen can join a political party. Joining a party is a good place to start if you want to get involved in politics. All parties welcome new members and anyone interested in joining pays a small annual fee and receives a membership card. Members are placed on the party mailing list and receive information on the party platform and coming events. They have the right to vote at a nomination meeting to choose the candidate in their riding for election. They may also be chosen to attend a party convention where the party platform is decided and where the national leader is chosen.

Bloc Québécois leader Lucien Bouchard talks with students during the 1993 federal election campaign. What was his party's platform?

SOCIETY AND SOCIAL CHANGE

Federal and Provincial Governments—A Comparison

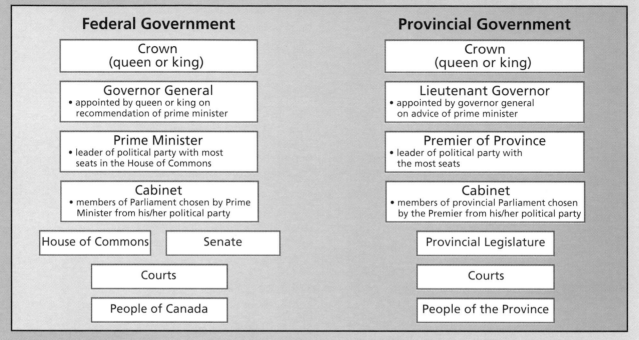

The federal and provincial governments in Canada are largely independent. The provincial government has its own executive, legislative, and judicial branches to govern the province. Provincial governments make their own laws, which do not have to be approved by the federal government. Provincial governments and all people in the provinces, however, must follow federal laws.

The provincial government is located in the provincial capital. The lieutenant governor is the monarch's representative and signs all provincial bills into law. Like the governor general, his or her duties are largely ceremonial: giving the Speech from the Throne at the opening of the provincial Parliament, greeting important visitors, and opening new schools and hospitals.

Bills are debated and passed in the provincial legislatures in the same way as in the House of Commons. However, bills do not need to be sent to the Senate. The provinces do not have a Senate. The judicial branch is made up of the provincial courts.

Separate elections are held for provincial governments. Some provincial parties are the same as federal parties. For example, many provinces have Liberal and Progressive Conservative candidates, but the provincial parties do not necessarily follow the same platform or policies of the federal parties. Many provinces also have parties with no federal equivalent.

1. a) Who is the premier of your province? Which provincial party is in power? If
   you do not live in a province, what is the form of your territorial government?
   b) Which party is the official opposition?
   c) Who is your provincial representative in the legislature?
2. What are the most important political issues in your province at the moment?
   Explain why you think these issues are important.

ACTIVITIES

Check Your Understanding

1. Create a glossary of terms for this chapter. Include definitions of the following.

    federal system of government   caucus
    constitution   Senate
    democracy   backbenchers
    Parliament   official opposition
    constitutional monarchy   bill
    governor general   majority government
    prime minister   minority government
    Cabinet   motion of non-confidence
    Cabinet portfolio   party platform

2. Identify the level of government—federal, provincial, or local (municipal)—which looks after the following activities.

    a) automobile licences
    b) metric system
    c) street cleaning
    d) motorcycle helmet legislation
    e) CBC
    f) regulating the drinking age
    g) restaurant and food inspection
    h) RCMP
    i) oil imports from Saudi Arabia
    j) local parks and recreation facilities
    k) customs duties
    l) immigration policy
    m) education policy
    n) sending an ambassador to France

3. Develop a mind map illustrating the three branches of government in Canada and their responsibilities.

4. Examine the imaginary job advertisement for the prime minister on page 380. Are there any qualifications and characteristics that should be deleted? Why? Are there any that should be added? Why? Rank the five most important characteristics and qualifications. Justify your ranking.

Confirm Your Learning

5. Read the problems that the following citizens face. With the help of the blue pages in your telephone directory, decide which level of government and department each one should call for help.

    a) Bob Russell has lost his poodle, Cuddles.
    b) Sarah and Bill Harrison are complaining about the smell and taste of their drinking water.
    c) Andrew Kim wants to sponsor his nephew coming to Canada from Hong Kong.
    d) Mary Sue Gallivan wants to investigate a career in the armed forces.
    e) Anatoly Jarozsek needs a patent for an insulated lunch bag that he has invented.
    f) Maria Sanchez wants to get her pilot's licence.
    g) N-P Window Washers Inc. wants to take a client to small claims court for not paying a bill.
    h) Joseph Singh wants to get a fishing licence so he can take part in the Great Salmon Derby.
    i) Dr. LaRoque wants to divide a house she owns into apartments.
    j) Elizabeth Cardor wants the potholes repaired on her street.

6. Governments not only provide services, they also put certain requirements on

people. Brainstorm a list of things that governments have the power to make us do (e.g., pay income tax). When you have completed the list, have a class discussion on whether the government has too much control over our lives.

7. Develop a comparison organizer to show the differences and similarities in Canada's federal and provincial governments.

8. Watch the televised Question Period from the House of Commons.
   a) What issue or issues were discussed?
   b) Were the questions asked by the opposition well thought out?
   c) How effectively did the government respond to the questions?
   d) Describe the behaviour of the members and the atmosphere in the House during Question Period.

9. Role play one of the following situations in your class. Decide on and assign appropriate roles. Remember to do some background research to prepare for your roles. Also decide on the issues that will be discussed beforehand.
   a) Question Period in the House of Commons.
   b) a debate between the federal or provincial party leaders
   c) a debate in Parliament over a particular bill
   Videotape parts of your role play and review the tapes afterwards.
   Evaluate your success.

Challenge Your Mind

10. Sir John A. Macdonald began the tradition of choosing Cabinet members to represent all regions of Canada. Find out the names of the federal Cabinet ministers today and their portfolios. From which province does each minister come? Are all provinces represented in the Cabinet today? How many women and visible minorities are represented in the Cabinet?

11. Choose a current issue you feel strongly about, such as funding for schools or damage to the environment. Clip newspaper articles related to the issue over a number of weeks. From the articles, determine the position of the government and opposition parties on the issue. Summarize the positions in a comparison organizer. Decide which party you would support on this issue.

12. Try to build a platform for a school election that will appeal to a large number of students. Include "planks" in your platform that will appeal to males and females, junior and senior students, athletes and non-athletes, etc. Present your platform to an interested group in the school.

13. Hold an election. As a class, select a problem as the key election issue. Divide the class into groups representing the major political parties in Canada. Each party should choose a candidate to run for office. Decide what your party's position will be on this issue. Make buttons, posters, and pamphlets to promote your candidate and the party. Each candidate should make a short speech outlining her/his position on the issue. Prepare ballots, a voters' list, and a ballot box. Set up a polling station in your classroom. Hold your election using the same procedures that would be followed in a federal election.

14. How is your local government organized? Ask a member of your local council to speak to your class about how your municipal government works.

CHAPTER 22

Law and Citizenship

UNDERSTANDING THE LAW

You and a friend are walking home from watching an evening basketball game at your school. It is dusk. As you pass your neighbourhood public school, you hear glass breaking. You see two figures breaking the windows of the school and spraying paint on walls and doors. An alarm goes off and the figures run off right by you. You think you recognize them—but you are frozen. What do you do? What should you do? You are eyewitnesses to a crime. The next day, the police come by your homes and ask to question you about the incident.

Do you know your rights and responsibilities? What do you know about Canadian law? Do you know how the law is enforced by the government and the police? Do you know that there are two types of law in Canada—criminal and civil?

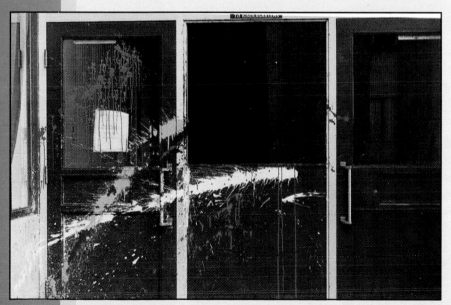

Breaking and entering and vandalism are criminal offences in Canada.

Criminal Law

Criminal law deals with what are considered offences against society, such as murder and theft. A person charged with a criminal offence can be taken to court. A person found guilty may be fined, imprisoned, or otherwise punished. The **Criminal Code of Canada** defines criminal offences and sets out penalties.

For an action to be considered a crime in Canada, it must meet the following three conditions:

1. It must be forbidden by the *Criminal Code of Canada*.
2. The accused must have intended to commit the offence, or have been aware that the action could result in breaking a law.
3. The accused must be of sound mind (able to understand the difference between right and wrong).

In Canada, a person is considered innocent until proven guilty. Action is taken against an accused criminal by the government or Crown. Before the accused can be found guilty, the Crown attorney must prove in court that all three conditions existed. Consider the following case study.

Case Study: A European Adventure

Sheena, a young Canadian woman, is returning from a month-long tour of Europe. On her travels, she met another young Canadian, Tracey, and they are flying home together. As they are getting off the plane in Toronto, Tracey asks Sheena to help her with her luggage. Since Sheena has only her backpack and Tracey has a lot of luggage, Sheena agrees.

Tracey goes through Canada Customs first. When Sheena goes through Customs, the officer finds something suspicious at the bottom of Tracey's bag. The bag is turned over to the RCMP for a closer look. Their examination shows that the bag has a false bottom and conceals packages of drugs. Sheena looks frantically for Tracey but can't see her anywhere.

Does Sheena's action constitute a crime?

Classification of Criminal Offences

The *Criminal Code* divides crimes into two classes: summary and indictable offences. **Summary offences** are less serious than indictable offences and carry lower maximum penalties. Summary offences are tried before a magistrate. Some examples are:

- traffic violations such as speeding tickets
- causing a disturbance
- breaking municipal noise by-laws
- cruelty to animals
- selling or possessing slugs for coin or token-operated machines

Indictable offences fall into three categories, and the *Criminal Code* has procedures for dealing with each one. The least serious indictable offences, such as theft under $1000, are tried before magistrates or provincial court judges. For serious indictable offences, such as armed robbery, the accused has the choice of being tried before a magistrate, a judge, or a judge and jury. The most serious indictable offences, such as murder, must be tried before a judge and jury in a provincial superior court. This occurs after a preliminary hearing before a magistrate.

The Police

Police usually make arrests only for serious crimes and they must have "reasonable grounds" before laying charges. For traffic violations or other less serious offences, a police officer may issue an "appearance notice." This notice states the offence and sets a date for a court appearance. No arrest is made.

Police officers must always inform people of the nature of an offence. When making an arrest, they may only use as much force as is "reasonable and necessary." Suspects under arrest are informed of their

Police make an arrest. What are the rights of the accused?

rights and may be questioned, searched, fingerprinted, and photographed. They have the right to remain silent and to get legal advice. A court date must be set as soon as possible and suspects are either released or held in jail until their trial date. Bail hearings are held to determine whether a prisoner can be released on bail. Bail is a sum of money paid for the temporary release of a prisoner until his or her trial. The amount of the bail depends on the seriousness of the crime and any past record.

Police may question any witnesses to a crime, but witnesses must give the information freely and knowingly. They cannot be forced to answer questions, but it is considered a citizen's responsibility to provide information about crimes.

What Happens During a Criminal Trial?

The most interesting and exciting way to discover what happens during a trial is to visit a courtroom as an observer. If it is impossible to visit a courtroom, you can ex-

amine a simulated trial, such as Gordon Mowbray's trial below.

Gordon Mowbray's Trial

You are attending the trial of the R. v. Mowbray. "R" is the Latin short form for Regina, which means queen. The Latin for king is Rex; therefore, the name of the trial would be the same if a king was on the throne. Mowbray is the defendant, the person against whom legal action is being taken.

This system of justice is sometimes called an **adversary system**. The Crown prosecutor presents evidence to find the accused guilty. The adversaries are the accused and the accused person's lawyer. They present evidence to prove that the accused is innocent.

Gordon Mowbray has been charged with arson. It is alleged that he willfully set fire to a neighbour's farmhouse. The house burned to the ground and the owner, Harriet Wright, and her daughter were seriously burned. Before Mowbray's trial begins, a number of preliminary legal procedures must be followed.

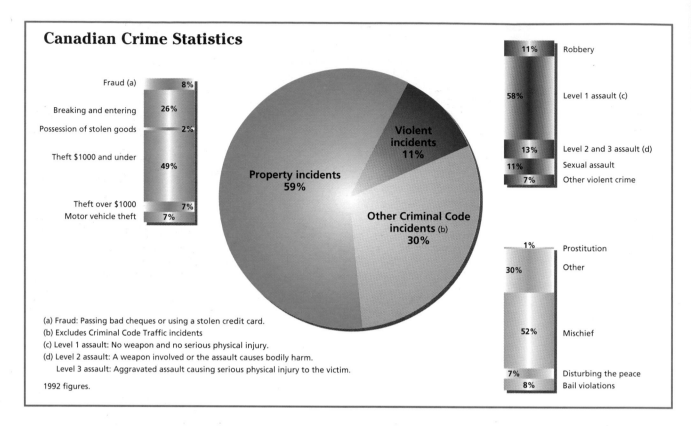

Canadian Crime Statistics

Fraud (a) — 8%
Breaking and entering — 26%
Possession of stolen goods — 2%
Theft $1000 and under — 49%
Theft over $1000 — 7%
Motor vehicle theft — 7%

Property incidents 59%

Violent incidents 11%

Other Criminal Code incidents (b) 30%

Robbery — 11%
Level 1 assault (c) — 58%
Level 2 and 3 assault (d) — 13%
Sexual assault — 11%
Other violent crime — 7%

Prostitution — 1%
Other — 30%
Mischief — 52%
Disturbing the peace — 7%
Bail violations — 8%

(a) Fraud: Passing bad cheques or using a stolen credit card.
(b) Excludes Criminal Code Traffic incidents
(c) Level 1 assault: No weapon and no serious physical injury.
(d) Level 2 assault: A weapon involved or the assault causes bodily harm.
   Level 3 assault: Aggravated assault causing serious physical injury to the victim.

1992 figures.

First, Mowbray was brought before a magistrate. At the preliminary hearing, the magistrate decided there was sufficient evidence to bring Mowbray to trial. Mowbray chose to be tried by a judge and jury. Many months elapsed before the case actually came to trial.

Before the trial date, Mowbray's lawyer, Elizabeth Sullivan, and the Crown attorney, Zahid Singh, prepared their cases. A **jury** was chosen. A jury is a group of 12 local people, chosen at random, to hear evidence during a trial. The selection of a jury is a time-consuming and difficult process. Both the defendant's lawyer and the Crown attorney question the potential jurors. Each has the right to accept or reject individuals for the jury. They might reject someone because of suspected prejudice or bias toward the accused. Only a few professions are exempt from jury duty. They include doctors, lawyers, clergy, members of the Armed Forces, and anyone working in the court system.

Once the jury has been selected, the trial is ready to begin. The charges are read and the accused enters a **plea**. This means that the defendant formally states whether she or he is guilty or not guilty. Gordon Mowbray pleaded "not guilty" to the charges. The judge instructs the jurors to listen to all the evidence and decide whether the accused person is guilty or innocent. The judge also tells the jurors not to discuss the case with anyone.

Trials are quite formal in Canada. Mowbray's lawyer has told him to dress neatly. Ms. Sullivan has also warned Mowbray that verbal outbursts, eating food, chewing gum, drinking coffee, and smoking in the courtroom might lead the judge to cite him for contempt of court. **Contempt of court** means disobedience or disrespect for court laws.

First, the Crown attorney presents his summary of the case. The evidence against Mowbray is presented and witnesses are called. Each witness is sworn to tell the

Cameras are not permitted in Canadian court-rooms, but reporters can make sketches of proceedings. In this sketch from the case of R. v. Bernardo, the accused is stating his plea—"Not guilty."

truth. A witness who lies on the stand will be charged with perjury. It is a serious offence, and the person could be sent to jail.

Sometimes, the evidence includes an eyewitness account. In this case, the eyewitness is the farmer. She testifies that she was at the barn when she saw Mowbray pour gasoline on the front porch and set fire to it. She was badly burned while saving her daughter.

Two witnesses identify Mowbray as the man they saw running from the burning house at the approximate time of the fire. However, they didn't see him light the fire. This is **circumstantial evidence**. It links facts or events to draw certain conclusions. Another neighbour testifies that he had seen many old rags and gasoline cans in Mowbray's garage. This is also circumstantial evidence.

Another witness says that she heard, from a neighbour, that Mowbray had want-ed Harriet Wright to sell her land to a developer. The developer would only buy if both farmers sold their land. Apparently, Mowbray had threatened Harriet Wright if she did not agree to sell her land. This is **hearsay evidence**. It is based on testimony of another person, not first-hand knowledge. The judge would not accept this evidence as the witness did not actually hear Mowbray make these threats.

After each witness has testified, the defence lawyer, Ms. Sullivan, may cross-examine the witnesses. **Cross-examination** tests the reliability of the witnesses and the truth of their evidence. After all its witnesses have been heard, the Crown rests its case.

Now, it's Ms. Sullivan's turn to call witnesses on Mowbray's behalf. The Crown is entitled to cross-examine these witnesses. Mowbray has been sitting beside Ms. Sullivan throughout the trial. He has the right

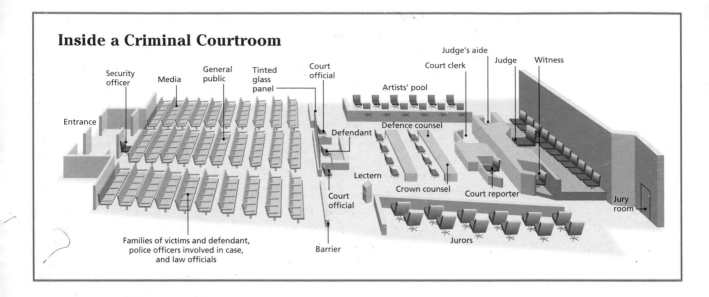

Inside a Criminal Courtroom

Entrance · Security officer · Media · General public · Tinted glass panel · Court official · Artists' pool · Court clerk · Judge's aide · Judge · Witness · Defendant · Defence counsel · Lectern · Crown counsel · Court reporter · Jury room · Court official · Barrier · Jurors · Families of victims and defendant, police officers involved in case, and law officials

to be present at his trial, but is not required to give evidence. However, Ms. Sullivan puts him on the witness stand. Mowbray's defence is that he was intoxicated and had no idea what he was doing. He desperately needed the money and Harriet Wright would not sell. He had hoped to pressure her into selling.

After all the witnesses have been called, the lawyers make their closing statements. They try to convince the jury to agree with their view of the facts. The judge instructs the jury in the legal meaning of the charge against the accused. The judge tells the jurors they must reach a **verdict**—a decision on whether Mowbray is guilty or innocent of the charge.

The jury retires to a private room. The foreperson leads the discussion. The jurors discuss the evidence they've heard and try to reach a unanimous decision. All 12 members of the jury must agree on the guilt or the innocence of the accused. This can take a long time and require several votes. Sometimes, the jury cannot agree upon a verdict. Then they are a **hung jury**. When this happens, the jury is dismissed and a new trial is ordered.

The jurors at Mowbray's trial have reached a verdict. They file back into the courtroom. If they've found Mowbray not guilty, he is free to leave. However, if he is found guilty, the judge will decide on an appropriate punishment. The foreperson informs the court that the jury has found Mowbray guilty.

The judge must impose a sentence upon Mowbray, within the limits of the law as set out in the *Criminal Code*. The punishment should accomplish three objectives. First, it should act as a deterrent. It must persuade Mowbray not to commit any further crimes for fear of the punishment. Second, the punishment should try to rehabilitate Mowbray. Today, prisoners are offered psychiatric, medical, and religious help while in prison. They can learn trades in the hope that they will have a better chance of finding employment when they are released. Sometimes, criminals do community service work. Third, if the guilty person is considered dangerous, the punishment may have to segregate him or her from the rest of society in prison.

The accused or the Crown may appeal the decision within 30 days of the trial's conclusion. An appeal court hears requests to change or overturn decisions made by other courts. What do you think Mowbray's punishment should be?

A Criminal Record

The consequences of a criminal record are quite serious. If you are sent to prison, many of your liberties are taken away. You will probably have difficulty finding a job upon release from prison. Some employers may be reluctant to hire people who have broken the law in the past. Some jobs, such as a bank teller or security guard, require employees to be bonded. A bond is a guarantee of trustworthiness. A person with a criminal record cannot be bonded. Although you can still obtain a Canadian passport if you have a criminal record, it is difficult to enter some foreign countries.

The Young Offenders Act

In recent years, a great deal of media attention has been focussed on youth crime, particularly violent youth crime. One reported incident occurred in Calgary in the spring of 1992. Thirteen-year-old Ryan Garrioch was stabbed in the school yard. He died a few hours later in hospital. His friends and teachers described Ryan as a good student, but a loner who was sometimes ridiculed by his schoolmates. A 15-year-old student was charged with first degree murder.

Has the media been exaggerating the incidence of youth crime? Most teenagers are not involved with crime at all. Other crimes committed by young people are not of such a violent nature as murder.

These crimes may include stealing from school lockers or shoplifting, the destruction of property (vandalism), verbal threats or abusive language, or running away from home or school. But statistics show that the number of crimes committed by young people is increasing in Canada. In 1992, youths accounted for 13.7 percent of all persons charged with violent crime. This was up from 10.5 percent in 1986.

How should young people who break the law be treated? Should they be given a second chance? At what age should a youth be considered an adult and be held fully responsible for her or his actions?

In 1984, the federal government introduced the **Young Offenders Act**. This act defines "young offenders" as all persons between the ages of 12 and 17 who break the law. It determines the way young people are dealt with by the police and law courts. The Young Offenders Act prohibits charges being laid against young people under the age of 12. A 10-year-old suspected of murder or other crimes, for example, cannot be charged or tried. The act has two major aims. On the one hand, it states that young people must be held responsible for their actions and the community must remain safe from crime. On the other hand, it recognizes that young people have special needs and require help and guidance to change their lives, rather than punishment in all cases.

Young offenders must be told their rights when they are arrested. They have the right to a lawyer and the same right to

Rates of Youth Charged With Violent Incidents, 1986-1992							
	1986	1987	1988	1989	1990	1991	1992
Youths charged in violent incidents per 100 000	415	458	520	633	720	863	900
Year-to-year percentage change	—	10%	14%	22%	14%	20%	4%

Source: Statistics Canada.

bail as adult offenders. To protect the identity of a young offender, the media are not allowed to print the names of the accused. Only if the youth is considered dangerous to the public can he or she be named. Witnesses or victims under 12 years of age also cannot be named.

Police can fingerprint and photograph suspects charged under the Young Offenders Act, but these records must be destroyed if the defendant is found not guilty. Once the young offender has served the sentence or disposition, as it is called in Youth Court, and has not committed another offence for two to five years, the police must destroy all records. These safeguards are meant to protect the privacy of young offenders and to ensure that they do not have to carry a criminal record for life based on mistakes made in their youth.

Young offenders are tried in Youth Court, which is a division of provincial courts and is presided over by a judge. Often, the Children's Aid Society, probation officers, and social workers are called upon to assist the court. First offenders and those found guilty of less serious crimes are generally not sent to jail where they will be with tougher criminals. In these cases, a young offender may be placed on probation or given a fine. Sometimes, young offenders are required to work for the victim to restore damages done to property.

The Young Offenders Act, however, has stirred controversy. Many Canadians demanded that the courts be tougher on young offenders who committed violent crimes. For example, Ryan Garrioch's parents circulated a petition demanding that the act be stiffer in murder cases. In 1992, the Young Offenders Act was changed with respect to murder. Before 1992, for a youth convicted in Youth Court of first degree murder, the maximum penalty was a three-year term in a youth jail. Now, the Youth Court sentence is longer: five years, in-cluding three years in youth jail and two years under community supervision. Youths charged with serious crimes such as rape or murder may be tried in adult court and face the same penalties as adults. The maximum penalty for murder in adult court is life in prison. Judges can choose to send a young offender convicted in an adult court to either an adult or youth jail.

Civil Law

Civil law deals with disputes and disagreements between people. Its purpose is to make sure people honour their agreements and do not violate another individual's rights. In criminal cases, it is the government or Crown that takes the accused to court. In a civil suit, one individual or group takes another individual or group to court. The person suing is known as the plaintiff. The person being sued is the defendant. The court acts as the referee. The court can order the winner in a case to pay damages to the loser, but it has no power to punish anyone. Let's look at some aspects of civil law.

Contracts

More people get into trouble over contracts than any other aspect of civil law. A **contract** is a bargain or agreement between two or more parties. Every time you exchange money for a service, you are performing a contract. You, the purchaser, and the seller are called the parties to the contract.

Contracts can be verbal. Both parties can make a spoken agreement. Suppose a college student offers to shovel your driveway after a mid-winter blizzard and agrees to $20 for the work. When she has finished shovelling, you give her the money. This is a simple verbal contract. You can't decide to pay her less once you have agreed upon the price without breaking the contract.

Contracts can be implied. If you go out

The Canadian Court System

Supreme Court of Canada

- final appeal court for all civil and criminal cases
- appeals come from provincial courts and Federal Court
- gives advisory opinions to the federal government on constitutional issues such as the powers of the federal and provincial governments

Federal Court of Canada

- deals with cases such as income tax, patents, and customs

Supreme or Superior Court of Province/Territory

Appeal Division

- hears requests to change or overturn decisions made by other courts; these requests are known as appeals

Trial Division

- has jurisdiction over serious criminal matters
- deals with more serious civil actions including contract and property disputes, damages for personal injury, and divorce

Provincial Court Criminal Division

- deals with people charged with minor criminal offences

Provincial Offences Court

- deals with minor offences contained in provincial laws such as the Highway Traffic Act, the Fish and Game Act, and other laws on matters such as pollution & consumer products

Small Claims Court

- settles claims worth less than $1000
- court costs may be kept to a minimum

Family Court

- deals with family matters such as child custody and family support

Youth Court

- deals with youths charged under the Young Offenders Act

Surrogate Court

- deals primarily with the wills and estates of deceased persons

Provincial court systems vary from province to province. The diagram above shows one example. In general, higher provincial courts look after more serious cases than lower provincial courts. Provincial supreme or superior courts also consider appeals from lower provincial courts.

In 1982, Bertha Wilson became the first woman appointed to the Supreme Court of Canada.

Judge Julius Isaac is Chief Justice of the Federal Court—the first African Canadian to be appointed a chief justice in Canada.

for dinner with friends, it is taken for granted that when you have finished your meal you will pay your bill. It is an implied contract between the diner and the restaurant.

Contracts can also be written. Maria and Janet went to their travel agent to book a holiday. The price included their flight, accommodation in a luxury hotel on the beach, and some meals. Maria and Janet signed a contract agreeing to pay for this vacation. When they arrived, nothing was as they had been promised. The hotel was full, so they were given alternate accommodation in a run-down hotel 5 km from the beach. The meals were unfit to eat and the swimming pool was closed for repairs. The holiday was a disaster!

When Maria and Janet arrived home, they complained to their travel agent. He said there wasn't much he could do. He pointed to the fine print on the contract. It said the company reserved the right to substitute alternate accommodation if necessary. The moral of the story is *caveat emptor*, a Latin saying that means "Let the buyer beware."

Do you think they had a case against the travel agency? Small Claims Court can make awards, usually up to $1000, but the amount varies from province to province. Maria and Janet decided to take the travel agency to Small Claims Court. Typical cases handled in Small Claims Court involve broken contracts, bad debts, disputes over wages, and the recovery of personal property. The procedure was simple, so neither Maria and Janet nor the travel agency needed a lawyer. Both sides discussed the details of the case with the judge. Do you think Janet and Maria will be awarded any money?

Young People and Contracts

Youths are not considered adults under the law. In some provinces, youths are people under the age of 18, while in other provinces the legal age is 19 or 21. Youths are treated differently from adults under

contract law to give them protection. They cannot make legal contracts.

Case Study

Bob and Leo, both 15, are friends. They enjoy watching martial arts films and want to learn *kung fu*. One day, as they are walking downtown, they see a martial arts studio. A sign in the studio's window offers a special two-for-one deal. Two people can get 15 weeks of *kung fu* instruction for the price of one person. Bob and Leo decide to check it out.

A high-pressure salesperson talks them into signing a contract on the spot. It sounds like a good deal, but when Bob and Leo are walking home, they begin to get a little worried. They've signed up for $300 worth of lessons, and neither of them has a job.

Issue: 1. Are Bob and Leo legally bound to their contract?

2. Are their parents legally responsible for their sons' contract?

Decision: 1. No.

2. No.

Reason: People under the legal age are not bound to any contract they sign. Parents or guardians cannot be held responsible for contracts signed by youths, except in the case of necessities. A martial arts course wouldn't be considered a necessity.

Renters and Leases

The Landlord and Tenant Act sets out the rights and responsibilities of tenants (renters) and "landlords" (owners of the property). The rental unit can be an apartment, house, mobile home, or townhouse. The act protects both parties in case of a disagreement. The contract between a property owner and a tenant is a **lease**. A lease does not need to be written, but it is a good idea if it is. The lease states the conditions of rental, such as the amount of the rent, the length of tenancy, and who pays for heat, hydro, and water.

A tenant has the right to:

- a place in good state of repair (the heating and plumbing must work)
- privacy (the owner can enter only after receiving the tenant's permission, in an emergency, or after 24 hours written notice)
- 90 days written notice of a rent increase.

The owner has the right to:

- expect the tenant to pay the rent in full and on time
- have the property kept clean and be informed of needed repairs
- not have damage done to the property
- have the rights of other tenants respected.

Owners cannot evict tenants without following an involved legal process. Tenants can be forced to leave only by a court order. An owner can try to evict a tenant for:

- failure to pay rent
- disturbing other tenants
- using the property for illegal purposes
- causing damage
- overcrowding.

Before court action is started, the owner must give the tenant written notice. The notice must state the reasons for eviction and allow 20 days for the tenant to leave.

Case Study

Sylvie and Carol are college students. They decided to share an apartment. Sylvie and Carol signed a lease as joint tenants. Their lease was to run for one year, and they were each to give the landlord $425 per month. However, after four months, Carol moved back to her parents' home. It was much cheaper and she didn't have to do her own laundry or cook her own meals.

Sylvie didn't have enough money to pay for Carol's share of the rent. Carol refused to pay Sylvie any money. Mr. Hoy, the building's owner, claimed that Sylvie was re-

sponsible for Carol's share of the rent. Sylvie argued that Mr. Hoy knew that half the rent was coming from Carol.

Issue: Is Sylvie responsible for half or all of the rent?

Decision: Sylvie is legally responsible for the full rent.

Reason: The lease says that Sylvie and Carol were joint tenants. If one tenant does not pay the full share, the other is responsible for the full amount. Sylvie could sue Carol in Small Claims Court to recover the money.

Discrimination in the Workplace

Provinces in Canada have laws to make sure that no person is discriminated against in the workplace. The *Ontario Human Rights Code*, for example, states "no person shall be refused employment because of race, creed, colour, age, sex, marital status, nationality, ancestry, or place of origin."

If a person feels discrimination might have occurred, a complaint can be filed at an office of the **Human Rights Commission**. The complaint will be investigated and, if necessary, a board of inquiry will be set up. At the inquiry, the commission's lawyers will argue on behalf of the victim. The person or company accused may also bring a lawyer. Evidence is heard and witnesses may be called.

Case Study

Anne Adams had just finished taking an auto mechanics course at a community college. She saw a job in a newspaper that said:

Junior Auto Mechanic
Required for east end garage.
Must be a good worker with
community college background.
Apply: MMM Garage

Anne went to apply for the job, but she was told it had already been filled. However, one week later, the advertisement was still running in the newspaper. Three weeks later, Anne went by the garage and found out that a man had been hired. Anne filed a complaint with the Human Rights Commission.

The owner of the garage told the commission the job was too physically demanding for a woman. Anne worked in a garage in her hometown during the summers and never had difficulty performing any task. Her teacher at the community college said Anne was the best student in the course.

Issue: Is being a male a genuine requirement for the job?

Decision: No. Anne was discriminated against.

Reason: During the investigation, evidence and witnesses demonstrated that Anne could fill all the job requirements.

Recovering Damages From a Wrongdoing

Another branch of civil law deals with people who go to court to recover damages from a wrongdoing. Sometimes, the wrongdoing comes from intentional actions. Other times, it comes from carelessness or negligence. Consider this case and see whether damages should be recovered or not.

Case Study

The 15-year-old plaintiff, Kyle O'Banion, was a student with limited athletic ability. The defendant was his physical education teacher, Mr. Smylie, who had 21 years' teaching experience. Mr. Smylie had noticed that Kyle was shy, had few friends, and often did not socialize with his classmates. One day, Kyle was placed in a group with three other boys and instructed to practise for the United Way three-legged race. All the boys were given instruction on how to do this safely. Kyle followed the instructions but, nevertheless, fell and broke his leg.

Issue: Was Mr. Smylie negligent in having Kyle participate in an activity where he might get hurt?

Decision: No, Mr. Smylie was not guilty.

Reason: The judge held it was reasonable for a 15-year-old boy to participate in a three-legged race as part of a supervised physical education class.

Why Laws Change

Attitudes and values change over the years and so do our laws. Laws that were acceptable to our great-grandparents are not necessarily acceptable to us today. For example, in the late nineteenth century, young children, 10 to 12 years old, were often sent to work in factories and coal mines. Today, that is totally unacceptable and we have laws to make sure it doesn't happen. Changes in laws come only when society is ready to accept them.

Sometimes society needs a bit of help to accept changes in laws. Canadian women went through a struggle to gain the right to vote and hold public office. At the turn of the century, women were not allowed to vote. Women could not be elected to federal or provincial offices in government. A man had a great deal of control over his wife and children. It was assumed that the views of married women were adequately represented through their husbands' votes. Over time, these laws were changed. Manitoba was the first province to grant women the right to vote in 1916. Other provinces followed. On 24 May 1918, women won the right to vote in federal elections.

Laws continued to be changed to reflect changing attitudes. For example, in the early decades of the twentieth century, it was extremely difficult for women to leave an unhappy marriage. Legal grounds for divorce were very limited. Changes were made to the Divorce Act in 1968

In the nineteenth century, this boy worked as a miner in dangerous conditions. In the early twentieth century, laws were enacted to stop child labour and ensure safer working conditions in mines and factories.

er we wish. We have the right to move, live, and work in any province in Canada. However, in many countries of the world, citizens do not have these rights.

These rights, and many others, are guaranteed in the **Charter of Rights and Freedoms**. The Charter was an important part of the Constitution Act of 1982. Some of the basic rights written down in the Charter are outlined in the box on the next page.

Rights impose responsibilities. If you have the right to freely express your ideas, then you have the responsibility to let others freely express theirs. If you have the right to protection under the law, then you also have the responsibility to obey the law. Consider the list of the basic rights a group of high school students thought they should have.

which made it easier to obtain a divorce. Further changes to the law were made in 1985 so that a divorce could be obtained after a one-year waiting period. People will continue to demand that governments revise or create new laws to accommodate the changing needs of society.

Rights and Responsibilities of Citizenship

Many Canadians take their rights for granted. We have the right to speak out and criticize our government. We have the right to hold demonstrations and demand new laws or changes to existing laws that no longer meet our needs. We have the right to practise any religion or none at all. We are free to travel outside Canada whenev-

We have the right to:
- choose our own friends
- go out with and marry the person of our choice
- say what we please
- go where we like
- read and see what we wish
- be educated
- be safe from muggings or beatings
- enjoy our privacy
- keep our personal property
- keep our cultural heritage
- live in an unpolluted environment
- practise our own religion
- be treated with respect by the police
- be treated with respect by our parents and teachers
- vote in an election at age 18.

What obligations are imposed upon the students by these rights?

SOCIETY AND SOCIAL CHANGE

The Charter of Rights and Freedoms

1. Fundamental freedoms
   a) freedom of conscience and religion
   b) freedom of thought, belief, opinion and expression, including
         i) freedom of the press
         ii) freedom of peaceful assembly
         iii) freedom of association.

2. Democratic rights
   a) the right to vote
   b) the right to run for election.

3. Mobility rights
   a) the right to enter, remain in, and leave Canada
   b) the right to live in, move to, and work in any province.

4. Legal rights
   a) the right to life, liberty, and security
   b) protection against unreasonable search and seizure or arbitrary detention or imprisonment
   c) the right to be informed quickly about the charges, if arrested
   d) the right to hire a lawyer
   e) the right to trial within a reasonable amount of time
   f) the right to be presumed innocent until proven guilty according to law in a fair and public hearing
   g) the right not to be subjected to cruel and unusual treatment or punishment.

5. Equality rights
   a) protection from discrimination on the basis of race, national or ethnic origin, colour, religion, age, sex, or mental or physical disability.

6. Official languages
   a) the right to use English and French in the government and courts of Canada and the province of New Brunswick.

7. Minority language education rights
   a) the right to education in English or French where there are sufficient numbers of students.

8. Aboriginal rights
   a) recognition of the existing aboriginal and treaty rights of the Native peoples (Inuit, Indian, and Métis).

Enforcement

Anyone whose rights or freedoms, as guaranteed by this Charter, have been infringed or denied, may apply to a court to obtain an appropriate and just remedy.

1. a) Rank the following rights, from the Charter of Rights and Freedoms, in order of importance to you. Give reasons for your choices.
   - freedom of assembly
   - mobility
   - freedom of association
   - freedom of the press
   - vote
   - freedom of conscience and religion
   - run for political office
   - aboriginal rights
   - legal rights
   - equality
   - language
2. Broaden your study by conducting a survey to find out which rights other Canadians value most. Ask people to rank the following four fundamental freedoms from most important to least important—freedom of religion, freedom of speech, freedom of peaceful assembly, and freedom of association.

Responsibility: Get Involved and Vote

Elections give you a chance to participate in the governing of your country. Your vote counts in the people's choice of government. Voting is an important right. Yet, in some elections, the turnout of voters is very low. Federal and provincial elections sometimes draw only about 60 percent of potential voters. In municipal elections, the turnout may drop as low as one-third. An election victory may be decided by only a few votes, so every vote does count.

Some Canadians have suggested that the right to vote (franchise) should be taken away from citizens who do not vote in each election. In Australia, eligible voters who do not vote in each election are fined. It is easy to take the right to vote for granted. We forget that many people, even in Canada's history, went through a long struggle to gain the right to vote. The timeline at the beginning of this unit tells the story of this struggle for some groups.

Ideal voters are informed voters. They examine closely the different parties and candidates. They know the issues and make a careful decision on how to vote. One way to become a well-informed voter is to get involved in a political party. You can participate more fully in an election by contributing your time and labour. To encourage Canadians to take part in the election process beyond voting, the Income Tax Act allows a tax credit for contributions to political parties.

You may even consider becoming a candidate. To run for federal office, you must:

- be 18 years old by election day
- be a Canadian citizen
- give a $200 deposit (which is returned if you win more than 15 percent of the votes cast in your riding).

The money qualification is intended to make sure candidates are serious. Although some candidates have no hope of winning, they are still willing to run. Some are looking for a chance to express their ideas or raise certain issues in the campaign.

Opportunity: Write Your Member of Parliament

Citizens have the right to make their views known to their elected representatives. Members of Parliament do a better job when they know their constituents' views. If you write to your federal MP in care of the House of Commons in Ottawa while

Canadian citizens have the right to hold peaceful demonstrations. In the early 1990s, thousands of students rallied to protest cuts in education and higher tuition fees.

the House is in session, it's not necessary to put a stamp on your envelope.

Think about the issue of capital punishment, which has caused great debate among Canadians. In 1976, the death penalty was abolished. However, some Canadians are in favour of bringing it back. They believe that violent crimes, such as murder, are occurring more frequently, and the only way to do anything about the situation is to bring back the death penalty.

In 1987, the House of Commons held a free debate on capital punishment. A free debate allows MPs to vote according to their conscience and not party policy. In the months leading up to the debate, thousands of citizens wrote to their MPs expressing their views. People supporting the return of the death penalty gave these arguments:

Capital punishment is a deterrent. Potential killers will think twice if they know they will lose their own lives if they are caught.

A police chief wrote:

I think if you have taken a life, the death penalty is the only answer. The cost of keeping criminals in jails is a tremendous cost to the taxpayers of Canada. It is estimated that it takes at least a half a million dollars to keep a convicted killer in jail for 50 years.

People opposing the return of the death penalty wrote letters showing a different side of the argument.

It is ridiculous to think the death penalty is a deterrent for any murderer. Most murders occur in the heat of an argument or fight. People who are exploding with anger do not stop to think about the death penalty. They act instead.

A leading civil rights lawyer wrote:

When you analyze the statistics in countries that still have the death penalty, you find that the murder rate is no lower than it is in Canada. It appears that capital punishment does not effectively reduce the number of violent crimes that are committed.

A member of Amnesty International, a human rights group, wrote:

Life is sacred. It should always be respected. As long as a convicted murderer is kept alive, there is still a chance that a human life can be rehabilitated.

Political analysts predicted the Parliamentary vote on capital punishment would be very close. It could go either way. Newspaper polls indicated that 60 percent of Canadians were in favour of capital punishment. But Canada's MPs surprised the pollsters and voted against the return of capital punishment.

After the vote, commentators said that one of the decisive factors influencing the vote was the well-organized letter writing blitz by opponents of the death penalty. These people used their influence and power to convince enough MPs to defeat the motion.

DEVELOPING SKILLS: WRITING TO YOUR MP

Some day you may feel strongly enough about an issue that you decide to write to your Member of Parliament about it. Such a letter is more formal than a personal letter to a friend. Its purpose is to conduct business and to state your opinion.

Members of Parliament have a duty to take seriously all letters from the people they represent. But to be taken seriously, you must be sure that the opinion you express is well supported.

Writing a letter to your MP involves several skills: forming and stating an opinion, supporting it in an essay of several paragraphs, and practising good business letter writing techniques.

With the help of your teachers, review models of how a business letter should be set up. Consider these elements.

- A heading with your address and the date. This is important if you expect your Member of Parliament to reply.

- Inside address, including the name, position, and address of the receiver of the letter. Remember to address your MP as "The Honourable." If the House of Commons is in session, send the letter in care of the House of Commons in Ottawa, Ontario, K1A 0A6. No stamp is needed. If it is the summer holidays or Christmas recess, it might be better to send a stamped letter to the constituency office.

- Salutation. Be formal and be polite.

- The body of the letter. This part of the letter states your opinion. It should be logically arranged and well supported. A good way to approach it is to review and apply your essay writing skills. Refer back to pages 322–323 in Chapter 18 for the steps in writing an essay. State and support your opinion in an essay of three to five paragraphs.

- Closing salutation. Again, be formal and polite.

- Signature. A written signature with your name typed below it. If you are writing on behalf of your class, indicate this as well.

You can follow the same format if you are writing a letter to the editor of a newspaper.

Do It!

Choose an issue you feel strongly about, such as the rising incidence of youth crime or gun control in Canada. Practise writing a letter on the issue to your MP or a newspaper editor. Publish the letters written in your class in a school or class newspaper or newsletter for other students to read and comment on.

As part of the Forum for Young Canadians program, a student asks questions in the House of Commons. Why is participation in government decision-making a responsibility of citizenship?

Opportunity: Speak to a Parliamentary Committee

On important issues that have a far-reaching impact, governments may establish special **parliamentary committees**. Members of these committees travel across the country or the province hearing the views of citizens. From these views, the committees make recommendations to the government. Appearing before a parliamentary committee provides an opportunity to influence government policy and laws.

In 1995, for example, a parliamentary committee held hearings on the federal Liberal government's plans for tighter gun control. Why was this committee established? Many Canadian citizens were becoming concerned about increasing violent crimes committed with firearms. The government announced sweeping reforms to regulate the use of firearms. The key measures included the following:

- all guns and owners must be registered
- Canadians will be banned from owning handguns unless they are collectors or use them for target-shooting
- anyone committing a crime using firearms will face a jail sentence
- many types of assault weapons and paramilitary rifles will be banned.

The committee on the gun law heard speakers from both sides of the issue. Hunters and gun collectors argued that they use firearms safely and responsibly. They were against having to register their guns. They see this legislation as taking away their rights as citizens. On the other side, people told the committee that restriction on firearms is necessary to curb rising crime rates, particularly in urban areas. When the parliamentary committee had finished hearing from concerned citizens and groups on both sides, recommendations were made to the government. The government instituted some changes to the bill in response to the committee's recommendations. For example, penalties for failing to register were reduced, and the bill would not overrule treaty rights of Native peoples.

Opportunity:
Join a Pressure Group

We have examined how an individual can influence the government decision-making process. If individuals join forces, they may be even more effective.

Suppose a group of neighbours is concerned about plans to open a dump site in their area. They decide to support the candidate running for mayor who has stated her opposition to the dump site. Their support helps to ensure she wins the election.

The neighbours could also join a pressure group. **Pressure groups** are people who get together to promote a particular interest or cause. Pressure groups can organize peaceful demonstrations or they can influence government decision-making by lobbying people in government. **Lobbying** involves making personal con-

tacts with government officials and making the group's ideas known to them. Lobbyists hope to exert enough influence so that legislation is favourable to their cause.

Where does the word "lobby" come from? Groups of business people used to wait in the lobby of the British House of Commons. They hoped to get government contracts as the members of Parliament passed through the lobby. Sometimes the most effective lobbyists are people who already have contacts in Ottawa and the provincial capitals. Lobbyists are often former government officials or former politicians. They know who is making the decisions and have access to them. A pressure group can hire a lobbyist to keep its interests constantly in front of the decision-makers.

Another way to apply pressure is to gain public support and attention through the media. The environmental group Greenpeace, for example, has spent hundreds of thousands of dollars on advertising directed against companies that use and produce chlorofluorocarbons (CFCs). Through the media, Greenpeace focussed worldwide attention on the destruction of the ozone layer by CFCs. The ozone layer is a blanket of gas that acts as a sunscreen for the Earth. Greenpeace warned that holes in the ozone layer were exposing the Earth to harmful sun rays that cause skin cancer in humans and can reduce harvests of important food crops. Until recently, chlorofluorocarbon compounds were used in aerosol spray cans, refrigerators, air conditioners, and foam packaging. Through the efforts of environmental pressure groups such as Greenpeace, the use of CFCs has been reduced.

Community members protest against a dump site in their neighbourhood. In what other ways can groups make their views known to government decision-makers?

The Inuit of the High Arctic became concerned when they heard through television about the depletion of the ozone layer over the North Pole. They have 24 hours of sunlight in summer and spend long hours outdoors hunting. The Inuit asked why they do not receive public health advice similar to that issued to Canadians in the south. Greenpeace planned an outreach program to inform the Inuit about the increased danger and the precautions they should take.

Opportunity: Participate in Peaceful Demonstrations

Peaceful demonstrations and large meetings not only bring a cause to the attention of the legislators, but to other Canadians. This increases the pressure on the MPs to take action on the issue.

Demonstrations can be held on issues of local or national importance. When Pierre Trudeau was working to "bring home" Canada's Constitution in 1982, the original proposals contained no mention of aboriginal or treaty rights. Native peoples wanted to safeguard their rights by having them written into the Constitution. They decided to hold a demonstration in Ottawa to make their views known. Two transcontinental trains travelling on different routes from Vancouver were also organized to pick up as many passengers as possible. In Winnipeg, the two trains came together to form the Constitution Express. All along the route, the Native people received support and publicity. By the time the Constitution Express arrived in Ottawa and the demonstration had been staged on Parliament Hill, most Canadians were aware of the issue. A clause that recognized "existing" aboriginal and treaty rights was inserted in the Constitution.

More recently, Native peoples have continued to demonstrate for their rights. People have also demonstrated against tax increases, cuts to education and other social programs, and cuts to arts programs. The demonstrations are an indication of what concerns people at all levels—local, provincial, and national.

Pressure groups such as Greenpeace can have an effect on government decision-making and laws.

Native peoples have held peaceful demonstrations to ensure that their rights are recognized. They succeeded in having aboriginal and treaty rights written into Canada's Constitution.

Activities

Check Your Understanding

1. Add to the glossary of terms you created for the last chapter. Include the following.

criminal law	Young Offenders Act
Criminal Code of Canada	civil law
summary offences	contract
indictable offences	lease
adversary system	Human Rights Commission
jury	Charter of Rights and Freedoms
plea	parliamentary committee
contempt of court	pressure group
circumstantial evidence	lobbying
hearsay evidence	
cross-examination	
verdict	
hung jury	

2. Briefly explain the differences between criminal law and civil law.

3. Referring to Gordon Mowbray's trial in this chapter, develop a diagram to outline the steps in a criminal trial.

4. What are the three objectives that a judge must consider as he or she chooses the penalty to be imposed?

Confirm Your Learning

5. a) How does the Young Offenders Act attempt to balance the special needs of young offenders with the need to take responsibility for their criminal action?
   b) Do you think the Young Offenders Act is a fair act for young people? Explain your point of view.

6. In each of the following situations, who is in the wrong? Explain your reasoning.
   a) Chantal is surprised when she comes into her apartment after work and finds the superintendent just leaving. The superintendent says she was just checking to see if all the windows were closed as it looks like rain. Chantal is quite angry and tells the superintendent not to go into her apartment again without permission.
   b) Bob celebrates his promotion by throwing a wild, noisy party. His neighbours complain and call the police to quiet the crowd. The next morning, the owner of Bob's building brings him a written eviction notice that states Bob has seven days to get out of his apartment.

7. The law says that a buyer has the responsibility to check out what he or she is purchasing. In other words, a buyer of a used car should take it out for a test drive and have it checked by a mechanic before buying it. If you do not take these steps, the law says that it is your own fault if you find out later that the car is a "lemon." Is the idea of *caveat emptor* fair? Outline the pros and cons.

8. a) What is good citizenship? Brainstorm criteria and then decide on the characteristics your class or group considers essential.
   b) Develop a list of Canadians, historical or contemporary, who you believe meet these criteria, and justify your choices.

9. Discuss what happens when the rights of an individual conflict with the rights of society in the following cases:
   i) smoking in a public place
   ii) censorship
   iii) noisy party that disturbs the neighbourhood.

Challenge Your Mind

10. a) Watch a Canadian television program that deals with criminal trials. Make notes on the proceedings of the trial. Comment on the role of the judge, jury, Crown attorney, defence attorney, and the trial procedures.
    b) Do you think the drama was accurate and realistic? Explain.

11. Debate:"Young offenders, even those under the age of 12, who are accused of serious crimes such as murder should be tried in adult court and be subject to the same penalties as adults."

12. In groups, make laws for your history class. Be prepared to explain why your laws are necessary. Select one of the laws and hold a class discussion on its merits and faults.

13. Simulate a trial in your classroom. Suppose two students were involved in a fight. In the course of the fight, one student was knocked down, hit his or her head on a locker, and suffered a concussion. The other student involved in the fight is charged with assault. A few students witnessed the fight after it started, but no one knows why it started. Assign roles, including a judge, Crown attorney, defence lawyer, witnesses, and accused. Assume it will be trial by jury. Go through the jury selection process and then hold the trial. Students not assigned specific roles should act as observers or media reporters. Hold debriefing sessions after key points in the trial as it progresses.

14. Statistics show that about 75 percent of paroled prisoners do not commit another offence. Only about 25 percent commit other crimes and are returned to prison. Some Canadians believe that criminals should not be released until they have served their full sentence. It is argued that one of the main reasons for putting criminals in prison is to protect society. What is your opinion on parole?

15. What should be the purpose of prisons—to punish or to help rehabilitate criminals? Support your point of view.

16. In groups, compose a "Students' Bill of Rights" or a "Children's Bill of Rights." Compare your bill with those of other groups, and discuss similarities and differences.

Wrapping It Up

WHAT WOULD LAURIER THINK?

If the ghost of Sir Wilfrid Laurier were to return to Canada today, how do you think he would react? What changes would strike him most? What would he think of present-day Canada? Consider these famous remarks that Laurier made in his lifetime:

> *My object is to consolidate Confederation and to bring our people, long separated from each other, gradually to become a nation. This is the supreme issue. Everything else is subordinate to that idea.*

> *The best and most effective way to maintain friendship with our American neighbours is to be absolutely independent of them.*

> *The nineteenth century was the century of the United States, the twentieth century will be the century of Canada.*

Laurier's comments touch on some of the themes that are central to twentieth century Canadian history—Canadian-American relations, French-English relations, our national identity, and our growth and diversity. Keep these themes in mind as you consider these questions.

1. To what extent do you think Laurier was correct when he predicted that the twentieth century would belong to Canada?
2. Would Laurier be happy with the present state of relations between English and French Canadians?
3. How would he view our cultural diversity?
4. What would be his opinion of Canadian-American relations today?

Use the following activities to help you reflect further on the history of Canada in the twentieth century that you have explored in this book.

ACTIVITIES

Check Your Understanding

1. Slogans are brief, catchy phrases that get people excited about an idea or cause. They have been used to stir support for a war effort or to win votes for a political party. Throughout history, slogans have been used as rallying cries.

   Match each slogan in the list below with the idea, event, or person to which it refers. Then choose three of the slogans and discuss what they mean.

Slogans

1 The "Iron Curtain"
2 "No truck or trade with the Yankees."
3 The "Just Society"
4 *Maîtres chez nous.*
5 "Peace in our time."
6 "The last best west."
7 *Vive le Québec libre.*
8 "Conscription if necessary but not necessarily conscription."

a) Prime Minister Chamberlain
b) General De Gaulle
c) Clifford Sifton
d) Pierre Trudeau
e) W. L. Mackenzie King
f) The Quiet Revolution
g) The election of 1911
h) Winston Churchill

2. Now that you have discussed these slogans, make a collection of others from the past or present. Bumper stickers are one place to look for modern slogans. Discuss the collection in class. Which are used most frequently? Classify the slogans into those that have to do with politics, social problems, sports, etc.

Confirm Your Learning

3. Think back over the Canadian history you have studied in this book.
   a) Which decade in this century would you most like to live through? Why?
   b) What do you think of the times you are living in now?
   c) Do you think that this decade will be remembered as one of the most important in Canadian history? Explain your point of view.

4. This text was published in 1996. Prepare a timeline of major events in Canadian history since then. You may decide to use a long roll of paper and put it on the bulletin board of your classroom. Include political, social, cultural, and economic events.

5. Styles of art change from one period to another. Make a collection of Canadian art in different periods of this century. Write a short report describing these styles.

6. Make a fashion history of Canada. Collect pictures of clothing styles from Canada's past. Mount the pictures on large sheets of paper and write a short essay to explain the changes and what they reveal about Canadian lifestyles.

7. In groups of five, prepare pantomimes which illustrate dramatic events in Canadian history. Let the rest of the class identify the event being dramatized.

Challenge Your Mind

8. Imagine you had the chance to put 10 objects into a time capsule to be opened by Canadians in the year 2500. What would you place in it to show people of the future what life is like today?

9. What do you think Canada will be like in the year 2067? Write a short essay describing your ideas.

10. Some historians have pointed out that Canada has struggled since its beginning to form a nation independent from the United States. This struggle has continually involved some kind of American challenge and a Canadian response to that challenge.

   In the period 1860-1880, the Americans seemed to be threatening a political takeover of Canada. This challenge certainly helped to hasten Confederation and our birth as a nation. It also encouraged the building of the CPR and the settlement of the West. From 1920-1940, there came the American cultural challenge. The influence of the American media was having a growing effect on Canadian styles, sports, and entertainment. From 1950 to the present, a strong economic challenge has been felt in Canada.

   Do you agree with the "challenge and response" theory? What do you think was the Canadian response to the American cultural and economic challenges?

11. Discuss the truth of the following comment by Wilfrid Laurier: "Compromise created this nation, nothing but compromise will hold it together." Think of as many examples from our history as you can in which compromises have played a part in keeping Canada together.

Text Credits

87-88 *The Winnipeg Tribune*; **89-90, 91, 111** *The Great War and Canadian Society: An Oral History*, Daphne Read (ed.), Toronto: New Hogtown Press, 1978; **96** From Erich Maria Remarque, *All Quiet on the Western Front*, William Heinemann, 1978; **160, 172** Reprinted from *Ten Lost Years* by Barry Broadfoot, Doubleday, 1973; **192, 213** Reprinted from *The Diary of Anne Frank* by permission of Vallentine Mitchell Publishers; **209, 227, 234-235** Reprinted from *Six War Years* by Barry Broadfoot, Doubleday, 1974; **210** Corvette illustration reproduced courtesy of DND (Department of National Defence); **217** *Hitler and Germany* by B. J. Elliot. Used by permission of Longmans, London; **222** Time Capsules/1945, courtesy Time-Life Books, Inc.; **230** Map adapted from Plate 48, *Historical Atlas of Canada*, Volume III, by permission of University of Toronto Press, Inc.; **238, 239** Reprinted from *Years of Sorrow, Years of Shame* by Barry Broadfoot, Doubleday, 1977; **268** From *The War Brides* by Joyce Hibbert. Reprinted with the permission of Stoddart Publishing Co. Limited, Don Mills, Ont.; **314-315** Reprinted by permission of the author; **341** Graph from *Maclean's Magazine*, Maclean Hunter Publishing Ltd., 2 January 1995; **343** Reprinted with permission—The Toronto Star Syndicate; **365** Map source: *Canadian Geographic*, November/December 1992; **382** From *In the Rapids* by Ovide Mercredi and Mary Ellen Turpel. Copyright © Ovide Mercredi and Mary Ellen Turpel, 1993. Reprinted by permission of Penguin Books Canada Limited; **400** Reproduced from *Canadian Crime Statistics*, Catalogue 85-205, Statistics Canada, 1992, by authority of the Minister of Industry, 1995; **402** Illustration reprinted with permission—The Toronto Star Syndicate.

Photo Credits

t = top;   c = centre;   b = bottom;   l = left;   r = right
Baldwin/MTRL = Baldwin Room/Metropolitan Toronto Reference Library
Canada Post = Stamp reproduced courtesy of Canada Post Corporation © 1995
CTA = City of Toronto Archives
CWM = Canadian War Museum/Photography by William Kent/ © Canadian War Museum 1995
Glenbow = The Glenbow Archives, Calgary, Alberta
Granger = The Granger Collection, New York
Malak = Malak Photography, Ottawa
MTRL = Metropolitan Toronto Reference Library
NAC = National Archives of Canada

Index